Growth and Risk in Infancy

of related interest

Six Theories of Child Development
Revised Formulations and Current Issues
Edited by Ross Vasta
ISBN 1 85302 137 7

Emotional Milestones
Ruth Schmidt Neven
ISBN 1 85302 456 2

Educational Psychology Casework
A Practical Guide
Rick Beaver
ISBN 1 85302 364 7

Growth and Risk in Infancy

Stephen Briggs

Jessica Kingsley Publishers
London and Bristol, Pennsylvania

First published in the United Kingdom in 1997 by
Jessica Kingsley Publishers Ltd
116 Pentonville Road
London N1 9JB, England
and
1900 Frost Road, Suite 101
Bristol, PA 19007, U S A

Library of Congress Cataloging in Publication Data
A CIP catalogue record for this book is available from the Library of Congress

British Library Cataloguing in Publication Data
Briggs, Stephen C.
Growth and risk in infancy
1. Infants – Development
I. Title
305.2'32

ISBN 1-85302-398-1

Printed and Bound in Great Britain by
Cromwell Press, Melksham, Wiltshire

Contents

Introduction 1

Chapter 1: Theories of Infancy 4

1.1 Different views of infancy 4
1.2 Rational development in infancy 5
1.3 Intersubjectivity 8
1.4 The 'third route': applications of developmentalism to psychoanalysis 10
1.5 A 'rational' or 'precarious' infant 16
1.6 The 'fourth route': operationalisation of Object Relations Theory 18
1.7 Summary 21

Chapter 2: Methodology 23

2.1 Epistemology 23
2.2 Esther Bick's method of infant observation 26
2.3 Application of Bick's model to research 28
2.4 The role of the observer 29
2.5 Advantages and disadvantages of the Bick model of infant observation 31
2.6 Summary 34

Chapter 3: The Study: Five Infants at Potential Risk 35

3.1 The study families; selection; risk; ethics 35
3.2 Observations; primary database; data analysis 39
3.3 The model 41
3.4 Categories in the grid 48
3.5 Risk 55
3.6 Summary 57

The Case Studies

Chapter 4: Hashmat 61

4.1 The family 61
4.2 Quality of containment 62
4.3 Hashmat's early development 65
4.4 Development from 3 to 12 months 68
4.5 Development from 12 to 24 months 71
4.6 Ending 76
4.7 Summary 77
4.8 Grid 78

Chapter 5: Michael 90

5.1 The family 90
5.2 Quality of containment 91
5.3 Michael's early development 93
5.4 Development from 3 to 12 months 98
5.5 Development after 12 months 104
5.6 Ending 108
5.7 Summary 108
5.8 Grid 109

Chapter 6: Hester 120

6.1 The family 120
6.2 Quality of containment 121
6.3 Hester's early development 123
6.4. Development from 3 to 12 months 128
6.5 Development from 12 to 24 months 133
6.6 Ending 139
6.7 Summary 141
6.8 Grid 142

Chapter 7: Samantha 154

7.1 The family 154
7.2 Quality of containment 156
7.3 Samantha's early development 158
7.4 Development from 3 to 12 months 162

7.5 Development from 12 to 24 months 168
7.6 Ending 178
7.7 Summary 179
7.8 Grid 179

Chapter 8: Timothy **193**
8.1 The family 193
8.2 Quality of containment 195
8.3 Timothy's early development 198
8.4 Development from 3 to 12 months 203
8.5 Development from 12 to 24 months 210
8.6 Ending 217
8.7 Summary 219
8.8 Grid 220

Chapter 9: Findings **233**
9.1 Methodology 233
9.2 The role of the observer 237
9.3 The basis for comparison: continuity and change in development 245
9.4 Evaluation of the model: infant development 248
9.5 Internalisation 256
9.6 Risk 269
9.7 Conclusions 271

Bibliography **274**

Subject Index **284**

Author Index **290**

Acknowledgements

Amongst the many people who have helped me throughout my studies and the final version of the book my deepest thanks are due to the following: to the five families who so generously let me share such an important part of their lives, and who provided me with such unique opportunities; to Professor Michael Rustin who inspired and encouraged me throughout; to Dr Gianna Williams who supervised the observations and offered thoughts and reflections on the material; to Dr Cathy Urwin who helped significantly to formulate ways of analysing the observational material and who read and commented in detail on the manuscripts; to Dr Amal Treacher who read and commented on the manuscripts.

I am grateful to the staff of the Adolescent Department of the Tavistock Clinic who supported my studies in many ways and, before this, to Croydon College who generously gave me the time to undertake the fieldwork.

Last, but not least I am grateful to Beverley and my children, Matthew and Oliver, who endured my preoccupation with these studies and who helped in many ways.

Introduction

This book is based on detailed and regular observations of five infants from soon after birth until two years. The form of observation used is based upon the method developed by Esther Bick (1964) and described by Miller *et al.* (1989). The method, which is explored in detail in Chapter 2, has been developed primarily as a training method for child psychotherapists. It is rooted in the psychoanalytical tradition, in which the purpose of enquiry is the emotional world and its impact upon individual development and relatedness. The observer of infancy, in this method, is expected to take into account the emotionality of the experience of observing.

Compared with the traditional developmentalist approach to child research, this is a quite different approach, though it does continue recent attempts to link psychoanalytic and developmental theories. It is chosen here because the primary aim of the study is to analyse closely the adaptations the infants make to their circumstances, and to come to some conclusions about the developmental progress of these infants. I am interested, not only in their cognitive development, but also in how the infants' states of mind, their behaviour, interaction and play can be seen to have meaningfulness, and how these can then be informative about their overall development.

This of course poses the problem at the outset as to whether such aspects of development are in fact reliably observable in such young infants, and whether the data obtained can in fact be analysed in a way that is useful for furthering understanding infant development. One of the aims of the study is therefore to assess whether this is possible, and therefore to comment upon the value of psychoanalytically based enquiry into infancy based on direct observation.

The methodology used here is, however, a variation of that developed by Bick. First, through studying a sample of five infants, the aim is to make a comparative analysis of the ways in which these infants develop. This has meant developing research instruments for making comparisons, through producing categories that permit comparison across the sample. Methodologically and theoretically this study is placed at the intersection of two traditions, the developmental and psychoanalytic. Recent attempts to make links between these two methods form the theoretical background to the book, and they are discussed in Chapter 1. Unlike many attempts to 'make empirical' psychoanalytic findings, this study does not primarily apply established empirical models to test psychoanalytic hypotheses. Rather, a more radical approach is taken, which is to analyse the data from the observations in a way whereby new theoretical ideas may emerge. The Bick method is then used through the operationalisation of some key psychoanalytic concepts, from which new grounded theory (Glaser and Strauss 1967) is encouraged and a conceptual framework, or model is developed (Chapter 3). The aim here is to explore, with regard to the data from the observations, how far this framework contributes to an understanding of infant development. The approach is primarily innovative and exploratory.

The second variation of the Bick model is that a specific group of infants were observed, namely infants who were in some way vulnerable, or 'at risk'. Indeed, the idea for the study came from a preoccupation with the problems of accurately predicting and assessing 'risk' in infancy. Some of these difficulties appeared to stem from the problems of implementing 'checklists' in a mechanical way.[1] The method of study used here, namely, detailed regular observations in the home settings, would, it appeared to me, produce detailed, multi-layered conceptions of developmental processes, which would offer the possibility of producing models and theories of development which could be more accurately used predictively than more simplistic linear or cause–effect models. Individual development is much more realistically seen as a multi-layered process.

By studying vulnerable infants, the material gathered would focus on the factors which led either to more 'healthy' or secure development, on the one hand, or to more difficult, disturbed, or problematic development on the other hand. The study is focused on 'risk' rather than 'child abuse'. By this I mean that concentration on the presence of potential problems in development, in a close study of infant–parent relationships concentrates inevitably on the formative patterns of personality for the infant and role of the parent. The ancestor of the study is not – say – Kempe's work on child abuse, but rather Escalona's (1969) on the origins of individuality. Studying infants in naturalistic settings she aimed to discover some of the characteristics that may make a difference to the quality of individual development (Escalona, pp.58–59). That is no more and no less than the intention here. Studying these five vulnerable or potentially at risk infants is intended to lead to a contribution to the understanding of difficulties in development in infancy, through close observation and comparative study, and second, to explore how far the theoretical framework developed for this study will provide the generation of concepts which will be established by the study as significant for understanding the nature of difficulties which

1 This concern is summarised by Dingwall: 'The amount of scientifically validated research on child abuse and neglect is vanishingly small. The value of any self-styled predictive checklist is negligible. Indeed, such tools do more harm than good because of the way they undervalue and undermine professional judgment.' (Dingwall 1989, p.51)

lead to 'risk'. Individuality, Escalona suggested, is seen through understanding developmental processes. This enquiry 'does not seek to elucidate the processes of cognition, perception, communication and the like in their own right, but rather to discern the mechanisms that propel developmental change in any and all areas in which change occurs' (p.51).

The discovery and description of 'mechanisms', or perhaps configurations of change propels this study. Its aims are, therefore, to explore the possibilities of systematically observing infant development from the point of view of the psychoanalytic tradition; second, to assess the methodology as a research instrument, that is the Bick method and the variations of it used in this study; third, to develop a theoretical framework from the observed material and to assess its contribution to furthering understanding of infancy and fourth to analyse in this methodology and theoretical framework, the factors which contribute to vulnerability and 'at riskness' in this sample of infants.

The study is structured around the detailed case histories of the five infants. These form five chapters in the centre of the book (Chapters 4–8). Chapter 1 discusses theories of infancy from the point of view of the differences between developmental and psychoanalytic positions, with a view to establishing the underpinning of a model which will be useful for applying to the observations, and to issues of risk. Methodological issues are discussed in Chapter 2, and the study is described in Chapter 3. Here the development of the methodological instruments and the model are essential parts of this discussion. The case studies are followed by a detailed comparative account of the findings of the study (Chapter 9).

CHAPTER 1

Theories of Infancy

1.1 Different views of infancy

The study of the consequences of problems in infant development demands a framework provided by a conceptualisation of 'normal' development. In an era when the proliferation of baby studies lead Bower to complain that 'some of us know more about infancy than we ever wanted to know' (Bower 1989, p.1), it could be assumed that a detailed understanding of infant development would be easily acquired and applied as a basis of comparison to any sample of infants. This is not the case. Controversy over infant development remains very much the essence of intellectual progress in this field of study. Thus when Daniel Stern explained his ideas to an audience consisting mainly of London psychotherapists, he was questioned by his audience about the differences between babies in London and Geneva. Though a lot may be known about infancy, studies of infancy have followed different theoretical routes. The perceived differences between babies in London and Geneva reflects the fact that theories about babies are constructed by different theoretical paradigms (Kuhn 1962), with different aims in mind.

The 'kind of baby' this study wishes to see is one in which problems that develop in infancy, especially those problems which are connected with the infant's relationship with his caregivers in his family setting, can be assessed, predicted and changed. There is a clinical and therapeutic goal to this study. For such an enterprise to have any foundation, the descriptions and assumptions about infant development need to be grounded in theoretical frameworks which have validity. These would then form 'routes' to the understanding of difficulties in infancy.

In the broadest sense, theories of infancy are based on the two paradigms of developmentalism and psychoanalysis. These are different in terms of method and aims, embodying a 'pervasive split between emotion and cognition' (Urwin 1986, p.259). Recent studies suggest that the two paradigms may be subdivided into four sub-paradigms; developmentalism which maintains a primary interest in cognition, and 'rational' development in infancy; developmentalism which is increasingly interested in emotions, through the study of 'intersubjectivity' in relationships infants develop with caregivers; psychoanalysis which maintains a non-empirical clinical methodology (though in which cognition has a larger part to play);[1] and psychoanalysis which is linked with forms of empirical testing, through making contact with developmentalist approaches.

In thinking about understanding infancy in a way in which cognition and emotion are included, it is necessary to cross the paradigmatic boundaries. There are two possible starting points. The first is to describe each theoretical framework and establish the 'points of correspondence' (Urwin 1989, p.224) between them. This approach is perhaps best exemplified by Daniel Stern's work (Stern 1985). The second approach, which will be taken here, is to look at influential studies from each sub-paradigm. The approach is therefore not to collect a review of all 'findings' produced by the developmentalist approach, as in Stern's approach to the subject, but rather to explore method and the language which is used to describe processes. This has the advantages of offering an evaluation of the developments realised and problems discovered by these studies, and suggesting how future studies may be linked with them. The four sub-paradigms form the basis for four different 'routes' to a theory of infancy which can be applied to clinical and preventive settings. I propose to survey each of them briefly.

1.2 Rational development in infancy

In developmental research, inspired by Piaget's theories, the emphasis has been, first, on the development of individual rational and intellectual qualities of the infant, second, though relating more to older children, on the relation between intellectual development and social context, and third on the very early development of relationships between the infant and others. The impact of these three approaches has been to significantly revise Piaget's account (1955) of development in stages. In this theory, the infant moves through six sub-stages of the sensori-motor stage, through learning by assimilation and accommodation. Ways of organising knowledge, or schemas, become increasingly more complex, as the infant learns. Initially, the infant views the world as from a two-dimensional position, responding to the world with reflex actions. Object permanency, the continuation in the infant's mind of an object's existence in its absence, has to be learned and this is a prerequisite for the capacity to think symbolically, which arrives in the second year.

---

1 Spillius (1994) comments that 'In constructing a hypothetical infant, Klein is not alone. Freud, Abraham, Winnicott, Mahler, indeed virtually all analysts are very free in constructing hypothetical accounts of the mental development of infants. I believe that these accounts are mainly derived from what happens in clinical work with adult and child patients, supplemented by some rather unsystematic observations of infants and by general reasoning and ideas of what is plausible. In other words, the theories are derived from one set of data but expounded as if they were based on a different set' (p.13).

In considering the idea of rational development in infancy I shall concentrate on the work of Bower (1974, 1979, 1989a, 1989b). Bower has constructed an infant whose perceptual capacities indicate considerable competence: 'the more the perceptual world of the young infant is investigated', he writes, 'the more competent the infant seems to be' (Bower 1989a, p.24). The essence of the infant's competence is found by exploring the infant's capacity to perceive distance and to locate objects, particularly through sound and vision, outside themselves (Bower 1989a, pp.13, 14). Bower came to the conclusion that new-born infants have a built-in capacity for the third dimension, that is a capacity to locate objects in space and time, and that they could experience shape and size constancy in objects. Further, this capacity enabled infants to act on the environment with intentionality (p.14), have an awareness of the 'world beyond the skin' (p.11) and to partake in perceptual experiences of a three-dimensional nature.

Bower distinguishes between the infant's perceptual world and that of the older child and adult through emphasising that the infant's perceptual world is largely composed of form and shape, rather than content: 'My new-born's perceptual world is form without content, a structure of places and events, without the rich sensory bloom that so characterises our own perceptual world' (1989a, p.37). The infant he says responds to these 'formal, higher order properties of stimulation' (p.26), that is shape and form, rather than the sensory content of stimulation. He showed that blind babies could learn as well as sighted babies. Using operant conditioning, and the knowledge that babies react to an approaching object through the use of three perceptual modalities (sight, sound, and touch), infants learned that the noises transmitted by an approaching object, the 'sonic guide', related to the position of the approaching object. Blind babies were able thereby to make the same defensive adjustments as sighted babies (p.18). Bower's description is: 'the full pattern included head retraction, eye widening, interposition of hands between face and object, and finally a blink' (p.18).

The infant's defensive reactions to an approaching object demonstrated that all five senses (and the sixth, proprioception), were employed to receive information and stimulation, and that the infant was capable of transferring information from one sensory modality to another. Infants, in other words, are able from the beginning of life to perform a cross-modal transfer of information. This gives a different model from Piaget's theory. If the idea is taken further, as Bower claims, the infant appears to be able to abstract shapes, intensities and temporal patterns from information gained by sight, sound and touch, through an innate general capacity. This may more accurately be called amodal perception, since the processes involve an internal coding of information by the infant, in a way which makes it recognisable to all sensory modes, and then effecting the transfer of information across modalities. Stern calls this the 'still mysterious amodal representation' (Stern 1985, p.51). Amodal perception is, indeed, an important outcome of the work of Bower and others.[2] The implication of this for understanding infant development is that a model for learning is thus proposed which is based on a process of differentiation, a gradual de-yoking of experience, rather than a laborious, in comparison, stage by stage building of schemas, as Piaget proposed. Since initially the new-born infant yokes experience in and across all sensory modalities, as the infant grows he develops the capacity to differentiate input received by all perceptual modalities. In the relationship between form and structure, on the one hand, and content, on the other hand, it is the content which introduces specificity and differentiation (Bower 1977, p.84).

Second, the influence upon Bower of information theory (e.g. Attneave 1959) led him to suggest a process of development that moves from openness to becoming more closed. At birth the infant is relatively 'open' to the infinite number of stimuli that might occur. Some he may never meet with: 'the new-born must be preset for many stimuli that he will never encounter' (Bower 1989a, p.36).

Rather like Eliot's (1944, p.13):

> Footfalls echo in the memory
> Down the passage which we did not take
> Towards the door we never opened
> Into the rose-garden

this is a vision of unfulfilled potential. On the other hand, some stimuli, via imitation (Meltzoff and Moore 1983), are encountered in the infant's actual experience: 'The baby has been rehearsing a wide variety of movements, including facial movements from well before birth. Suddenly there is a match for these internally known stimuli' (p.36). Bower adds that this explains the preference of infants for human rather than inanimate stimulation (Bower 1989b). He then develops a theory of the impact of the early on the late, which emphasises the traumatic and long-lasting impact of particular stimuli which are 'matched'. (Bower 1989a, pp.37–8 and chapters 7 and 8.)

In describing the continuities and change in his model of learning, Bower has to bring in the infant's relationship with others. He does this minimally and without developing the concepts he derives in any consistent or rigorous way. Nevertheless, the idea of 'matching' of external and 'internally known' stimuli is the third process he identifies in his model of learning. Bower also leaves a sense of the rational, competent infant, whose capacities in the perceptual sphere indicate their potential to impact upon the relationship with others. The more the infant is competent, or has competent potential, the less the infant is passive, subject to the 'moulding' of others. If the infant is 'inbuilt'

2 Stern cites in particular Moore and Meltzoff (1978) and Meltzoff (1981) in addition to Bower.

with learning potential and processes, rather than simply reflexes, he will take part in the first relationships in a much more organised way.

1.3 Intersubjectivity

In contrast with Bower's one-person psychology the discussion of the theory of infant intersubjectivity has placed the infant's relationship with mother at the centre of the field of study. Instead of concentrating on the capacity of the infant to relate to the physical world, but building on the findings of the perceptual world of the infant (Trevarthen 1982, p.86) the emphasis is placed on the capacity of the very young infant for relationships and relatedness, coming to the conclusion that 'a human is born with a readiness to know another human' (Trevarthen 1980, p.318).

Through the technique of microanalysis, infants up to two months (Murray and Trevarthen 1985; Murray and Trevarthen 1986) are seen to partake in complex interactional exchanges with mother, who, for her part appears to be in synchrony with the patterns of interaction. The 'readiness to know another human' has specific sequential components. For example a six week-old is illustrated (Trevarthen 1980, p.319) in the following sequence:

1. the baby smiles at mother's face
2. mother responds with gentle baby talk
3. baby makes 'cooing vocalisation and a conspicuous hand movement', and ceases to smile when 'expressing an utterance'
4. mother imitates baby.

The infant transfers information across modalities in this communication sequence, uses the mouth, tongue and lips to make 'pre-speech' sounds, and substitutes one set of gestures (smiling) by the attempts at vocalisation. Similarly, the important aspect of maternal behaviour is 'the unselfconsciously intended interpersonal quality of the maternal utterances' (Trevarthen 1980, p.324). Trevarthen shows the musicality of the sequential patterns of mother–infant interactions. Throughout the world, he says, the rhythm of mothers' and babies' communications is allegro (Trevarthen 1991).

Given the capacity of the infant to be in such synchronicity with mother, it is a not surprising conclusion that infants under two months differentiate people from things, and prefer people. (Trevarthen 1980, p.324). This first phase of life Trevarthen calls the period of primary intersubjectivity (Trevarthen 1979, p.???). Exploring the motives of infants, he describes the early capacity not only 'to do things in adjustment to the world' (1980, p.318) but also to make 'purely communicative movements that can never have effect on the physical world except by influencing a human mind: remarkably rich facial expressions for change in emotional state, gesture like hand movements and lip and tongue movements that are evidently precursors of verbal expression' (1980, p.318).

The period of primary intersubjectivity is then the 'most social' (Trevarthen 1991) period of infancy, when the motive of the infant is simply to relate to another and, in turn, to be related with. Turn taking, perfect timing and the richness of these orchestrated interchanges between mother and infant are closely similar to other descriptions of intersubjectivity, notably Brazelton's 'reciprocity' (Brazelton, Koslowski and Main 1974), Stern's 'virtuosity' of mother infant 'exquisitely intricate dyadic patterns' (Stern 1977) and Braten's 'dialogic' dyadic organisation (Braten 1987).

In Trevarthen's theory, there are two significant changes in intention and mode of relating. First, after the intensity of the primary interpersonal period, infants and mothers tend to turn to games in which a third object (toy) is increasingly important: 'Games tend to arise as a result of systematic variation in the interpersonal contact (person–person games). Then objects are increasingly introduced to catch a baby's attention and are manipulated as toys by the partner (object–person games)' (Trevarthen 1982, p.98). Interest in the 'third thing' is built on the foundations of primary intersubjectivity. Second, after 30 weeks – 40 weeks in Trevarthen and Hubley (1978) – the infant becomes more interested in the 'purposes of others and their utterances. In particular, there begins to dawn in the child's mind a new kind of interest in what others know about or are doing to objects. Truly co-operative activity with a toy or set of toys becomes possible' (Trevarthen 1982, p.100).

In secondary intersubjectivity, as Trevarthen called this period ushered in by the baby's interest in other person's motives the co-operative play and interactions

> A deliberately sought sharing of experiences about events and things is achieved for the first time. Before this objects are perceived and used, and persons communicated with – but these two kinds of intention are expressed separately. Infants under nine months share themselves with others but not their knowledge or intentions about things (Trevarthen and Hubley 1978, p.184).

Comparison between secondary intersubjectivity and Piagetian developmental stages shows that all the elements in Trevarthen and Hubley's case example are present in Piaget's theory, except the capacity of adjusting attentions to the mother, an omission caused by Piaget's lack of differentiation of an infant's distinction between human and non-human relations (Trevarthen and Hubley 1978, p.216). Drawing on object relations theory, particularly that of Klein (using Segal 1964) and Winnicott (1965), Trevarthen and Hubley comment on the similarity between secondary intersubjectivity, through the infant's development of interest in motives in others, the depressive position (Klein) and the stage of concern (Winnicott). The infant's passage from dependency on others to greater independence is therefore linked with the infant's 'ability to master objects in acts of developing intentionality' (Trevarthen and Hubley 1978, p.225).

1.4 The 'third route': applications of developmentalism to psychoanalysis

Trevarthen's correspondence with object relations theory leads towards ways in thinking about infants empirically that are linked with psychoanalytic theory. Bower's work is essentially intellectually centred, and socially and interpersonally naive; Stern, Trevarthen and Brazelton, however, all placed increased emphasis on the role of emotion in infant development. Trevarthen, quite simply, described the 'abundant and usually very clear expressions of feeling [demonstrated by babies]. Their feelings, as expressed in facial movements, vocalisation, body movements, orientating movements, are closely integrated with the expression of what they want to do in exploratory or prehensile behaviour and in communication' (1982, p.89), which suggests that the observation of infants could easily become linked with observations of emotional states and intentions. The increased interest in emotionality, affective relationships, and the relationship between these and cognitive development have led to a number of theories and models about infancy that combine, to some extent, developmentalist and psychoanalytic perspectives. Four different treatments of this theme of combination of theories exist:

1. The application of developmentalist findings to psychoanalytic theory with the purpose of influencing the latter.
2. The development of a derivative of psychoanalytical theory and its application via other paradigms to empirical infant study.
3. The development of developmental psychopathology, through the empirical testing of psychoanalytic hypotheses.
4. The combination of developmentalist and psychoanalytic models, both as a theoretical exposition and applied to clinical situations.

1.4.1 Application of developmentalist findings to psychoanalytic theory

The main impetus of this amalgamation is to indicate how the 'revolution' in child developmental research impacts upon psychoanalytic theory. More specifically, the aim is to show that empirical studies modify psychoanalytic concepts, which are formed through clinical reconstruction. This is the first of Stern's aims in his influential project (1985). A Mahlerian (Mahler 1968), Stern, probably with mixed feelings, felt forced to abandon Mahler's view of symbiosis in early infancy: 'can infants experience non-organisation? No! The "state" of undifferentiation is an excellent example of non-organisation. Only an observer who has enough perspective to know the future course of things can even imagine an undifferentiated state. Infants cannot know what they do not know, nor that they do not know' (Stern 1985, p.46).

Through the application of Bower's findings on perception, and Meltzoff and Borton (1979) on imitation, Stern argues for the development of infant organisation through the processes involved in amodal perception. The sense of an emerging organisation of self, in terms of subjective experience of the world and others does not imply the presence of a process of disorganisation (Stern 1985, p.45). This questioned, effectively, the assumption of early symbiosis and the consequent 'undifferentiated' states in infancy, notably the stage of 'normal autism' (Mahler, Pine and Bergman 1975). Though primarily concerned with North American psychoanalysis, Stern also 'catches' Winnicott's model of early mother–infant relatedness, which was similarly positing an 'undifferentiated' early state of 'fusion' (Winnicott 1960, p.45).[3] On the other hand, Stern does not deal with the commonness of his and Klein's position, in that Klein posits an object-relating part of the baby from birth (Klein 1952b, and see Shuttleworth 1989 p.24).[4] Stern goes on to use this confrontation of psychoanalytic hypotheses to develop a model for a developmental pathway and to illustrate the differences between a 'clinical' and an 'observed' infant (1985, chapter 9). This is then used as the basis for his subsequent work of constructing a 'clinically relevant baby'. The achievement of his approach includes an integration of a Bower-like approach to infancy with an intersubjective view of mother–infant relationships. He develops a model of mother's role with her infant, namely affect attunement (1985, pp.138–149). Affect attunement describes a number of responses a parent uses in order to be involved with the infant in an exchange of emotion. Stern emphasises that imitation is insufficient to achieve intersubjective sharing of affect. Additionally, the parent has to intuit the infant's feeling state from his behaviour, to respond in a way which corresponds to the feeling state of the infant and, third, to do this in a way in which the infant can experience the parental response as relating to the infant's original emotional communication (Stern 1985, p.139). Affect attunement is restricted in Stern's usage to the time when the infant begins to be aware of the motives and intentions of others, that is, after about nine months, the period of secondary intersubjectivity. It is used to understand mother–infant interactions in this phase of development, in which the central intention is the mediation of shared internal states. Affect attunement relies upon the infant's capacity to use amodal perception, so that the parent can respond to the infant either in the same modality or another,

---

3 Both Mahler's and Winnicott's accounts derive from Freud's views on auto-erotism and narcissism (Freud 1905 and 1914a).

4 Shuttleworth's chapter performs the operation of comparison in reverse, outlining Klein's theory, the points of contact with developmentalist positions and conducting a defence of the Kleinian argument.

and the emotion of the communication can therefore be amplified, or in other ways emphasised. Thus: 'Imitation renders form, attunement renders feeling' (p.142).

This formulation of mother's behaviour as modifying and 'expanding' the infant communication is close in form (though not in content) to Bion's idea of the mother as 'container' (see below, 1.6). Stern's model of a developmental pathway in infancy leading to 'a sense of a subjective self' places affect in the centre of the model. He then (Stern 1994) constructs a model in which the infant is thought to organise experience at different levels. In particular he emphasises the qualities of shape, time, contour and narrative. There is here a correspondence with Bower's terminology, particularly in the contrast between shape and content. Stern however describes a continuing development of the different levels of experience, which continue to build alongside each other, in 'envelopes', as he calls them. Thus the baby develops patterns of experience in discrete, but interrelated qualitative packages, and these develop from the experiences of relationships, in which emotional states shared with the parent, and with which the parent has been attuned, take central place.

1.4.2 Derivatives of psychoanalysis: Attachment Theory

Bowlby's (1969, 1973, 1980, 1988) conjunction of aspects of Freud's psychoanalysis[5] with ethology has been extremely influential in producing an empirically useful model of infancy. Particularly with the developments by Ainsworth, Bell (Ainsworth *et al.* 1978; Ainsworth and Wittig 1969; Bell and Ainsworth 1972) and Mary Main (1991), Attachment Theory is able to operate as a systematic way of describing infant behaviour, in terms of attachment or proximity-seeking behaviour, a laboratory type-test for infants for assessing the quality of attachment (Ainsworth's 'Strange Situation');[6] Mary Main's (George, Kaplan and Main 1985) Adult Attachment Interview has created adult attachment categories which cross-reference with the Ainsworth infant categories,[7] and the theory carries predictive value across the life cycle (Murray-Parkes, Stevenson-Hinde, Marris 1991), in which the determinants for future behaviour, sense of security and parenting capacity are predicted through one underlying configuration, the quality of the infant's attachment to his caregiver.[8]

---

5 to which he maintained he was being faithful, through taking one aspect of Freud's theory of anxiety, namely signal anxiety (Bowlby 1969, pages 391–392).

6 Infants are observed whilst in a sequence of separations and reunions with mother. Reactions to these events can be categorised in terms of the quality of attachment.

7 Namely Autonomous–Secure; Dismissing–detached; Preoccupied–entangled.

8 Though belatedly, Attachment Theory also commented on the father's relationship with the infant (Lamb 1981).

Following Ainsworth's work on the Strange Situation, there emerged descriptions of the mother's task which is described as 'sensitive parenting', (Ainsworth *et al.* 1978; Main 1991, p.140) a perhaps unnecessarily value laden term,[9] but one which was chosen to indicate the quality in the mother – sensitivity to infant distress – which was necessary to provide secure attachment. Main's later distinctions, formed through work with adults, indicate the quality of attachment which the parent has internalised (Main 1991, p.142) and therefore indicate the continuity of development from infancy through childhood to adulthood, and which indicate the parent's predisposition to provide 'sensitive' parenting. In order to reach this position, Bowlby returned to object relations theory (Bretherton 1991, p.25) to introduce the concept of 'internal working models of mother' (Bowlby 1973, chapter 14), and to begin a process of interest in and elucidation of the nature of internal representation, of relationships within relationships.[10]

The amalgamation of psychoanalysis and ethology has resulted in a free-standing theory. It could have been thought of as such here, as a theory of infant development in its own right, though it suits the purposes of this chapter to see it emerging from a cross-fertilisation of two paradigms.[11] The motivation for infants – proximity seeking – appears critically simplistic in view of the child developmentalist research, though it does give a point of entry into the world of the infant where the state of 'alert inactivity' is not assumed. Trevarthen's list of motives for infants in the primary intersubjective phase includes: 'To maintain a coherent state of well-being whilst [getting to know the physical world]' (Trevarthen 1980, p.326).

The emphasis in Attachment Theory of seeking contact with a 'sensitive' parent indicates one way in which this might be obtained. However, a more sophisticated range of possible motives and behavioural methods of achieving them will be needed before the relationships between infants and their caregivers in states other than alert inactivity can be fully explored. Attachment Theory has little to say about very early development. Attachment behaviours do begin before the mid-first year when they become more easily observable. Internal working models of mothers begin to be formed before attachment is clearly observed. Yet the range of early infant gestures, emotions and contact seeking gestures have more purposes than Attachment Theory suggests. Stern, for example, emphasises the 'motive' of building shared subjective states. Object

9 And the 'avoidant' mother is termed, equally strongly, 'rejecting' (Main 1991).

10 This was the title of a conference in 1990, organised by the Tavistock Clinic which combined views of the nature of 'representation' from the different schools of infancy studies.

11 The inspiration for Bowlby was his differences with Klein's emphasis on the internal world. His insistence on the role of the 'real' mother (Bowlby 1969) formed a virulent and eventually productive 'argument' in the Tavistock Clinic in the 1950s.

relations theory increases this view of early intentions, in infants who are experiencing discomfort or anxiety, rather than the 'alert inactivity' of the laboratory testable baby.

Attachment theory has itself been 'yoked' to other theoretical viewpoints in recent research. In conjunction with hypotheses from contemporary Freudian psychoanalysis, the amalgamation has been used to form developmental psychopathology. It is used as an outcome indicator in research into the experiences of infants with depressed mothers (Murray 1992, 1993), and as a selected part of a combination of theoretical positions in linking developmental research with clinical application (Brazelton and Cramer 1991).

1.4.3 Psychoanalysis and developmentalism combined

Brazelton and Cramer (1991) aimed to explore the relationship between developmental understanding of infancy and clinical situations. A collaboration between a developmentalist – Brazelton – and a clinician – Cramer, the theoretical foundations were Brazelton's work on reciprocity (Brazelton, Koslowski and Main 1974; Brazelton *et al.* 1975; Brazelton *et al.* 1979; Brazelton and Yogman 1986): 'interaction is a mutually regulated system in which both partners modify their actions in response to the feedback provided by their partner. It is surprising how early the infant plays a role' (Brazelton *et al.* 1974, p.147).

This idea of mutual adjustment was closely linked with Attachment Theory, and Freiberg's (1980) idea of the 'ghost in the nursery'. The clinical exposition produced a series of compelling short case studies, in which assessment of infant development, through Attachment Theory, was linked with understanding the disturbance in 'reciprocity' in the relationship between mother and infant in terms of the nature of the parental 'ghost'. Freiberg described the impact of the 'ghost' as varying from an intrusion in an 'unguarded moment', 'and a parent and his child may find themselves re-enacting scene from another time with another set of characters' (Freiberg 1980, p.387), to taking up 'residence and conducting the rehearsal of the family tragedy from a tattered script' (p.388).

The infant's activity in the relationship through making a claim on his parent's love – the reciprocity – usually helps to banish the ghost. When the ghost takes a grip, the result is distortion of the mother–infant relationship. Identifying the ghost in mother–infant brief psychotherapy relieves the situation (Brazelton and Cramer 1991, p.139).

Fonagy and his colleagues (Fonagy *et al.* 1991b; Fonagy, Steele, and Steele 1991; Fonagy *et al.* 1993 and Fonagy 1994) also make use of Freiberg's 'ghost' and Attachment Theory in their programme. Their aim was to discover if a prediction of parent–infant relationships could be made through an assessment of the 'quality of parental internal object relations and habitual modes of defence' (Fonagy *et al.* 1991a, p.117). A psychoanalytic question, in other words, was being addressed by empirical methods, principally Main's Adult Attachment Interview (AAI).

The approach enabled Fonagy and his colleagues to arrive at some interesting conclusions. The development of a reflective self, that is, the capacity of the parent to accurately reflect on his/her own history was a prime factor connected with infant security, as measured by infant attachment patterns in the Strange Situation. Further, the stronger the parental defensive stance, the more likely patterns were to repeat themselves, through 'ghosts in the nursery'. Through the close affective relationship between parent and infant, the child 'internalises his perception of his mother's reaction to his own affective signals' (Fonagy *et al.* 1991, p.126) and 'the child needs to resort to defensive strategies in the face of the caregiver who is incapable of responding accurately to his affective signals' (p.126). This supports empirically the relationship between parental self-awareness and parenting patterns, and the relationship between secure attachment in the infant, and defensive strategies, which could be further described and delineated. In other words, this develops a hypothesis about parenting qualities and the effect of these in influencing the 'internal representations' in infants. The term 'defence' is used in its psychoanalytical sense, having been transformed through the process of application of the AAI.

Fonagy and his colleagues approach the idea of why particular relationships may be subject to difficulties, and suggest a relationship between parental awareness, and defence. Developmental psychopathology, it follows, offers the possibility of empirical testing of psychoanalytical theoretical concepts. (Fonagy 1993).

Lynne Murray (1988, 1991) was more ambitious in her application of psychoanalytic concepts. Intersubjectivity and Braten's 'dialogic' model of the relationship between the 'actual' and 'virtual' other are seen as bridges between psychoanalytic concepts and developmental psychology (Murray 1991, p.229). This enabled her to think about some of the more abstract of psychoanalytic conceptions. Beginning with a variation of intersubjectivity, the discovery that if the mother does not respond in synchronicity with the infant's communications, the infant becomes distressed, it was posited that this 'perturbation' (Tronick *et al.* 1978; Murray and Trevarthen 1985) closely resembled the impact on the infant of maternal depression. In an empirical study of depressed mothers and their infants (Murray 1991, 1992, 1993) Murray used microanalysis of mother–infant relationships at two months (Murray and Trevarthen 1986), Bower's object concept tasks (Wishart and Bower 1984) and the Strange Situation to assess developmental progress. The Life Events and Difficulties Schedule (Brown and Harris 1978) was employed to assess maternal depression. Murray's findings significantly link Object Relations Theory, Intersubjectivity and Attachment. Infants whose mothers were depressed were less able to 'integrate the distress of separation from the mother and instead responded with avoidance and disorientation or resistance' (Murray 1991, p.229).

The capacity of infants to distinguish self and other (as seen through the object concept tasks) was related to the capacity of the mother to identify with infant experience rather than being preoccupied with her own concerns. Citing Object Relations Theory's emphasis on the infant's vulnerability to difficult experiences of distress unless the mother actively responds to help the infant, Murray comments that the study emphasises the 'potentially precarious nature of the mother's capacity to relate appropriately to her infant' (p.229). She has in mind formulations by Winnicott (1974, p.104) of 'falling for ever' and 'going to pieces' and by Bion (1962), 'nameless dread'. Her earlier view (Murray 1989) that these experiences could not be empirically operationalised, despite their importance for development, was therefore amended by the way the 'bridges' of intersubjectivity and the 'dialogic' model allow the subject to be approached. The discussion of infant–mother precariousness suggests that the Object Relations emphasis on the infant's vulnerability plays a significant part in early relationships. Murray also found that the quality of mother–infant relationships was formed through a whole range of moments of intimacy, and not just from experiences of distress: 'Difficulties in relating are not confined to periods of infant distress, but may also be apparent in other forms of contact, such as play, that demand intimate involvement' (Murray 1991, p.229).

Thus models of infant intentionality broader than Attachment Theory are necessary for understanding the range of configurations which influence infant development, especially the development of internal representation. Perhaps the clearest summary which includes multiple motivation is that provided by Emde (1988). He suggests motivation in infancy comes under the four headings of activity, self-regulation, social fittedness and affective monitoring. Parenting, therefore, would normally address all four of these needs. This suggests the need to address how different kinds of parenting are experienced by the infant, and how they meet the needs of these different motivations. Murray lists three – the capacity to tolerate distress and remain engaged with the infant's experiences; switching off; turning against the infant with hostility (Murray 1991, p.223).

1.5 A 'rational' or 'precarious' infant?

Murray's discussion of infants of depressed mothers introduced the idea of the 'precariousness' of the mother–infant relationship, and vivid expressions of infants states of mind, such as 'falling for ever'. These concepts, though familiar to psychoanalytic clinicians are diametrically different from Bower's notion of the rational and competent infant. When the context – mother's depression in this case – is introduced to infancy studies, the infant appears less balanced and competent in his relationships with the physical world. Similarly the idealistic patterns of mother–infant synchronicity are tempered by the perturbation studies and applications to family situations where mothers are in difficulties.

The role of emotion in context appears to introduce a dampener on the world of the laboratory. Developmental psychopathology shows that the concept of defence is an important part of the infant's repertoire of relationships with others. This has its parallel in Bower's clear description of an infant's defence against an inanimate object in the approaching object test. These discussions all suggest the need to further explore the concepts currently used in Object Relations Theory, and their potential application to empirical studies.

Before turning to this task, it is important to consider how far, from this discussion, the different models of infancy can be reconciled. First, many studies now produce amalgamations of ideas across paradigmatic boundaries. The empirical model is used to evaluate the more subjective hypotheses from psychoanalysis. Subjectivity and intersubjectivity form a central focus for studies of infancy, and there is a common theme of mother–infant reciprocity, or mutual adjustment to each other. Psychoanalytic hypotheses have been applied with some caution, except in Murray's willingness to bridge the different descriptions of infant experience described by Object Relations Theory. Partly this is a problem associated with operationalising such concepts; partly it is to do with how emotion is viewed methodologically. Testing an infant in a state of alert inactivity clearly fails to take into account other infant states of mind, notably those of distress. Criticisms of the developmentalist methodology include questioning the observer's objectivity (Urwin 1989), and the narrowness of the range of experience viewed in this way (Bradley 1989). The problem of emotionality is centrally to do with the place it is accorded in the scheme of things. For Bower and others interested in cognition, emotion *is* treated as a non-variable, minimally used to decide whether an infant has responded or not. Nevertheless, emotion *is* registered (Urwin 1989). However, in order to view infants in the round so to speak, a model in which emotion and cognition are dynamically related is necessary. This, to some extent, is the aim of Trevarthen.

Murray suggests that the problem is not simply of introducing infant distress into the equation. Mother–infant activities require from the mother a quality of attention on the experiences of the infant. This is important for the development of the infant. This state of attention is consistent with the kind of responses Trevarthen suggested the mother employed in her synchronistic interactions with the infant, and the kind of emotional involvement Stern described in attunement. It is also a very familiar concept for object relations clinicians, and is central to Bion's model of the mother–infant relationship. Similarly, mother–infant relationships require some forms of categorisation of the part that mothers play. Attachment Theory has gone furthest in this direction, but the categories refer only to the acts of the mother in response to the attachment behaviours of the infant. Infant intentionality, and the range of responses required by the parent are both broader than this.

These features need further attention if a picture of infant development and infant–mother relationships is to be constructed. Such a picture would include cognition and emotion; moments of distress, 'alert inactivity', and, indeed, a full range of emotionality. It would also include relationships between mothers and infants in different states of openness to each others communications. To this one should add mothers, and fathers, in different socio-economic and cultural settings. As current developments across paradigms emphasise the development of internal relationships, or representation, these too, it follows, are the product of an interrelationship of some kind between all these factors. How early internalisation takes place is still not systematically studied. The most detailed accounts remain those emanating from psychoanalytic work with children and adults.

1.6. The 'fourth route': operationalisation of Object Relations Theory

The potential 'fourth route', the empirical study of infants through psychoanalytic object relations theory, has not as yet been realised, partly because the conceptual framework of the theory aims to describe emotional processes of great complexity, and partly because the clinical aims of psychoanalytic practice are achieved through theory generated from clinical settings. The theory depends on models of hypothetical infants, as Spillius describes (see footnote 1, page 5 above). Psychoanalytic theories of infancy have therefore developed a number of models of infancy, some of which differ from each other in important respects. As I have already mentioned (page 10 above), Mahler (1968) and Winnicott (1960) emphasised a lack of differentiation between mother and infant in the early weeks, whereas Klein posited the infant's rudimentary capacity to object relate from birth, that is to relate to others in moments of 'alert inactivity':

> I have seen babies as young as three weeks interrupt their sucking for a short time to play with mother's breast or look towards her face. I have also observed that young infants – even as early as the second month – would, in wakeful periods after feeding lie on mother's lap, look up at her, listen to her voice and respond to it by their facial expression. (Klein 1952c)

Shuttleworth points out (1989, p.23) that this aspect of Klein's theory is a point of contact with the views of Bower and Trevarthen. Klein added that the infant maintained a precarious hold on object relating, limited to periods of freedom from hunger and tension (Klein 1952b, p.62), because of the impact of anxiety, which has both internal and external sources. External sources consisted of any situation of discomfort or frustration, whilst internally, continuous processes of taking in and expelling – introjection and projection – are established from birth and these are linked with emotional states. Thus loving and hating impulses are both projected on to the mother. Good and bad, loving and hating experiences are also taken in and become the starting point for emotional and mental life.

The infant employs all perceptual modalities for these processes of introjection and projection, though, in Klein's theory, emphasis is given to the constant and inevitable emotional content of these operations. Second, the impact of processes of introjection and projection is to create a state of confusion between inner and outer, agent and recipient. Third, the experiences of reality are distorted by the infant's phantasies, that is, his inner images of the other and his projections on to her. A recent exposition of these processes is provided by Brenman Pick:

> Our receptors – eyes, ears, mouth, nose and touch – all that with which we take in from outside, are parts of our living and evolving selves. Because we project so much – and then take in – we are not sure how much of what we are perceiving is really there, and what has been added to, either with love or hate, of what comes from ourselves. We receive experiences, and also in phantasy or reality express or expel feelings and parts of ourselves, good and bad, as well as our own internalised history... [In Klein's work] the emphasis was placed on the idea that these forces were operative from the very beginning of life. (Brenman Pick 1992, p.24).

The infant's precariousness is the cause of the confusion and complexity since anxiety is ever present and likely to be experienced as catastrophic; the experience is described in terms of 'falling for ever' (Winnicott 1974, p.104); 'liquefying' and 'falling apart' (Bick 1986, p.296). In the face of such overwhelming anxiety infants develop defensive strategies, which are based on processes of introjection and projection. In particular, the idea of projective identification was designated by Klein (1946) as an omnipotent unconscious phantasy for expelling the unwanted and unbearable feelings from inside the infant, out into the person of the mother.

Bion (1962) added to this picture a theory which identified the mother's role in relating to her infant, which he called 'reverie'. Reverie comprises a state of mind in the mother (or parent) in which she allows the baby's experiences to enter her mind, so that she can think about and gather a sense of the meaning of these infantile communications. These are then used to formulate, consciously and unconsciously responses to the infant's communications and needs. The baby experiences containment from the mother's emotional work of first allowing the infant's experiences to permeate her, making sense of these communications before responding to the baby, through her words, gestures, and deeds, conveying her understanding of his needs.

The idea that the mother, through her reverie, transforms the infant's emotional experiences, is based on a three-dimensional model of the container and contained. This was clearly related to and built upon Klein's ideas about projection, introjection and projective identification.

For Bion, projective identification was not simply a defensive strategy, but also a primitive form of communication. From this he proposed a model of learning, and of thinking (Bion 1962). In terms of the discussion in this chapter as a whole, there are four features which follow from Bion's contribution to psychoanalytic theory, that have a bearing on the relationship between Object Relations Theory and the other three 'routes' to a theory of infancy.

First, Bion brings cognition into the psychoanalytic theory. The container–contained relationship is a 'link' between thoughts and thinking (Bion 1967, p.102). The mother/container aims to get to know her infant and the infant seeks from the mother an understanding of experiences which are beyond his capacity to name and differentiate. The infant has a preconception of the kind of experience he will receive and these are either realised or frustrated. Thoughts develop from sensations and feelings through the mother's reverie, which will modify or reduce frustration, and the infant develops a mixture of realised or frustrated experiences, leading to conceptualisations (Bion 1967, pp.110–119). There is a kind of correspondence with Bower's model. The infant's expression of sensation is similar in quality to Bower's description of sensory inputs, whilst the mother's function as a container is to provide a bounded space for the communications, to offer a means of organising the 'higher order variables' of shape and form. Bion therefore distinguishes between two components – the container and contained. Unlike Bower these two parts of the 'system' are primarily a relationship between two people; the 'container' is made, not given.

Second, the images of shape that are involved in the process of container–contained are, like the preoccupations of Stern and Fonagy (both 1994) descriptive of spatial relations. Similarly Meltzer's work on autism (Meltzer *et al.* 1975) and Bick's (1968) theory of 'skin formation' employ images of shape and spatial relationships, namely the movement from two to three dimensions of internal relations. Again, unlike Bower, these theories postulate processes whereby the development of and retreat from three-dimensionality may occur, particularly in experiences of unbearable bodily and mental separation from the mother.

Third, the containing function of the mother, which Bion called her 'reverie', is used to describe the processes that occur in interaction between mother and infant, using the Kleinian theory of projection and introjection as their driving force. Bion's elucidation of the failure of the mother's reverie (Bion 1967, pp.116–117) was taken up by others (e.g. Harris 1975) to suggest consequences of problems of internalisation, thinking and symbol formation. The theory addresses Emde's motive of self regulation, describing how mother achieves this with and on behalf of the infant, through her containing the infant's emotional experiences. Reverie is similar to Stern's attunement and Ainsworth's sensitivity, but it has the differences of, first, being applied to very early functioning, and, second, of being linked with a particular process of emotional transformation in interactions.

Fourth, the theory delineates a developmental pathway, which being based on an analogy with the digestive system, describes mental formations arising from bodily experiences, moving, in other words, from a state of body to a state of mind. From physical holding the infant is 'held in mind'. The infant then internalises the containing function of the parent. The containing process gives rise to the capacity to maintain a link with the mother in her absence. Internalisation of the mother's containing function and therefore of her capacity for thinking, leads to the infant developing for himself the capacity to think. This is an essential prerequisite for symbolic modes of thinking in the infant. The developmental pathway suggested by Bion is therefore towards the capacity to think, and contain feelings, through the capacity to symbolise.

These elements of Bion's theory have bearing on risk in infancy. First, there is a hypothesis that links the quality of the early container–contained relationship with the infant's later developmental achievements, particularly with regard to symbolisation, thinking and internalisation; a satisfactory early container–contained relationship leads to a more satisfactory developmental outcome whilst problems in the early container–contained relationship lead to difficulties in thinking and symbolising. Second, the description of mother's function – her reverie – provides a concept for evaluating the effect of maternal care on the infant. Failure in the function of maternal reverie contributes to infant developmental failure. Third, there are suggestions as to some of the processes, such as the retreat from three- to two-dimensionality, and the failure to move from 'states of body' to 'states of mind', through which the infant may manifest responses to the quality of the container–contained relationship. In this framework, the possibility of describing risk lies in thinking about the particular qualities of the maternal function – the qualities of the container – and the particular adjustments the infant makes to contend with the experiences presented by the containing function, whilst attempting to maintain developmental needs and progress. These qualities of the relationship between container and contained need further elaboration in order to operationalise them as a framework for exploring risk. A model is therefore required (see Chapter 3.3) which will lead to a refinement of the particular qualities of risk which are to be investigated.

1.7. Summary

Bion's theories and their points of contact with the other three 'routes' represent what Urwin has called 'some of the distinctive or challenging aspects of psychoanalysis' (Urwin 1989, p.275), which can be lost in any attempt to empiricise the conceptual framework. The challenge is twofold; first, to ascertain how the operations of projection and introjection can be observed. If they are not observable, do they not exist? The second problem is equal and opposite. Brenman Pick's description of early processes in adult language is precisely that the attribution of adult functioning, or at least functioning at a verbal level, to a non-verbal infant commits an anachronism. Bion was aware of this potential problem – arising in his case from an abstractness, not to say abstruse mode of expression, as his cryptic footnote in *Learning from Experience* shows:

> Yet it is but a short step... to the absurdity of attributing to the infant ideas, thoughts, concepts about what the grown up calls a 'feeling' that would do credit to a Kant. Perhaps the answer is that only a Kant has such problems and can solve them. Those who are not Kant (a) do not have these problems or (b) have these problems and develop disorders of thought. (Bion 1962, p.103)

Methodological problems are thus raised which require discussion. Nevertheless, the possibilities for providing a distinctive framework for the study of very early development, and the dynamic relationship between emotion and cognition within the theory of container–contained holds the possibility of adding to understanding of infancy in general and risk in infancy in particular. The means for accomplishing this task lie in the operationalisation of an Object Relations model based on Bion's theory. Discussion of methodological issues and the process of operationalisation are the subjects to which I shall now attend.

CHAPTER 2

Methodology

The operationalisation of psychoanalytical concepts from the object relations school is an innovative, exploratory approach to understanding infancy. The newness of this approach raises issues concerning the scientific status of psychoanalytic theories and requires the development of a suitable method of observation, which will need to be compared with other more traditional forms of observation and analysis of infant development, particularly the laboratory techniques of the developmentalists. The form of observational study, developed by Esther Bick for training purposes, provides a possible method which with adaptation could provide the means for developing the study of infants in the direction I am aiming. Here I shall consider these methodological issues and discuss how the Esther Bick method can be adapted to become a method of research.

2.1 Epistemology

So far, I have alluded to, and occasionally introduced, methodological differences between the different theories of infancy. I shall now summarise these as a prelude to a wider methodological discussion. In developmentalism observational methods exist alongside the experimental. The Piagetian observational method has been described as a 'form of psychiatric interview' (Urwin 1986, p.262) and as a detailed form of interviewing which Piaget thought needed at least two years' training (Bradley 1989, p.101). Technological innovations in the use of video recording have led to laboratory-based techniques known as microanalysis, and these methods, in common with experimental work in general, are detailed, available to scrutiny and easily repeatable. These techniques reduce to a minimum the interaction between the observer and his subject. Both Attachment Theory and developmentalism apply a mixture of methods, a multistrategy approach (Layder 1991, p.107) combining direct observation, structured interviews (e.g. the Adult Attachment Scale) and predetermined sequences of observation (e.g. the object concept tasks). Those programmes (e.g. Murray, Fonagy) which move across paradigms also employ a mixture of methods.

Throughout the discussion in Chapter 1 a distinction has been made between 'empirical' and clinical. The former is used to describe direct observation of babies or testing via structured interview or tasks; the latter implies the construction of a hypothetical infant from clinical work with adults and children (Spillius 1994, see page 5 above). Clinical reconstruction is occasionally illustrated by direct observation, for example Freud's 'boy with a cotton reel' (Freud 1920) and Klein's descriptions of babies from direct observation, from which I have quoted (Chapter 1.6 above). The scientificity of the psychoanalytic view of infancy then rests on the efficacy of the clinical method. Unlike microanalysis, the clinical method is always open to the 'interference' of the clinician, through his interpretative work and other roles (Rustin 1991, p.120). Psychoanalysis – like Marxism – has fared badly in the hands of the empirical philosophers of science, particularly following Popper's (1963) falsification principle, the idea persists that, under an epistemology of empiricism, psychoanalysis fails to meet the requirements of rational scientific enquiry.

A vigorous defence of psychoanalysis as a science has been made by Will (1986) and Rustin (1991), principally through questioning the hegemony of empirical epistemology in the event of the emergence of alternative epistemologies. Drawing particularly on Bhaskar's (1978, 1979, 1986) theory of transcendental realism, both Will and Rustin make this the basis for developing grounds for the scientific underpinning of psychoanalysis. Will is particularly harsh on theoretical positions – such as Bowlby's – which accept the dominance of empiricism, and therefore reduce the importance of concepts such as phantasy, the unconscious, and the inner world; a piece of 'epistemological identification with the aggressor' (Will 1986, p.167) is his judgment. Hermaneutics are also severely treated, since, Will claims, the effect of splitting causes and meaning is solipsism, and maintains the prioritisation of and distinction between, in empiricism, natural sciences over human sciences. This is ''very dubious ontologically' (p.167).

Bhaskar's realism – which is derived from Kant's fourth parologism of pure reason (Kant 1964, pp.345–6) – emphasises the independent existence of the subjects of scientific enquiry: 'Things exist and act independently of our descriptions, but we can only know them under particular descriptions… Science…is the systematic attempt to express in thought the structures and ways of acting of things that exist and act independently of thought' (Bhaskar 1978, p.250).

Thus Bhaskar posits 'deep structures' of theoretical knowledge which describe observations. The problem caused by leaving an empirical world is not only that of solipsism, but also of relativism. If the 'thing in itself' can be approached from any position, then any description will do. For Wittgenstein, this was part of a particular 'language game' (see Phillips 1977, pp.74–92). The realist view is that, first, reality is stratified, and that scientific theories are similarly stratified, through the operation of what Bhaskar calls 'generative mechanisms'. Different kinds of generative mechanism are needed to describe different kinds of knowledge.[1] Second, the existence of generative mechanisms is known by their effects, a factor which suits psychoanalysis very well, but is also true of natural science, since: 'It seems impossible to formulate a coherent model of science based on direct observation alone, as opposed to inferences from the observed effects of structures. All perception depends on choices of material and physiological effects emanating from phenomena which are known only through such effects' (Rustin 1991, p.127).

The realist view validates the kinds of description that psychoanalysts make. It does not obviate the need for observation or linking empirical-type work with and in addition to the clinical. For one thing, the effect of clinical 'interference' necessitates the application of non-clinical methods. There is also the requirement to build what Rustin calls 'Networks of interlocked and interdependent theories supported by observational data at many points' (p.120) in any scientific theory, rather than relying on a 'single observational pillar'. 'Triangulation', as Denzin (1970) described it, is an important criteria in scientific endeavour. Psychoanalysis *qua* science therefore needs the availability of observational support for its tenets; the idea of 'generative mechanisms' provides the philosophical underpinning for exploration through operationalisation of the kinds of questions about infants raised in Chapter 1, particularly the relationship between emotion and cognition. Operationalisation of psychoanalytic concepts for direct observation takes place then in a climate in which the concepts themselves through a realistic epistemology have some scientific standing.

The discussion in Chapter 1 raised other questions for which methodological considerations are necessary. First, it was not simply the case that there was a need to include emotional hypotheses, but also that a method was needed in which infants could be studied in all emotional states. Second, the issue of continuity, or 'history' of infant development was important in order to address the significance of patterns or configurations of infant development and mother–infant relationships over time to assess the relationship between earlier and later development. All the variations of approach to infant development proposed some form of developmental pathway, in which the earlier organisation led into or was superseded by a later one. Specifically, for infants in families where there were difficulties, the issue of continuity addresses the relationship between the 'passing phase' of difficulty, moments of distress and of 'missing' in the relationship, and the crystallisation of patterns as significant for infant development. Finally, in any non-laboratory method the role and impact of the observer on the subject needs to be taken into account.

---

1 Will uses the example of Bion's work on groups, and the relationship between this and knowledge gained from individual psychoanalysis. These are complementary, and do not replace each other (p.164).

For this study, then, these considerations require that the method needs to be, first, naturalistic, second, longitudinal, and third, able to employ a framework for thinking about the observer's role. Bick's observational method appeared to have the potential for meeting these requirements..

2.2 Esther Bick's method of infant observation

The programme of infant observation was devised for child psychotherapy trainees, and it has been suggested (M.J. Rustin 1989, 1991) that this has the potential for meeting requirements for research. The aims of the programme, as Bick herself described them, were to include the fact that therapists, when faced by their child patients in the clinical setting, would have an actual experience of observation of an infant to support their experiences of relating to the infantile anxieties and object relationships of their patients: 'It would give each student a unique opportunity to observe the development of an infant, more or less from birth, in his home setting and in his relation to his immediate family and thus to find out for himself how these relations emerge and develop' (Bick 1964, p.558). Within this statement is the belief that extensive and intensive exposure of the student, or trainee, to the observational procedure can be a central part of the overall training objectives. It is indeed an extensive training method. Students are required to observe an infant at home weekly for one hour from birth to two years. Each hourly observation is recorded after the event (note taking at the time is eschewed, as it is felt to detract from the task of observation). These detailed descriptive accounts are then discussed in a small seminar group of usually five members, who present usually two recordings in a seminar in rotation. There is considerable emphasis placed on the importance of description; the observer is encouraged to record as nearly as possible everything that happened in the hour. Theoretical and other forms of speculation are left until the seminar discussion. Bick was clear about the difficulties of 'objective' recording, whilst optimistic that the essential task of separating description from interpretation could be accomplished. She wrote:

> As soon as these facts (i.e. the observational events) have to be described in language we find every word is loaded with a penumbra of implication... In fact the observer chooses a particular word because observation and thinking are almost inseparable. This is an important lesson for it teaches caution and reliance on consecutive observations for confirmation (Bick 1964, p.565)

The need for repeated observations to confirm assessment is one which justifies the massiveness of the project, namely the regularly repeated observations over two years. In turn this regularity and relatively long time-scale of observations leads to the development of emotionally powerful relationships between the observer and observed, together with an appreciation of the depth of the relationships between parent and infant. For newcomers to observation, both the discomfort in adopting an observational or non-interventionist role, and the quality of the relationship between parent and infant provides an experience which can be surprising in its intensity.

This is now an extensively-used model, being a central part of the MA in Psychoanalytical Observational Studies at the Tavistock Clinic, and incorporated in other Tavistock trainings. There have been some developments whereby observation is included in social work training programme (see Briggs 1992; Wilson 1992; Trowell and Miles 1991).

It has been found in the course of these developments that the learning provided by observation is essentially pluralistic. That is to say that the observation provides the student with an extensive opportunity to learn from experience about infants and young children. He also learns how the family members experience the crucial events of the infant's first two years, and the quality and nature of relationships that develop between them. He is subject to the emotional impact of these events and relationships. In learning about this impact, the observer is part of a process in which his awareness and sensitivity are also developed. The observer's role is not that of the 'fly on the wall'. Although required to refrain from initiating activity and interaction, he is expected to maintain a friendly and receptive attitude to the family, of whom he is a privileged guest. He is also expected to be active emotionally and mentally (Henry 1984), and the observation of the events in the family is coupled with digesting the emotional impact of the encounter. It is in any event not possible to be an observer in a family and not be noticed, or to have no impact on the family system. Thinking about the quality of this impact, in both directions, between observer and observed is an important part of the process of understanding the observational material.

Here the seminar discussions have the function of holding or containing the emotional dynamics in which the observer is involved. (See M.E. Rustin 1989). The observer also has a potentially containing function in the family, relying on the parent to help to define the boundaries of the observation, and to accommodate him in this role, but also being available for the family – both parent and infant – through being emotionally attentive to the interaction in the family.

So the development of this kind of infant observation has many potential uses, and has thus emerged as a flexible tool for teaching and learning, where the original method has been demonstrably capable of adaptation to different settings, time-scales and consumer groups.

2.3. Application of Bick's model to research

The teaching and learning function of this observational method has predominated, permitting the accumulation of some 45 years' experience of infant observation without much attention being paid to the qualities of data from observation that could contribute in a systematic way to knowledge about infancy. On the other hand some writers have included observation in an attempt to influence theory, notably Bick herself. There are three variations of the attempts so far to use infant observation in this way. First, there is the insertion of observational material to illustrate or supplement clinical data such as Bick's work on skin formation (1968, 1986) and Symington's (1985) extension of this. Here a 'snapshot' of observation is used alongside some generalised comments about infant behaviour and its meaning in relationship with clinical hypotheses. Second, there is a small but growing body of case studies which are based on observation (Meltzer 1984; Miller *et al.* 1989; Miller 1987; Piontelli 1986; Waddell 1988). These accounts combine description of context of the observation, the family circumstances, some aspects of the infant's development, the relationship between mother and infant and a linking with an aspect of psychoanalytical theory. Third, there is some recent research using infant observation as part of the study, in which specific aspects of infant development are discussed. These include aspects of the parent–infant relationship and the context in which the infant lives. Therefore studies have focused on the relationship between eye contact and feeding in young infants (Rhode 1993), on the role of the nanny's relationship with mother and how this impacts upon the baby's development (Magagna 1993), and cross-cultural mother–infant relationships (Ellis 1993). These studies, which were part of the Tavistock Conference in Infant Observation (Reid 1997), persuade Rustin that the method is beginning to have an impact on theory generation and understanding of infant development in its social context (Rustin 1993). Piontelli (1987, 1992) has made significant contributions to the understanding of early development through employing an observational methodology. Combining ultrascan observations with the Bick method of infant observation and extracts from clinical sessions of psychoanalysis with young children she provides persuasive evidence for the continuities of configurations of development from pre-birth into young childhood. She shows, particularly, patterns of activity which persist from pre-birth into childhood. Twins are seen to occupy similar spatial relationships to each other throughout her period of study; one infant has a predilection for licking from pre-birth to early childhood. Her observational material is seen through the extensive presentation of some chosen sessions of ultra-scan, infant observation and child analytic sessions.

These observational studies then have some significant correspondence with other forms of the ethnographic or case study approach. Rustin (1989) suggests the parallels are that the observations take place in naturalistic settings and that the observational reports aim to achieve descriptions of the subjects in ordinary language. It follows that there is a task involved in operationalising psychoanalytic theory for naturalistic observation purposes.

The other central feature of Bick's method concerns the role of the observer. Since the method of observation as a teaching and learning tool is essentially a two-way process; that is to say that the focus of study is both the infant in his family and the observer's capacity to manage the emotional impact of this exposure to this emotionally charged arena of early development, it follows that these two have something to say about each other. Rustin (1989, p.61) comments on the inevitability of being a 'participant' observer in this method, which again compares with ethnographic methods. Moreover the explicit sense in which the observer is helped in seminars to think about the meaning of the responses he/she experiences, and the quality of language he uses to describe what he has been seeing, focus the observer on the application of the clinical concepts of transference and countertransference. It must be emphasised that these concepts are adapted from the clinical use and applied to the transactions between observer and family members. Understanding the function of the observer in infant observation in this way leads to thinking about the parallels, and differences, between the psychoanalytical and social science theories of observation.

2.4 The role of the observer

If empiricism suggests that the presence of the observer is a disturbance to the practice of scientific endeavour, an aside by Stern (1977) indicates the potential value. He comments on the 'old' method of recording mother–infant interactions by hand-operated take-up reels on the camera and playback equipment: 'It [the hand-held camera method] brings the researcher into very intimate contact with the material. Much as I came involved with the process between Jenny [the infant] and her mother so through this method did I become a participant observer of the interaction between the twins and their mother' (Stern 1977, p.138).[2]

Bick, too, as we have seen, wrote about the difficulty of steering a path between the 'participant' and 'observer' parts of the role, and the overall method is somewhat delicate, involving the observer's regular and fairly long-term presence in the family home, with many implications for the family's relationships. It is common, especially in times of stress and difficulty for the observer to be seen in a supportive way, or alternatively as an intruder. The psychoanalytic meta-theory for the management and understanding of the dynamics between observer and observed adapted from clinical practice, transference and countertransference, would indicate also that the kind of emotion and relationship

---

2 Incidentally the whole of Stern's very innovatory chapter is packed with examples of countertransference!

channelled through these observer-observed interactions embraces powerful emotional issues. The theory of transference and countertransference permits the characterisation of observer–observed relationships.

The presence of transference in observations is suggested by the capacity of the subject of observations to 'transfer' expectation, hopeful and fearful, on to the observer (Wittenberg 1970). Following Melanie Klein's idea of projective identification (Klein 1946), Heimann (1950) suggested that understanding, through reflection, on the analyst's state of mind may be both analytically useful and informative of the state of mind of the patient. In observation it is possible that the combination of transferred expectations and the observer's receptiveness may be an additional source of information for the observer. There is a danger, of course, in that the 'countertransference' may be much more to do with the observer's own pathology, as was intended by Freud's original formulation of countertransference as a distortion of understanding (Freud 1910). The implication is that countertransference evidence in observations requires corroboration from other levels of material – the descriptive narrative of interactions and the parents' verbal reports.

There is also a case for suggesting that countertransference is always present in ethnographic studies. Taken to mean the researcher's attitude to his subjects, Bradley (1989) suggests 'it is always a crucial part' (p.158) and Hunt (1985) introduces the terms into general application for fieldwork. Recording the interactions between observer and observed and the controlled or systematic recording of observer emotional reactions provides the method with the means for assessing the impact between the observer and observed at both a macro and micro level. By macro I mean the overall attitude created between the subject and researcher through contact, what each represent for the other;[3] micro is meant to suggest the momentary or persistent passing of projections from observed to observer and the feeling states evoked in the observer at any moment during observation.

As a research method, therefore, the ethnographic, historical, longitudinal and naturalistic perspective will be accompanied by descriptions of the quality of observer–observed transactions, the qualities, in other words, of transference and countertransference. There will also be information about what was 'done' by the observer, and relations between description and generative structures will also be made explicit. These demands on the methodology require a careful

3 Rosaldo (1986) suggests the same with regard to Evans Pritchard's classic work on the Nuer (1940). Evans Pritchard's irritation with the Nuer's unwillingness to communicate with him is seen as a characteristic of the Nuer. Rosaldo suggests it is more likely a failure of Evans Pritchard to take into account how he is identified with the imperial regime to which the Nuer are subject. However, the fact that this is open to scrutiny some 40–50 years after the writing provides an incidence of the usefulness of recording in such explicit detail.

discussion of strategy (2.5 below) and operationalisation of theoretical concepts (3.3 below).

2.5 Advantages and disadvantages of the Bick model of infant observation

The Bick method of naturalistic observation can be demonstrated to be a naturalistic method of observation similar to other ethnographic forms of study, the kind of data produced to have scientific value in terms of realism and the role of the observer to be understood in terms of transference and countertransference. It is rich in individual details of development in one family, and is unproven as an objective source of research data. There are no intrinsic mechanisms for comparison and these will need to be devised for this study. There are, nevertheless, some advantages and disadvantages of this method which need to be stated and evaluated.

Compared with laboratory-type methods, this method of observation includes problems of reliability connected with the emphasis placed on the observer's recall. Unlike microanalysis techniques where the video recording stores the observation for repeated playback, the observer has a once-only opportunity to record what he sees. Moreover, the observer's recall may be subject to selectivity and unreliability. Though observers do develop a particular skill in recall, the data from this method is restricted to the observations of a single observer. This is continually born in mind in this study and it follows that any hypothesis is subject to confirmation by interreliability testing. The aim must therefore be to make conclusions which can be further tested either by the same methodology, or by others which will act as forms of triangulation. The study is primarily exploratory, and the aims of the book are consistent with this.

The method permits considerable repetition of observations over a substantial period of time, and the findings from this method never rest on one particular observation alone. It is potentially possible to introduce into the method measures which would increase the reliability, or even to find subjects who would accept multiple observers. The use of video and review of the transcripts on a systematic basis are both possible. The possible application of video in using the method will be born in mind during the discussion of the findings, but it was not used here in this study because it was felt to interfere unduly with the unobtrusive observational method. The aim was to provide a constant framework for observations and the consistency of the regular weekly hour for observation; that every observation was unstructured and the observer's role was unobtrusive 'friendly receptivity' provided the elements of such a framework.

Similarly the method does not include systematic microanalysis, formalised coding and sequential analysis of the observational transcripts. Interpretations of these rely on a holistic reading of the transcripts which the observer has produced, through, as it were, observing with a moving rather than a fixed lens. Each recording then takes in a 'wide angle' and it is possible to 'zoom' for a close-up – indeed this is often an essential part of the process when observing the minute movements involved in mother–infant interactions. Formal analysis of the data is provided here through the development of a grid which was administered to the data on a regular basis and which contained consistent categories for comparison.

On the other hand the Bick method offers a number of advantages for the observer. Observing the baby in naturalistic surroundings, which the presence of the observer distorts only to a minor degree, permits the baby to be observed in all emotional states, whilst the observer, for an hour a week, observes the normal ebb and flow of infant–parent relationships. Ethically, the naturalistic environment provides few problems when observing disturbed or unhappy circumstances compared with laboratory methods.[4] The method is sensitive to transactions between the observer and the family members and these transactions can be recorded and made explicit.

Second, the openness of the method, that is to say, the absence of prestructured protocol makes this form of observation a potential source of new theoretical perspectives. This possibility is best described by Glaser and Strauss (1967) and their development of the concept of 'grounded theory'. The application of grounded theory, through the development of middle range classifications and categories is ambitious in its assertion that the 'social world must be *discovered.* This can only be achieved by first-hand observations and participation in "natural" settings, guided by an exploratory orientation' (Hammersley 1990, p.598).

The aims of grounded theory conflict with those of ethnography (Glaser and Strauss 1971, p.183; Layder 1992, p.44). Its application means an active sampling of the data, rather than an immersion in the subject to produce the fullest data possible. However, in that grounded theory is formed through the development from the empirical material of 'substantive' theory, which has a relationship to the deep structures of formal theory in terms of the level of abstraction and generalisation, the twin aims of ethnographic immersion and theory generation can be achieved through the development of research instruments which act on the data. Since 'grounded theory' concentrates on the generation of new approaches and perspectives, the outcome of the approach is much more likely to be concerned with what Rudner (1966) calls 'the context of discovery' rather than the 'context of validation'. The aim of the study must therefore be more directed towards the formation rather than the testing of hypotheses.

---

4 Ethical issues in this study are discussed in detail below, Chapter 3.1).

The aim, therefore, in using this method of observation must be to produce hypotheses which have the possibility of testing on a wider scale. This consideration – the development of 'grounded theory' and the requirements of this approach – led to two important decisions with regard to the process of this study. First, a case study approach was taken to the data produced from each observation and the presentation of the data was primarily descriptive. This is consistent with the ethnographic and participant–observer type of study that is being undertaken. Second, a grid was developed which was used to develop the 'grounded theory' concepts, and to provide categorisation which could be used for the basis of comparison between the cases. Comparison focused on changes over time – the longitudinal aspect of the study – and between cases.

The main variations of the Bick method adopted by this study were, therefore, first, the development of a case study approach, and second, the introduction of a grid for purposes of comparison within the sample. Case study design needs to have distinct characteristics, in order to be effective as a research design. Fonagy and Moran (1993) comment on four particular qualities. First, that 'The attention to repeated observations, more than any other single factor permits knowledge to be drawn from the individual case and has the power to eliminate plausible hypotheses' (p.66). These case studies were all based on repeated observations. Second, Fonagy and Moran suggest that qualitative data should attempt to support conclusions using data from multiple sources. Given that the single researcher raises the problem of interreliability testing, as discussed above, the possibilities of 'triangulation' were given some thought. First, there is the possibility of referring to different levels of evidence. Direct observations of infant behaviour, for example, were complemented by comments from mother, and other family members, and the observer's countertransference experiences. Fonagy and Moran make a claim that triangulation is a widely based concept, including, even, the inclusion of different kinds of theoretical material: 'A broader interpretation of triangulation is the supplementing of clinical psychoanalytic data with anthropological observations from other fields, such as literature or the visual arts' (p.66). Here, holistic reading of transcripts, the development of the grid and the inclusion of different levels of evidence aim to support any observations that are made and from which findings are drawn.

Third, Fonagy and Moran recommend that hypotheses are formed clearly enough to permit the derivation of appropriate counter examples and fourth, they require clarification between the personal connection of the researcher and the possible threats from this to objectivity. Both of these are attended to in the design of the case studies which follow.

2.6 Summary

In this chapter the methodological issues affecting this study have been discussed. The main emphasis of this discussion has been to establish the place – or potential place – in research methodology of the kind of observational method employed in this study. This discussion, incorporating epistemological issues, the aetiology and main methodological pillars of the Bick method, and the role of the observer led to an evaluation of this method compared with other forms of observational study and laboratory-based methods. These methods are clearly different, and purport to accomplish different aims and tasks. In this study the emphasis is on developing a new perspective, through, especially, the use of grounded theory, and on extending the Bick method through the processes of comparison, for which the grid is developed, and through the systematic writing of case studies.

CHAPTER 3

The Study
Five Infants at Potential Risk

There are two parts to this chapter. In the first part I describe the five families whose infants were chosen to be intensively studied. I describe the development of primary data from these observations and the development of an assessment grid as a research instrument for masking comparisons over time and between the infants studied. In the second part of the Chapter I return to the discussion of Chapter 1 and demonstrate how a 'model' was developed from the observational data seen as grounded theory and the operationalisation of concepts from psychoanalysis, particularly Bion's theories. I then show how the model can be used qualitatively and quantitatively to provide a structure for the writing of case studies from the observations of the five infants.

3.1 The study families; selection; risk; ethics

The study is based on observations conducted over a two-year period with each of five families. In each case the infant was observed weekly, usually at the same time each week for one hour, from soon after the birth to two years.

One infant, Timothy, was observed initially in order for the observer to familiarise himself with the method. The other four infants were observed more or less concurrently. In each case a link person – a health visitor, nursery officer, social worker, psychotherapist – was approached and the nature of the observation required was explained to them. This was put in simple terms, that I wished to study development in infancy from experience, and that it was entirely a matter for the family to agree to this. I explained that I wished to meet with the parents before the baby's birth, and that it would be easier, perhaps, for the parents to decide whether to accept the observation after having met me, so to speak, in the flesh. They would then be more able to ask me questions and get a feel of what was involved. This was an approach that was consistent with the normal way families are sought for the 'training' application of Bick's method.

In fact, the recruiting of families was a lengthy process. Whereas Timothy's parents Sally and Neville had been recruited from a health visitor serving a general population the other infants were recruited from sources where it was known that potentially 'at risk' populations were predominant. Moving from a general source to one more directly concerned with difficulties therefore made the task of recruitment more onerous. At the time of discussing the potential observation with Sally and Neville, another quite eager family was kept on hold and there was a choice of two infants available to me. However, when families with potential risk were sought, numerous visits to organisations took place. A sequence of difficult negotiations with the link agency occurred, and two initial visits to families resulted in both declining to take part. A third mother agreed to go ahead, but discontinued after the first observation. The four study families were chosen from the following sources; a health visitor, a social worker, a psychotherapist and a day nursery.

Some of the difficulties in negotiating the observation with the families need to be considered. Two factors appeared to be prominent. First, there was a suggestion that the agencies were protective of families they felt might be likely to feel scrutinised in a negative way by the idea of an observation. The families themselves did seem to experience the suggestion in this light. Second, there was the issue of observer gender, that a male observing babies increased suspicion. On more than one occasion these two factors were present simultaneously. For example one father communicated to me via his partner that 'He didn't want no bloke staring at his baby'. This neatly encapsulated the sense of negative scrutiny and threat from another male.

The trawl of agencies was probably an uneconomical way of recruiting. Much more effective was the contact made by an individual known to the observer and who therefore had a sense of the observer's role and either personal or professional knowledge of him. The reason for the attempt to locate families within these agency settings was to locate possible risk factors without unduly skewing the introductions and therefore the aims of the study.

Five families did agree to be subjects for the study, and were accepted as suitable within the framework of the study. These were[1]

Infant	*Mother*	*Father*
Timothy	Sally	Neville
Hester	Yvonne	Kevin
Hashmat	Rani	Javed Ahmed
Samantha	Anne	Martin
Michael	Mary	Dave

These parents agreed to the weekly observations. The families who agreed to an initial discussion with me were all asked if they would take part in an observation in which I said that I hoped to study infants from experience, rather than books. The essence of the observer's role was described to them, as was the duration of each observation and the frequency. I attempted to see both

1 All names have been changed for the purposes of ensuring anonymity.

mother and father together but only in two cases (Timothy and Hashmat) did this happen. Yvonne told me her partner Kevin 'would not object' and Anne arranged a second visit for me to meet Martin. It was not possible to see Mary's partner Dave as his whereabouts were unknown at the time of Michael's birth. Discussion of the nature of the observation was accompanied by an opportunity for the parents to ask questions of me. Whilst I maintained a particular stance, as a student of child development who wished to learn from experience, I answered directly any questions put to me about the observation and my own professional and personal situation. These questions were, on the whole, not unduly intrusive, and it was not difficult to answer them within the guidance of Bick's dictum to maintain a stance of friendly receptivity.

The families were recruited from a fairly wide cross-section of cultural and social backgrounds. To a great extent this was deliberate; as wide a range as possible of social and cultural factors was sought, given the limitations of the small sample. This permitted observations within a range of family structures and parental role organisation (Bott 1957). Similarly there was a wide range in the infant's place in the family; from first to ninth! These background factors are summarised as:

> *Timothy.* A first child of university-educated parents; father has a professional occupation; mother works in an administrative capacity. The family are British, and white.
>
> *Hester.* The second child of parents who both came from large, working class families. Father is a tradesman and mother worked as a secretary. They are white. Older brother, Sid, is two years older.
>
> *Hashmat.* He is the ninth boy of a Bengali family. Father was unemployed and had a disability (loss of sight in one eye). Mother's extended family live nearby.
>
> *Samantha.* The second child (Donald is 23 months older). Parents were university educated, and father holds a professional job, necessitating a mobile lifestyle. Both are white, and English speaking.
>
> *Michael.* Mary's third child. Darren and Colin are 11 months and five years older respectively. Mother and father come from London working class families. Father Dave works as a taxi driver. Mother's employment history is not known. She has not worked since Colin's birth.

Recognition of potential 'risk' in all the families took place without overt discussion with the family or referrer, between the initial contact and the end of the first observation. This raises issues of the definition of 'risk' and issues of an ethical nature. Administering a structured interview before the observations could have predicted subsequent attachment patterns (Fonagy, Steele and Steele 1991) but such an intervention would have interfered with the methodological aims. It was difficult enough to enable parents to function in as 'natural' a way as possible during the observation, and the avoidance of specific tasks during the observation was important for the functioning of the observations as a whole.

The literature suggests that factors of risk would be found in a large number of aspects of family functioning, including parental childhood experience (Spinetta and Rigler 1980), experiences in past and current relationships (Dingwall 1989), socio-economic circumstances (Jones *et al.* 1987), levels of support networks available (Brown and Harris 1978) and the attitude to the baby before birth and throughout infancy (Kempe 1978). Similarly, a number of factors were associated with the events surrounding the birth, particularly the experience of childbirth itself (Trowell 1982) and the presence or absence of maternal depression (Murray 1992, 1993). Information about potential risk was assessed through information gained during the initial contacts with parents, the observations of other children with parents, and the communications made by the parents during the first observation of their states of mind. During these initial contacts with the families parents talked about their situations and their hopes, fears and expectations for the birth of the baby. The following constituted areas of potential risk for the study sample:

> *Timothy.* Though Timothy was expected to be a non-risk infant from the initial contact, Sally experienced a difficult birth and Timothy was placed in special care, following jaundice. The parents experienced a significant disillusionment of hopes for a natural childbirth.
>
> *Hester.* The link person saw the family as non-risk; during the initial meeting Yvonne expressed fears of her aggression towards her baby. The birth was difficult and Yvonne was then depressed.
>
> *Hashmat.* The link person saw the family as not open to influence about child care issues. Poor socio-economic circumstances and a large family were possible problematic factors. Mother was depressed postnatally, possibly through producing another boy.
>
> *Samantha.* Mother was initially isolated socially. She described her own childhood difficulties in a disrupted family. Her first child, Donald, had manifest difficulties. Samantha was not planned and was born by Caesarean. Mother was depressed postnatally.
>
> *Michael.* Mary had a history of previous difficulties with her children, especially Colin. Her life situation was unstable, through Dave's disappearance. Michael's pregnancy was unexpected and she was significantly depressed postnatally.

These factors, which are discussed fully in the case studies, suggest the presence of a degree of difficulty for all the mothers with the infants who are being observed. The severity of the experiences of these difficulties, and the impact on the infant were very much open questions at the beginning of the observations. The sample therefore was commensurate with the aims of the study.

Ethical issues arose from the down-playing of the observer's preoccupations and status. This is a common feature of 'participant observation', in which:

> playing down or even disguising a professional sociological interest, the participant observer has unique access to the otherwise somewhat 'closed world' of a social group. By gaining the trust of the people in the group the participant observer is initiated into the values, routines and social meanings that the group holds dear. Thus the sociologist is able to observe first hand the typical experiences and attitudes of group members, and is able to describe their world in terms of the same language and expressions. (Layder 1992, p.40)

Though some aspects of my personal and professional experience were played down, and the role of risk in my thinking was not made explicit, I would strongly contend that this did not amount to a deception. It was important to enable parents to have as unstructured a view of me and the observations as was possible. Discussion of risk would have clearly weighted the parents' expectations of the observations in an unhelpful way, and possibly hampered the development of non-problematic aspects of their relationships. Parents did get to know about some aspects of my study though it was thought prudent not to talk about other babies in the sample, for reasons of confidentiality and that the awareness of other babies could prove a provocative issue to the parents.

A second ethical consideration was the awareness that in situations of risk it may be necessary to intervene in order to protect the child. The ultimate intervention would be to make contact with social services or health professionals. Though this did not happen I had the possibility firmly in mind at the outset. The regular discussion of the observations of these infants in seminar groups and individual supervision created a 'containing space' for thinking about all aspects of the infant's development including potential risk. Strategies for dealing with situations of risk included discussion of the situation with the parent (and this did happen) and responding in a way in which the observation could attempt to contain the difficulties that were observed. This, again, became very much part of the observational method with these families.

3.2 Observations; primary database; data analysis

3.2.1 Observation reports and discussions

The observations of each infant were all recorded in detail so that between 2000 and 2500 words were written for each hour observed. The primary database was formed from the following number of observations of each infant:

Timothy	83
Hester	83
Hashmat	80
Samantha	73
Michael	48

An essential part of the process was the supervision of these reports in seminar groups of four to six members throughout the observational period. Notes were taken on each seminar presentation recording the main points of the discussion.

The data was analysed through, first, a process which began whilst observations were taking place, of operationalising key aspects of the deeper theoretical structures that were needed to address aspects of infant development and parent–infant relationships relevant to the aims of the study. In particular, Bion's container–contained and Bick's skin formation were subject to this procedure (see Chapter 3.3 below). This was consistent with an aim to make explicit the preconceptions that were taken into the observations (see Chapter 2.3) and developing the Bion theories into an operationalised set of categories (see Chapter 1.7). Simultaneously, activities consistent with the development of grounded theory addressed the emerging data to form descriptive categories relating to infant development and parent–infant relationships which contributed to the formation of the model.

3.2.2 The development and administration of an assessment grid

Alongside this procedure of model building a reflexive assessment grid was designed. This had a primary aim of providing points of comparison for the sample of infants, between infants and over time. It consisted of a range of categories; from those which were self-evidently empirical (such as recording the development of mobility in infants) to those which were an inherent part of the model (such as the components of internalisation).

The idea in the development of the categories of the grid was to provide points of comparison at a number of levels, including – in general terms – parenting, parent–infant relationships, and the infant's development. By choosing categories that were applied to all infants and their parents, a consistent framework was built. By applying the grid to the data of the observations at regular intervals, consistent comparisons over time were facilitated. Although the study set out with a qualitative methodology in mind, it became apparent that as in the observations mothers and infants did similar things, that is to say categories of things, each week, I found it was possible to compare closely across the sample. It therefore emerged that it was possible, and worthwhile, to produce a quantitative study of the categories which were part of the grid.

A simple and appropriate design for quantitative comparison was a five-point rating scale. This was relatively simple to apply to the data collected by the grid, and the scoring was always within a similar range where the highest value (5) constituted a rating of very frequent, strong, high and the lowest value (1) was the lowest, least frequent or weakest. The administration of the grid was undertaken through detailed reading of the transcripts which were then summarised under each category. The ratings for each category were established from the summaries. Repeated practice at defining and applying the ratings to each category was part of this process. There was no independent reading of the transcripts in this way,[2] though the regular discussion of material in seminars contributed to this method of thinking about the data. Detailed descriptive case studies were needed in order to substantiate and triangulate the ratings. The presentation of both grid ratings in the form of graphs and the descriptive case studies are therefore made in full knowledge that reliability testing of the conclusions of this book is a future task. Here the aim is to establish whether such categories can be meaningfully quantified and to assess how this may contribute to understanding of the questions I am asking about infancy.

The detailed categories of the grid were formed from the model, and the rest of this chapter is concerned with three discussions: first, a detailed exploration of the model; second, the development of grid categories and ratings; and third, the relation of the model to issues of risk.

3.3 The model

To describe the model of infant development which was constructed it is necessary to return to the discussion of Chapter 1. There it was seen that an increased interest in the emotional content of infant development led various writers to link developmental concepts with those from psychoanalytic Object Relations Theory (Chapter 1.5). More specifically, Bion's development of Melanie Klein's work led to the idea of a relationship between mother and infant which was likened to that between container and contained. This theory offered possibilities for the operationalisation of psychoanalytic concepts for empirical study (Chapter 1.6), and for the study of not only 'healthy' development but also risk (Chapter 1.7). Through the observation of the infants and the analysis of the data from these observations a more specific analysis of Bion's theory was indicated.

The model of the container–contained relationship, which Bion developed in *Learning from Experience* (Bion 1962) arose from the observation that the 'understanding mother' (Bion 1967, p.104) does more than attain and retain proximity to the infant: '[the mother] should have treated the infant's cry as more than a demand for her presence. From the infant's point of view she should have taken into her, and then experienced, the fear that the child was dying. It was this fear that the child could not contain' (Bion 1967, p.104).

---

2 The issue of interreliability is discussed in the conclusions in Chapter 9.

The infant then uses projective identification to relieve himself of this experience, and the mother's 'reverie' becomes 'the receptor organ for the infant's harvest of self-sensation gained by its conscious' (p.116); and the function of the reverie is to transform the projective identifications of the infant 'in a manner that makes the infant feel it is receiving its frightened personality back, but in a form which it can tolerate' (p.115).

Bion is therefore dealing with the infant imagined to be in an anxious state of incipient collapse, to be, in other words, precarious (Chapter 1.5, above), and the emotional content of the transaction is fear. He wished, however, to be more general in his application of the model, and limited reverie

> only for such content as is suffused with love or hate. Using it in this restricted sense reverie is that state of mind which is open to the reception of any 'objects' from the loved object and is therefore capable of reception of the infant's projective identifications whether they are felt by the infant to be good or bad. In short, reverie is a factor of the mother's alpha function. (1962, p.36)

Bion further abstracted the dynamic of the container–contained relationship, using the symbols ♀♂ to indicate a relationship which was: 'susceptible of conjunction and permeation by emotion' (1962, p.90). The 'link' as a function (1967, p.102) is then developed to show the purpose of the link being understanding, that is 'K', which in this case means the mother's wish to know and to get to know the baby: 'The earliest and most primitive manifestation of K occurs in the relationship between mother and infant. As a part object relationship it may be stated as a relationship between mouth and breast. In abstract terms it is between ♀ and ♂' (p.90).

Emotion is conveyed via the function of the link and the content of the emotion is decided through the quality of the link between ♀ and ♂. Bion suggests there is a 'commensal' quality to the relationship, describing the means for internalisation:

> The activity that I have here described as shared between two individuals becomes introjected by the infant so that the ♀♂ apparatus becomes installed in the infant as part of the apparatus of alpha function. A model is provided by the idea of the infant who explores an object by putting it into his mouth. What talking was originally done by the mother, possibly a rudimentary designatory function, is replaced by the infant's own baby talk. (p.91)

The container–contained relationship as described by Bion in these terms has four components which can be thought about in conjunction with later theoretical elaborations of the model, principally by Bick and Meltzer, and the data from the observations in this study to form a model. These four elements are, first, the 'commensal' mutually interpenetrating system of ♀ and ♂, second, the mother's capacity for reverie, and ways in which she performs that function, third, the communications made by the infant, described by Bion in terms of projective identification, and fourth, the suggestion that the model is the means, or mechanism, for internalisation.

3.3.1 The 'commensal relationship'

The relationship between ♀ and ♂ provides a model for how the mother and infant 'fit' together, both in terms of the quality of link which is made, that is to say, the quality of understanding provided (K), and the possibility of recording the emotional content of the link. The process of understanding, which Bion suggests is internalised by the infant through this process, is the consequence of the development of conceptions and thoughts from preconceptions. In the 'theory of thinking' Bion discussed the arrival of conceptions from 'the mating of a preconception with a realisation' (1967,p.111), whereas 'thought' was the result of the 'mating of a preconception with a frustration' (p.111) or a 'negative realisation' (p.112). This provides a dynamic model for the establishment of the currency of the mother–infant relationship. Repeated experience of which elements were 'contained' within the relationships, and those which were outside (negative realisations) constitute the kind of commensality appertaining to individual parent–infant relationships. The term parent is used here, because though Bion is normally talking about the 'mother' the model provides for a multiplicity of parenting figures, all 'realising' the preconceptions of the infant. This would certainly include the father, though the impact of Bion's work on linking, and the infant's relationship to both parents, in the early Oedipal relationship (Bion 1967, chapter 7), emphasises much more than the summation of the qualities of individual caregiver–infant relationships, the relationship between the infant and the parents, an idea which was taken up subsequently by Bion (1970) and Britton (1987).

The commensality of this relationship also implied that, so to speak, very different kinds of meals could be partaken of, and that the discourse over the preparation and eating of the meal was open to many variations. Bion himself envisaged situations where the mother and infant both derive benefit from the relationship (1962, p.91) and where the outcome was disastrous in different ways:

> the verbal expression can be so formalised that the idea I want to express can have all the life squeezed out of it OR the meaning I wish to express may have such force and vitality, relative to the verbal formulation which I would strive to contain it that it destroys the verbal container. (1967, p.141)

The former seems to equate with a lifeless, compact communication, a 'flattened' state of being and the latter to an incoherence, which is potentially explosive or forceful. In his Commentary in *Second Thoughts*, he emphasised that he was attempting to describe a configuration, an underlying pattern in the link between two part objects, or two people (Bion 1967, p.141). Other writers have commented on the idea of a 'fit' between mother and infant. Harris (1975) emphasises the constitution of the infant, and the temperament of the parent in the matching of mother and infant together. Segal (1991, p.61) refers to a mutually cruel 'fit'. This is a quite sporadic literature. Developmentalists make use of the idea, particularly Escalona (1969), Stern (1977) and Bower (1989a) provided a model for the development of a 'fit' through the process of differentiation and the decreasing potential for the infant to meet with 'realisations' (see Chapter 1.2 above). Chess and Thomas (1984) develop the idea most fully. They stress the importance of conflict and some stress in the relationship, whilst defining 'consonance' and 'dissonance' as the qualities of 'goodness of fit' and 'poorness of fit' respectively. These are close to the descriptive categories adopted here.

The quality of the 'link' between mother and infant could therefore be observed through attention to the ways in which mother and infant come to develop patterns of relating with and through emotional and developmental issues. The content of the emotional issues could also become identifiable, that is to say that shared emotional problems and preoccupations could be seen. From the data of this study, three kinds of 'commensal relationships' could be identified, namely 'containing', 'accommodating' and 'conflictual'. These in general were the 'kinds of meal' that were observed. The model, here, then is of the operation of the container–contained relationship to develop particular qualities of mother–infant relationships, characterised by the way the 'matching' or 'fit' between them comes to form a configuration. However, the operation of this dynamic can only be observed if parts of it, namely the mother's role and function, and the infant's, are explored. The 'fit' is composed of the individual elements brought to the dyadic patterns. This requires the elaboration of other concepts within the ♀♂ system.

3.3.2 The mother's reverie; containing 'shape'

Bion's view that the understanding mother provides the means for transforming the infant's projective identifications through her reverie, also raises the issue of what would be the impact of the mother's lack of reverie. Bion himself elaborated one variation of the model, namely the mother who is unaccepting, or blocking of projective identifications emanating from the infant. Failure of maternal reverie leads, through blocking the ingress of infant primitive communications to the projections being returned in a more frightening form: 'It [the infant] reintrojects not a fear of dying made tolerable, but a nameless dread' (1967, p.116), and the infant internalises a 'wilfully misunderstanding object – with which he is identified' (p.117). The growth of the contained (♂), he adds: 'is a medium in which lie suspended the "contents". The "contents" must be perceived of as protruding from a base which is unknown. A two-dimensional image is provided by the parabola'.

This suggests that in the two variations supplied by Bion, that of 'reverie' and the 'projective identification blocking object', the parabola moves from a concave to a flat shape, the former admitting the projections; the latter keeping them out. These two 'shapes' have a different impact on the infant through the capacity to transform emotional communications in different ways. In general terms:

the concave – identifies and mediates the emotion

the flat – ignores and diffuses the emotion (flattens the affect)

From the data, moments of 'reverie' (concave maternal shape) and of 'flat' maternal shape were recognisable in sequences of interaction. Additionally, it was found that these two categories did not cover the total phenomena and a third category was needed. This was to account for the situations where the mother not only did not fail to respond, through 'blocking' communications, but also invested the infant with projections of her own. This is a situation where the mother indicates her unavailability to the infant's communications through her preoccupations and her actions which are either forceful or directly in contradiction with the infant's communications. The internalisation that follows is not of a 'wilfully misunderstanding object' but rather of an unwanted state of mind of the mother's and or a perversion of the meaning of an action. So, for example, feeding which is forced upon the infant becomes an unwanted intrusion rather than an experience of love and warmth. The infant thus becomes a recipient of the mother's projections (Williams 1991). The presence of a 'ghost in the nursery' (Freiberg 1980) would come into this category.[3] In terms of the maternal shape, this would be convex and therefore, the third maternal shape is:

the convex – which adds the mother's unconscious projections, perverting meaning and conflicting with the infant's states of mind.

This view of the different container shapes provides a model for the presentation of the mother to the infant within the ♀♂ relationship. Put together, I would represent the mother as three-dimensional, a potential 'container', and with the option of three different surfaces contacting the infant's communications. The emotional meaning can be discerned through the context of the contact between the mother and infant through the kind of contact made between them.

3 It is of interest why Bion did not include this third possibility. Two reasons exist. First, as he was reconstructing mother–infant relationships from clinical experience he would probably not think of the analyst acting this way. Second, in his autobiography, he records an incident with his daughter where he does not respond to her distress, but remains passive; a clear example of 'flat' container shape (Bleandonu 1994, pp.97–8).

3.3.3 The infant's communications: 'grip relations'

So far, the operationalisation of Bion's theory has maintained fidelity to his description of the infant's function in the relationship between container and contained. That is to say that the infant's part in the relationship is confined to descriptions of 'communication' and 'projective identification'. For operationalisation to be effective these terms need to be translated into observable categories. This process of operationalisation to form a model is effected by the conjunction of this theory with Bick's development of it. Surfaces are important for this conjunction.

For Bick, the first function of the containing mother was to provide a 'psychic skin' for the infant. This was taken to be concretely experienced, and the function of early contact with mother was the internalisation of the mother's containing function, through the physical activities of the mother: 'The optimal [containing] object is the nipple in the mouth together with the holding and talking and familiar smelling mother' (Bick 1968, p.484). The failure of the containing function of the mother could be observed through the 'frantic search for an object – a light, a voice, a smell or other sensual object' (p.484).

This activity is elaborated in her later, posthumous, paper (Bick 1986) where the infant aims to prevent the 'predominant terror...of falling to pieces or liquefying' (1986, p.296). Both Bick and Symington (1985) describe the gripping, grasping and clinging contact. In the absence of a containing mother, the infant would 'hold himself' (Bick 1986, p.297). Symington describes three ways in which the baby holds himself together: focusing on a sensory stimulus; engaging in constant bodily movement; muscular tightening or clenching (p.181).

These means of gripping the mother or other objects were seen in these papers of Bick and Symington as defensive measures from which a 'second skin' took the place of the primary skin, and which constituted a two-dimensional hold on the surface of another in the absence of the mother's transforming the infant's internal anguish through her 'reverie'. The infant's 'gripping' of another object could therefore be in the service of survival (Bick 1986; Symington 1985), through re-entering object relations or defending against the primary anxieties through 'pseudo-independence' (Bick 1968, p.484).

Drawing on her infant observation model, Bick devised a theory which was ready-operationalised, and the descriptions of the baby's behaviour could be directly observed. On the other hand the underlying anxiety or phantasy needed to be inferred from the material, either through clinical material or the observer's countertransference (Bick 1986, p.296). If, as Bion suggested, it is assumed that the infant is attempting to communicate through projective identification the sensory modalities would be used as the vehicles for the communications. The quality of gripping, or grasping an 'object' would therefore be more ubiquitous. The emphasis placed by developmentalists on the perceptual capabilities of the infant in 'alert inactivity' suggests that the sensory modalities will be used to convey the more varied aspects of the infant's relationship motives. In the observational data of this sample, the infant's capacity to use the perceptual qualities, and to do this sequentially, meant that the emotional preoccupations of the infant could be followed by observing these qualities of grip. The early relationships of the infant are then characterised by what can be called 'grip relations'.

If 'grip relations' is a term which is used inclusively, to mean any particular indication of communication through any modality, the observations of infants' behaviour show the infant's willingness to object relate (Klein 1952c), to use perceptual capacities for a variety of motives (Bower 1989a; Emde 1988) and to be involved in dyadic patterns of rhythm and timing (Stern 1985; Trevarthen 1991). What is of particular interest is the meaning of the 'grip' and the nature of the relationship assumed by the particular grip employed by an infant. In this model, that is to say, the interest is not simply on the achievement of proximity,[4] but also the quality of understanding which is made of the communications, by the mother, and which is then internalised. In the data from the observations here, the notion of 'grip relations' was seen to show the discrimination of the infant; the direction of the infant's attention (towards or away from a particular person or thing), and the relationship between contact with another and the state of mind of the infant, as shown by the appearance of new modalities of 'grip', and by a change in the infant's emotional state. Quite clearly, in this model, the grip relations demonstrate the qualities appertaining to the container–contained relationship, and the 'realisations' of the infant's 'preconceptions'. These relationships may be connected with the process of internalisation and the outcome of internalisation processes.

3.3.4 Internalisation

Both Bion and Bick present particular difficulties for the operationalisation of the concept of internalisation, though the developmental outcome in terms of the inner representational world is seen as important in almost all theories of infancy (see Chapter 1). Internalisation of a 'container' or 'skin-container' are inevitably difficult to operationalise and observe empirically. In this model, the qualities of the mother's shape, the grip which the infant makes on others (people and things) and the emotional qualities that are contained in the relationship, through the realisations in the commensal relationship (or fit) provide the basis for the procedure of internalisation. The hypothesis is that the 'grip' on the mother needs to be made, and then relinquished, before internalisation can take place (Williams 1991). Qualities of internalisation will be studied as outcome measures, through the evidence provided by the

---

4 This would give the notion an evolutionary context, namely the loss of the human infant's capacity to 'grip' or 'grasp' the mother (Harlow and Zimmermann 1958).

components of internalisation which were operationalised in the grid. In general terms, evidence of a trusting, secure relationship with mother would be the outcome of a 'good' internalisation. 'Good' is an evaluative shorthand for what Melanie Klein defined as an internalisation of 'an object which loves and protects the self, and is loved and protected by the self' (Klein 1957).

Similarly, evidence of a suspicious, distressed or conflictual approach to mother would suggest the internalisation of a persecutory nature. The elements that appeared to be observable aspects of internalisation process included the infant's capacity for memory, recognition, for tolerating absence from the mother, discrimination of people and things, and the emotional qualities embedded in these elements of developing personality. Particularly, from the observations it was possible to distinguish between the infant's capacity to recall with affection or, on the other hand, recollections (or recognitions) which prompted distress or other signs of persecution.

Bion's theory suggests a pathway for development in which the capacity to think is linked with the capacity to tolerate absence (Bion 1962, p.35), and, second, that symbol formation depends on the establishment of an early link between two objects (Bion 1967, p.48). The evidence of symbolic ways of thinking, playing and relating are therefore related to the quality of the 'link' between container and contained, for which the case studies provide longitudinal evidence of the quality of the internalisations of the infant, in the context of the patterns or configurations within the container–contained system (including parental shape, grip relations and commensal relationships).

3.4 Categories in the grid

The grid categories were designed to address all the aspects of the model; the 'fit' in the relationship between mother and infant (and father and infant); the qualities of mother's (and father's) containment; the infant's development, including the capacity to develop grip relations and the quality of these, and characteristics of the quality of internalisation.

3.4.1 Parent–infant relationship

Parent–infant relationships were categorised in the grid according to the qualities of the 'fit' or commensal relationship described above. Ways in which parents and infants made a link (♀ ♂) were studied through the rating of the strength of the grip relationships between them, at all modalities – mouth–nipple/teat, eye–eye, voice–ear, body–body and mind–mind. The quality of the emotionality in the parent–infant links was assessed through categories which measured levels of attentiveness, sensitivity, understanding, intimacy and conflict. Third, there was assessment of the intensity of the contact, the capacity to maintain emotional contact (rather than subduing or muting emotionality) and the matching of each other's emotional wavelengths. This last was a dissonance–consonance measure (Chess and Thomas 1984; Chapter 3, p.10 above).

The overall quality of the 'fit' was assessed in terms of the three categories – containing, conflictual and accommodating. Finally, the category of the mother's shape belonged in this section of the grid as it was concerned with the shape mother presented in the interaction with the infant. These were then rated according to the frequency with which each shape appeared in the observations.

The mother–infant grid consisted of five categories in all:

1. Qualities of relationship.
   (Key: 5=most; 4=a lot; 3=moderate; 2=some; 1=little)
   a) Sensitivity.
   b) Attentiveness.
   c) Conflict.
   d) Intimacy.
   e) Understanding:

2. Mutual grip.
   (5=very strong; 4=strong; 3=moderate; 2=somewhat weak; 1=weak)
   a) Mouth–nipple.
   b) Eye–eye.
   c) Voice–ear.
   d) Body–body.
   e) Mind–mind.

3. Quality of stimulation/timing rhythms.
   (5=very high; 4=high; 3=moderate; 2=some; 1=low)
   a) Intensity.
   b) Being 'in tune' with each other.
   c) Maintaining emotional contact.

4. Quality of fit.
   (5=very high; 4=high; 3=moderate; 2=some; 1=low)
   a) Containing.
   b) Conflictual.
   c) Accommodating.

5. Containing shape.
   (5=very high; 4=high; 3=moderate; 2=some; 1=low)
   a) Concave.
   b) Flat.
   c) Convex.

3.4.2 Parenting

The central issue for parenting in the model is the extent to which the mother offers a containing (concave) or not containing (flat/convex) shape in interactions with the infant. Reverie, or concave shape, is the function of the mother's availability for receiving communications from the infant and through this being able to transform the emotionality. Availability was measured through summarising mother's emotional preoccupations, ranging from positive to anxious and persecutory. Mothers dealt with their preoccupations through talking about them or allowing them to impinge on the infant (convex container shape) or through expressions of conflict between the need to be available and the need to find the means for dealing with her preoccupations. The characteristic way she would do this depended on her internal and external resources. The latter could be measured through assessing the levels of practical and emotional support she received.

In talking about her infant, and in her actions, mother expressed her view of her infant's development as he/she reached key milestones. She also represented her infant's states of mind, character and development. The degree to which and the consistency with which she made representations, and the quality of the representations – positive or negative – all gave some measures of her states of mind and her availability for thinking about her infant.

The qualities of availability and transformation led to the mother's capacity to be able to show understanding of infant communications of need, awareness of the infant's emotional needs and the capacity to meet his/her physical and emotional needs.

The categories in this section of the grid were, therefore:

1. Mother's resources.

    a) Levels of practical and emotional support.
    (5=very high; 4=high; 3=moderate; 2=fairly low; 1=low)

        i) Partner.

        ii) Extended family.

        iii) Friends.

        iv) Professional support.

    b) Quality of internal resources.
    (5=very well resourced; 4=good resources; 3=moderate resources; 2=somewhat under-resourced; 1=low resources)

2. Mother's emotional availability.

    a) Primary emotional preoccupations.
    (5=very positive; 4=positive; 3=mixed/neutral; 2=somewhat anxious and /or persecutory; 1=anxious and /or persecutory)

    b) Conflict experienced in her role.
    (5=very high; 4=high; 3=moderate; 2=some; 1=low)

    c) Capacity for verbalisation (talking about feelings).
    (5=very high; 4=high; 3=moderate; 2=some; 1=low)

    d) Impingement of emotional preoccupations on infant.
    (5=very high; 4=high; 3=moderate; 2=some; 1=low)

3. Mother's representations of infant states of mind.

    a) Mother's experience of key events in infant's development.
    (5=very positive; 4=positive; 3=mixed/neutral; 2=somewhat negative; 1=negative)

    b) Type of mother's attributions of qualities of infant (characteristics, states of mind).
    (5=very positive; 4=positive; 3=mixed/neutral; 2=somewhat negative; 1=negative)

    c) Frequency of mother's representations of infant state of mind/character/development.
    (5=very frequent; 4=frequent; 3=moderately frequent; 2=fairly infrequent; 1=infrequent)

d) Persistence/consistency of mother's attributions of qualities to infant.
(5=very persistent/consistent; 4=persistent/consistent; 3= moderately consistent/persistent; 2=fairly inconsistent/unpersistent; 1=inconsistent/unpersistent)

4. Mother's meeting of infant's containment needs.
(5=very high; 4=high; 3=moderate/partial; 2=fairly low; 1=low)
   a) Meeting of baby's physical needs.
   b) Awareness of emotional needs.
   c) Understanding infant communications/needs.
   d) Meeting of infant emotional needs.

3.4.3 Parental relationship and its functioning to meet infant containment needs

Bion's model emphasises mother–infant relationships. In describing the model it was noted that the containing function of the father and the infant's relationships to both parents needed to be taken into consideration. In naturalistic observations there was contact with father and other members of the family. The father–infant relationship was accounted for by using the same grid as for mother–infant relationships. Similarly, the parenting grid for mother was used for father. Following Bion's description of the quality of the emotional link between parents, which was amplified by Britton (Chapter 3, p.9 above), categories were devised to assess this issue. Levels of harmony and conflict and characteristic ways of addressing conflict – verbalised, acted out, seemingly unaware – were assessed and specific ways of linking were categorised. Parents were seen to think together about the infant's containment needs, leading to attempts to solve problems and make links. This was called 'bridge building'. Second, parents could complement each other to make the best use of their internal resources for working with the emotional needs of the infant. This interchangeability of extremes was likened to the nursery rhyme of 'Jack Spratt'. Between them, parents covered a wider range of emotional needs. Third, one parent could be seen to increase the receptivity of the other by undertaking some practical or emotional tasks. The prototype for this was that whereas the mother fed the infant, the father would change the nappy.

There were styles of parental link which had an adverse effect, that is to say, that the effect of the parental link was to decrease receptivity. First, one parent could actively undermine the other; a specific process of undermining was that of projecting painful issues (undigested, uncontainable or spilling over emotions) on to the other parent, overloading their emotional capacity to be available for the infant. Second, parents could reduce availability and receptivity through flattening or muffling the emotionality between them ('flattening the affect'; a flat combined container shape) or through 'sticking together', an adhesive link where the aim was to maintain a common front against a perceived threat from outside the couple, and which projected on to the infant a sense of outsidership (convex combined container shape).

The parental relationship's functioning to meet infant containment needs grid then consisted of:

1. Levels of harmony/conflict.
   (5=very frequent; 4=frequent; 3=sometimes; 2=fairly infrequent; 1=infrequent)
   a) Observations of parental harmony.
   b) Observations of parental conflict.
   c) Types of conflict.
      i) Verbalised.
      ii) Acted out
      iii) Seemingly unaware.

2. Parental interaction types (to meet containment needs of infant).
   (5=very frequent; 4=frequent; 3=sometimes; 2=fairly infrequent; 1=infrequent)
   a) 'Bridge building'.
   b) Interchangeability of extremes ('Jack Spratt').
   c) Other parent='nappy changer': increase of receptivity.
   d) Undermining/undermined: loss of receptivity.
   e) 'Sticking together'.
   f) Flattening of affect/muting.

3.4.4 Infant development

The development of each infant was compared across the sample and over time through a grid which was designed to include measurements of physical characteristics – physical development including mobility milestones, sleeping, feeding and physical health – and, second, the qualities of development emphasised in the model, especially 'grip relations' and the qualities of internalisation.

Since the model proposes that the infant developed and used grip relations to make links with others, and to provide a sense of holding the self together, these purposes were assessed by measuring and rating the frequency with which the infant was involved in object relating and defending. Qualities of grip relations, such as the strength with which the infant developed a particular grip at each modality and the texture and direction of the grip were important considerations for the relationship between container and contained to be followed over time and across the sample. The strength of grip relations was recorded in the grid; texture and direction were discussed in the case studies.

In addition to the frequency of object relating and defending, the grid included assessments of the extent to which the infant was expressive and protesting and the degree of flexibility (varied use of a number of defensive grip relations) – or rigidity (prolonged, repetitive use of one recognisable defensive manoeuvre) – in the defences that developed.

The qualities of internalisation were measured and compared as described in 3.3.4 above. There were two sections to this category; first there were measures of characteristic developmental achievements such as the capacity to develop memory, to recognise, to recall with affection, to seek proximity, manage experiences of separation and to think. The second section concentrated on achievements in the sphere of language development and symbolic play, both of which were important to the hypothesis about the effects of early containment qualities on later development.

The infant development grid then consisted of the following categories:

1. Characteristics of physical development.
   a) Physical development.
   (5=very advanced; 4=advanced; 3=in time; 2=somewhat delayed; 1=delayed)
   b) Physical health.
   (5=very good health; 4=good health; 3=OK; 2=some illness; 1=consistent or serious ill health)
   c) Feeding.
   (5=very well; 4=well; 3=OK; 2=some problems; 1=considerable problems)
   d) Sleeping.
   (5=very well; 4=well; 3=OK; 2=some problems; 1=considerable problems)

2. Strength of grip relations.
   (5=very strong; 4=strong; 3=moderate; 2=fairly weak; 1=weak)
   a) Mouth.
   b) Eye.

c) Voice.

d) Hand.

e) Body.

f) Mind.

3. Qualities of relatedness.
   (5=very high; 4=high; 3=moderate; 2=fairly low; 1=low)

   a) Frequency of object relating.

   b) Frequency of defending.

   c) Strength of protesting/expressiveness.

   d) Flexibility of defences.

4. Qualities of internalisation.
   (5=very high; 4=high; 3=moderate; 2=fairly low; 1=low)

   a) Capacity for memory.

   b) Capacity for recall with affection.

   c) Capacity for recognition.

   d) Capacity for discrimination/fidelity.

   e) Reactions to separation.

   f) Demonstrations of proximity seeking.

   g) Capacity to think.

   h) Language development.

   i) Capacity for symbolic play.

   j) Evidence for unconscious phantasy.

   k) Quality of internalisation.
   (5=very secure/'good'/benign; 4=secure/'good'/benign; 3=mixed; 2=somewhat persecutory; 1=persecutory)

3.5 Risk

It was suggested in Chapter 1 that Bion's theories have relevance not only as a conceptual framework for 'normal' or 'healthy' infant development, but also – and this makes it especially relevant to this study – about development where difficulties in development and parental functioning lead to risk. Not only is there a conceptualisation of the way in which the mother–infant relationship functions to develop qualities in the infant, especially thinking and symbol formation, but also ways in which the failure of the maternal containing function results in developmental difficulties (Harris 1975). Bick's ideas about the defensive operations that infants employ describes how the infant may become defended as a reaction to the experience of difficulties in the container–contained relationship. The model developed these ideas further, and proposed specific descriptions of parental states of mind and parent–infant relationships that have within them a propensity for risk. The containing shapes of flat and convex, in contrast to the concave, suggest that parental states of mind lead respectively to unreceptivity to infant communications and the spilling over of preoccupations in intrusive and/or bombarding modes of relating. The potential for risk may then be thought of as the inability to contain and/or the overspilling of emotional experiences. These are suggestive of parental over-identification with particular aspects of themselves, or situations which lead to enactments of emotional issues, which are potentially damaging for the infant, both physically and emotionally. The parental link is also important in this respect, since it can be activated by the parents together to contain 'bridge building', to reduce or muffle receptivity (flat combined container shape) or to be at a point from which projection on to the infant can occur (convex combined container shape).

The model also suggests the different ways in which the infant may respond to the modes of container shape provided by the parent. Through their grip relations infants make different qualities of contact with parental communications and actions. The qualities of internalisation which infants develop constitutes the primary factor in understanding a question central to risk, namely what resources infants need in order to manage difficult and stressful circumstances, particularly those in which there are deficiencies in parental care. The second part of this question addresses individual differences in infant development; namely how these resources are acquired and maintained. Thus the capacity to maintain development in the face of – for the infants – stressful circumstances suggests resilience, whilst failure or partial failure to do so amounts to vulnerability. The qualities of internalisation, measured through the categories developed in the grid and elaborated in the case studies, provide a starting point for this discussion.

There are, therefore, two main points which connect the model developed here with the aim of exploring the question of risk. First, the model provides a framework for thinking about parental difficulties in containing emotional experiences, and second, it provides a framework for the analysis of the infant's acquisition and maintenance of resources. These are therefore specific hypotheses about risk which it is the task of the case studies to explore and evaluate.

3.6 Summary

This chapter has been concerned with the development of the study, the sample of five infants who were studied in their families, and the acquisition and organisation of data. The model used here was elaborated, and the grid, developed as a way of making comparisons between infants and over time, was described. Finally the relevance of this method to a study of infants at potential risk was elucidated. This then prepares the way for the presentation of the data in the form of case studies. Following the methodology described here, each case study can now be presented through the application of the model. First, detailed descriptive accounts qualitatively describe the development of each infant within the framework provided by the model, and the categories of the grid. Points of reference are made with the graphs of the grid and these are reproduced in full after the descriptive account. The five individual case studies (descriptive and grid) are followed by a discussion of the findings in Chapter 9. These are based on a comparison of each case study. The functioning of the model is evaluated, as is its capacity to develop the hypotheses of risk which have been described in 3.5 above.

The Case Studies

CHAPTER 4

Hashmat

Hashmat was the ninth boy in a Bengali family. His parents spoke very little English and they adhered strongly to a traditional way of life. The family size, the cultural difference between the family and the observer, and the fact that there was little common ground in terms of verbal communication created an unusual observational context. As observer I found it necessary to suspend judgement; the task of contending with ambiguous communication was powerfully present.

4.1 The family

I was introduced to the family through a health visitor, whose comments to me suggested that she had no particular concerns about this baby, nor about the family as a whole; no other child in the family had caused particular problems, nor had there been stillbirths, or infant deaths. Therefore, risk was not identified by the referral source.

I was taken to meet the family – by appointment – by the health visitor and an interpreter. I was told that neither parent spoke much English, father being more able than mother in this regard. The family live in a four bedroom flat on a large estate which is almost totally Bengali. In this part of London there is a community of some 40,000 Bengali. The pattern of Bengali migration is poorly documented;[1] there was a particular influx after the war with Pakistan, though many, like Hashmat's father, came to this country much earlier, in 1960.

The flat I described at the time as 'cavernous'; a long corridor off which there were bedrooms led to a warm living room. Javed, the father, spoke in Bengali through the interpreter, impressing on us his role. His wife waited until permission was given to sit down, and father spoke about his wife's view of the observation. I was especially keen to think about some boundaries with them, but Javed assured me, for example, that his wife would not breast-feed as 'she did not have enough milk' and that they were quite happy for me to observe. Indeed, he added, if I came later in the day I could observe all his children.

1 Watson (1977) however describes the experiences of Bengali males, and their separations and reunions with their families.

They were aged 18, 15, 14, 13, 11, 8, 5 and 3. I said I would be pleased indeed to meet his children, but that I wished to concentrate on the new baby. Javed was quite portly, about 50, with a damaged eye. He did not work outside the home and throughout was a significant presence in observations. Rani was darker skinned, with a warm smile and looked quite younger than her husband – under 40 I guessed. Both were traditionally dressed and Rani's pregnancy showed very little.

After the initial visit it was arranged that the health visitor would let me know when the baby was born and then I would contact the family. In fact I was contacted two months ahead of time, the health visitor announcing that the baby was born. She was somewhat surprised but told me the baby was full term. 'They must have got their dates wrong,' she added, and thus purveyed a sense of frustration – as though the family had made her feel incompetent. This was the first of a number of key events that occurred in my association with this family, where the element of total surprise, lack of preparation or of communication about the event were features, raising the ambiguous issue of the quality of communications between white professionals and the family; who did not understand whom? Or did the family not know themselves? The problem I was to encounter as an observer on these occasions was in assessing the quality of meaning of the events themselves for the family. What was the significance of the narrative, the history of family life for them?

4.2 Quality of containment

It is difficult in this family to summarise the quality of parental containment for this infant, Hashmat, within a family gestalt where each member had a role and function in terms of parenting the infant Hashmat. In order to think about the kind of containment experienced by Hashmat, we have to take into account the contribution of the family members as a unit, as well as the direct evidence of the way in which mother and infant relate. It is worth adding that it is into this culture – small c – that the observer appears and impacts. Three distinct and different family patterns were observed at different times during the observations.

First, there was a 'group' culture, where, with many family members present, the experience within the family group was of free-flowing projections, potential (and actual) violence, intrusion, dealt with through a paternalistic authority, based on the adherence to (cultural) rules and the threat of violence, to which individuals submitted. A variation of this pattern occurred when no adult was present, when siblings as a group interacted together. In this pattern the infant was at risk, and the observer on occasions intervened physically to protect the infant, or younger sibling.

Differentiating individual need and thinking were more or less absent in these periods. The notion of individual attention was not present. For example, there were occasions (observations (O) 4,13,58) when the infant was subject to responses which had the effect of communicating that anyone could care for him as well as anyone else. As the observer I was initially invited to join this shared phantasy, being asked to feed Hashmat, hold him and to be similarly involved with the other children. Parental functions were delegated to different family members. For example, one sibling would be delegated to care physically for the infant; another would appear as the attacker of the infant, either – more usually – physically hurting the baby, or – more rarely – inflicting some emotionally cruel situation upon him. Mother's approach was characterised by, first, not thinking, not noticing, or passing the baby to someone else, and father's by attempts at authoritarianism; cracking the whip (literally). It was of interest why parental authority was absent when parents were physically absent. At these times, the notion of a protecting parent, held in the mind by the child, was also absent. In that the attack was usually directed towards a baby, the meaning of the culture became at times that of a 'gang', in Meltzer's (1984) definition of this term. He suggests: 'The gang-family, by virtue of its ambiguous relation to the community, at once defiant, and yet seeking acceptance, greedy and at the same time scornfully proud, imposes a confusing task on its members' (p.166).

These elements were certainly present, though I may invert the emphasis; the relationship with the community was ambiguous, as was the community's relationship with the families of which, at this level, this family was representative. In the categories I have developed, mother's containment was mainly 'flat' (Graph 4.9), and father's was 'convex' in that his shouting and aggression was directly taken in by the infant. This approach was also displaced into one of the siblings, who also therefore offered a convex shape to Hashmat.

Second, by way of contrast, there were passages of time where, with most of the older boys out of the house, with both mother and father and perhaps two or at most three infants/young children in the home, the family resembled much more a nuclear family, and where individual attention was possible. In contrast to the first pattern of relating, these passages seemed extremely peaceful, and included interaction between parent and child, and play. In these periods mother was capable of a vigorous containment. She seldom demonstrated this capacity (see though O11, page 69); for large parts of the observation she was much more passive than this, undeniably depressed and dealing with the very great burden of her situation by not thinking (Graph 4.2), and through escape into a phantasy world. For example, she was completely captivated by a video of an Asian woman as heroine, the portrayal of whom was so far from her actual situation as could possibly be imagined.(O7: Hashmat at 10 weeks). On other occasions if she did let herself think, especially about the dependency needs of the infants, she became very easily overwhelmed, and portrayed real helplessness. (O40: Hashmat at one year two weeks). In the second year when I was more actively involved with Hashmat, she was at times more responsive and able to observe his behaviour and interactions with me.

It is clear, however, that the portrayal of herself, initially, as a 'role', unsubstantial and passively assenting to her husband's authority, was a caricature of herself. Much more evident as time went by in the observations was the importance for her of defending against overwhelming need, through switching off and through relying on the 'group' to complete her task of mothering.

Father was to an extent supportive in this second 'mode' of parenting (Graph 4.1). Tasks were divided between them; he dealt with the outside – shopping, collecting children from school. She prepared the food and fed the children. Father would hold the infant, smile at him, sing a soothing lullaby to him (Graph 4.10).

Third, though this was seen much less often, there were periods of time when the adults outnumbered the children, namely when mother's mother, other relatives and friends were present. These events produced different reactions in terms of the quality of the containing environment. When mother's mother was present there appeared to be a more vigorous approach not only to the children but also to the quality of communication (Graph 4.3). Mother on these occasions found the wherewithal to talk clearly in English. It was also when other adults were present that the family – and particularly the parents – moved into a most 'switched off' mode of functioning, where the children were left literally to attend to themselves (Graph 4.4). For example in O13 (Hashmat at 16 weeks), both Hashmat and Shakil (3) were left to cry without being attended to, as mother was involved in a kind of ritualistic food preparation, imbued with sensuality.

A fourth dimension to add to these three modes of parenting was the history of events as they unfolded during the observational period. Most notably I observed the arrival of two babies (Hashmat and his younger brother Fashmat, born just before Hashmat's first birthday). During his second year, the Bangladesh cyclone took many lives and this was followed by father's visit there. One of the older boys told me that 'Bangladesh is slipping into the sea'. This is then an uprooted family with a relationship to another country, Bangladesh. Probably pertinent here is the impact of previous history; Javed's parents had died in Bangladesh whilst he lived in England (but before the observations started). He may have lost relatives in the cyclone. In the immediate environment I heard from time to time – from inside the family and outside sources – of race-fuelled conflicts. During the observational period the older boys were leaving school and starting work. Four of them were wage earners before the end of the observation. All of these events I heard about in passing; a child would mention something to me – for example, that the oldest boy now lived away from home. Often the impact of events was gleaned from the experience of observing before the event was named. Naming of things was not a family forte. The task of naming things rested with the eight-year-old, a benign soft-featured boy who had the capacity to give names to feelings, on behalf of the family. I shall refer to his part later.

The impact of the historical dimension on the modes of parenting can be thought of in terms of Bion's notation of Ps<->D (Bion 1963, p.35), symbolising the movement between the paranoid schizoid (PS) and depressive (D) positions (Klein 1952b). The family functioning was shifted by these events from the more depressive 'family' style to the PS group/gang style; and/or to an increase in the level of PS in the group/gang. For example, at the time of the Bangladesh cyclone, the boys were attacking each other with sticks and receiving no parental response, as if to suggest that if tens of thousands were dying at home then a boy hitting another with a stick was a negligible event, requiring no intervention.

4.3 Hashmat's early development

Hashmat was then born into these patterns of relating. I should like to turn now to consider his early development. As with all the infants I observed, the problem to which I have paid attention was how, and with what success, there was a capacity in the infant to develop object relations in the face of the deficiencies of containment I have described. In thinking about Hashmat I wish to focus on three themes:

1. The problem of feeding difficulties; his difficult relationship with the bottle (Graph 4.14).
2. That he developed a distinctive defensive pattern, which was characterised by withdrawal (Graph 4.16).
3. That his 'grip relations' involved a complex pattern of relating with the hand (Graph 4.15b).

Mother reported Hashmat not to be feeding well, to be regurgitating feeds; to be sick. In the first observation she fed him, after father had shown him to me. This is my first view of him:

> He has a shock of dark hair, pale fingers, and seemed delicate, but full-term. I asked mother Rani if she wanted to take him as he continued to cry, and she did so, holding him, then sitting down on the sofa. Baby stopped crying and Rani asked father Javed Ahmed to pass the bottle, and she gave the bottle, cradling baby on her right arm, her large hand held out open palmed. Hashmat took the bottle and sucked, closing his eyes. Rani looked at him and then at me, smiling a little self-consciously. (O1:Hashmat at nine days)

It is interesting to note from the beginning – he is nine days – Hashmat's co-ordination of mouth and eye. That his eyes closed when the bottle was found opens the way to two hypotheses. First, that Hashmat has already learned from experience how to secure the bottle. Second, it is not easy for him to locate both the bottle and mother's eye, or mind. Here mother briefly smiles at him, but she is clearly self-conscious. This would not be a problem in itself at this age, but the pattern continued, to become a feature, whereby the idea that there is no eye, or emotional contact between them is jointly accepted (Graph 4.6a). This way of feeding was so regularly repeated that it held the quality of a sculpt. For example, when Hashmat is nine weeks: 'Rani looked up and smiled and continued to feed Hashmat. She held him loosely, watching TV, her large hand open and then just touching his arm. His eyes were open and looking also in the direction of the TV. He sucked quietly' (O6: Hashmat at nine weeks).

The accommodation in the 'fit' between mother and infant (Graph 4.8) has them sharing a third object – the TV – with their eyes. The eye-seeking relationship is with a third person, the TV, me, brother; the emotional contact in feeding lies outside the mother infant couple, in the 'group', the family nucleus. Here there are a wide range of objects of different qualities. The TV, in this example, has a mindless quality. Father contributes a well-meaning but noisily intrusive presence. The other character is Shakil, the three-year-old, who is noisily murderous, particularly when supported by the older (five-year-old) Chalaak. Both father and Shakil appear as the observation continues. Shakil climbed on the coffee table, father shouted to him to get down. Then:

> ...Hashmat seemed to splutter over his milk and mother tried to keep the bottle in his mouth, but he continued to splutter and she took it out and seemed to grapple with him, pulling his legs and then sitting him up and patting his back firmly, then putting him over her shoulder and patting him, still firmly. Hashmat continued to cry and struggle, his hands and legs pushing against her, and she seemed to hold him tight. He kept crying and she put him down on the sofa, where he kept crying and she spoke to him, soothingly, saying 'alla, alla'. (O6)

Mother seemed slow to respond to Hashmat's spluttering and appeared to insist he took the bottle. His protest is quite vigorous, communicating the indigestibility of the experience for him. As with the other infants in the sample, there was little sense of Hashmat's own rhythms being responded to in feeding, and it is not surprising that he vomited so much (Graph 4.9). The protest that is observed here is not pronounced during the first weeks of his life, and he appeared quite withdrawn, peering at the world through closed, or nearly closed eyes, showing signs of alertness through barely imperceptible movements, appearing frozen, a frightened animal in a threatening world. For example: 'Shakil started playing with a football. He said, with menace, "no baby" and Hashmat lay with his eyes very slightly open as if peering or pretending to be asleep' (O5: Hashmat at seven weeks four days).

Hashmat's defence against the convex shape of containment was to withdraw from object relations. He does not grow, he is not thriving (Graph 4.14).

The experiences of assault on his bodily integrity, through noisy intrusion and the lack of emotional space for him in mother's mind, as shown by her lack of sympathy for his timing and rhythms, lead to question how he holds himself together (Bick 1968). He is not a muscular child, though I do notice on occasions he arches his back and stiffens, flaps his legs and arms, suggesting an unintegrated state. What does emerge is a complex relationship between his hand, himself and other people.

We have already seen how his eye contact and the grip of his mouth on the bottle are kept separate, in order, I suggest, to separate the relationship between feeding and relating to his needs to be held together. Now we can follow how he uses his hand to make a grip on his world of relationships. First, when asleep, his hand makes contact with the blanket:

> I watched Hashmat, and his hands touched one another so that the right one was resting on the left wrist. He was still for a time until he brought his right hand up and over his head; then he took it down and it caught the lip of the blanket. He shuffled this across his mouth. He twitched his head, eyes closed, from side to side and then cried. He cried once and was quiet, and neither mother nor father reacted. Hashmat resumed sleeping with his hand on the left wrist. Then he repeated his movements, his right leg moving under the blanket, his right hand moving towards his face but catching the blanket which he seemed to pull against his chin uncomfortably. He began to cry, his mouth wide and his hands shaking a little against the blanket. He cried once, and then again, then continuously. (O8: Hashmat at 11 weeks)

This affords something of a precarious grip on himself, providing probably a phantasy or dream. He also makes gestures which convey a clear meaning; his hands came over his eyes as if to shield them (O8). He makes a grip with his hand on Shakil's finger (O6). This hand grip is developing strongly with variety. It shows he has at least a notion of an object which can hold another, in a three-dimensional way, one containing another. These quiet gestures permit some psychic survival in the face of a mother who is clearly depressed and lacking emotional space for him, and a family setting which is dangerously intrusive. They also form prototypes of relationships which are seen throughout the observations. It seems to me that these are in the service of differentiating container and contained.

That Hashmat has reason to be wary of the family is indicated by the experience of sibling attacks. When he is five weeks (O4) he is nearly caught by a flying foot from Chalaak who was engaged in horseplay with the 14-year-old Miral. When he is 12 weeks (O9) he is attacked in a more chilling way by the combination of Shakil (three) and Chalaak (five):

> With his fingers Chalaak started poking Hashmat's face, rubbing his finger down his cheek. He then got hold of his bib and twisted it with

> the effect of twisting as if to throttle him. I looked at Chalaak and he stopped. He got off the sofa and started to play his violent game with the other two boys and then Shakil came next to Chalaak on the sofa and grabbed both Hashmat's legs. He started to pull the legs towards him. I said 'no' to Shakil. Hashmat started to cry loudly and persistently. Shakil held on to Hashmat's legs, looking very angrily at me, and I leaned over him while Shakil swore at me a couple of times. I picked up Hashmat as he continued to cry and held him on my lap. His head went back and he cried, looking at me with a frightened look in his eyes. The boys opened the door and ran out. (O9: Hashmat at 12 weeks)

The murderous intent is evident. I intervened to protect Hashmat, and draw the event to the attention of the absent mother. One is struck by the contrast between the vulnerable Hashmat, whose development is so retarded, and the rumbustious pair of Shakil and Chalaak. The former has the attributes of a gangster; Chalaak is the epitome of toughness. Is Hashmat one boy too many in this family, or is there a family pattern whereby survival in a particular way – namely of developing a tough, fighting skin – is part of the culture of development? It appeared significant that this attack occurred after I witnessed (O8: Hashmat at 11 weeks) Hashmat's first smile during the observations, and that this was directed at me. The attack appeared to be precipitated by the sense of specialness that the observation of Hashmat was affording him. In this family, individual attention is eschewed, and the danger of it is manifest, a consequence of the total absence of modulation of sibling jealousy.

Negotiating an observational position had been difficult. With verbal communication being minimal, I have had to try to demonstrate my role in a concrete way. I was drawn into situations from which I would then try to set boundaries. For example, when Hashmat was five weeks (O4) I was asked to feed him. The following week I was asked again and I told mother that it was difficult for me to observe and feed Hashmat; I added something about her being in the best position to do this, rather than me. However, the sequence where Hashmat is attacked by his brothers indicates that the observer's act of attention is not neutral. It clashes directly with the first mode of parenting, that of the group or gang. In these circumstances, since I could not desist from emotional attention upon Hashmat, my intention was to communicate about my activity, to Hashmat and his brothers; to respond, but not to initiate, but clearly communicating to them. I shall give examples of this below.

4.4 Development from 3 to 12 months

Between three months and a year, Hashmat's behaviour was characterised by sudden spurts of development, which countered the feeling – and fact – that his development was markedly backward. He continued to be remarkably unadventurous. He was not sitting unaided until eight months and he began to attempt crawling after nine months. In fact development occurred, as it were, from the outside. Parents put him in a bouncing chair, and later a baby walker, though he had shown no movement towards sitting up, raising his head, or trying to move about. But there were grounds for optimism. At 14 weeks I saw him for the first time sitting in a baby walker. This elevation was accompanied by a greater sense of curiosity. His hand grip was still evident: 'He looked alertly around the room and in my direction, his hair shaved and his very dark eyes looking out. His legs kicked a little and his arms moved also, his hands touching each other' (O11: Hashmat at 14 weeks).

Mother is more vigorous in this period. Later in this observation she offers a soothing containment when changing Hashmat:

> Hashmat quietened down as soon as Rani started to stroke his legs and bottom with the cotton wool. She cleaned him very thoroughly, quite vigorously at times and then she seemed to clean him with quite smooth movements with the cotton wool, all in her usual unhurried slightly slow way. (O11: Hashmat at 14 weeks)

Her attention to his skin appears to give him a sense of his boundaries, of himself. Later she is almost tender when she holds him, and at five months one week (O17) he bounces on her lap. He greets me with a smile when I arrive for observations, he seeks me with his eyes, and there is developing a considerable interaction in the relationship with me. It is particularly notable that this relationship hinges around a particular kind of grip, often with the use of the hand, and accompanied by his making sounds.

> Rani rubbed his back more, and then she picked him up and put him in the bouncing chair, and went out, and Hashmat made his high-pitched noises with Shakil riding his bike around. Hashmat seemed about to cry and I leaned forwards and touched his foot and his hand reached down so I put my finger in his hand and he held on to it tightly and pulled my hand towards him and he made noises ranging between content, accompanied by a suggestion of a smile, to distress. (O16: Hashmat at four months two weeks)

I have acknowledged his solitary struggle towards relating inner states. Attempts at language and sharing a wide range of emotions follows. This willingness to communicate continued. When he was six months three weeks:

> Hashmat sat and looked at me with a long look. His eyes focused on me steadily, with his face on the brink of tears. His hands moved on the table and he had a small, hard plastic whistle which he held. He cast his eyes in the direction of the door where Rani had gone out. I smiled at him and felt there was something very delicate in his mood, so he could easily shift from smiling to crying. The look he was giving me was held on a gossamer thread. He made a little shrieking noise

> and I made a soothing one back. He put his finger in his mouth, and he poked with it behind his top gum, his mouth wide open. He took his finger out and held the toy which he dropped over the side. I retrieved it and he looked surprised to see it again, and he held it. (O21: Hashmat at six months three weeks)

He seems to be communicating to me something about his teeth, to be saying 'it hurts'. There followed a weekly ritual where he made lip-smacking gestures to me, which I imitated. His communication of pain is also seen when he was nine months two weeks. Here the communication indicates the nature of the source of his distress:

> [He is trying to crawl, but gets his leg caught]. He cried a little and then gently banged his head on the floor some few times. [Father then picked him up and after comforting him passed him to me] He was hesitant and then touched my hand, grasping my finger, holding it quite tightly. He reached out to me and poked his finger into my mouth... He leaned against my chest and banged his head against it, lightly but with a feeling of wanting to make a space – concave – there (O28: Hashmat at nine months two weeks).

Hashmat's interest in internal spaces, and his complaint that there is no space inside, is the first communication I have received that mother is pregnant. From the course of the observation so far, the state of pregnancy has been seen as a metaphor of a mother who has no mental space for Hashmat's individual needs, rather than as a concrete and factual state of her condition. Yet there is further evidence:

> Hashmat crawled under the table near Rani's feet, his head nearly touching the underside of the table top. There was no room for him to move unless he dropped down. He seemed to get stuck, and became motionless, frozen, unable to move. Rani's mother leaned down and gently pulled him out backwards, while Rani guided his head to stop it bumping the table. (O33: Hashmat at 10 months 17 days)

This sequence has all the hallmarks of a role play of a forceps delivery, with Hashmat playing the baby and his grandmother the midwife.

The birth of Fashmat was one of the most peculiar events in the history of this observation. This was partly because I failed to spot her pregnancy! Partly, too, it was because of the family's reaction to it. Father announced the birth in this way:

> Javed Ahmed came in and sat at the table and began to peel an onion with the curved knife. Then he said he may have to go to the hospital and added that his wife had a baby yesterday at 2.30pm; another boy. He was looking pleased, a smile on his face as he spoke to me. Then

> he carried on peeling the onion. (O37: Hashmat 11 months 3 weeks 1 day)

Meanwhile, the children – Chalaak, Miral (14) and Belal (10) – played a game of counting fruit: 'Belal said "apples, bananas, grapes, pears", and Miral added "apples, oranges, grapes, bananas, grapes" to which Belal rejoined, with giggles "apples, oranges, grapes, pears, bananas, melon, grapes" (O38: Hashmat at one year less one day). As the list grew longer and in random style, with repetition, one had the inescapable feeling that they were counting babies! Humour turned to violence in the hands of Siral, the 15-year-old. In the absence of his parents, he enacted the mindless rage against the family's babies, with Hashmat as victim:

> Hashmat, sitting on the windowsill, seemed to wriggle and Siral got up and hit him across the face several times. Hashmat cried, his head shot back and he banged it against the window. He again wriggled and again Siral slapped him across the face. Hashmat cried, looked at me and I suggested I had Hashmat for a time. Siral assented without expression and Hashmat cried and held on to my neck. (O37: Hashmat at 11 months 23 days)

After mother returned from hospital with Fashmat, Hashmat responded with a spurt of development and he showed his mother his accomplishments: 'Javed Ahmed stood Hashmat on the floor and he walked a few steps towards us, and said "mama". Rani, with Fashmat on her lap, looked at him and smiled to me and repeated "mama"' (O38: Hashmat at 11 months 29 days).

Hashmat's earlier unadventurousness was seen through delayed development and lack of curiosity. Now he has caught up, developing some muscularity and the capacity to verbalise, precipitated by mother's absence. Now he is a mixture of confidence and fragility: 'He walked a couple of steps across the floor – looking fragile, but seeming confident. He looked round and walked across to the sofa, again taking fragile but confident steps (O38). He emphasises he is no longer the baby by repudiating his drinking bottle: 'Hashmat took the bottle in his hand and tipped it up, letting it drip behind the sofa. Belal stood it up, and Hashmat, standing on Belal's lap, tipped it up again. As it dripped down behind the sofa he called out loudly, "ahh, ahh, ahh"' (O38).

4.5 Hashmat: Development from 12 to 24 months

In the aftermath of the arrival of Fashmat and the adaptation of the family to another baby, Hashmat's experience approximated to a choice, between, on the one hand, accepting the family norm that babies are like fruit – and as common, and that the vulnerable, dependent attitudes of infancy should be violently shed. On the other hand the possibility existed of maintaining a relationship to a maternal object, with all that implied in terms of experiences of individuality, uniqueness and the capacity to communicate internal states of mind. The precariousness of this struggle is seen as Hashmat negotiated the passage between these two alternative ways of relating. Suddenly he is a toddler, not a baby. Developmental progress, taking his first steps and saying 'mama', gives him added capacity and separateness. It also confirms his 'toddlerhood'. He can now join the boys.

During this second year he charts a course through three predominant states of mind. First, there is a boy in pain, who has the capacity to communicate his pain, demand a place with mother and hold on to her (there are occasions when I see him standing by her, holding his hand on her knee – the hand continues to be important for him). There is a developing curiosity. My presence was increasingly linked with this process. He became attached to some of the trappings of my role: my glasses, watch and briefcase. The glasses symbolised the observer's function and his play with them was multifunctional. He wore them (in imitation or identification with me) and he would explore their properties, touching them and looking through them:

> He climbed on the chair and sat next to me. He looked at my face, and then my glasses and he gently leaned over and took them off. He passed them back to me. He took them off and passed them back, and I put them on. He did this again and put his face to the lens and sucked lightly. (O60: Hashmat 18 months 11 days)

This greater curiosity appeared linked to a phantasy of space inside mother, which I mediate. The watch was clearly a symbol of my coming and going. He would come to me at the beginning of observations and ask to wear it. It appeared to help him work through the issue of separation and reunion (Graph 4.18). As he reached two and the observation neared its close, he tried to prevent me leaving. In an act reminiscent of 'John' in the Robertsons' film (Robertson and Robertson 1969) he put on his coat and shoes as I was leaving. (O76: Hashmat at 22 months 2 weeks) He was proprietorial with the briefcase, sitting on it, carrying it round, and preventing Fashmat from reaching it. He was most preoccupied with opening it – which he could not – and his possession of the briefcase and preoccupation with it suggested a relationship with a mother–observer figure. I talked to him a great deal in this second year, and as the quality of his curiosity indicated, his language began to develop (Graph 4.19). He seemed for a time to be bilingual, and his saying 'oma, mama' (mother in Bengali and English) appeared apposite. This also amused Rani, who, when Hashmat was in this state of mind – shall I call it that of a family child? – and the parents were also in a 'family' mode, both of them watched his play benignly, and with interest (Graph 4.3a). Rani in particular became capable at times of responding to Hashmat with some concern and protection.

In contrast to this picture, Hashmat's second state of mind was aggressive and sadistic. He joined the 'group' and his attacks focused on Fashmat (or a baby substitute) and the feeding bottle in equal measure. He thus held the family core phantasy of the attack against the mother–baby couple/link. His shifts from one state of mind to the other could happen quite quickly, in the course of a single observation.

Hashmat's third state of mind was claustrophobic; he spent periods of time looking out of the window, in a rigid and 'switched off' mode. He became transfixed on these occasions (and I held him), unaware of my presence. This appeared to be a continuation of the withdrawn infant, who became mindless in the face of external threats, and whose primary relationship was as if to a doubly-pregnant mother. What was particularly interesting from the point of view of the observer's role was how the observer modulated these states of mind, acting as it were, as a 'connecting tissue' between the 'Russian dolls' of this internal world. The following sequence from an observation when Hashmat was one year three months and one week (O49) demonstrates both the shift from one part of his self to another, the observer's role in providing the 'connecting tissue'. It occurred early on in the process that ensued through this second year, and the observation ended with a demonstration of the quality of risk to which Hashmat was vulnerable:

> Mother showed Hashmat a tank on the living room floor and moved it, playing. Hashmat pushed the tank and then stood up. Rani went out and Hashmat looked at me and held his finger in his mouth with a pained expression. I imitated him and asked if it hurt. He smiled and moved his finger round his mouth. He moved across the room and picked up a toy, went to the doorway and picked up a belt and then turned round, looked at me, showed me the belt and went out of the room.

...so far he is in 'family' mode, though the objects have ominous symbolism...

> I followed him and found Shakil and a friend in a bedroom, and Hashmat stood on a chair. They seemed to stop playing as I went in and then carried on. Rani came in behind me and Hashmat picked up a pair of scissors, a large dressmaking pair. Rani reacted with a worried expression, saying 'no, no' and took them off him. He threw some pegs on the floor and then Rani picked him up and carried him into the kitchen. She gave him a tin (baby food) which had a string making a handle and some pegs in it. Hashmat took this and threw the pegs on the floor. He came up to me, shaped as if to throw the tin and then passed it to me. I took it and passed it back.

...here there is some modulation; Hashmat appears to think as he is approaching an attack...

> He went down the corridor. Shakil and his friend went out to play and Hashmat cried and pointed to the door. He then turned to Rani and reached out to hold her sari. She did not respond and he cried and held

> his arms higher seeking to be picked up. She did not respond and he turned away and went into the bedroom where there were two bikes. He touched them quite gently and picked up some papers, studied them and then put them down, letting them fall to the floor. He looked up and saw me and moved sideways a few steps until he was out of sight, then he moved back and smiled when I came into view. He looked at me again and walked up to me and touched me on the leg, quite tenderly, and then walked backwards still looking at me until he hit the bed. The force of this knocked him over and he looked quite shocked, on all fours. He stayed there for a moment and then stood up.

...he stays related to me, with a hint of a 'peek a boo'... Provocation follows...

> The sound of Fashmat crying came into the room and Hashmat picked up the tin and went out of the room and into the kitchen. Rani called out to him 'no, no, no, hey hey hey'; he followed her into the living room as Fashmat still cried and Hashmat climbed up on to the sofa and reached up to get his bottle which was resting on the back of the sofa. He turned to me and held the bottle tightly between his teeth, pulling the bottle. Rani looked at him and got up and fetched a pillow for him, seeming to understand what he wanted. She laid this on the sofa and sat down on the adjacent chair with Fashmat still crying, on her lap. Hashmat lay down on the sofa with the bottle and sucked it. He lifted his left leg up in the air and looked straight ahead and tensed his leg as he held it in the air. He twisted round so he lay on his side still sucking his bottle which he held in his right hand, while his left hand covered his ear. Fashmat stopped crying but Hashmat still covered his ear. He twisted right round so he was lying on his tummy, his head on its side in a contraposta. He was now sucking more air than milk. He turned again and looked at Rani and passed her the bottle.

...it was rare to see such muscularity...he is preoccupied with babies; murder is in the air...

> She held a biro out to him and he climbed to his feet and slid off the sofa, landing on an empty lemonade bottle, crushing it. He exchanged the bottle for the pen and took it to one of the toys on the floor, bent over and started to push the pen into a hole on the surface of the toy. Rani went to answer a knock at the door, carrying Fashmat. Hashmat followed. A friend came in preceded by her little boy, and he went to play with the toys in a bin. Hashmat went up to the boy, and took a toy himself. Then gently and deliberately he hit the other child with it, several times. The boy cried and called his mother's attention. Rani said something to Hashmat and Hashmat got another toy and hit the boy again.

...Hashmat left the room and I followed him...he is at risk now...

> I found him in the bedroom, kneeling on the bed and hanging out of the open window. I put him down on the floor and he protested, then he ran round the bed and came up to me with a smile and then sat next to me and I held him as he looked out of the window. He called out repeatedly 'mama' pushing the window to and fro. We stayed like this for a time and then as it was time to go I picked him up and he complained at me carrying him away from the window. I went to the living room and told Rani he had been hanging out of the window. Rani registered shock and concern and said to me he was very naughty. (O49)

Holding him had helped him verbalise the problem he is demonstrating in a concrete way – feeling, or being, lost and outside... Here was risk with some emphasis. It seemed quite incongruous that the small, delicate, almost fragile Hashmat could attempt to be so tough. The identification with the older brother crystallised by the time he was two, a consequence it would seem of the constant attacks from Shakil (to which he rarely reacted) and the event of Fashmat's arrival. Toughness, the antithesis of strength, is commonly the defence of the deprived child, (see for example Williams 1983). Belal, the 10-year-old, told the family story in the form of an allegory:

> Belal sat on the chair by the table and told me a story about finding a golden eagle in the flat opposite; the eagle had many babies and they fight each other. The eagle had bitten his hand and he had to go to hospital. He was having to go to stay with his cousin for two weeks because he had been in trouble for tearing the wallpaper off the wall. He was in trouble for fighting here but he would fight with his cousins there and be in trouble again. (O58: Hashmat at 18 months less 5 days)

In the conflict between the siblings, humour could replace deadliness, leaving a sense of horseplay rather than grievious bodily harm. This was exemplified by Hashmat's fight with Shakil:

> Hashmat followed Shakil, calling 'oma' and 'uhh'. Gritting his teeth he hit Shakil on the back and arm. Shakil pretended to be dead and lay on the chair. Hashmat watched him and then hit him several times on the back, as if to stir him. Shakil got up with a big grin (O62: Hashmat at 18 months and 25 days)

I found that as the observations continued, and as the two boys played out their fights, I became less antagonised by the behaviour. I could say that my countertransference changed, moved by Shakil's humour. I wondered in particular how toughness, the capacity to fight, to maintain a possession, or even one's own body boundaries was crucial to the existence of young Asian boys living in contemporary British society.

Hashmat's identifications with big brother figures were evident as he approached his second birthday. He imitated Shakil's tone of voice, the way the older boys brushed their hair, and he got into Miral's shoes, literally: 'Hashmat had left the room and now he came back in wearing big brother Miral's shoes. He grinned broadly and then seriously tried to concentrate on walking in them' (O74: Hashmat at 22 months 6 days). The movement from grinning to seriousness could be said to indicate a conflict between introjective identification and projective identification (Meltzer 1984); Hashmat is not only trying them on for fun, he is aspiring to the position they represent. His identifications flourished, as his play became richer. Just before his birthday he played in a manner which suggested he was relating to identifications with both parents. First he imitates mother in applying face cream:

> Rani intercepted Hashmat and rummaged in his pyjama breast pocket and produced a jar of face cream. She took it from him and rubbed some cream on her face. Hashmat raised his hands and asked for the cream to be returned to him. Rani gave him some cream on his finger and he came over to me. Gently and deliberately he rubbed the cream on to his face, forehead and round his ear, exactly as Rani had done. He finished and looked at me with a 'look how clever I've been' expression (O78: Hashmat at 23 months 13 days)

Second, he imitates father, illicitly helping himself to the betel-nut:

> He leaned over the betel-nut tray and looked at it for a long time. He looked at me warily as if asking permission and I tried to keep my expression neutral! He carried on, taking some leaf and a piece of biscuit. He offered it to me and I shook my head. He put the leaf and biscuit in his mouth, stood very still and chewed, completely taken over by the event, and sporting a slightly glazed expression. He pointed to where Javed Ahmed's jacket hung on the wall and went over to it. He pulled a penknife from the jacket pocket, almost furtively put it back in the jacket pocket and climbed down. He pointed to the window and spoke in Bengali, including the word 'abar' (father/outside). (O78)

In the midst of this he had time to claim an object from Fashmat, and ensure Fashmat had a replacement, an act of considerable generosity.

4.6 Ending

The end of the observation, after two years, was difficult to contemplate, and to work with. With much repetition, there was some working through before the end of the observations. The last observation was a moving occasion, where Hashmat joined me in a meal. I should like to end by describing some of this.

> Rani cleared the table and invited me to sit there. Hashmat looked up at me and called me 'moma'. Rani laughed and spoke to Miral (14)

> who told me Hashmat was calling me 'uncle'. Rani said 'Bengali "oma"; English "mama"; English "uncle", Bengali "moma"'. Hashmat looked up at me eating and then pulled a chair for himself and sat on it. Rani gave him a plate and he ate his rice and curry with his fingers. He pointed to the water jug and I poured him some water in the glass. He drank some and pointed again and I refilled it for him. He raised his glass and I raised mine and he said 'cheers'. I said 'cheers' and we touched glasses. This was repeated several times, each time he said 'cheers' and smiled at me. (O80: Hashmat at two years two days).

4.7 Summary

The context provides an intercultural setting for the observation and a sense of unfamiliarity for the observer. Communication between myself and the adults took place very concretely; there were few and limited verbal exchanges. Actions became important communications. Hashmat made a considerable recovery from difficult early experiences, influenced by hostility from siblings and his parents' inattention. With mother he was loosely held. Fashmat's arrival served to confirm the family's core phantasy – ambivalence towards babies. Through identification with his big brothers, Hashmat attacked the new baby and also the dependent, vulnerable baby part of himself.

The circumstances of the observation demonstrate the impact of flat and convex containing shapes, to which Hashmat responded with a (literal) hold on object relations with his hand. In the process of discussing Hashmat's development some new descriptive categories are introduced. First, there is a description of the idea of an 'unadventurous' defensive pattern, which operates between the experiences of containment and his grip relations. Second, there is evidence that his internalisation includes the capacity to make links between three distinct parts of himself. These are described as 'Russian dolls' of experience, since they develop alongside each other but from different 'historical events' in early infancy. The concept relates to the deep theoretical structure of Anzieu's concept of 'psychic envelopes' (Anzieu 1990), which emerged from Bion's later work (Bleandonu 1994, p.286). The fact that there is a link between them, in Hashmat's mind, suggests he possesses a 'connective tissue' to make the links. My attention for Hashmat appears to have helped this process. The implication is that the observer can have a direct role with the infant in preventing risk.

The observer's role is described as purposefully active, particularly with attempts to respond to Hashmat's communications. The positive link between myself and Hashmat is shown in the farewell meal, and Hashmat's internalisation includes a sense of an object that is able to understand his emotional states (Graph 4.20).

4.8 Grid

4.8.1 Mothering

Support for Rani, Hashmat's mother, centred on the availability of her husband Javed Ahmed, and the presence of extended family and friends. Contact with professionals leading to support from them scored lower than the other categories (Graph 4.1). Rani's preoccupations were rated as mixed, or neutral, and her internal resources were scored as moderate (Graph 4.2a). The grid recorded moderate to fairly low levels of impingement of mother's emotional preoccupations on to Hashmat, and a similar level of conflict in her role. Her verbalisation was, on the whole, fairly low (Graph 4.2b).

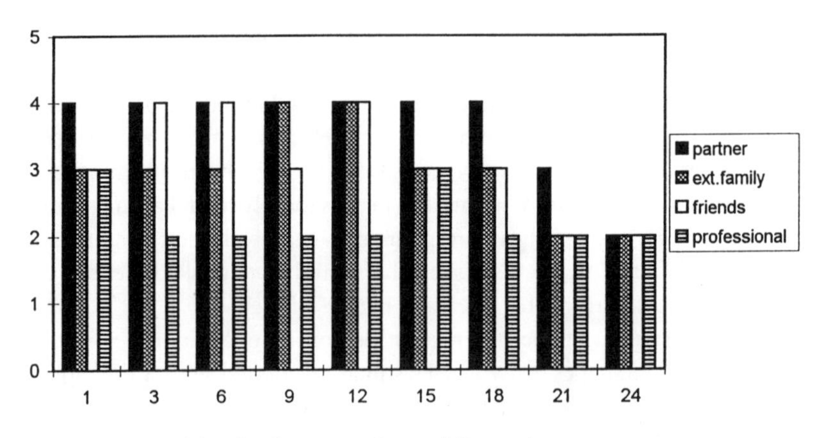

Key: 5=very high levels of support; 4=good; 3=moderate;
2=fairly low; 1=low

Graph 4.1

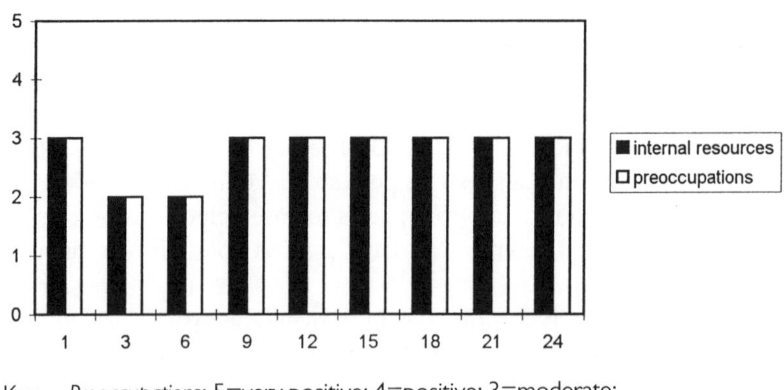

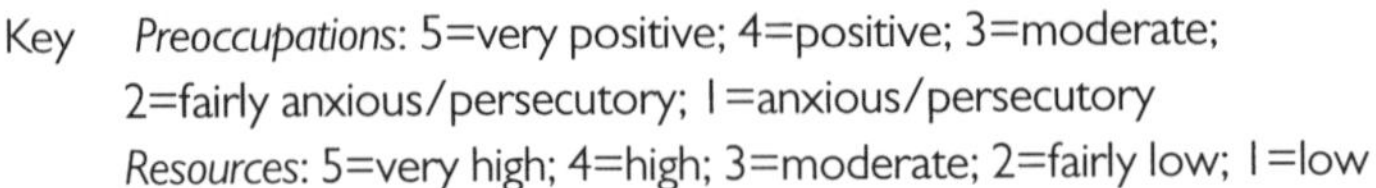
Key *Preoccupations*: 5=very positive; 4=positive; 3=moderate;
2=fairly anxious/persecutory; 1=anxious/persecutory
Resources: 5=very high; 4=high; 3=moderate; 2=fairly low; 1=low

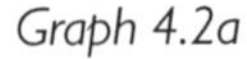
Graph 4.2a

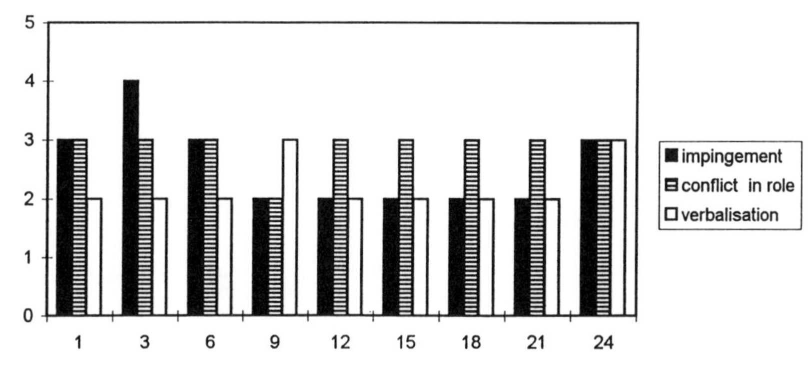

Key: 5=very high; 4=high; 3=moderate; 2=fairly low; 1=low

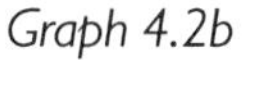
Graph 4.2b

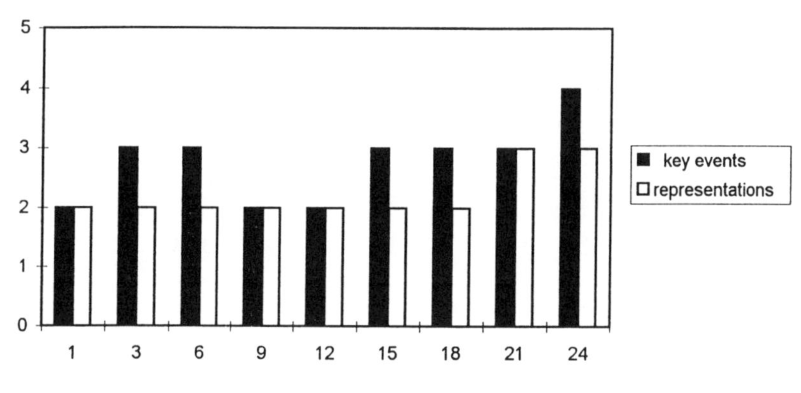

Key: *Experience of events*: 5=very positive; 4=positive; 3=moderate; 2=fairly negative; 1=negative
Representations: 5=very frequent; 4=frequent; 3=moderate; 2=fairly infrequent; 1=infrequent

Graph 4.3a

The key events in Hashmat's development were responded to in a mixed or neutral way, and Rani was rated as making fairly infrequent representations of his states of mind and character (Graph 4.3a). Consistency/persistence of representations was fairly low, and the representations tended towards the negative (Graph 4.3b). Rani's meeting of Hashmat's physical and emotional needs, her awareness of his emotional needs and her understanding of his communication of needs were all recorded as fairly low to moderate. The ratings showed a small increase in these in Hashmat's second year (Graph 4.4).

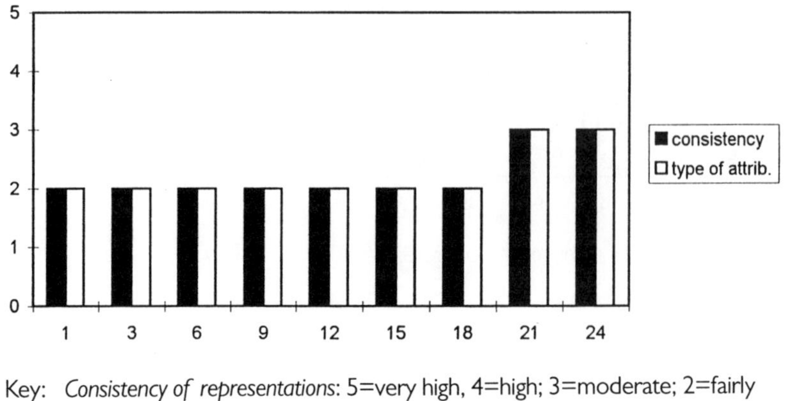

Key: *Consistency of representations*: 5=very high, 4=high; 3=moderate; 2=fairly low; 1=low
Type of representations: 5=very positive; 4=positive; 3=moderate; 2=fairly negative; 1=negative

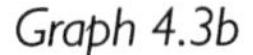
Graph 4.3b

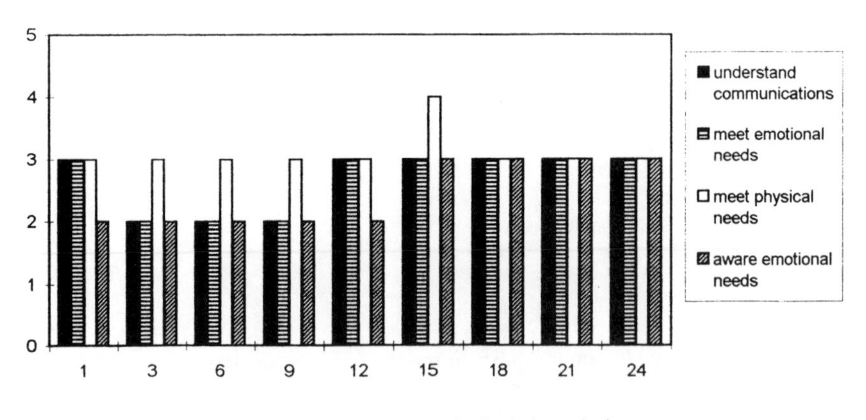

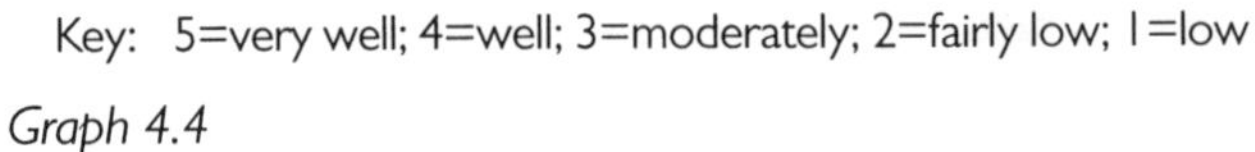
Key: 5=very well; 4=well; 3=moderately; 2=fairly low; 1=low

Graph 4.4

4.8.2 Mother–infant relationship

The categories for the mother–infant relationship were rated consistently at moderate to fairly low levels. This included the levels of attentiveness, sensitivity, understanding, conflict and intimacy (Graph 4.5); the strength of mutual grip relations (Graph 4.6); the levels of intensity, the capacity to maintain emotionality and the levels of 'in tuneness' (Graph 4.7). There were ratings of moderate to fairly low with regard to the 'fit' in the relationship; these ratings show a slightly higher degree of accommodation rather than containing or conflict in the relationship (Graph 4.8). Concave, flat and convex containing shape were rated as present in almost equal measure (Graph 4.9).

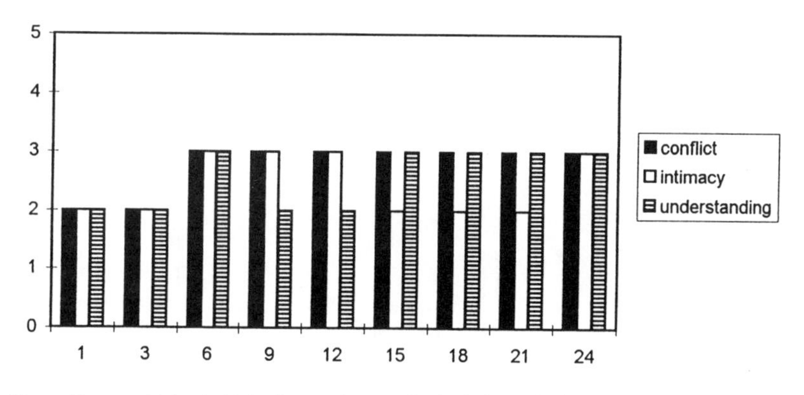

Key: 5=very high; 4=high; 3=moderate; 2=fairly low; 1=low

Graph 4.5a

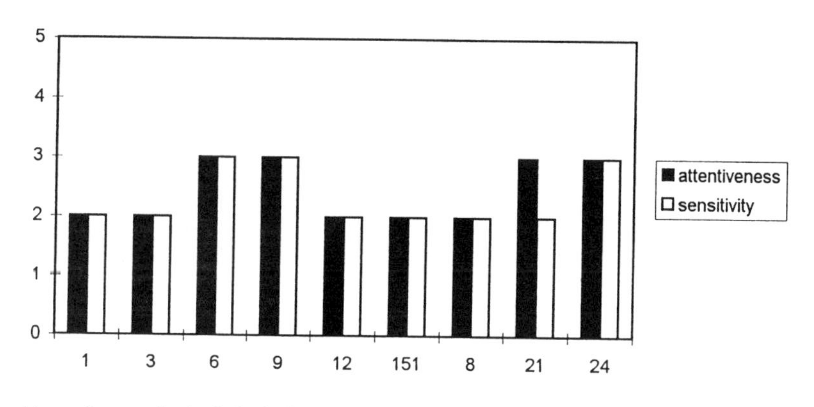

Key: 5=very high; 4=high; 3=moderate; 2=fairly low; 1=low

Graph 4.5b

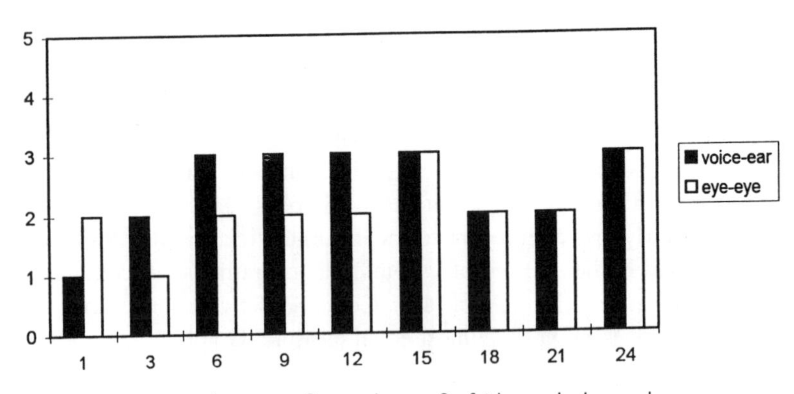

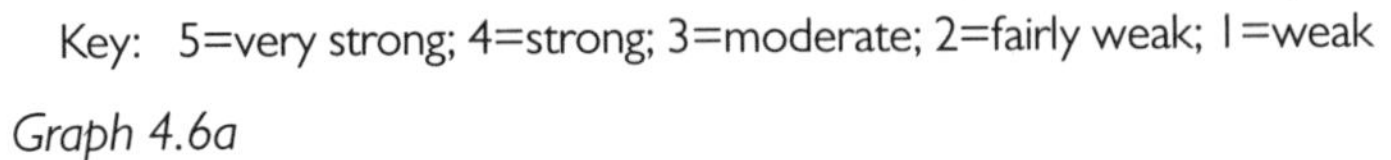
Key: 5=very strong; 4=strong; 3=moderate; 2=fairly weak; 1=weak

Graph 4.6a

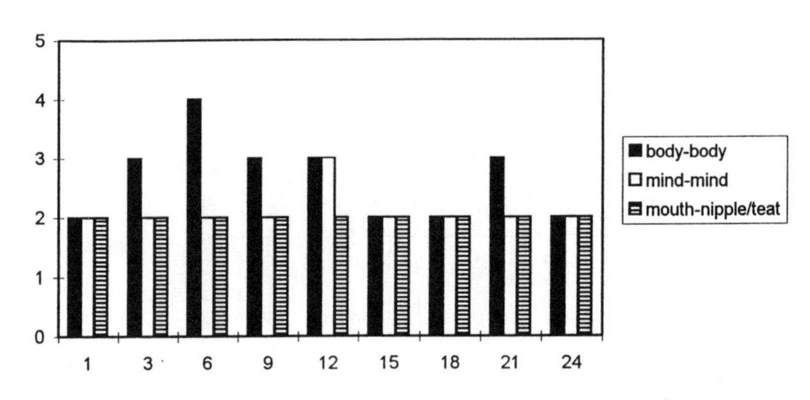

Key: 5=very strong; 4=strong; 3=moderate; 2=fairly weak; 1=weak

Graph 4.6b

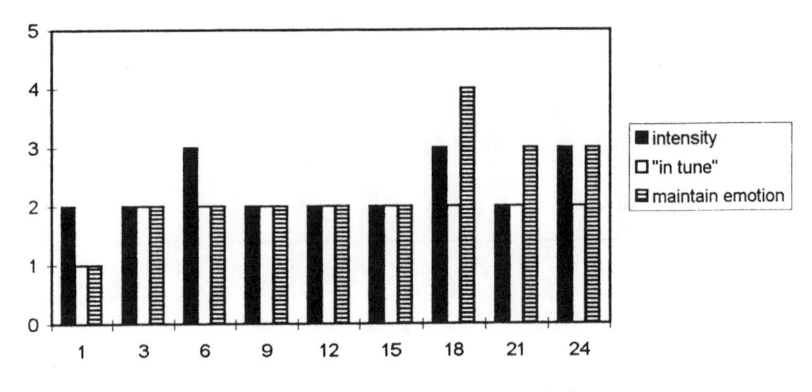

Key: 5=very high; 4=high; 3=moderate; 2=fairly low; 1=low

Graph 4.7

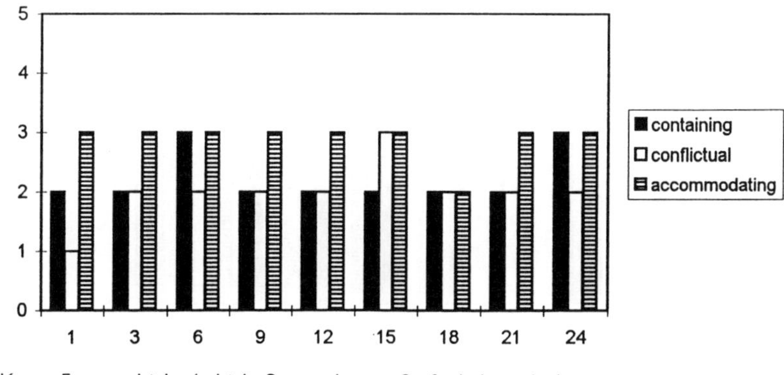

Key: 5=very high; 4=high; 3=moderate; 2=fairly low; 1=low

Graph 4.8

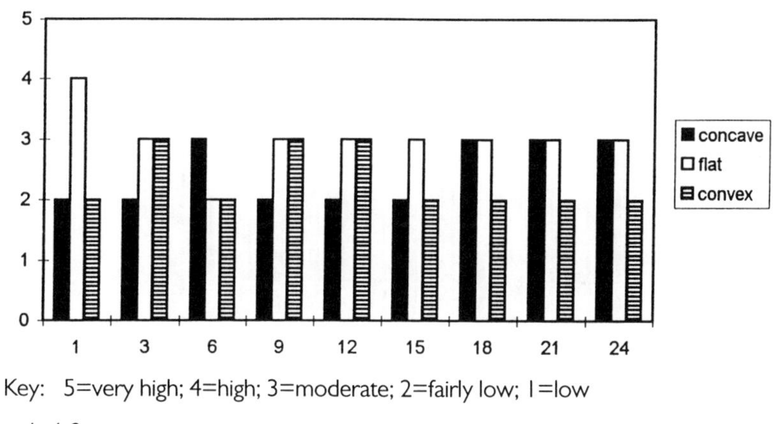

Key: 5=very high; 4=high; 3=moderate; 2=fairly low; 1=low

Graph 4.9

4.8.3 Father and father–infant relationship

Javed Ahmed was a very present figure in observations; his relationship with Hashmat was rated as moderate to fairly low in terms of sensitivity, attentiveness and intimacy (Graph 4.10). Grip relations were also scored in these categories (Graph 4.11).

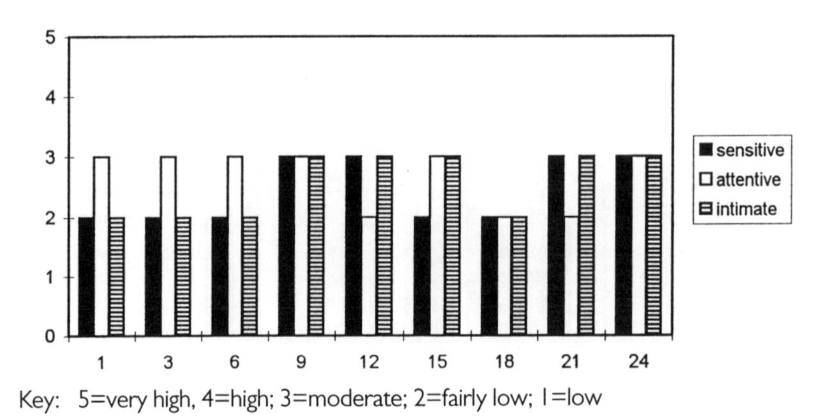

Key: 5=very high, 4=high; 3=moderate; 2=fairly low; 1=low

Graph 4.10

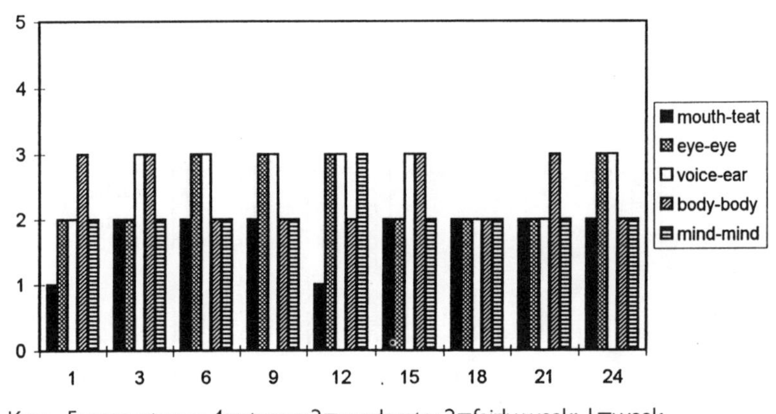

Key: 5=very strong; 4=strong; 3=moderate; 2=fairly weak; 1=weak

Graph 4.11

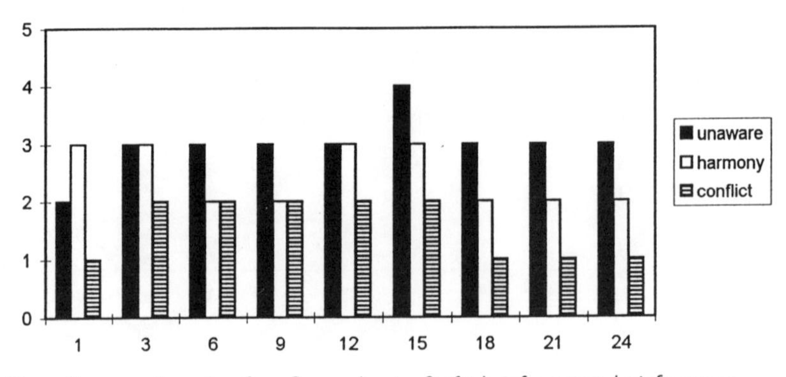

Key: 5=very often; 4=often; 3=moderate; 2=fairly infrequent; 1=infrequent

Graph 4.12

4.8.4 Parental relationship

The relationship between Rani and Javed Ahmed was characterised by ratings of fairly low levels of conflict, a moderate to fairly low level of harmony. There were moderate levels of unawareness of conflict between them (Graph 4.12). High levels of 'flattening of affect' were recorded when it came to scoring the way the parents worked together to meet Hashmat's containment needs. In contrast the thinking or problem solving link ('bridge building') was rated fairly low. Javed Ahmed's role in sharing parental tasks ('nappy changer') was scored as moderate for the first 18 months (Graph 4.13).

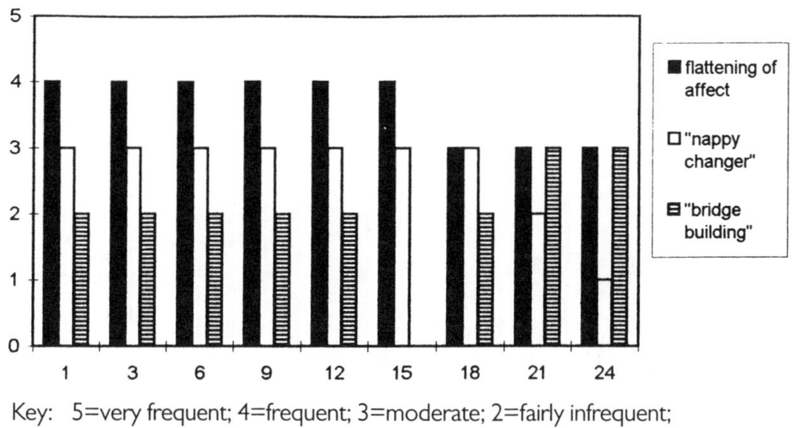

Key: 5=very frequent; 4=frequent; 3=moderate; 2=fairly infrequent; 1=infrequent

Graph 4.13

4.8.5 Infant Development

Hashmat's physical development was scored as moderate to somewhat delayed (see Table 4.1). He was scored as experiencing some poor health, some difficulties sleeping, and some feeding difficulties (Graph 4.14).

Table 4.1

sitting	8 months
crawling	9 months
standing	11 months
walking	12 months

His grip relations were rated as showing a strong hand grip, and an increasing strength of body grip (Graph 4.15b). His eye, voice and mouth grips appeared to be subject to fluctuating strength; eye and voice were rated as falling below moderate strength from 9–15 months. (Graph 4.15a). Hashmat was rated as demonstrating moderate to high frequencies of object relating; moderate frequencies of defending, and his defending was moderately flexible. He developed moderate to high levels of expressiveness and protest (Graph 4.16). Hashmat was rated as having moderate to high capacities for memory, recognition and recall with affection (Graph 4.17). He was rated as showing moderate levels of seeking proximity, showing discrimination and fidelity towards people, and reacting to separation. His thinking was rated below moderate in his first year and moderate thereafter (Graph 4.18).

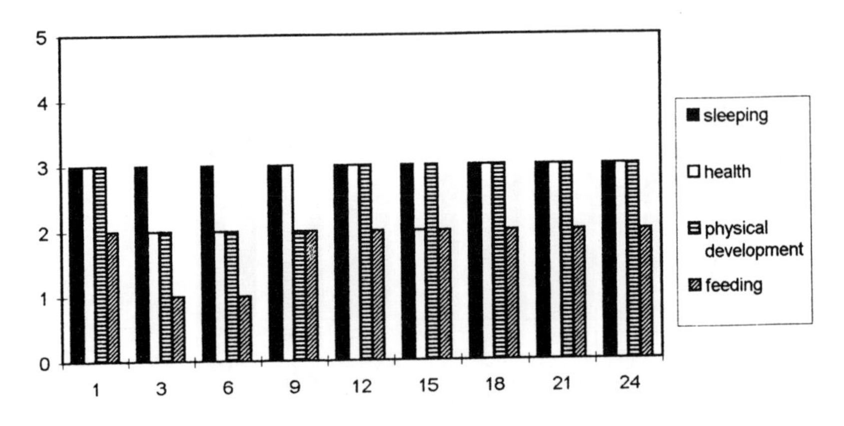

Key: *Physical development*: 5=very advanced; 4=advanced; 3=in time; 2=slightly backward; 1=backward
Other categories: 5=very well; 4=well; 3=OK; 2=some difficulties; 1=difficulties

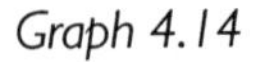
Graph 4.14

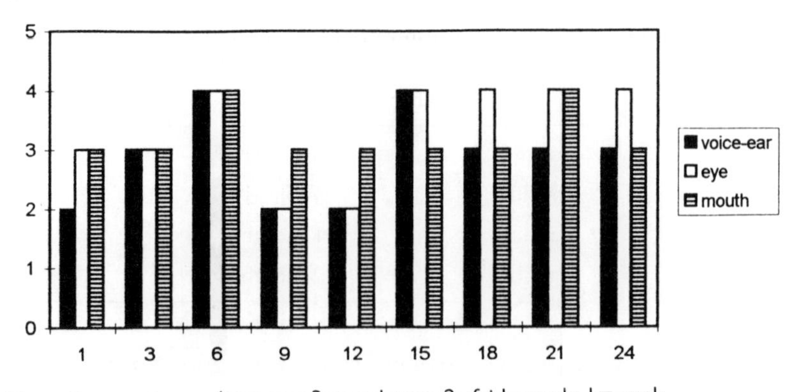

Key: 5=very strong; 4=strong; 3=moderate; 2=fairly weak; 1=weak

Graph 4.15a

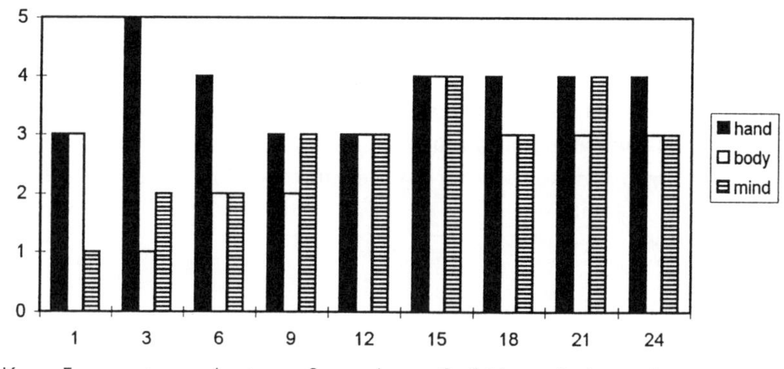

Key: 5=very strong; 4=strong; 3=moderate; 2=fairly weak; 1=weak

Graph 4.15b

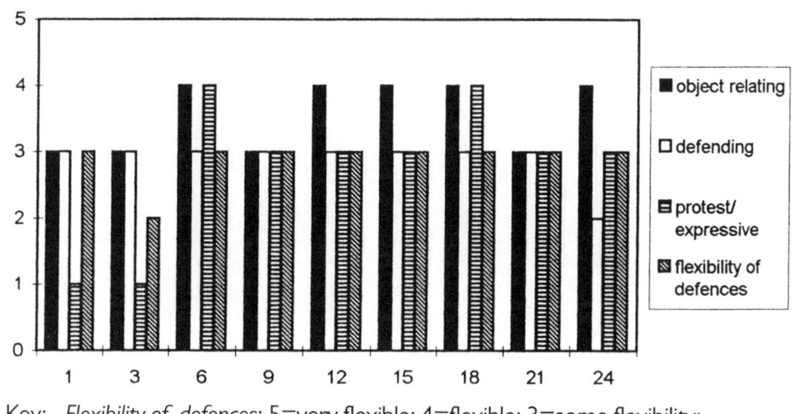

Key: *Flexibility of defences*: 5=very flexible; 4=flexible; 3=some flexibility; 2=tending to rigid; 1=rigid
Other categories: 5=very high; 4=high; 3=moderate; 2=fairly low; 1=low

Graph 4.16

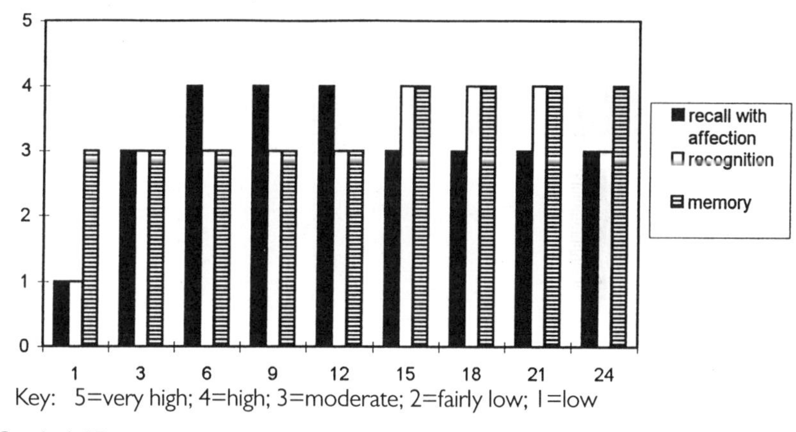

Key: 5=very high; 4=high; 3=moderate; 2=fairly low; 1=low

Graph 4.17

Hashmat gained a moderate level of language development, and his symbolic play began to appear in his ratings after 18 months. He was rated as demonstrating a high level of play which was connected with expressions of unconscious phantasy (Graph 4.19). Overall the quality of internalisation was rated throughout the two years as including both benign, secure and 'good' qualities on the one hand, and some persecutory elements on the other hand (Graph 4.20).

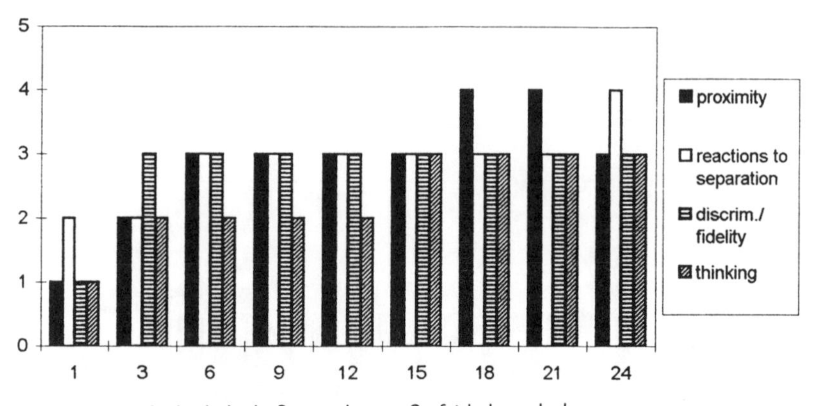

Key: 5=very high; 4=high; 3=moderate; 2=fairly low; 1=low

Graph 4.18

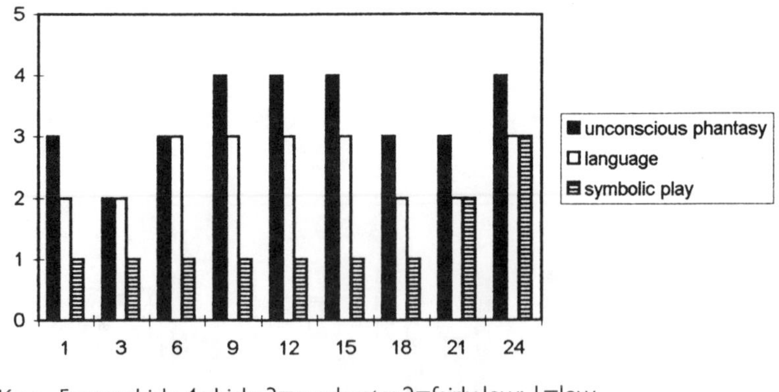

Key: 5=very high; 4=high; 3=moderate; 2=fairly low; 1=low

Graph 4.19

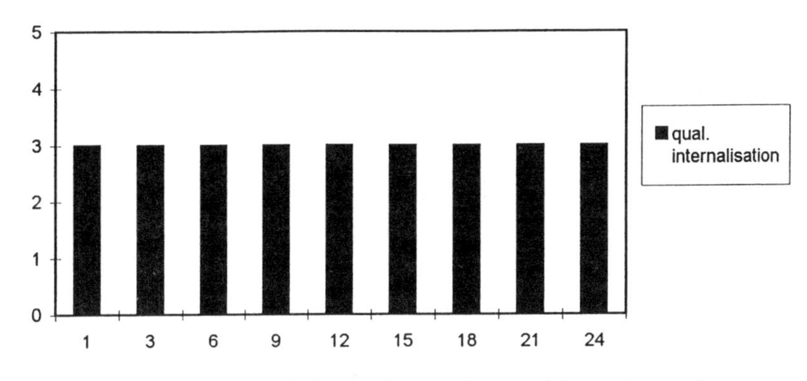

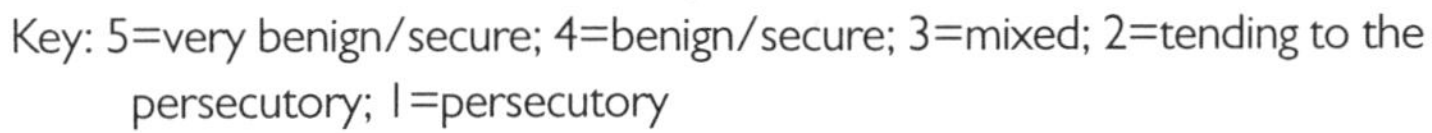
Key: 5=very benign/secure; 4=benign/secure; 3=mixed; 2=tending to the persecutory; 1=persecutory

Graph 4.20

4.8.6 Summary of grid

The grid for Hashmat provides categories for structuring the descriptive case study, and confirms the overall picture of moderate development. That is to say that there are categories which indicate areas of positive development, and those which suggest some problematic features. Capacity for positive development is seen through Hashmat maintaining object relations, despite a high degree of defensiveness (Graph 4.16), an increasingly positive pattern of internalised qualities (Graphs 4.17, 4.18) and the capacity to maintain a range of grip relations (4.15a and 4.15b). The prominent early hand grip is seen vividly in the graph, in contrast to the relatively low scores for eye and mouth grips.

Problematic aspects of development were recorded in the consistent moderate to fairly weak/low recordings for parent–infant sensitivity and attentiveness and mutual grip (graphs 4.5, 4.6, 4.7 and 4.10, 4.11). Recordings of moderate concave container shape, moderate flat/convex container shape and moderate accommodation in the mother–infant 'fit' (Graphs 4.9, 4.8) confirm the mixture of containment and propensity for risk that were recorded in the descriptive case study. Some slight increase in parental capacity was recorded, for example in the increased parental representations of Hashmat's states of mind (Graph 4.3) and these are in accord with some recovery in the second year and a moderate capacity for symbolic functioning by his second birthday (Graph 4.19).

CHAPTER 5

Michael

The observation of Michael was the most difficult in the sample and it came to a premature end when mother placed Michael, and his brother in foster care when he was 16 months. As with Hashmat there were limited resources available for Michael's parenting. Hashmat seemed for some time to be 'one too many' and Michael's arrival also had this meaning for his mother. Unlike Hashmat's experience, the limitations of parental resources and the precariousness of the family structure prevented recovery during Michael's infancy and the ending of this observation could not present a greater contrast with that of Hashmat. Michael's development contained some similar features to that of Hashmat, particularly the development of a defensive pattern which I have called 'unadventurous'. In Michael the constellation was more marked, more exaggerated, and he gave concern that he was failing to thrive. The observation therefore concentrates on an infant's development in very difficult circumstances.

5.1 The family

Michael was Mary's third child, and was born when his next older brother, Darren was just 11 months. Mary's pregnancy with Michael was unplanned and almost unnoticed, for Mary said she was not aware of being pregnant until her sixth month. She was then worried she may have damaged the baby through not being aware of his presence, by over-exerting herself and carrying heavy items up the stairs to her flat.

My first meeting with Mary took place six weeks before the baby's expected birth. She was a tall, fair woman in her mid-twenties, with a bland baby-face appearance. She sat across the doorway of her narrow kitchen and I had a sense of being hemmed in as she talked in a rather seamless way. This held the sense of a projection as she told me about feeling trapped by this pregnancy and her life as a single parent.

I was put in contact with Mary by her social worker who told me there had been concern about Colin, Mary's first baby, who was five at the start of the observation. Mary had requested Colin be placed in foster care in his second year, as she found him very difficult and she and his father had separated. Though the social services tried to help Mary continue her parenting of Colin rather than being separated from him, there was concern that Mary was inattentive, leaving him for periods of time unattended, and therefore placed him in some risk. To me Mary said that, when a baby, Colin cried all the time and she 'screamed back and that seemed to make matters worse' (O4: Michael at five weeks six days) Since Darren's birth, Mary appeared to have enjoyed motherhood with the support of the social worker, and Mary told me she felt she had a 'love affair' with Darren. Colin had seemed to cause less concern since starting school, though he maintained some characteristics of difficult development, an indiscriminate displaying of affection and enuresis. Mary's third pregnancy complicated the picture and there was concern how Mary would respond to this latest challenge.

Mary told me that her mother had died when she was four, and that she felt she had not been accepted by her father's second wife, who she told me was a childminder. This limited the support she received from her family. Her father did keep in contact with her, as did Colin's father. Her current partner, Dave, the father of Darren and Michael, had not been seen since hearing about her pregnancy. Her flat was at the top of six flights of stairs; an impossible task, almost, for a single parent with a five-year-old and two babies in a double buggy! She hoped to be moved by the council to somewhere more appropriate.

Mary readily agreed to the observation taking place, but did not contact me after Michael's birth. I heard from the social worker that he was born and telephoned Mary. She was reluctant to start the observation saying things were 'too hectic' for her to have time for me. She suggested I phone again in a few days. In this second phone call Mary talked to me extensively about her situation – which was still 'hectic' – and about Michael's birth. She said this was very painful, but also quick – a two and a half hour labour. He was a large baby, weighing 10lb. Mary was still hesitant about starting the observation and I said that perhaps the observation could be helpful for her. This was certainly a tentative suggestion, but Mary at this point agreed to the observations and we made a time for me to visit.

5.2 Quality of containment

Mary took some months to accept Michael, and her initial responses to his presence were dominated by a murderous depression, a wish to have him quiet or absent. She suggested that I should spend the whole observation time with him whilst she went out (O8), and that I should take him away (O7). Though it was not stated, the feeling was evoked that she would, in retrospect, have had him adopted or even aborted had she been able to think about this when she was pregnant with him. There was considerable regret and recrimination that Michael had disrupted her relationship with Darren. Similarly she was raging against Dave, for his absence and the conception of Michael.

In these circumstances, Mary's containment of Michael was characterised by paucity of attentiveness (flat container shape) and intrusiveness (convex container shape) (Graph 5.9). She found it extremely difficult to achieve any thoughtful and attentive contact with him (Graph 5.5). These features and their impact on Michael are described below.

Her relationship with me was quite ambivalent and precarious. Mary found it difficult to keep to the weekly observation schedule, and they were often more than a week apart. When I was away for one week, Mary was away for two. Her deprivation was very much to the foreground, as she clearly placed me in the role of her father (O2) and the absent or abandoning partner (O2). I had been able to begin the observations through suggesting that the observational time might be helpful for Mary; her interpretation of the observational role had three aspects. First, I was to have the function of holding the baby; second, of listening to her seamless talk; and third, of interpreting for her the current needs of the baby. By this I mean that she would call to me asking what I thought the baby needed; was he hungry? was he asleep? was he taking the dummy? etc. By this means she seemed to delegate to me the function of reverie. She could then parent at a distance, without the same intensity of emotional involvement, and at the same time, through me, experience both the sense of containment of having someone else there, and the problems that were associated with the limitations of my presence; for one hour only each week.

She had a torrid time in these first three months, and was able to say how difficult it had been when she reflected on the early weeks with Michael:

> Mary said things were a bit better now and there were times when she had reasonably good days. There were times when she felt she could not cope. The beginning, when she had come back from hospital with Michael, was awful, but it was not as bad as that now. (O7: Michael at two months one day)

Dave returned when Michael was five months. I do not know how the reconciliation was effected. His presence did, for a time, provide some semblance of solidity to the parenting of the children (Graph 5.1). Dave helped with practical issues, buying furniture, helping with the shopping and looking after the children. He was able to feed Michael with some attention (Graph 5.10), but he was impervious to the infant's distress (see O20, O27 below). He was also an inconsistent presence in his children's lives.

Mary seemed to relate to both Dave (Graph 5.12) and myself in similar ways, in which we moved from usefulness to uselessness. Both of us were 'ejected' at different times. Mary told me that Dave was inhibiting her chances of being rehoused (O20) (Graph 5.13). Her wish to be rehoused was one with which one had considerable sympathy. Mary had a vision of living in a house with a garden, and which would solve all her problems. This idealism excluded Dave, myself and everyone else she knew. Her preoccupation with rehousing ran throughout the observation period. When she was offered a house and the offer did not then materialise, she fell into a hopeless depression, precipitating the end of the observation.

The early death of her mother left Mary experiencing life as an abandoned child, and her life appeared to consist of insurmountable hurdles which 'happened' to her – not least amongst these was her pregnancy with Michael. Her main support during the period of the observations was the social worker who was my source of initial contact (Graph 5.1). This was a helpful relationship for her, someone whom she kept in mind as a supportive presence. When the social worker left, Mary could not replace her, and this coincided with her decline. Again, the social worker seemed to thoughtfully communicate after her leaving, to minimise the sense of abandonment Mary experienced.

In the observations I took an active role with Michael, and attempted to make myself available for Mary in a supportive way. This did have some impact on the quality of containment. Mary became more interested in the task of parenting (see O34 below) as she became more accepting of Michael's presence. Occasionally she accepted my thoughts about what was ailing the children (O34) and about her difficulties. Just as often my comments would be dismissed – or ejected. Nevertheless the failure of the containing environment leads inevitably to reflections on the role of the observer in these circumstances. Particularly, the question of whether I could have done more within the role is the one with which I have been preoccupied. Like the Robertson's (J. and J. Robertson 1969), the process involved inevitably attracts criticism and highlights the limits of the observer's potency in such circumstances.[1]

5.3 Michael's early development

My first view of Michael occurred at the beginning of the first observation. He appeared to be an alert baby, seeking contact, whilst Mary demonstrated how limited were the emotional resources she had available for him (Graph 5.2). The first moments of the observation graphically revealed the dilemma both of them had:

> Mary opened the door saying 'hallo' and that she had a problem. Colin was ill and the school had phoned to say he needed to come home. She had arranged for his father to collect him. She took me into the living room where Michael was lying on the sofa in the middle of a

---

1 There was certainly criticism – largely sympathetic – when I discussed this observation in Rome (Briggs 1993). This centred on the extent and direction of my interventions with mother, particularly in containing her experiences in relationship with me, where I became another potentially abandoning figure. I shall explore this issue as I proceed. The contrary argument is that the observation enabled Mary to continue as long as she did.

> nappy change. Mary sat down beside him and completed changing his nappy whilst talking to me about the difficulties of managing all three children. Michael, a fair-haired baby, was awake and alert with his arms moving, kicking a little. Mary wiped his bottom with cotton wool and then put on a clean nappy, tucking his legs into the Babygro. He turned his head to the side and made sucking movements, his eyes closed. He turned his head again, to face upwards, opened his eyes and moved both arms away from his body, and he shook a little.
>
> Mary picked him up and put him straight in the pram. He lay on his back and cried and she rocked the pram backwards and forwards. She put a dummy in his mouth saying she had resorted to a dummy and he quietened. He sucked at the dummy with his eyes closed. (O1: Michael at two weeks six days)

Mary attended to Michael almost mechanically, whilst his sucking and then shaking show his need for holding containment. He continued to show a willingness to make a grip through crying, sucking and his eye contact. Similarly, he has the need to hold himself together in the face of Mary's limited attentiveness. In the next observation I was enlisted by Mary to hold Michael and to inform her of his needs and state of mind:

> Michael started to cry and Mary asked me to fetch him. I found him crying softly, eyes shut, and mouth wide open. He was red in the face. I picked him up and he quietened straight away. He moved his head and I looked into his eyes. He looked back at me and this expression felt distant. I took him to where Mary was busy in the kitchen and his eyes followed her. He closed his eyes and turned his head back into my clothing, and then looked up at me lying very still. He burped quite loudly and Mary commented on it. (O2: Michael at three weeks six days)

Michael actively sought mother with his eyes and his distress is eased by being held. He conveys to me in my very active role the need to be held tightly, and firmly. When Mary was more directly involved with him she used me to express her intensely unhappy feeling, and to indicate that I am offering some containment for her which was, however, tantalising:

> She laid Michael on his back on the bed. He turned his head towards the window, holding his hands, fists clenched, up in the air, and he made some gurgling noises. Mary inspected his nappy with her finger and said it did need changing. Darren walked round Mary, picked up a nappy, and she passed him a bottle. He took this and came and sat on my lap. He drank from the bottle, looked up at me, and sat quite comfortably. Mary said she could do with someone being there permanently to help her. She turned to Michael and undid his nappy,

> talking as she did so. She said that she felt she was being punished for what she had done, that is, getting pregnant. She said that she had felt like 'cracking up' the previous evening, when all three children had been crying. (O3: Michael at four weeks six days)

The containment experienced by Mary when 'someone is there' is in stark contrast with her state of nearly 'cracking up' the previous evening when she is alone. The attention I give to Darren frees her to attend to Michael. Whilst she contemplates the nappy change, her guilt about her pregnancy comes to the forefront (Graph 5.2). There is a barely concealed wish that Michael was not there. The impact of this has a dramatic effect as the observation continued:

> Mary came in with Darren and said would I like a coffee, and would I continue to hold Michael because that stopped him crying, while she gave Darren his dinner. Michael sat in my arms holding very tightly on to my finger; his eyes looking ahead, unfocused. We sat like this for some time, and I got him comfortable by holding him quite close and tight. I could hear Mary in the background feeding Darren. (A feeling I had at this point was wanting to throw him across the room and this felt quite puzzling.) Mary came in with Darren and she said she could kill the children's father if she saw him; she was very angry and really could kill him. He knew she could be violent; she did not lose her temper very much but when she did it was very strong. I made a comment about how difficult this was, and Mary said she just wished she knew where she was with him. If he said to her he did not want to have anything to do with the children she would accept this, but not knowing was difficult, but she also wanted to give him the benefit of the doubt in case anything had happened to him, and she was worried about him too. (O3)

In this extract two features are important; first there is Michael's very tight grip on my finger, which seemed to confirm the feeling I had of his need to be tightly held. It has a flavour of 'holding on for dear life'. There is a drowning quality to this communication, perhaps under the impact of projections from mother he cannot assimilate. Second, there is the feeling aroused in me of wanting to 'throw him away', which is experienced in a particularly strong way because I am holding him. It has the quality of a projection of which Michael is attempting to rid himself, and is closely in line with both Mary's murderousness towards the father – and this baby? – and her ambivalence about his existence. The hypothesis following from this is that Michael is internalising this sense of being a 'thrown away baby'.

Michael's activity is seen through the way he uses all his modalities – mouth, ears, eyes, voice, hand and body – to attempt to make a grip on his object. Predominantly he made sucking gestures with his mouth (nine occasions), cried (nine occasions), searched with his eyes (20 occasions) and held on to me with his hand (five occasions). In the first six observations I was able to record, in all, 80 occasions when Michael made a grip-seeking gesture. In the same observations, there were but four occasions when mother and infant reciprocated. There was repeatedly, one could say, using Bion's phrase, 'the mating of a preconception with a negative realisation' (Bion 1967) for Michael in regard to his relationship with his mother. This was an elemental source of conflict in the relationship (Graph 5.5). Mary hinted that she wished Michael to be asleep, quiet or otherwise invisible. She left me to observe him alone whilst she was preoccupied with Darren. She went out, leaving me baby-sitting (O8: Michael at two months three weeks) and suggested I spent all my time alone with him (O7: Michael at two months one week). She had little attention for Michael and most strikingly did not feed him when he was crying and making sucking gestures (O4: Michael at five weeks six days; O6: Michael at six weeks six days). On the latter occasion he sucked the back of his hand. He was seen to focus on a light (O4) and the development of defensive constellations could be predicted from this analysis (Graph 5.16).

Michael's defensiveness was characterised by a striking withdrawal which was dramatically and worryingly observed. I watched him lie quietly with only the faintest signs of life and liveliness:

> He was asleep with his pacifier in his mouth and I watched him lie on his back with his right hand near his ear. He sucked 11 or 12 times, paused and then repeated, sucking lightly. After ten minutes like this his right fist moved, clenched and loosened, then his left hand came closer over towards his face. He sucked and his mouth slightly opened, not gripping the dummy hard. His eyes slightly opened and closed, then opened. He eventually looked at me but did not seem to take me in and there was a glazed and unfocused look on his face. The pacifier fell out of his mouth and his mouth opened. He was very still and almost comatose. His hands moved a little and he started to stretch, and there was a sense of something being stuck, like wind or indigestion, not quite coming through. He stretched both his arms up and there was a flick as his arm came down and flicked the coverlet, a quite sudden movement in the midst of this 'never never land'. He then shivered a little. (O8: Michael at two months three weeks)

The vagueness of his eye contact (Graph 5.15) was repeatedly seen in other observations, where he looked at the world with barely open eyes, conveying fearfulness, like a frightened rabbit: 'Michael had his eyes very slightly open as if peering out from the very smallest gap in his lids. His dummy fell from his mouth and he started to wriggle uncomfortably, his mouth open' (O7: Michael at two months one week), and 'Michael was lying on his back with his eyes open the slightest amount. His mouth was open making some sucking movements. He lay still and moved his feet, turned his head slowly, still with his eyes open the merest crack' (O9: Michael at three months five days).

He seemed quite empty in O8, and he began to decline feeds when they were offered: 'Mary gave him his bottle. Again his open mouth took it in but he would not suck and seemed to push the bottle out with his tongue' (O10: Michael at three months one week five days). He was sick in almost every feed I observed (O7, O9, O10) and in the last of these he regurgitated almost the entire feed. When Mary did feed him she did this intrusively and mechanically: 'Michael sucked at the bottle which Mary pushed backwards and forwards in and out of his mouth in a mechanical way, with impatience' (O9). Similarly she was intrusive, and hostile, when wiping his mouth: 'Michael was sick and Mary vigorously mopped the corner of his mouth and his neck with tissue. He cried while she rubbed and stopped crying when she finished. He was sick again, and when Mary rubbed his mouth vigorously he cried' (O7).

When feeding, he focused away from mother, usually looking at Colin or Darren, both of whom actively interrupted his feeding or any other time he had with Mary. He maintained his hand grip on my finger (O4, O6, O7, O9) which appeared to suggest his continued notion of a grip on another which was three-dimensional (Graph 5.15b), despite the desperate feeling this grip activated in me. However, his other grips – his eyes and particularly his mouth – became quite slack, and limp. In O7 (above) he was observed with an open mouth and this was first seen in O4: 'Michael was asleep in his pram, lying very still with his mouth wide open' (O4: Michael at five weeks six days). Later in this observation he went limp: 'His finger held my shirt tightly, then he equally tightly gripped my finger. Quite suddenly Michael let the dummy fall from his mouth, continued to hold my finger, but seemed for a moment to go very limp, and closed his eyes' (O4).

This limpness of mouth, and his whole body in this sequence, seemed to suggest a real loss of contact, or expectation of contact, again raising feelings that this was concerned with issues of life and death. The interchangeability of grip modalities – holding with his hand led to letting go with his mouth – gave cause for thinking that a considerable dissociation was taking place. His survival seemed to depend on this retreat into suspended animation, or mindlessness, and from this very withdrawn state he did make contact with his voice and his hand. First, as I am watching him and he loses his grip on the dummy:

> I leaned over and popped the dummy back into his mouth. As I did so his fingers caught hold of my finger and held on. He put both hands in front of his face and I let him hold my finger for a time until the grip eased and his eyes closed. (O7)

Then on two occasions (O8 – above – and O9) he makes a contact with his hand in a way which evokes suddenness, and a sense of falling:

> He lifted his right arm up and caught the string of the cover of the cot, and pulled it, which caused the cover to fall over his head. At this point Mary came in and asked if he was awake. She picked him up and once in her arms he opened his eyes more widely. (O9)

The contact showed the capacity to make contact with another. When held he emerged – passively – to a responsiveness in which he nearly smiled.

At three months Michael was not thriving (Graph 5.14). He could lift his head but seemed disinclined to do so. His physical movements were restricted to the slightest movements of turning his head and kicking his legs. Only the capacity to grasp with his hand gave a sense that he was growing. His feeding was becoming very problematic, he was thin and not gaining weight. He had a capacity to make contact with others but he had become very passive, waiting for Mary to attend to him rather than having the expectation of contact which he could seek or activate. He protested less, and his grip relations had been reduced to a slack limpness of expression, especially in his mouth. Hashmat has been described as 'unadventurous', and Michael shares some of these characteristics – only more so. He seemed to be fulfilling Mary's wish that he should become an invisible baby.

As the observer in this difficult situation I have developed some contact with Michael through the hand grip, and through frequent spells of holding him. As Mary began to use me as part of a system through which Michael could be forgotten about, or put on one side, I spoke with her about the need for her to continue to relate to Michael as in the rest of the week. I also found it important to speak frequently about what I had noticed about Michael, his being awake or not, and I would relay in some detail what I had seen, and Mary was welcoming of these reports from me.

5.4 Development from 3 to 12 months

Soon after Michael was three months Mary experienced some relief from her depression and hostility towards Michael, and became more available for him. Some interactions were observed between them and Michael demonstrated his greater alertness when held by mother:

> Michael looked up at the light which Mary had just turned on. He made 'ooh' and 'ahhh' noises which Mary imitated. He looked at her and she looked back at him. He held her eyes and she said he smiles a lot. He continued to look alert, but he did not smile. (O11: Michael at three months three weeks)

His difficulties continued, however. He continued to refuse to feed and to be sick. He refused the bottle with an open mouth, by turning his head away: 'Mary held him on her lap for a moment, laid him back and gave him the bottle.

He kept his mouth open and turned his head away' (O13: Michael at four months ten days).

This open-mouthed expression became quite dominant. I described this feature in various ways; as 'like a cuckoo in the nest, making him look a bit stupid' (O13) and in O19 as 'wide eyed and expressionless, mouth open and tongue forward' (O19: Michael at seven months three days) and as 'blank alertness' (O20: Michael at seven months 17 days). In his baby walker, and after a break in observations he demonstrated this 'stupid' expression:

> He held his gaze on me unblinkingly for a time, turned the baby walker away, and crossed to the doorway. He turned round again and looked at me wide mouthed, a suggestion of some pleasure in his face, suggesting a 'what can I do with him' kind of thought. He wheeled the baby walker towards me, looking, turned away and put his head over the back of the baby walker, looking at me upside down. He stared at me, mouth open and tongue forward to the point where it merged with his lower lip. (O19)

Mary too commented on his appearance though her thought was rather clinical:

> Mary said she was worried about his tongue; she thinks he is tongue-tied. She had mentioned it to the doctor who had said they would not do anything until he was two and in the meantime would see how his language would develop. Mary thought he needed to have his tongue cut where it is very tight. She knew a friend who had had her child's tongue cut and this had not been as bad as Michael's. She knew his tongue was not right. (O19)

The expression seemed quite clearly related to his experiences. In fact his language by 12 months consisted of 'uhh' and 'ahh' sounds which do not need the lips to meet. On two occasions only did he make sounds that emanated from the lips being closed (see O27 below).

At six–seven months he stopped regurgitating his feeds, and instead he and Mary seemed to apply a hit and miss method to his taking solids:

> Michael held a Mickey Mouse rattle in one hand, and a car in the other one. Mary started to feed him, putting a spoonful through the gap – almost between the car and the rattle, with Michael looking at the rattle. She rapidly gave him some spoonfuls; some went into his mouth and some went on his face. The first spoon movement gave him some food, the second wiped his face and the third put the food collected in this manner into his mouth. (O25: Michael at nine months 11 days)

Michael feeds through a 'gap' as though the toys were offering the protection his mouth could not. Similarly when eating a biscuit he used his hand to 'protect' the biscuit: 'He sucked his biscuit which he hid behind his hand, cupped around the biscuit. He looked at me over the top of his hand' (O19).

This appeared to be the reaction of an infant living in a dangerous environment. The inattention and hostility of mother was matched by the hostility of his siblings. Colin dropped him on the stairs causing him to be bruised. Mary said this was not Colin's fault, but it added fuel to her demands to be rehoused.

Michael was dispensing food rather than digesting it. He was 18lb at seven months and under 20lb at ten months. From a birth-weight of 10lb this was a marked failure to thrive.

He did make some progress physically (Graph 5.14: Table 5.1). At three and three quarters months he tried to sit up (O11); he was sitting propped up at four and a half months (O14) and he could sit in the high chair from six months (O18) and he used the baby walker effectively from six and a half months (O21). He could not sit unaided until eight months, and at this time he began rolling over and putting himself in the crawling position. He was crawling at 11 months and trying to stand (O31).

These milestones were however complicated by the fact that he could suddenly lose his grip on himself and topple over, as though his musculature suffered complete power failure. In O20: 'He sat on the floor holding on to my finger and foot and then quite suddenly let go and fell backwards, banging his head on the leg of the coffee table' (O20: Michael at seven months 17 days), and again: 'He crawled towards the kitchen and sat there for a time. Without warning he went limp, and leaned backwards, bumping his head in the doorway' (O31:Michael at 10 months 30 days).

The loss of grip evoked his earlier experience when he seemed to go limp when I was holding him (O4). Although the slack mouth and the loss of motor control or 'tone' suggested the inability to hold on to his sense of his own body, or muscularity, he did show some capacity to make a grip on others. He became increasingly curious about me, looking at me (as seen in O19 above) and showing some signs of recognition after a break (Graph 5.17):

> He was asleep on his back. He opened his eyes, closed them, yawned and opened his eyes again. He looked up at the mobile over the bed, turned his head and looked at the pictures on the bumper at the side of his bed, turned his eyes and saw me, and was quietly startled for a second. He closed his eyes, opened and looked at me again. He studied me for a few moments and then smiled a little, mouth open and tongue forward. He turned his head away and quietly looked at his mobile again. (O18: Michael at six months 11 days)

This was a quite touching, if low key, reunion, and his studying expression suggested an attempt to locate memories. One can perhaps forgive the startled reaction in a six-month-old who wakes to find an observer present! The quality of recognition – almost another example of 'blank alertness' – uncannily replicates the behaviour of Mary and Michael's father, Dave, (who was present after Michael was five months). Mary answered the door head down, either to avoid contact or in the expectation that the contact will not occur. Similarly, I found Dave did the same: 'There was a knock at the door and I picked Michael up and took him to the door. Dave was there, looking down, so that when he looked up he was surprised to see me' (O31: Michael at 10 months 30 days).

Dave's reappearance, coinciding with my summer holiday and school holidays which Mary said she 'survived', brought some moments of greater containment for Michael. First, there was a feed in which there was some acknowledgement of Michael's rhythms:

> Michael took the bottle and sucked and Dave looked down at him and smiled. After taking about a third of the milk in the bottle, Michael pushed it away and tried to sit up. Dave let him and rubbed his back. Michael looked at me blankly and Dave laid him down again and he took some more of it, sucking, his arms by his side. After sucking some more he pushed the bottle away with his hands and mouth, and pushed himself up. Dave let him sit up and rubbed his back, and he brought up some wind loudly. (O20: Michael at seven months 17 days)

Second, Dave fed him with a spoon and Michael made a word:

> Dave said he thought the dinner was hot. He tasted some and held the spoonful to cool, with Michael looking at him quietly, and then taking the food on each spoonful as it was offered. He cried for a moment and said 'mama'. Dave said 'mummy has gone shopping'. Dave offered Michael another spoonful but he would not take it. Dave got a balloon and patted it to Michael and Michael smiled. (O27, Michael at 10 months one day)

Dave appears attentive in this sequence (Graphs 5.10; 5.11), and Michael responsive. Lest an idealised picture of Dave is presented, it is important to note that he was unresponsive to Michael's distress, leaving him to cry in his cot (O23: Michael at eight months 7 days).

Michael's increased curiosity in me was shown by his recognition of me and his curiosity about my glasses and face. In O14, he removed my glasses: 'He looked at me with curiosity and alertness and he reached out with his hands and grabbed my glasses' (O14: Michael at four months 15 days). This became a regular occurrence. A further dimension to this exploration was seen when he explored my face and mouth in an intense kind of way:

> Michael reached out with his hand and touched my face. Then his hand held my finger very tightly, and he put my finger in his mouth very greedily, ramming it into his mouth with both hands. He started to explore my face, looking at me, staring almost. He grabbed my beard and pulled it; let go and held it and pulled again. (O20)

Michael's intensity as he pulled my finger to his mouth suggested a very hungry baby, invoked Tustin's 'mouthful of sucklings'.[2] It also seems to make sense that Michael is repeating, almost in a symbolic way, his experience of feeding. The powerful intrusion for which he has no effective defence, and the hunger with which his refusal of food leaves him. The urgency of his possession of my hand, greedily as I put it, suggests this may be connected with an urgent survival need in Michael, similar to that described by Hoxter: 'Complete possession of the object, or at least a segment of the object, was felt to be an urgent necessity to preserve the life of both himself and the object' (Hoxter 1975, p.176).

The greater curiosity Michael showed towards me was also seen in his interest in the insides of objects (Graph 5.19: unconscious phantasy). The prelude was again an exploration of my face:

> He poked his hand around my beard and mouth. I sat down with him and he continued to explore my face looking at me continuously. Mary said I could put him on the floor as he was sitting more strongly now. I sat him between my feet and he rolled on the floor. He opened a cupboard door, and then shutting it, banging his fingers. He did not react. (O21: Michael at eight months)

Later he explored the insides of some objects – a box and the washing machine – and the quality of the exploration is distressing for the way he bangs his head. The sequence was preceded by Darren banging Michael's head:

> Michael looked at me with his dummy in his mouth, and Darren banged his head with his own. Mary said 'don't do that, you'll hurt him, say sorry'. She looked at Michael and added. 'That's it give him a bump, make him feel better'. She put Michael in the walker and he moved round the room while Darren stayed on Mary's lap. He bumped his head on the table, moved away, and then came back and bumped his head again. He seemed not to react. He peered into the container box for the set of McDonalds' food.[3] He put his head close to the box and looked in. He moved his hands around the edge of the box and then put one hand inside. He moved the walker backwards and then sideways round the room until he came to the washing machine. He put his hand up and touched the door and then the switch. He poked the switch and then looked inside the door. He ran his hand round the

2 Tustin (1990) suggests the link between autistic children and feeding difficulties, particularly the difficulty of the infant in keeping hold of the nipple, and 'limp' holding on the part of the mother. This is not to suggest that Michael is autistic, though his defences (and those of his parents) are not dissimilar from Meltzer's (1975) description of autistic defences. Michael seems to be more an infant who 'lies in wait', but who never loses the capacity to object relate, despite the costs, particularly to the mouth.

3 A toy in which there were plastic imitations of burgers, fries etc.

> rim of the (concave) window. He moved across the room in the walker. He banged his head lightly against the table, stopped, went backwards, banged his head sharply and cried. He banged his head again. (O28: Michael at 10 months eight days)

Michael's banging of his head, like his ramming my hand in his mouth (O20) seems to mirror, in activity, something he has received passively. In this case the head bumping immediately and in a magnified way, repeats the insult Darren delivered to him. There are two other possibilities that flow from this sequence. First, Michael has identified with his brother and joins with him in an attack on the baby – using himself as the target. Second, the link between the head-bumping and the play with the insides of the box and the washing machine is an expression of a perception of a mother who is permanently pregnant, through her attention lying elsewhere. In all cases there is a loss of an awareness of physical boundaries for Michael, and his frequent head bumps, hitting against the object, reverse the sense of the experience of a mother who has no space for him in her mind, and who projects into him her hostility to his presence. The counterpart of this is seen where his internal state is either hollow or two-dimensional:

> I passed him his dummy. He did not grip it and it fell out of his mouth. He crawled over to me and took my glasses off. He put them in his mouth, passed them back, took them again and put them in his mouth. He passed them back and I hid them under a toy. He turned to the telephone and when I showed him the glasses he said 'ahh' and took them back. I hid them again and he turned to another toy. I uncovered the glasses and he saw them and with an 'ahh' took them. (O31: Michael at ten months 30 days)

The repeated taking into the mouth, which, with his singular expression, epitomised a hollow state, was combined here with a refusal or inability to recognise an absent/hidden object. This unofficial object concept test took place in the absence of his mother whilst I looked after him alone. He had cried forlornly as she left and had been consoled only by going to the door, standing there (with my support) and playing with the lock and keys (Graph 5.18).

Michael's grip thus oscillated between a very loose contact with the object and a tight, desperate grip on the other which appeared intrusive or lacking entry. His boundaries between himself and others were uncertain, both in terms of the physical spaciality and the sense of an inside mental space. At a year, he was failing to thrive physically and mentally. He was primarily limp and lacked muscularity. Only the occasional hints of development gave limited hope for his future. His firm grip on me was seen also in his grip on his mother: 'Michael leaned back and held Mary's face, gripping her mouth and lip and the other hand grabbed her hair' (O28: Michael at ten months eight days). The firmness of this grip, and his development of a firmer grip on others suggested that his continual willingness to object relate, despite the costs this involved for him, would enable him to maintain development (Graph 5.16). It hints too at splitting processes taking place, and therefore a greater organisation within Michael (see Meltzer 1975, pp.11–12). These hints appear tantalisingly during this period from four months onwards. In O13 he bit Mary's finger and refused to settle on my lap, instead of hers. These hints bubbled under the surface, so to speak, appearing and then receding from sight.

In this period, Mary did achieve moments when she could reflect on her parenting, and times when she seemed to be getting more of a grasp of the needs of the situation (Graph 5.4). She bought a book by Penelope Leach, and talked to me about this. She was able to use the observation to reflect on a current difficulty. Here, for example, Darren has been in distress, the day before Michael's first birthday:

> Darren was still kicking and screaming and Mary got up to go to him. As she went, Michael cried and reached over to me. Mary asked me to take him out of the high chair. I lifted him out and he sat on my lap and played with a toy for a moment or two. There was quiet in the bedroom and Michael reached away from me to go on the floor. I sat him down and he crawled into the bedroom. Mary said she had to change herself and Darren because he had spilled juice over her. She picked Darren up and they went out. Michael stood himself up against the cabinet and pulled at a book. I helped him get it and showed him the pages, then he picked up Darren's bottle. I fetched his bottle and Michael took it and drank from it. He came over to me and picked up a car which he pushed towards me. I pushed it back and his mouth opened wide with pleasure. Mary returned with Darren who sat sobbing on her chest. She said she wondered what was the matter and I talked to Darren about Michael's birthday, and he quietened. Mary said perhaps it was about Michael's birthday, though she would not have believed it was possible for him to be affected by it at his age. There were a few moments of quiet and it was time to go. Mary took Michael and he cried and reached his arms out towards me as I left. (O34: Michael at one year less one day).

Darren is a very different child from Michael. In contrast with Michael's passivity, limpness and unadventurousness, Darren is passionate, tormented and protesting. He conveys a sense of unbearable loss, and jealousy. Mary could name the feeling – jealousy – but she could not contain his distress and sadness (Graph 5.2).

5.5 Development after 12 months

Observations ended when Michael was 16 months three days. In the four months that I was able to observe him after his first birthday, the themes of his development continued. Feeding continued to be confusing, and he put on little weight. At 15 months (O44) Mary told me he weighed 23lb. He looked very thin. At 13 months three weeks I described him thus: 'He looked very thin, wearing a vest Babygro which seemed to hang off him and emphasised his thin arms and legs' (O38: Michael at 13 months three weeks three days). There was some developmental progress (Graph 5.14). He began to walk during the time I was away over Easter, that is by 13 months two weeks. He made some words (Graph 5.19): 'bye' (O44, Michael at 15 months five days; O45: Michael at 15 months 12 days); 'lora' (O45); 'oma' (Mama) (O48: Michael at 16 months three days). In his play with me he seemed to have developed a sense of an identification with me, which Mary supported:

> He pointed at my glasses, calling 'ah, ah, ah'. I let him take them and he put them on himself. He passed them back and then took them again, repeating this several times and then put them on himself again. Mary said she had got him some glasses. She fetched them and put them on him. He smiled and she said 'glasses suit him'. He took my glasses and passed his to me, and we swapped glasses several times. (O44)

As Michael's development continued to cause concern, and Mary's attentiveness seemed to decline further following her disappointment that she was not rehoused, I increased the level of activity with Michael. At times I fed him, paying attention to him as I did so, and found that he would take the food on these occasions. As his language development was very backward, I talked more and more to him. I engaged in play with him, as I have illustrated. His play oscillated between that in which he showed poor contact with an object and that in which there was a three-dimensional content. He played with a football:

> He looked round the room and walked over to a football. He held it, pushed it, made contact with it, and he followed it, every contact pushing it away, and he went after it again. He seemed to slip against it, with movements that were indecisive, neither trying to hold it nor move it. (O38: Michael at 13 months three weeks three days)

This football is a very slippery or elusive object, on which Michael makes a very loose grip, reminiscent of his loose grip with his mouth. Later in the same observation he puts himself in a box and then tries to put an object in a cupboard:

> Michael pulled out a toy box, and sat in it. He spent some time sitting here, looking quite tiny. He looked over the side, down at the floor and then his foot appeared at one corner of the tray. He looked at the bottom of the box and found a felt shape. He climbed out of the box, and walked over to me carrying the felt shape. He walked into the kitchen. I followed him and found him trying to open the doors under the sink.

> He looked round at me, walked over to me and lifted up his arms to be picked up. (O38)

There was clearly an attempt at representative expression in this sequence, an unconscious phantasy (Isaacs 1952) in which he first places himself as the object in a container, and then takes a toy from one container to another. He shows he has a concept of internal space and that this is a space with some meaning. It is poignant that he also, albeit vaguely and 'loosely', communicates with me (as though I am like the football he has earlier played with?). I speculate about this partly because the other babies in the sample also played in this way,[4] and also because I later became aware that one of the reasons Mary felt unable to continue was because she was again pregnant.

Michael continued to show moments when he could achieve greater tone and concentration in his play. In O44 he engaged in some give and take play with me which had a 'pretend' quality:

> He passed me an egg cup and I pretended to drink out of it. I passed it to him and he held it and imitated drinking from it. He turned, stood up, and looked into the cupboard. He took a cup and passed this to me. I 'drank' from it and passed it to him, and he 'drank' again. (O44)

As he played in this way he needed a continuous holding. He frequently fell, and bumped himself. So did Darren:

> Darren pointed to his head and said 'look'. He had a substantial red bruise on his forehead. Mary told me he did this on the way to school, chasing the other boys. Michael then pointed to his head and he had a similar bruise in an identical position. Mary said he had fallen twice and landed in the same place. (O44)

Were these 'accidents'? It seemed most likely these were inflicted indirectly, through the internalisation of an object which attacks the capacity in the infant for self-protection. There were frequent occasions in the observations where 'bumps' were likely to occur:

> Michael lifted up his arms to be picked up, and I sat him on the table, and he seemed to sway towards the edge, so I held him firmly throughout. Michael tried to stand up on the table and I put my hand under his head to stop him hitting his head on the cupboard. Michael tried to walk off the table, as I held him, and I stood him on the floor. He went towards the washing machine, pulled the chair across the room and climbed on the chair (and I held him). He opened the powder compartment of the machine, looked at it and poked his fingers in. He walked off the chair, oblivious to the act, as I held him, and I put him

4 See particularly the observations of Samantha and Roger (below),

> on the floor. He pushed the chair to the cooker and climbed in it (and I held him). He opened the lighting compartment and put his finger in.

The combination here is of Michael's unawareness of physical space, my holding him, and his interest in the insides of compartments of the washing machine and cooker. The interest in insides and the way he pokes his finger into these spaces is reminiscent of the way he poked his finger into my mouth (see O21, above).

Bumps did occur, often through the conflict between siblings: 'Darren ran across Michael, knocking him over. He fell heavily and had a bump on his head. He cried. I held him and stayed with him till he calmed. Mary then came in and picked him up and held him. He looked at me tearfully as I left' (O46: Michael at 15 months 19 days).

This occurred at the end of the observation time, when I had been holding both Darren and Michael. Putting them down in preparation for leaving seemed to precipitate the incident. There was a strong feeling of being dropped. The end of the observations, precipitated by Mary's depression and the collapse of her capacity to continue to care for the children, was marked by a sense of collapse in the children. Even the hitherto passionate and determined Darren became limp (O45). Michael's limpness continued: 'Michael looked at me, mouth open, pointing at me, somewhat limply' (O45: Michael at 15 months 12 days).

His interest in insides included the toilet bowl: 'He walked into the toilet and tried to climb into the bowl. I followed him and lifted him down' (O46). This somewhat perverse interests in insides had its counterpart in Mary's increased claustrophobia, and she found it almost impossible to stay in the flat for the duration of the observation. Again, Michael communicated his painful situation to me when: 'He took the door handle out, and passed me separately the handle and spindle. He looked at me and I held them and then passed them back. He pressed the spindle against his forehead in quite a painful way' (O48 Michael at 16 months three weeks). He then sat on my lap and showed me his craving for a container, together with its almost suicidal meaning:

> He poked at my shirt and looked inside between two buttons. He looked inside the flap of the pocket and rubbed his fingers against the flap of the pocket. He stood up and followed Mary on to the balcony. He stood against the railings, giving the impression he could squeeze between the bars and fall through. (O48)

He seemed to be fulfilling his destiny as a 'thrown away baby'.

5.6 Ending

In the final observation Mary was unable to stay in until the end of the hour. She got the children ready to go out:

> She put Michael in the buggy and Darren said he wanted a carry down the stairs. I carried him down smiling and laughing. Michael turned his head to watch me go and Darren turned and waved, walked round the corner, came back and waved again. Mary said goodbye and looked ahead grimly as she left. (O48)

After this observation Mary was not at home when I called and I subsequently learned that she placed both children in foster care, whilst Colin went to live with his father. Mary herself moved out of the flat. I spoke to her on two occasions on the telephone, and tried to maintain contact through the social worker. I have heard that Michael remains in foster care, with his mother visiting him on a regular basis. He is said to be developing without major concerns to his carers, though he has needed speech therapy. My experience of the ending of this observation was primarily of a feeling of ejection, of being part of a world of which Mary wished to rid herself. In retrospect I remembered Mary telling me that when she moved, she would not let anyone know where she had gone.

5.7 Summary

Michael's early development took place in a family where the mother was precariously placed in her capacity to care for this new baby. In Michael's development three factors emerged as major themes; first, there was his failure to thrive; second, the relationship between his defensive constellations and his bodily organisation, especially his mouth; third, the tenuous capacity to maintain a hold – a grip – on object relations and thereby to procure developmental achievements. The defences, and the characteristics that were connected with them, have been likened to autistic defences, and are considered here under the category 'unadventurous'. They include a sense of limp passivity with intruded/intrusive aspects of his behaviour. Unadventurousness was later combined with a curiosity about inside space which yielded evidence of an unprotected state of his internalisation – the introjection of a 'bumping' or 'dropping' big brother/mother. In feeding there was a gross mismatch of timing rhythms, in which Mary's reluctance to feed, and her intrusive and mechanical modes of feeding 'fitted' with Michael's inability to take in from the bottle. This adds to the literature of failing to thrive. The repeated observations here indicate the steps in the process towards feeding being experienced in this way, uncovering the 'hidden' aetiology of non-organic failure to thrive (Drotar *et al.* 1990, p.49), and confirming Crittenden's view that: 'the child with non-organic failure to thrive is just one casualty in a family comprised almost entirely of hurt members' (Crittenden 1987, p.62), and Model's, that the mother's attitude to the baby – her convex container shape I would say – was a crucial component (Model 1987, p.137).

The study of Michael also draws attention to the consequences for development of this configuration, not only in terms of mother's difficulties, but also the qualities of internalisation. It also confirms the difficulty of intervening effectively (Model 1987, p.143). This returns us to the role of the observer and the relationship between myself and mother's limited capacity for reverie.

As Mary said at the beginning, she needed someone there all the time. The presence of the observer did increase mother's grip on her task but was insufficient to maintain states of mind that could help her effectively deal with her difficulties, or to sufficiently replenish her in these circumstances. Mary was not able to *think* about her feelings of abandonment, and to contend with absence and separations. The impact on me was to leave me with considerable feelings of regret and painful sadness that a greater impact was not made on her, from within the role.

5.8 Grid

5.8.1. Mothering

Mary was rated as having fairly low and low levels of support, and relying considerably on her social worker (professional support) during Michael's first year (Graph 5.1). Mary's containing capacity was rated to show she had fairly anxious and persecutory preoccupations, high levels of conflict in her role, fairly low internal resources and high levels of impingement of her preoccupations on to Michael. She was quite able to verbalise her emotions (Graph 5.2).

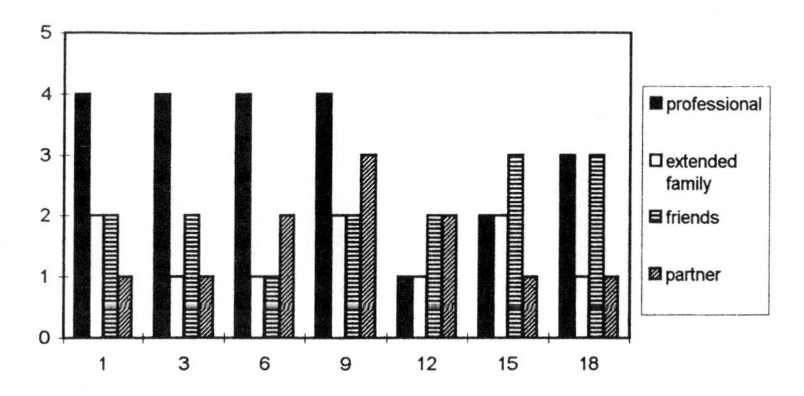

Key: 5=very high levels of support; 4=good; 3=moderate; 2=fairly low; 1=low

Graph 5.1

Mary was rated as making numerous representations of Michael's qualities, which were moderately persistent. Her view of Michael's development, and her representations about his development and states of mind tended to become much more positive between Michael's birth and six months. After this time she held a less positive view of his development, states of mind, and characteristics (Graph 5.3). Mary recorded fairly low levels of meeting Michael's needs, awareness of his needs, and understanding the communications of his needs (Graph 5.4).

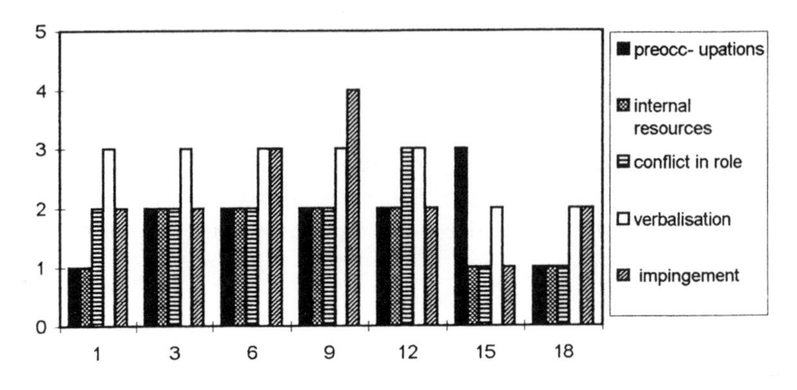

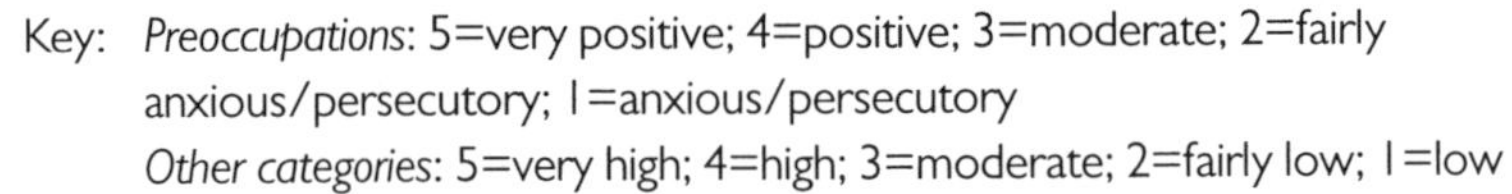
Key: *Preoccupations*: 5=very positive; 4=positive; 3=moderate; 2=fairly anxious/persecutory; 1=anxious/persecutory
Other categories: 5=very high; 4=high; 3=moderate; 2=fairly low; 1=low

Graph 5.2

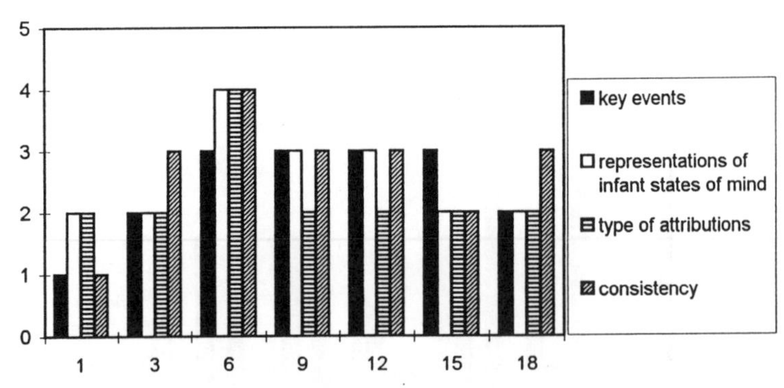

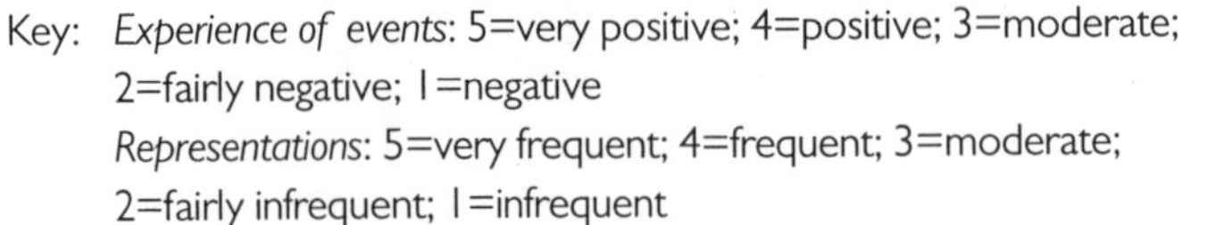
Key: *Experience of events*: 5=very positive; 4=positive; 3=moderate; 2=fairly negative; 1=negative
Representations: 5=very frequent; 4=frequent; 3=moderate; 2=fairly infrequent; 1=infrequent
Consistency of representations: 5=very high, 4=high; 3=moderate; 2=fairly low; 1=low
Type of representations: 5=very positive; 4=positive; 3=moderate; 2=fairly negative; 1=negative

Graph 5.3

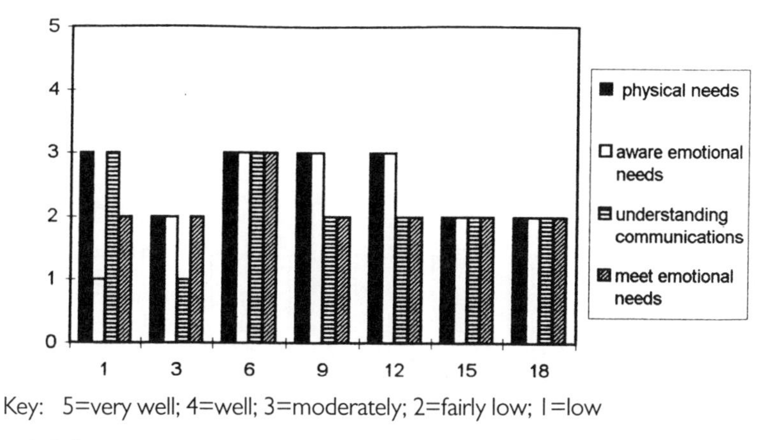

Key: 5=very well; 4=well; 3=moderately; 2=fairly low; 1=low

Graph 5.4

5.8.2 Mother–infant relationship

Mary's relationship with Michael was scored as having fairly low levels of attentiveness, sensitivity, intimacy and understanding between them. Conflict between them was high in Michael's first nine months, and then reduced (Graph 5.5). Mary and Michael were scored as having grip relations which were overall fairly weak. There was, in particular, a consistently weak mouth–teat link. The voice–ear and eye–eye grips showed an increase in strength over his first year, and were then rated at moderate levels (Graph 5.6). Michael and Mary's timing rhythms were scored at fairly low to low (Graph 5.7). The overall 'fit' between Mary and Michael was rated as low in containment, initially moderately conflictual but increasingly accommodating (Graph 5.8). Flat and convex containing shape were rated as moderate to high, whilst concave containing shape was fairly low (Graph 5.9).

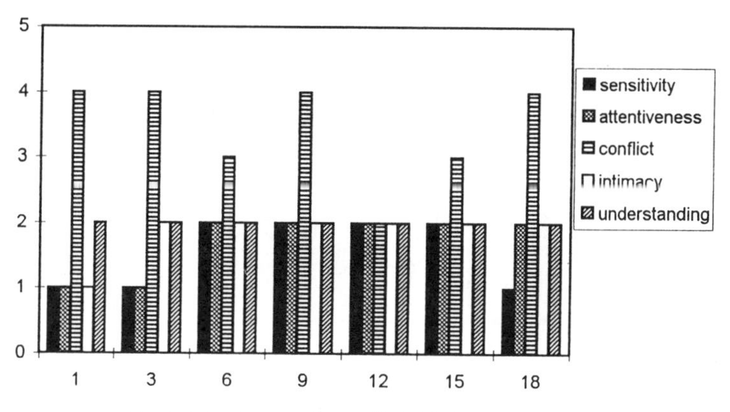

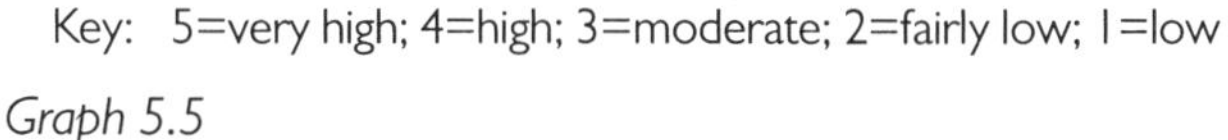
Key: 5=very high; 4=high; 3=moderate; 2=fairly low; 1=low

Graph 5.5

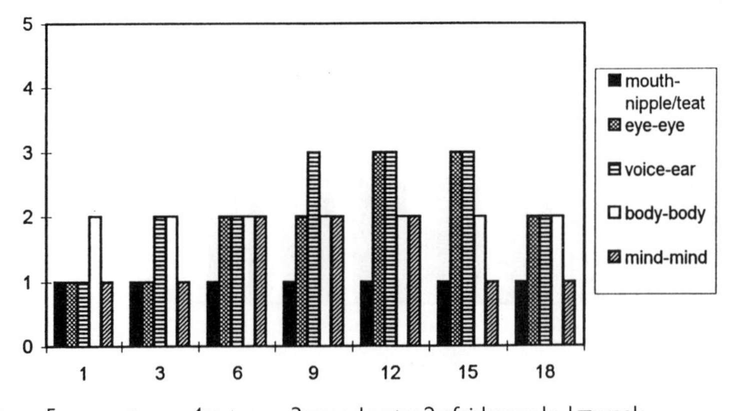

Key: 5=very strong; 4=strong; 3=moderate; 2=fairly weak; 1=weak

Graph 5.6

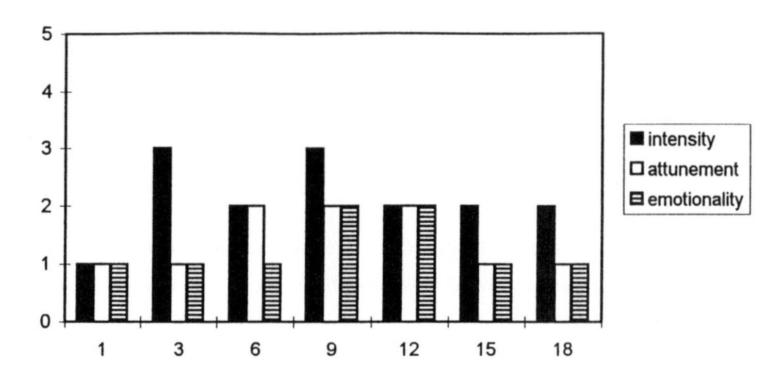

Key: 5=very high; 4=high; 3=moderate; 2=fairly low; 1=low

Graph 5.7

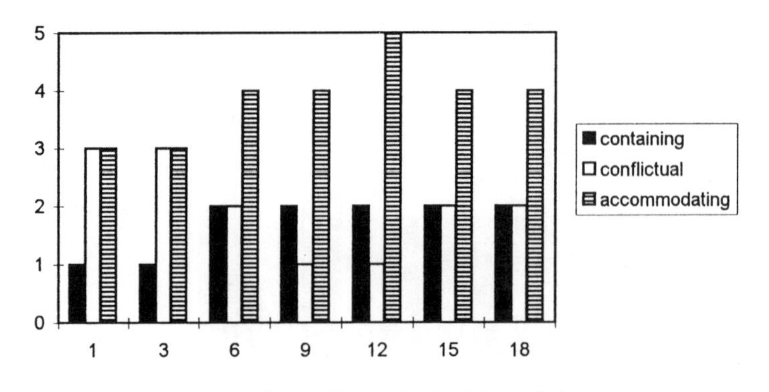

Key: 5=very high; 4=high; 3=moderate; 2=fairly low; 1=low

Graph 5.8

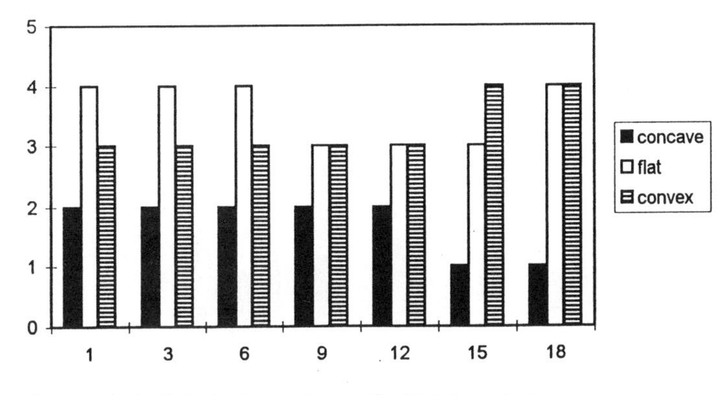

Key: 5=very high; 4=high; 3=moderate; 2=fairly low; 1=low

Graph 5.9

5.8.3 Fathering and father–infant relationship

Michael's father Dave was seen in observations only between five and 12 months. During the times he was present, he developed some qualities of relationship with Michael, including, in interactions together, a rating of a moderate degree of attentiveness, sensitivity, understanding, intimacy and conflict (Graph 5.10). Their grip relations were rated between low and moderate (Graph 5.11).

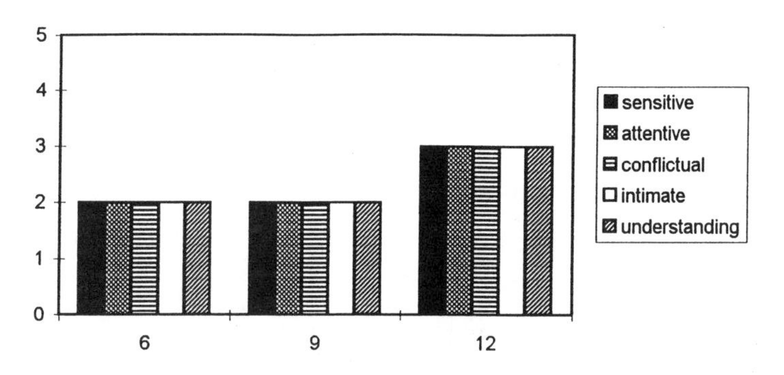

Key: 5=very high; 4=high; 3=moderate; 2=fairly low; 1=low

Graph 5.10

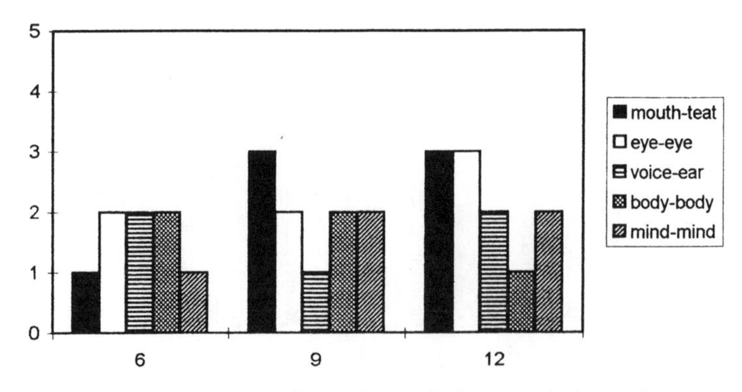

Key: 5=very strong; 4=strong; 3=moderate; 2=fairly weak; 1=weak

Graph 5.11

5.8.4 Parental relationship

Conflict was scored as ranging between moderate and high, and it was expressed, particularly early and late in the observation period, through action rather than words (Graph 5.12). The ways the parental relationship functioned to meet Michael's containment needs were rated as showing high levels of projection of painful experience on to the other parent, whilst problem solving ('bridge builder') was scored as low (Graph 5.13).

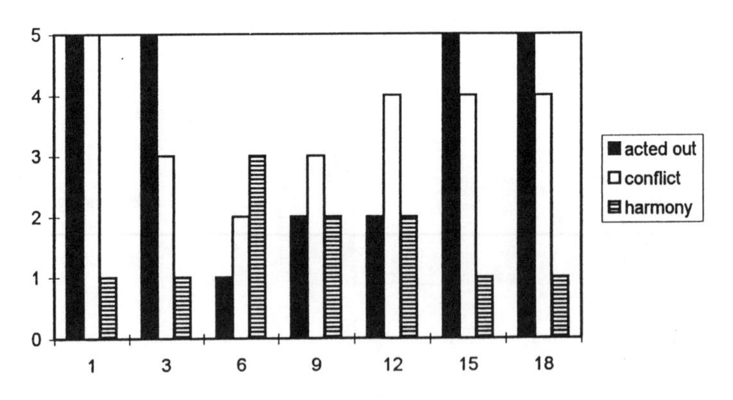

Key: 5=very often; 4=often; 3=moderate; 2=fairly infrequent; 1=infrequent

Graph 5.12

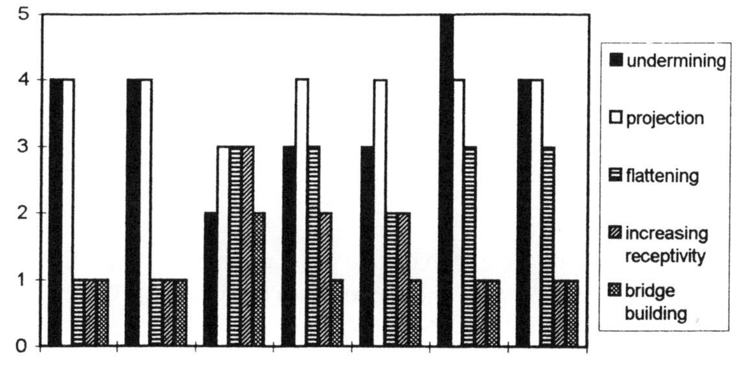

Key: 5=very frequent; 4=frequent; 3=moderate; 2=fairly infrequent;
1=infrequent

Graph 5.13

5.8.5 Infant development

Michael's development was rated to show difficulties in feeding, and some backwardness in physical development. There was some acceleration of mobility between eight months and one year. Health and sleeping were rated as moderate. (Graph 5.14, Table 5.1):

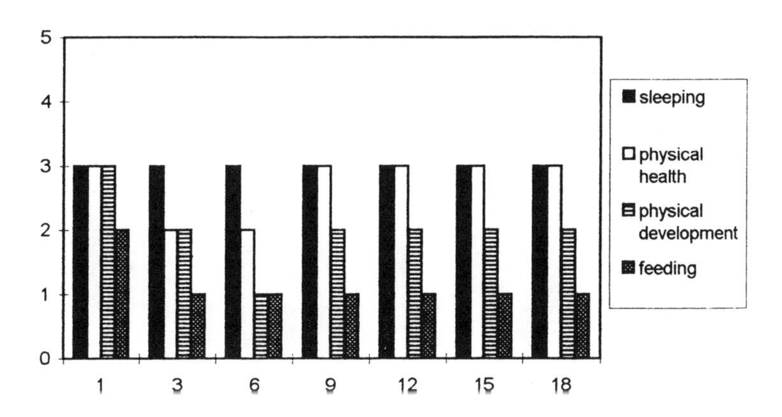

Key: *Physical development*: 5=very advanced; 4=advanced; 3=in time;
2=slightly backwards; 1=backwards
Other categories: 5=very well; 4=well; 3=OK; 2=some difficulties;
1=difficulties

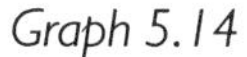
Graph 5.14

Table 5.1

Sitting unaided	8 months
Crawling	11 months
Standing	11.5 months
Walking	13 months

Michael's grip relations were scored showing a decline in the strength of his mouth grip, a strong hand grip, and moderate to fairly weak grips at the levels of eye, voice and body (Graphs 15a, 15b):

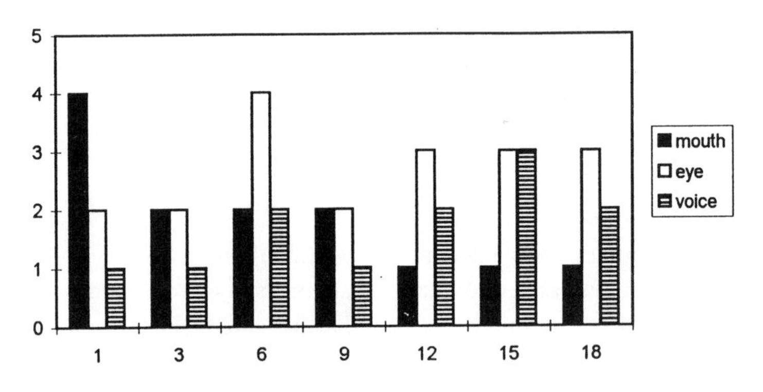

Key: 5=very strong; 4=strong; 3=moderate; 2=fairly weak; 1=weak

Graph 5.15a

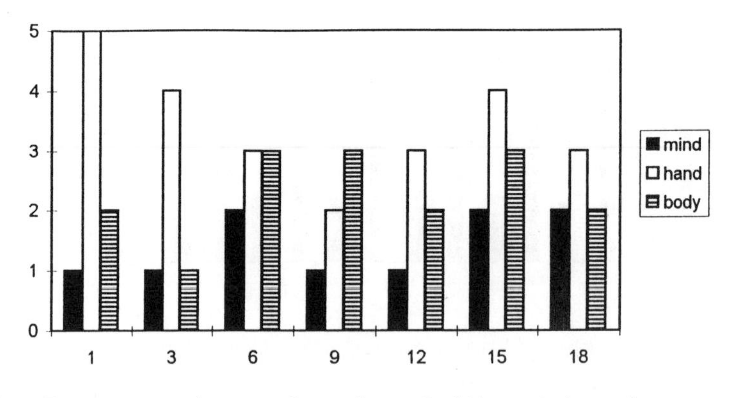

Key: 5=very strong; 4=strong; 3=moderate; 2=fairly weak; 1=weak

Graph 5.15b

Michael's capacity for object relating was rated as moderate to fairly infrequent. His frequency of defending was moderate to high. Defences were rated as rigid, and he was scored as protesting/expressing infrequently (Graph 5.16). Michael was rated as gaining fairly low to moderate capacities for memory, recognition and recall with affection (Graph 5.17). Moderate to fairly low levels of discrimination/fidelity, proximity seeking and reacting to separations were also recorded (Graph 5.18). Michael's language development scored fairly low to moderate, and symbolic play had not emerged at the end of the observation. His play was recorded as moderate levels of unconscious phantasy (Graph 5.19). Michael's overall quality of internalisation was rated throughout his development as somewhat persecutory (Graph 5.20).

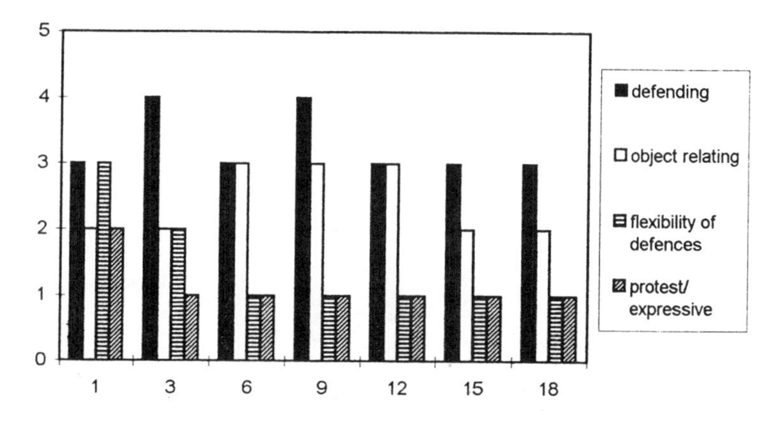

Key: *Flexibility of defences*: 5=very flexible; 4=flexible; 3=some flexibility; 2=tending to rigid; 1=rigid
Other categories: 5=very high; 4=high; 3=moderate; 2=fairly low; 1=low

Graph 5.16

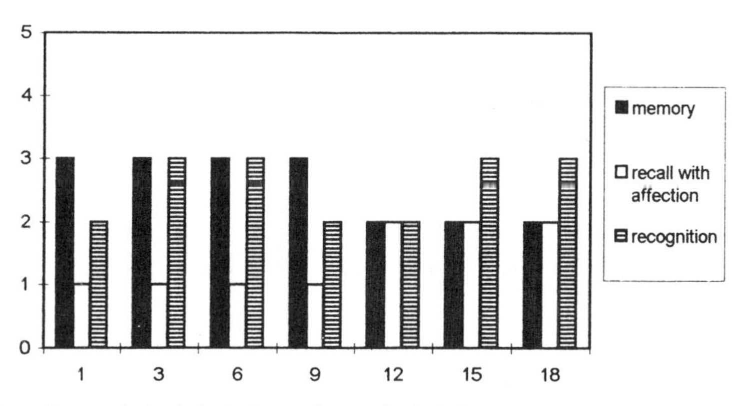

Key: 5=very high; 4=high; 3=moderate; 2=fairly low; 1=low

Graph 5.17

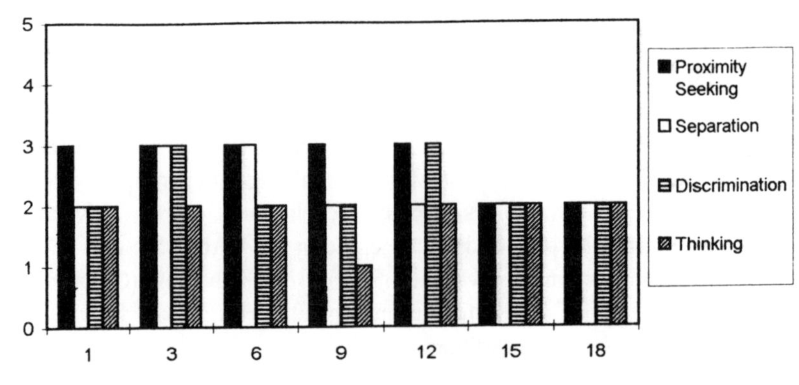

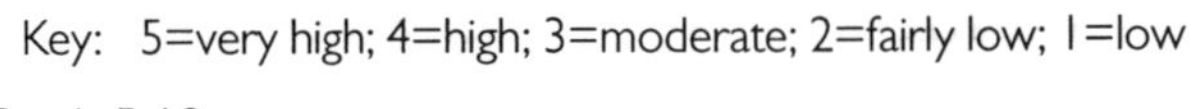
Key: 5=very high; 4=high; 3=moderate; 2=fairly low; 1=low

Graph 5.18

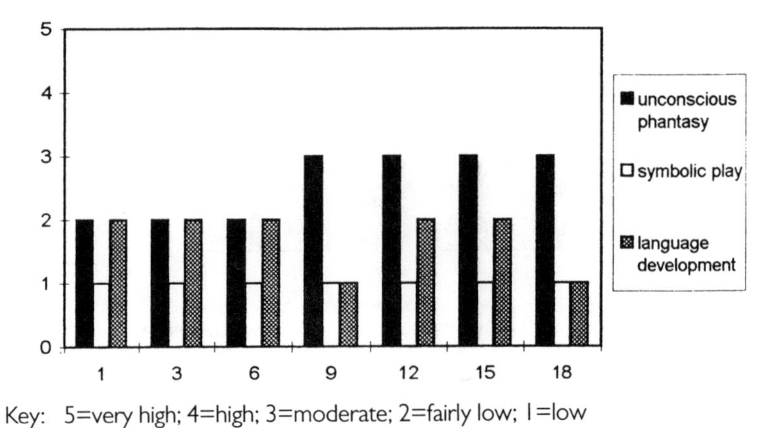

Key: 5=very high; 4=high; 3=moderate; 2=fairly low; 1=low

Graph 5.19

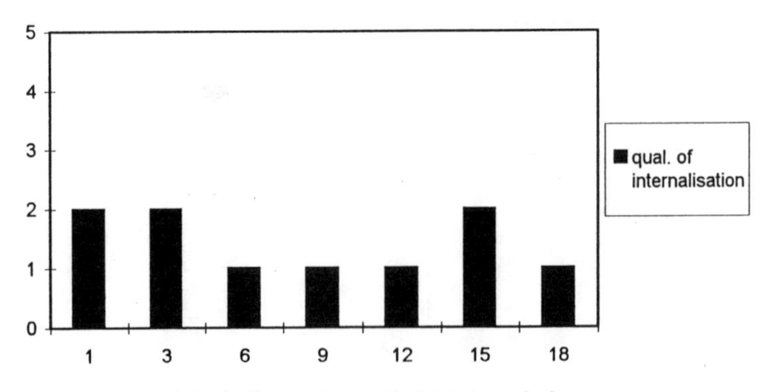

Key: 5=very high; 4=high; 3=moderate; 2=fairly low; 1=low

Graph 5.20

5.8.6 Summary of grid

These grids display the problems Michael encountered in his early development. The extent of convex and flat containing shape (Graph 5.9) provided by Mary, and Michael's defensiveness (Graph 5.16) are the cornerstones of the difficult experiences they both had during Michael's infancy. The descriptive case study elaborates these features. The grids record the extent to which Michael had difficulty maintaining a grip on mother (Graphs 5.15a, 5.15b) and his weak mouth grip is particularly clearly seen. His low to moderate levels of internalised capacities (Graphs 5.17 and 5.18) give evidence that he was not developing sufficient resources to maintain development in his circumstances. Mary's own difficulties are seen in the ratings and the overall picture provided by the graphs is of a high propensity for difficulties in development, and risk to developmental progress.

Whilst evidence for risk is clearly recorded the specific outcomes – problems in developing symbolic functioning (Graph 5.19), high levels of defensiveness and moderate to weak grip relations – are also seen in these grids. Equally, the suggestion of increased mutual contact between Mary and Michael between three and 12 months (Graph 5.6) and Michael's grip relation patterns – especially his hand grip and moderate eye and voice grips – are indicative of a potential source of resilience and recovery, for a time, in this mother–infant relationship.

CHAPTER 6

Hester

The third infant to be described, Hester, also had feeding difficulties, which culminated in a dramatic feeding battle with her mother in her second year. Hester displayed quite different characteristics from Hashmat and Michael in the course of these conflicts. In addition to the withdrawn, mindless defensive characteristics called 'unadventurousness', she developed conflicting, fighting qualities which were part of a 'muscular' defensive pattern. She recovered from the difficulties to a considerable extent, developing language, communication and other skills at a symbolic level of thinking before her second birthday. The discussion of Hester's development is therefore centrally concerned with the question of the quality of her resilience, in the face of experiences of parenting in which she was a recipient of parental projections which I have called 'convex containing shape'. The nature of this aspect of parenting and its relationship to mother's circumstances, past and present, can be carefully followed in the data from the observations.

6.1 The family

Hester was the second of Yvonne and Kevin's children. I first met Yvonne when she was seven months pregnant, at a créche where she took Sid, her two-year-old son. Yvonne was fair, warm featured, and she seemed very large in her pregnancy. She joked lightly with a créche worker about whether she was expecting twins. Sid was quiet, almost submissive and spoke to me politely. His face looked older than his two years. Yvonne quickly agreed to the idea of the observation, adding that her partner, Kevin, would also agree to the observation, and that she did not think it was necessary for me to see him. Yvonne looked forward to the birth of this baby, which was planned, saying she hoped to have a large family. She added that she did not like the waiting. She had gone past full term with Sid and expected the same with Hester. Towards the end of our discussion, Yvonne talked about a sense of foreboding about this birth and said that she 'hoped I would not be there when she felt like strangling the baby, or one of them'. This could have been a 'throw away line', expressed in the nervousness of the moment; or a harbinger of a dynamic, and a theme to follow in the course of the observation.

Yvonne telephoned ten days after Hester's birth. She immediately started to tell me how difficult the birth had been, and that Hester had got stuck with her shoulders during delivery. She had the strong feeling that she would never go through this experience again. She invited me to visit as soon as possible, preferably the next day. I was struck by how quickly and plaintively Yvonne had started to tell me about the event of Hester's birth, the anxiety in her voice as she described Hester getting 'stuck', and how keen she was for me to begin the observations.

When I visited the day after this phone call, Hester was asleep and Yvonne told me again about the difficult birth. She had an epidural, and had wanted to push before the epidural had taken any effect. She was very stiff and sore afterwards. While in hospital she had 'baby blues'. She told me 'it just came on her' but she was told to let herself cry, and she did. She said that in the next life she wanted to return as a man! She added that Kevin was in fact being helpful, making her dinner and 'even' changing the nappy, but he could not feed Hester. Yvonne was calmer than she had sounded on the telephone and she spent some time telling me about herself and her family.

She was the oldest of five children and her younger brother died a cot death. Her father had recently become unemployed and she was worried about her mother's ill health. She had lived in this part of South London all her life, as had Kevin. He was one of 11 children, a small, dark-haired man, who looked much younger than his 27 years, and who told me that his father had been ill with heart trouble. Kevin himself had been off work for some weeks with an ear infection. Yvonne told me that if I really wanted to know what her life had been like I should see the film *Poor Cow*; it had been filmed in the area where she had lived all her life, and illustrated how her life had been.

6.2 Quality of containment

Yvonne and Kevin both came from large families, the extended families lived near by, both sets of parents involved with the childcare of these children, Sid and Hester, and the home was open to a large number of visitors. Both were interested in childcare matters; Yvonne helped out at the créche and Kevin, whilst 'renouncing' – to use Raphael Leff's categorisation (Raphael Leff 1986) small babies, was very involved with Sid. They were quite liberal, anti-racist, interested in politics and the local community. Both grasped particularly the role of the observer, especially the notion of learning about infant development from experience.

It followed from the interest that both parents took in the development of children that there were times in the observation that I witnessed periods of attention to the needs and development of Hester and her brother. Yvonne would report to me about things that had happened during the week, and show the capacity to recall in detail the observations she had made. She talked about the characteristics she saw in Hester, the developmental moves she made, the way she herself felt about the relationship with her daughter and her hopes and aspirations for her (Graphs 6.3a and 6.3b). In the observations themselves, Yvonne showed times when she observed carefully Hester's emotional states and thought about what she needed. At best, she was capable of thinking about these, using her own receptivity to do so (Graph 6.4). For example, in O7, she spent a great part of the time thinking about Hester's needs and trying to respond to them. This was concave containment, or 'reverie'. In this mode she was capable of tender moments with Hester, and displaying affection and intimacy (Graph 6.5).

Yvonne rarely maintained the concave qualities of receptivity, and tender, thoughtful communication. Yvonne displayed three other patterns of relating; a quality of containment, that with additional support could reach the concave; a flat containment, characterised by lack of receptivity, or diffusing the communications of Hester, and a particular quality of convexity which amounted to a substantial emotional bombardment of her (Graph 6.9).

It seemed from the beginning that Yvonne achieved a greater capacity to be reflective when she was talking to me, and using me, in the observer role, as an aid to her own observing function. Her capacity to think about Hester was constricted through her difficulties in containing her own emotional conflicts.

Yvonne's partner Kevin preferred young children of Sid's age, when they became 'more interesting'. He was not responsive to infants crying, and he occupied a role in helping to support Yvonne's establishment of a pattern which reduced the demands upon her. Kevin became much more actively involved with Hester in her second year (Graph 6.10). In this period there were times when he helped her with some of the difficulties in the mother–daughter relationship and actively identified and responded to the emotional content of her communications between them, introducing a sense of vigour to the containment of the conflictual areas between them (Graph 6.13).

Family events – the birth, christenings and deaths of family members – formed a structure to the events and history of the family. Around these ritualised events, family functioning moved through bereavements and celebrations, and the effects of changes seemed to be mitigated by the invoking of the permanent capacity of the family to constitute itself despite the arrival of new members and the absence of others. Mourning appeared to be something which was not so much felt as taken to be a weakening of the member of the family who experienced most directly the loss. As Yvonne said, the funeral of Kevin's father was 'a beautiful event, but a sad occasion'. The christening – probably delayed because of the mourning for Kevin's father – was a notable social event in which the whole family gathered in a pub and celebrated, men together and women similarly together but separate from each other, in a way which commented on the gender arrangements within the smaller, nuclear unit of Yvonne and Kevin's family.

Larger societal events percolated without ritualistic or thoughtful intervention. Particularly, the Gulf War, which started when Hester was 17 months, seemed to pervade the family and affect the emotional dynamics of the relationships, through the mirroring of the family 'war' over food, revealing its impact in the images of the children's play. That these events appeared to percolate the family environment in an unmediated way demonstrated the need for the larger family to provide a container for the individual members through its group cohesiveness and ritualistic marking of events. This family 'skin' had the weakness of not affording Yvonne the internal supports of internalised working through of emotions.

6.3 Hester's early development

Towards the end of the first observation, Hester woke and this gave me a first view of her, and my only observation of her feeding at the breast.

> She took Hester and settled her in her arms and prepared to feed her. She said something about hitting Hester and her arms imitated hitting Hester with clenched fists. Then she said 'no, we would not do that'. It was near the end of the observation but Yvonne said she would like me to stay longer. She said this is the bit she hates, getting Hester on to the nipple. She laid Hester in a position to take the right breast. Sid asked for the TV to be turned up and Yvonne said he likes the singing. Yvonne concentrated on helping Hester to take the breast. She said she likes to take the drips and does not open her mouth. Imperceptibly, though I could not see clearly facing the back of Hester's head, she took the breast and Yvonne started to talk. She said the midwife had signed her off and that she had said that the vomiting may be due to an obstruction in the stomach. If it continues, Hester may need an operation. This was said without affect. A further knock at the door brought in a friend, and Hester continued to suck at the breast. (O1: Hester at 11 days)

Hester achieves a calm and steady grip on the breast while Yvonne is in the midst of many preoccupations, responding to Sid as well as to Hester. Yvonne implies Hester will not open her mouth to take the nipple and she says that she 'hates' the point of union between the nipple and the mouth. Her reaction to the proposed operation is noticeably without affect.

Her sickness was the reason Yvonne gave for weaning from the breast before the second observation. She said: '"Hester has been so sick it hardly seemed worth the struggle to breast-feed. She still brings up some milk but it is much easier with the bottle. I think breast-feeding is best for the child, but..."and she shrugged..."She's getting demanding" Yvonne added' (O2: Hester at two weeks three days). On one level, ceasing breast-feeding amounted to a realistic appraisal of her limitations, and she spoke about the greater time she had available to her when feeding with the bottle. She was depressed, and felt empty: 'Look at me, I'm terrible. I've the radio on in the bedroom, and the kitchen, and the TV on in here. I don't like the flat to be quiet because then it feels so empty' (O5: Hester at five weeks two days). Her depression was accompanied by a sense of her having limited internal and external resources (Graphs 6.1, 6.2). Her own account emphasised the difficulties of her early experiences – 'Poor Cow' – and her mother's illness and her father's unemployment left them needing Yvonne's support, rather than their being able to support her. She was ambivalent about Kevin's support. When he and Sid were away for the weekend she said: 'You want them to go away when they're here but then you miss them. Kevin phoned on Saturday night and I said I'd like him to come home. All he said was that he likes it there. Sid came on the phone and said he was on his holidays' (O7: Hester at seven weeks). In this way dependent feelings between Kevin and Yvonne were subject to miscommunication and misunderstanding, in which the emotion was 'flattened' or diffused (Graph 6.13b). From Sid's point of view the new baby did not have to be faced, and Yvonne was insistent on his lack of jealousy for the baby.

Following her weaning Hester developed four distinct ways of relating. First, with the bottle she developed a significantly blank expression, continued to regurgitate the milk and to take the bottle when bloated. It was her blank expression which was most evident. At five weeks:

> Yvonne cradled Hester in her arm and gave her the bottle. She took the bottle straight away and looked blankly ahead of her, her hands down and not holding Yvonne or the bottle. Hester appeared quite bloated and soon a trickle of milk came out of her mouth. She sucked slowly and spasmodically (O5: Hester at five weeks two days).

It is also apparent how little hold, or grip, she has on mother or her bottle when feeding (Graph 6.15a).

Second, Hester showed a capacity to become engaged with inanimate objects, maintaining her attention with a combination of hand, eye and voice, for considerable periods of time:

> Yvonne placed a toy, a small, bright tiger, on the edge of the changing mat in Hester's line of vision. Hester looked at it and gurgled, and tried to reach it with her hands. She did this for the next 20 minutes. Occasionally her hand would make contact with the tiger, toppling it and Yvonne would replace it. She gurgled intermittently and Yvonne and I both watched her. (O4: Hester at four weeks five days)

This seems very self-contained behaviour, which is maintained in the presence of mother's continuous observation of her alongside me. In this mode of relating Hester seemed to be becoming a sparing, undemanding baby. She slept for up to seven hours, Yvonne told me (Graph 6.14). In the presence of mother she was able to co-ordinate her 'grip' modalities, her eye, voice and hand (Graph

6.15a, 6.15b). When Yvonne was absent, however, Hester expressed her distress, being soothed by the skin-to-skin contact of mother holding her. For example:

> Hester began to cry, softly at first but then more and more insistently. Yvonne came past the door and said 'she's being naughty is she' and hurried back towards the bathroom. She returned a few moments later and went over to Hester picking her up and holding her until she stopped crying. (O2: Hester at two weeks three days)

Later, in company with the quite sparing mode of relating, Hester shows an increasing capacity to hold herself together, seeking contact with an object in the way described by Bick (1968):

> Hester lay on her back, her head turned vigorously twice, then her legs moved around and her arms, with mittens on her hands, came up together and moved in front of her face, touching her cheeks. She looked around and then her eyes came to rest in an upward direction. She looked at the light, which was switched on. Her eyes stayed focused in this direction, and her arms and legs moved more gently. (O6: Hester at six weeks three days)

The vigour of her muscular movements is reduced when she achieves an eye grip on the light. In contrast with the distress she showed earlier (O2, above) which brought her into contact with mother (object relating), here she turns to inanimate objects to perform the function of 'holding' her. Later (O7) she turns to music from the TV. Her muscularity is seen as 'flapping', and as arching her back and pressing her head downwards (O13: Hester at 13 weeks two days).

Her third mode of relating was to experience passages of time where she related with mother, who showed a capacity on these occasions to think about Hester's needs (Graph 6.16: object relating):

> Yvonne said 'what's the matter?' and 'are you hungry?'. She took the pacifier out of Hester's mouth and put the knuckle of her finger in her mouth. Yvonne looked at Hester's response and said 'she is not hungry'. Hester arched her back and cried strongly. Yvonne held her upright and said 'maybe she's wanting to go to the toilet – powder milk leaves her constipated.' I asked if there was anything she could do about it and Yvonne shrugged and said 'nothing'. She added that Hester goes every evening or if she misses she goes the following morning. Holding her upright, Hester stopped crying. She held her head securely and looked ahead and towards Yvonne. (07: Hester at seven weeks two days)

Yvonne's thinking about Hester's needs, and her trial and error approach, though still conveying something of her helplessness, is responded to by direct eye contact from Hester. Yvonne's curiosity about Hester's needs, her wish to understand (Bion's 'K') was enhanced by the observer's presence, providing a focus for Yvonne's 'wondering aloud'. Similarly she seemed able to take up an observing role in my presence (see O4, above).

The relationship between Hester's different modes of relating, the 'switched off', or mindless 'blankness', attention to object (animate and inanimate) and a muscular holding herself together, was suggested by sequences where Hester moved from one mode to another. She shows a warm contact with mother, in an intimate moment between them: 'Yvonne moved her on the changing mat, and Hester looked at her. Her tongue appeared several times and Yvonne looked down at her and smiled. Hester smiled back, keeping her eyes on Yvonne's face' (O8: Hester at eight weeks two days).

The mutual eye–eye grip between them is lost when Yvonne introduces a feed. The quality of contact between them is quite different:

> Yvonne picked up Hester and held her on her lap. For the first time in this observation Hester looked at me, turning her face away from Yvonne. She looked ahead, Yvonne placed the bottle in her mouth and Hester squirmed a little. She looked straight ahead, blankly, and sucked. Her hands moved but did not touch the bottle. (O8)

Here Hester turns away from mother, and reverts to a blankness of expression. Feeding appears a barrier to mother–infant intimacy, and an area of misunderstanding between them. Separation from contact with mother (when she goes out of the room) leads to defensive 'muscularity' in Hester.

The fourth mode of relating involved Hester employing her hand in making a grip on mother's finger:

> Soon she was smiling back at me, a wide-mouthed smile. She held her fingers as she smiled and kicked her legs...
>
> ...Hester then took her dummy and looked round the room and towards me, let her fingers entwine and held the forefinger of her right hand in the palm of her left hand. She let the dummy fall and looked at Yvonne...
>
> ...Yvonne held out her finger and encouraged Hester to hold it. She did so, gripping with the whole of her hand, while Yvonne and Hester smiled at each other. Then Yvonne asked for her finger back and it slipped out of Hester's grasp. Hester held her own fingers, then Yvonne gave her the ring and her finger again, quite abruptly getting Hester to hold her finger. Hester let it go. (O11: Hester at 11 weeks five days)

A game developed between them, in which the hand grip accompanies eye and voice contact. The game appears to include elements of holding firm, slipping and letting go, which suggest an issue of loss or separation is being shared by them. Hester is more interested in holding mother's hand than in the bottle, which brings on her mindlessness. Hester began to hold her own fingers, as though this contact with mother had been internalised, and when she gained mother's attention her eye and voice contact were preceded by her 'getting a grip on herself' in this way:

> Hester flapped her legs and sneezed. She held the finger of her right hand in the palm of her left hand and looked at Yvonne. She then made a long moaning sound – 'wow, wow, wow'. Yvonne turned to her and said 'isn't any one paying you any attention? Oh, Hessie!', and she smiled at her (O12: Hester at 12 weeks six days)

Yet this relationship of hand to hand also contained Yvonne's concern about scratching Hester, or in other ways hurting her. Hester was often dressed in mittens and frequently scratched herself: 'Yvonne said that Hester was still scratching herself, and pointed to the marks on her forehead. She leaned forwards and pulled Hester towards her. Yvonne then leaned over her, caught Hester in the eye and recoiled, saying "oops, I've poked her in the eye"' (O6: Hester at six weeks three days), and: 'Yvonne moved her hand to Hester's neck as if to tickle her. She then drew back her hand suddenly, saying with some alarm, "did I scratch you?"' (O13: Hester at 13 weeks six days).

The ambivalence in the relationship between them seemed located, to some extent, in the patterns of hand contact, with the hypothesis that through this, Hester was internalising both her contact with mother, and her capacity to hurt her. Alongside this, Yvonne called her 'greedy' and a 'greedy cow' (O5, O9) and verbalised her mixed feelings about Hester, who seemed big and greedy to her.[1] Hester was introduced to solids at nine weeks, and grew from a 9lb baby at birth to 15lb at three months. Yvonne was thus exposing herself to her own contradictory feelings about her daughter, hurrying development and then saying that 'she never seemed to have been a baby' (O7) when Hester grew. During this period Yvonne spoke about death. She described sudden deaths of those near to her; her sister's husband, a cousin, and her younger brother who died a cot death. Her worry about hurting Hester appeared connected with this preoccupation, and the brother's cot death had the quality of a 'ghost in the nursery'.

By three months, therefore, Hester showed a wide repertoire of grip relations, and in her object relating mode she had the capacity to link several modalities. Here eye contact with mother and her grip on mother's finger contrasted the blank limpness when feeding, and her development of a sparing, muscular mode of relating indicated an area where she was not contained.

---

1 Alongside 'greedy' and 'greedy cow' Hester was called 'stinker' and 'fatty' and at times quite cruel images were given to her: 'Fat Bessy', the 'ballerina' when she was a few weeks old, and 'Norma', referring to a motel waitress who was neither helpful, nor bright.

Accommodation (Graph 6.8) of an area of loss, of something missing, in which the early weaning from the breast appeared to be the significant experience in the emergence of these early defensive patterns, linked with depression in the mother and a 'sparing' to 'mindless' state of mind in Hester. Risk is focused on the potential conflict between mother's overspilling emotions, particularly those centring on a preoccupation with doing harm, or hurting Hester, and Hester's fitting in with this state of mind in mother, through her willingness to take in from her.

6.4 Development from 3 to 12 months

From three months to a year, Hester's development was marked by a continuation of the themes of the early grip relationships. In turn she was seen to be object relating, turning away from object relations, holding herself together in a muscular way and retreating from relationships into a blank, mindless state (Graph 6.16). Additionally, there emerged a provocative aspect of her, which linked with the capacity to be 'in touch', or understanding of the communications around her (Graph 6.15b). This was a disturbing development, as it held the notion of the development of a proto-masochistic way of relating, for which the precursor was the hurting and being hurt (scratching) hand grip. At six months one week one day (O24), Hester followed mother's hint that she 'likes banging' by banging her head:

> The TV started to play the theme for 'Home and Away' and Hester seemed transfixed by it. She stopped listened and looked at the TV, becoming very calm. I commented to Yvonne how calm she became. Yvonne said she should get a tape of it. The music finished and Hester pushed her chair backwards towards Yvonne. She started to lean right back, arching her back sharply. She sat up and verbalised, quite musically, then she arched her back again, going right down so that her head was in the tray. It seemed she was trying to see Yvonne but when she turned the chair so Hester could see her, Hester arched her back again and pushed her walker backwards so that she went across the room. When she came to a stop by the wall she again arched her back. Yvonne got up, offered me coffee and on the way out she said 'not for you' to Hester, who immediately started to cry and threw her head backwards two or three times, hitting her head on the wall and crying more loudly. I rubbed the back of her head but she continued to cry. (O24: Hester at six months one week one day)

These gestures suggest that Hester, who was clearly receptive to Yvonne's comments, was vulnerable to the double communications of a mother who could 'abuse her with words': 'Yvonne went over to Hester and put her head close to her. She blew a raspberry on her neck, and said "you stinker". She looked at me and said "you can abuse her and she smiles" and added, "I mean with words."' (O14: Hester at 14 weeks).

Hester was spending large periods of time in the walker, as mother was preoccupied with hurrying her development. There was a cruel, torturing feel to this experience. She banged her head again (O28: Hester at seven months one week three days), and though this did not develop into a regular pattern, the underlying theme of provocation continued. Hester stretched Yvonne's resources in a way which could lead to a strong reaction from mother:

> Yvonne said she had told Hester off for grabbing the glass bowl on the coffee table. Hester looked at her and then turned round towards the bowl. She reached out her hand towards the bowl, looking at Yvonne, and Yvonne said 'no' firmly and admonishingly. She went over to the walker and pulled Hester to the middle of the room. Hester looked at Yvonne and then banged her hand on the tray of the walker, twisted around in it and made it go backwards towards the other coffee table. She looked up at Yvonne reached out her hand to the drawer of the table, pulling it open. Yvonne looked up and said 'no' and added 'naughty girl'. Hester continued to open the drawer and Yvonne got up and shut it, looking down at her, saying 'no'. Yvonne shut the drawer and Hester looked up blankly at her. She opened the drawer again and Yvonne shut it, again saying 'no', and holding it shut (O27: Hester at seven months three days)

Later, at ten months six days (O38), Hester sang a soliloquy on the theme of 'daddy', after Kevin had taken her, with Sid, away for the weekend for the first time. Yvonne was quite incensed by this lack of fidelity (Graph 6.18), and Hester's proclamations were, at least, in the service of throwing caution to the wind.

This was a very difficult period for them all. Kevin's father died when Hester was four months, and Yvonne appeared to accept that she would receive little support from Kevin in the aftermath of this loss (Graph 6.1). She frequently talked to me about how she looked forward to the children feeding themselves and being in other ways less dependent upon her. On occasions she reached the point of overflowing, lashing out at Sid, and shouting at him to eat his dinner, which she described as 'food with no name' (O22, O32).

Sid was quite seriously ill after the last of these observations, being hospitalised with a chest infection. The parents were separated from Hester, who stayed with her maternal grandparents for five days while Kevin and Yvonne attended to Sid in hospital. Hester's reaction to the reunion was to cry, and Kevin commented that 'this was because we did not pick her up straight away' (Graph 13b).

Hester continued to move between her different modes of relating; in the observation when she was seven months three days (O27) these followed each other in sequence, beginning, as we have seen with the provocative conflict with Yvonne. She then turned away from mother, to relate to inanimate objects:

> Hester stood up in her walker, jerked and twisted, banged the tray with her hand, and twisting herself round she saw the activity frame, and Yvonne moved the frame a little so she could reach it. Hester reached out and took the Mickey Mouse in her hands and then leaning forwards she put it in her mouth and sucked it (O27)

She then related to me, with a combination of hand and mouth, involving food:

> She moved over towards where I sat, reaching her hand out towards the biscuits. I put my hand out and she gripped my finger and drew it towards her mouth. Yvonne said 'what is she doing?' and I said 'gripping my finger and sucking it'. 'Is she biting you?', Yvonne added. Hester sucked for a moment and then bit my finger (O27)

Again, Hester's understanding of her mother is evident; she bit on Yvonne's suggestion. Her muscular movements combined with a quite painful, proto-masochistic way of relating:

> Hester got her legs down as well, and rolled on to her side and then on to her back. She reached out with her hands and got her legs up in the air as well so that her legs and hands were touching the frame. Then she got hold of the legs of the frame and lifted it and put it over her face and then sucked the end of the leg which has a red ferrule with a flange, so that it is very nipple-shaped. She put this in her mouth and sucked it, her hands holding on to the leg of the walker, her feet in the air, her toes moving touching another part of the frame. She lifted the leg so that it came out of her mouth and then seemed to jab it down on herself, on her chin and the side of her neck, and then she lifted it again and put it in her mouth and sucked it, and then jabbed it down again on her neck. (O27)

Then, as mother left Hester with me, she reverted to the 'lumpish', sad mindlessness, holding on through a grip on my finger:

> Hester pushed herself backwards on her back, so she came near me, and I reached down and put my hand on her. Yvonne came back with a dummy, and put it in her mouth and Hester lay quietly sucking while pushing down with her feet and arching her back. I touched Hester's fingers and she held my finger tightly and pulled as if pulling herself up. I picked her up on to my lap, where she sat, a sad and inert figure (a bit of a 'lump'). She lay back, eyes looking straight ahead and lightly sucking, her feet kicked regularly at my arm, and I held her toes – which were cold – as she continued to kick. (O27)

The purpose of the modes of relating – still observed through the notion of grip but carrying a context of the emergence of personality structures – have an underlying content of the need to hold together the parts of her personality, dominated by a search for comfort, and freedom from the prevailing conflict. This view is confirmed by two observations; first, at five months three days, Hester is involved in a muscular sequence:

> Yvonne pulled her towards her, and put the mat over her head. Hester kicked her legs a little stiffly, and Yvonne took the mat off her, but Hester did not react and she put the fingers of both hands in her mouth. Yvonne repeated this, and tickled her through the mat, and again Hester kicked her legs in the same stiff way, then Yvonne took the mat off her, put it away and went back to TV, leaving Hester lying on her back with her hands in her mouth. Hester seemed to be distracted by music on the TV and turned her head in that direction, letting her hands come out of her mouth. (O20: Hester at five months three days)

The response Hester made to the TV (which, as we have already seen, was a source of comfort for her, evoking peacefulness) revealed the meaning of the grip of the hands, and holding her hands and foot in her mouth, namely that her preoccupation is with making contact with an object. In the absence of satisfying contact with mother, the sound of music from the TV serves this purpose. At times Hester could find no comfort for herself. For example, at nine months three weeks, she turns away from mother and the bottle and is inconsolable:

> Hester lay on the floor, crying, and rubbed her hand backwards and forwards on the carpet. Yvonne picked her up and sat her on her lap. She laid Hester back to give her bottle. Hester would not take it and pushed Yvonne away. Yvonne took the bottle away and sat Hester up and again she turned towards Yvonne and again pushed away. Still crying she pushed herself off Yvonne's lap and Yvonne sat her on the floor, sitting and crying. She looked towards me and back to Yvonne, still crying. Yvonne put the bottle on the floor next to Hester, and she picked it up and lifted it to her lips and started to suck it. The bottle was too heavy to lift far enough to get the milk and Yvonne laid her on her back. Hester lay sucking and her hand flapped at the side of her. She banged on the floor. She held the bottle again with both hands, kicked her legs, sucked at the bottle and was quiet. (O36: Hester at nine months three weeks)

After a break in observations of two weeks when she was eight months, Hester showed recognition of me (Graph 6.17) and used the reunion to express her preoccupations: 'She looked at me with a sense of recognition, crawled over to me and gestured to be picked up. I sat her on my lap. She looked at me and ran her fingers along my arm in a light scratching gesture' (O30: Hester at eight months four days). Hester made scratching communications with me in the next observation:

> Yvonne then put Hester down on the floor and Hester looking at me whilst sitting, put her finger in her mouth and moved it around her gums; then she scratched the back of her neck, replaced her finger in her mouth and her look – quite communicative – suggested she was explaining what was the matter. (O31: Hester at eight months two weeks one day)

Hester appears to be addressing her pain about teeth, reminiscent of Hashmat's communication with me (see Chapter 4.5). It also evoked Yvonne's fear of scratching her, and this aspect of their early hand grip. There is some evidence that this was internalised by Hester, and that she was using the observer to mediate the effect. Confirmation occurred later in the observation, where Yvonne was in her 'abuse her and she smiles' mode: 'She crawled across to Yvonne and tried to climb up. Yvonne lifted her on to her lap and tickled her legs saying "I could hit you" and "I could scratch you" in a sort of gleeful babytalk' (031).

Hester's capacity to communicate, to use her muscular skills to move towards and make contact with others offsets the moments when she was clearly persecuted by her internal world to the point that no object appeared contactable (Graphs 6.18; 6.20). Hester began to crawl, stand and then walk with some precocity, walking by the time she was ten and a half months (Graph 6.14). In the complex pattern of her development to this point, the act of walking was overdetermined. At one level, it was a sparing, accommodating fit with mother, who wished to effect some separation and separateness, and wanted Hester to be more independent. At another level, it was a further extension of the need to hold herself together and be active in seeking her objects. At a third level, it was – of course – a developmental achievement, which, with the development of language promoted hope for the future. Hester's first steps took place between her mother and myself:

> Hester crawled over to Yvonne, lifted herself to standing position and Yvonne said 'go away' with a smile. She turned her round and said 'walk to Steve' and I held my hands out and Hester took five steps across the room to me, looking delighted with herself. We applauded. She turned round, dropped effortlessly on to the floor and crawled back to Yvonne. Yvonne turned her round and said again 'walk to Steve' and she again took five steps and then reached me. Her face lit up with a smile as she walked. More applause from both of us and Hester sat down and crawled back to Yvonne (O39: Hester at ten months two weeks two days)

In the context of the sequence of the observation, Hester displayed a state of mind in which she was able to make the movement alone, across the room. It was an act of confidence, and development towards separateness, over which future conflicts would be drawn.

6.5 Development from 12 to 24 months

The primary theme during this second year was the conflict with Yvonne, especially, but also with Kevin, over food, a conflict which assumed the proportions of a battle with the connotation of a life and death struggle (Graphs 6.5, 6.8). The converse of this theme was that of resilience, as demonstrated through Hester's capacity to maintain object relationships. What I aim to show is that the conflictual/masochistic form of object relations grew out of the conflictual grip relations of Hester's early development. I shall therefore concentrate on four themes:

First, the conflict over food, its course and how this can be understood in terms of conflictual relationships between Hester and her mother, and in terms of mother's projection on to Hester of a particular form of 'convex containing shape' (Graph 6.8, 6.9).

Second, the continual observations of other kinds of defensive patterns of relating (Graph 6.16), already noted in her development, but now seen in particular patterns of relationships. These were Hester's turning away from her objects, suggesting infidelity or disillusion; her muscularity, or vigorous ways of holding herself together. Appearing when these forms of relating failed, was a depressed state of mind, which suggest the possibility of depressive collapse. She resorted in the face of this to mindlessness.

Third, the continued persistence in maintaining object relations (Graph 6.16) which led Hester to develop symbolic modes of relating, language and play which bordered on the symbolic (Graph 6.19).

Fourth, the relationship between the development of Hester and some softening in the container experience, after the food battle had reached its peak, and therefore during the second half of this second year. I mean by this that the hard, uncompromising, and confrontational approach of both parents to food was replaced by a more tender, less retaliatory way of relating.

The food battle was first observed when Hester was one year one month and 12 days, and continued until she was 19 months. From the outset, both Hester and Yvonne clearly demonstrated the factors involved. Yvonne anticipated the meal with sarcasm: '"This will be fun," she said, "Because Hester is really naughty and she won't take her food from me. She wants to feed herself all the time"' (O46: Hester at one year one month 12 days). Immediately, Yvonne's tone became crisp and the tension in the way she spoke to both Sid and Hester seemed to suggest difficulties would follow. Hester initially treated the food quite unkindly: 'She picked up a spoon and gave Hester a spoonful, standing over her. Hester let it in and then pushed it out with her tongue' (O46: Hester at one year one month 12 days). Then she differentiated the food she ate from her own fingers and that offered by Yvonne, as Yvonne had suggested she would: 'Hester put her fingers into her food, eating several mouthfuls. Yvonne gave Hester a spoonful and she took it into her mouth and then eased it out with her tongue. Hester put the spoon down and turned away' (O46) and, as Yvonne tried to leave her, Hester had a coughing or choking episode:

> Hester had some more food with her fingers, looked up at me and down at Sid and babbled some more – 'ba, da, bla' – and as Yvonne reached the doorway, Hester started to splutter and then to cough, wheezily. Yvonne said sharply 'stop it Hester, stop it' and patted her on the back firmly. Hester coughed more, turning to choking and she got red in the face and breathless. (O46)

This choking evoked an issue of life and death. Finally, Hester ate a yoghurt in a way which was both triumphant and seductive:

> Yvonne sat down with a yoghurt and offered Hester a spoonful. Hester backed herself to the wall, leaned against it and then went forwards to the spoon, took it and turned away and went back to the wall. She looked at Yvonne who smiled at her and offered her another spoonful. She came up again and again smilingly took another spoonful in a teasy kind of way, coyly bending down and smiling, and again retreated to the wall. Yvonne said 'one more' and Hester came again and took the spoonful of yoghurt. (O46)

The observer was a third person in this rivalrous triangle. Hester had already indicated evidence of sexualisation when she, bejewelled with a bangle and earring in her pierced ear, treated the present I had given her for her first birthday in a seductive manner:

> She picked up the cuddly toy again and started to suck the toy's head. She looked at me as she did this, a sense of a coquettish expression on her face, enhanced by the bangle and earrings, and there was a hint of her biting. Yvonne said 'don't bite it; don't bite it'. (O44: Hester at one year one week three days)

This sexual little girl might be preferable, from the parents' point of view, to the alternative of an aggressive little girl, and Yvonne is keen to point out that she does not want Hester biting.

Hester's refusal to eat when she was 13 months 19 days was accompanied by tears, and much smearing of the food, so that she became the object of contempt for both parents. She was left miserably upset, disconnected from her relationships and blank:

> She started to cry again and Kevin came in and looked at her, saying she needed a bath. He looked as if he was going to pick her up and then did not, saying he was not going to pick her up like that – and she cried again, loudly. Then Yvonne said recriminatingly to Kevin that

> Hester had expected him to pick her up. Yvonne suggested taking her jumper off, and then Kevin did reach over and with an unperturbed expression, lifted her out and carried her out, at arm's length and facing away from him, saying she was untouchable. Hester made a very sorry sight, caked in tears and shepherd's pie, and sobbing a little, eyes hopelessly open wide and blankly looking ahead. (O47)

Thus the battle was joined, with Yvonne and Kevin both unable to tolerate or think about Hester's state of mind, a state of misery, which she defended through her repertoire of muscularity and triumph based on rivalry with mother. For many months Yvonne had wished for Hester's independence; now she resented the lack of control she had. Underlying the paradox appeared to be the memory of the failure of breast-feeding, and the frequent glimpses of Yvonne's fear of her capacity to harm Hester. The battle appeared to be about control and separation, and a battle over the degree to which each participant – Yvonne and Hester – would accept the projections of the other. For Yvonne, too, the frequently recurring idea that this was a life and death struggle evoked the cot death she had spoken about, the scratching of Hester to which she reacted with alarm; all the archaeology, in other words, of the problems she had been faced with through the presence of this daughter who had 'never been a baby', and who was thought to be so 'greedy'.

Yvonne did seem to need to play out the battle in front of me. It seemed important to her that I witnessed these events, and preferable to maintaining a 'front' by not introducing mealtimes during the observations. Nor did she suggest changing the times of the observation so that mealtime could be avoided. These were very difficult events to observe, and maintain an appropriate response. The function I had was to contain the sense of damage, emanating from Yvonne in terms of hostility and control, and to provide a focus for Hester to work through the impact of these experiences.

The example which follows demonstrates, at the height of the battle, Hester's denigration of food, so that it was treated as contaminating. Yvonne had given Hester her dinner on a tray, and Hester had stood up and moved away from the meal:

> Yvonne snapped at her to 'sit down and eat your dinner'. Hester looked at her with a defiant grin. Yvonne came over, got her and sat her by the tray. Hester wriggled and Yvonne held her in place and then Yvonne got a spoonful of food and tried to give it to Hester who moved her mouth away. Yvonne said – crossly – 'eat your dinner.' Hester wriggled and moved away from the tray. Yvonne snapped 'sit still and eat your dinner'. Hester moved away from the tray again and Yvonne went after her, held her and sat her in front of the tray, holding her in place. Hester cried, tears rolling down her cheek. Yvonne held her and said to me that this happens every night and she was going to eat her dinner, she

> gets away with it far too often. She sat Hester on her lap and Hester wriggled to get away. Yvonne slapped her bottom, held her firmly and Hester cried. Yvonne got a spoonful of food and Hester put it towards her mouth. Hester twisted her mouth away, still crying. Yvonne persisted and got a little bit of food in her mouth and Hester spat it out straight away. Yvonne said forcefully, 'stop it; you're going to eat your dinner'. She sat Hester by the tray again, shouting 'sit still' and Hester still cried, Yvonne tried to give her a spoon of food, still holding her and Hester cried and moved her mouth away. Yvonne held her firmly and some food got in and Hester spat it out again. Hester tried to get away and stood up and came over to me and appealed to me crying tearfully and called 'di-ie, di-ie'. She put her hand on my knee and Yvonne came over and took her and sat her down by the tray. Hester's cries redoubled and Yvonne tried to get a spoonful of food into her mouth saying 'I shall force feed you'. Hester cried and shrieked. Yvonne said 'don't cry' and she slapped her fingers. Hester cried again and Yvonne said 'don't cry' and slapped her fingers again. Hester cried and Yvonne smacked her fingers; Hester cried and Yvonne slapped her fingers.

It felt at the time there was going to be no way out of this for either of them; Yvonne was really pent up, furious, and Hester crying and determined. Hester had a tightly clenched mouth, which would admit no food at all, and Yvonne had a single-minded forceful approach to gaining control over her mouth:

> Yvonne turned Hester round so she was sitting on her lap and tried to give her some more food. Hester turned her mouth away, spat out the bit that got in and cried loudly, shrieking. Hester leaned back away from Yvonne, rolled away from her and Yvonne let her go. Hester stood up and came over to me and cried saying 'di-ie', but looking angrily at me. I gently brushed my hand through her hair and Yvonne seemed to stop, looking on, eyes glazed a little. Hester lay on the floor crying, her head in the carpet and bottom in the air. She howled, turned and looked at me with a mixture of an appealing and angry expression.
>
> Hester came up to me and half gestured to be picked up. I looked at her with sympathy, and Hester turned and went over to Yvonne. She said she did not want to have anything to do with her. Hester smiled at her and she said Hester was not funny and they were not friends. Hester smiled and grinned at Yvonne and she put her arms out wide asking for a cuddle – very appealingly. Yvonne let her climb up and Hester wriggled about on Yvonne and wriggled off and put her head into Yvonne's lap. (O58: Hester at 17 months less three days)

This observation contained both the nadir of the relationship between Yvonne and Hester, and some of the elements that foreshadowed recovery. The theme of recovery from this crisis dominated the remainder of Hester's second year. First, Kevin began to take a more active part in proceedings: 'At this point Kevin walked in, saying hallo and commenting on Hester's boots. Kevin looked around and said "it's set up for dinner and it looks like a bomb has hit it". He tidied up.' (O58). Later (O63) he actively criticised the food, taking Hester's side, as it were, and took part in feeding her. Similarly, when Yvonne scratched Hester with her watch strap (O76: Hester at 22 months 13 days), he both named the event and repaired the damage. Kevin, until the end of Hester's first year a peripheral figure, now offered a quality of containment in his own right (Graph 6.10; 6.11). When linking with Yvonne in the combined care of Hester, the impact of Kevin's involvement was to offer both a sense of proportion, and a sense of noticing. However, rather than paint a portrait of Kevin as the 'good' parent, it should be noted that there were times when these roles became reversed. He could be fiercely unresponsive to Hester, for example laughing at her when she was crying. Yvonne would on these occasions make a comment about the interaction between them. The common factor was that there was verbalisation between the parents about the relationship of the other parent and infant, offering a counterpoint for the conflict between the parent involved with Hester and Hester herself (Graph 6.12).

Second, we saw in this observation (O58) how Hester attempted to gain closeness to mother, approaching her appealingly and forgivingly. Her persistence in relating to mother is striking, and when Yvonne relented – at first as if defeated, but later with more resilience – from her forceful position, there emerged the possibility for tender interaction:

> Yvonne pretended to snore and Hester climbed on the sofa with her, cuddled her and they both pretended to go to sleep. Yvonne smiled at me, clearly enjoying it, and said 'wake mummy up' and Hester pulled her head up by the hair. Yvonne got up laughing and cuddled Hester. (O70: Hester at 20 months five days)

Yvonne shared Hester's interest in words. Hester became quite verbal (Graph 6.19), though there was always a hint in her language development that it contained both a sense of real development and of finding another way to screen the depressed core of herself. Language development therefore was in the service of developing her object relationships and her defences; particularly her unfaithful flirtatious self, and her holding together muscular self. Nevertheless, her achievement was at times delightful, particularly in contrast to the misery of the feeding difficulties. First, we see her in conversation with mother, and Yvonne maintaining an interest, with an effort not to lose patience:

> Hester got on to the floor, pointed at the videos and said 'Turtles'. She went over to lie by the TV, and picked up a magazine and looked at it lying on her tummy. Yvonne sat down and Hester looked at the picture and said 'what's that?', and Yvonne said 'lady', and Hester pointed at

> another picture, repeating 'what's that?'; Yvonne answered. This was repeated many times. (O77: Hester at 22 months three weeks)

When Yvonne lost patience Hester showed her that, in her view, losing patience was not very maternal: she 'detitled' her: 'Yvonne answered shortly; "frog; frog's legs; frog again". Hester then said "what that Yvonne" and Yvonne said to me "did you hear that?" with a laugh' (O77).

Hester's language development contained a wide vocabulary, some sentences developed during the second half of her second year, and, significantly her curiosity was seen through her constant questioning. She could produce impressive combinations of words. Here, on cue, she performs for the observer:

> Terry, a friend of Kevin's, asked me what I was doing exactly, and Yvonne told him I was observing Hester, so I could learn about babies from experience. Hester sat down in the middle of the room and started to sing: 'rainy, pury, owd man nory; went a bed, banged he head cun get up in a morny. (O73: Hester at 21 months less three days)

In her play, Hester oscillated between a concrete, action-based form of play, and one which was more truly symbolic (Graph 6.19). This contained a strong sense of mediating difficult emotional experiences. First, there was an example where the play was quite clearly about babies, feeding, going away, and getting stuck:

> She walked gingerly over the pile of bricks on the floor like walking on tacks. She walked over to the bed and reached on to it, trying to get the doll. She could not quite reach and pushed herself between the ladder and the bed post. She could not get in and turned and looked at me appealingly. She persisted and did get in, took the doll off the bed and put the back pack, containing her feeding bottle, on it, carefully passing the straps round the doll's arms. Hester climbed up the ladder to get into Sid's bed, saying to herself 'get down' but ignored her own command. She reached the top and then climbed down until she reached the bottom step, put her foot down reaching for the ground, could not reach and looked round at me. I lifted her down. (O69: Hester at 20 months less two days)

Second, there was a moving sequence where I unwittingly 'refused' a biscuit Hester offered and she delightedly leaped on the opportunity to turn the tables:

> Kevin brought me a cup of coffee and Hester came over, took a biscuit and passed it to me to 'dunk' it in the coffee. Kevin told her it was hot and not to touch. Hester passed me a biscuit and I turned my head away. This captivated her and so we played the game of Hester offering a biscuit and me refusing to take it. She pushed it right up to my mouth until I did take it. She then got another one and repeated the game,

> with Hester smiling and enjoying it. (073: Hester at 21 months less three days)

The last months of the observation remained under the dominant influence of the theme of recovery from crisis and resilience. Her memory and recognition were good; she recalled people with affection, especially father (Graph 6.17), but at times she demonstrated a gap in her thinking connected with the concept of absence, and separation (Graph 6.18). For example: 'A friend of the family came to the window and waved. Hester waved back but when he then appeared at the door Hester looked most confused and continued to look at the window' (O73). After the family went on holiday when she was 21 months, her coolness towards me after the holiday was disconcerting, and not readily yielding to the assumption that I had 'turned bad' in her absence. When she showed me some photographs of where she had been on holiday, and then crumpled them up and dropped them, she conveyed that I had abandoned (dropped) her through not going with her (O75: Hester at 22 months two weeks). This also suggested that for Hester, when something is dropped, or lost, it is relinquished and not returnable. She was obliged to follow a tortuous path between different manoeuvres to re-establish, maintain, and then enhance the core of experience, to restore the lost heart of herself, and her relationships.

6.6 Ending

The observations ended almost as an epilogue, as the family holiday – which was arranged through Kevin's father's legacy – made a significant break in the observations during Hester's 22nd month. Neither Yvonne nor Hester were responsive to my comments about ending, as the event was overshadowed by Yvonne choosing the last weeks of the observation to wean Hester from the bottle. Undoubtedly, the two endings, of the observation and Hester's babyhood, were merged in this decision.

This second weaning of the observation period was both painful and reparative. Hester had the opportunity to persist in wishing to retain the object, to be pained and comforted, and Yvonne, for the most part, managed not to retaliate in the face of this protest by Hester. Yvonne showed much greater resilience, therefore, in her containment of Hester; Hester showed herself more consistently able to continue to mourn the loss of the bottle, without resorting to the easier ways out; the infidelity, withdrawal from relationship with mother, muscularity, and mindlessness. Here is Hester at 23 months 13 days:

> Yvonne returned and asked if Hester was still crying. She sat her on her lap and Hester continued to cry. Yvonne said 'stop crying, silly, there's nothing wrong with you'. Hester continued to cry and said, half audibly, 'kit' (biscuit) and Yvonne said she could have a biscuit after her dinner. Hester resumed her crying, sounding more angry now. Yvonne held on to her and said 'come and have your dinner'. She spent some

> time manoeuvring her around with Hester crying. Yvonne said 'do you want your dinner' and Hester replied 'yes'. Yvonne asked her if she wanted to eat it on the floor and Hester said 'yes'. Yvonne asked if she wanted it on the tray and Hester again said 'yes'. Yvonne put Hester on the floor next to her tray and then Hester cried and pulled away and held on to Yvonne's lap. Yvonne then got her comfortable on her lap and asked Hester if she wanted it on her lap. Hester said she did and then Yvonne brought the plate towards her and Hester pulled away and she cried loudly. Yvonne then tried to get her to sit with the blanket around her and Hester pushed it away. Yvonne then lost patience and told her she was a silly girl and she should stop crying. She pushed Hester away and Hester lay on the sofa and then turned and hit Yvonne on the hand several times, amidst cries. Yvonne then tried again and sat her down and put the food in front of her, and this time Hester took some, and quietened as she took her food. She ate a little and Yvonne asked if she wanted a drink now. Hester said 'yes' quietly, nodding her head slightly and Yvonne passed her the beaker. She quietly took a drink from her beaker and Yvonne told me that she was managing without the bottle. She added that she keeps her awake as late as possible in the evening and she then settles to sleep, with just a moan. Hester is dry during the day and asks for the potty. When she wakes in the morning she is a little wet. Hester had been 'very good' with putting her own pyjamas on and doing up her buttons. Yvonne said she was 'nearly there'. Yvonne talked to Hester and said 'where's your bottle?'. Hester said 'boken' (broken) and Yvonne said that was right, and 'you don't have a bottle any more, you have a beaker' and Hester said 'Heska'. (O79: Hester at 23 months 13 days)

In the last observation, three days after her birthday, Hester ate most of her dinner quietly, accepted the present I had given her, said goodbye, and as I was about to leave with a sense of healing between mother and infant, Yvonne told me Hester had spent her birthday at the caravan with Kevin and Sid, and that she, Yvonne, had therefore not seen Hester on her birthday. This absence appeared to be the last retaliation of the period of the observation, the final act I would witness of mother's resentment against this 'greedy cow' of a child, who had evoked for her experiences which were both painful, and beyond her capacity to experience as pain. As with many of these experiences, one had the feeling that Yvonne knew what she was doing, without knowing what it was that made her behaviour so compulsive. This seemed especially so when she said it was only this, her second, birthday that she would miss.

6.7 Summary

Hester's development was characterised by the impact of her early weaning from the breast, which was itself the first event in the relationship between Yvonne and Hester that told the story of a conflictual fit between them (Graph 6.8). Subsequently, both mother and Hester had to struggle to achieve a resolution of this conflict, Yvonne's limitations in terms of containing the emotional experiences of her daughter were painful to observe, and reached the point of dangerousness on occasions, particularly during the feeding battles. Overspilling of maternal emotions were observed in connection with the appellations Yvonne used – 'greedy', 'greedy cow' were clearly related to feeding, and to concepts of Hester's body. Yvonne expressed disillusion with her size. She had been born a large baby, who had 'got stuck' in the process of birth, and Yvonne needed reassurance that she was not too big, was not ugly. She spoke about her never having seemed to be a baby, and at times exaggerated her size. For example she placed her in a Babygro which was too big for her, but said Hester filled it. In her depression she projected her greed for contact with others on to Hester, building an image of her as a greedy, demanding baby.

Yvonne did not express directly her phantasies about a cot death affecting Hester. Rather, the theme recurred as a repetitive image in the observations. She conveyed the sense that, like the Ancient Mariner, she had a story to tell, which gripped her and to which she was compelled to listen, though condemned not to be able to speak. Particularly, this appeared in the observational material when she was overly concerned about hurting Hester. Her references to 'strangling' or 'hitting' Hester were followed by a reference to the cot death. Studies of the impact of cot death suggest the impact can be far-reaching and long-lasting (Reid 1992). Feeding difficulties, and therefore questions of indigestibility, were accompanied by questions concerning life and death. These were an essential part of the convex containing shape.

Hester's development was dominated by the struggle between the adaptation of defensive patterns that would lead her to be 'doubly deprived' (Henry 1974), and finding ways of holding on to object relationships. Her defensive pattern of muscularity was developed in the search for an object to hold on to and her unadventurousness was indicative of her awareness of an absence, or loss. Her grip relations, in contrast to Michael and Hashmat, were more varied, and employed more modalities in greater combinations (Graphs 6.15a; 6.15b). Particularly through play and symbolic activity, but also through the repetition and working through of difficult emotional experiences, again in play and also in the relationship with mother, there was clearly some development towards a more benign internalisation (Graph 6.20). The experience of weaning from the bottle appeared, with the aid of language, to give Hester the experience of internalising a more robust notion of absence and loss than had occurred in her primary experiences of weaning from the breast. If we take the image of 'Russian dolls' of experience used in discussing Hashmat's development, then, as her language and symbolic capacities emerged, Hester showed – to an extent – that later experience, or a larger 'Russian doll' can readdress the earlier, or smaller 'Russian doll'. In this connectiveness between levels of experience lies the possibility of resilience.

6.8 Grid

6.8.1 Mothering

Yvonne, Hester's mother, received good levels of support from her partner, Kevin, except for the period when Hester was three–six months, a period which coincided with Kevin's father's death (see 6.3 below). There was moderately good support from her extended family and friends (Graph 6.1). Yvonne's states of mind were somewhat anxious and persecutory. She was subject to some significant degree of conflict in her role with Hester, and her internal resources were limited, despite the reasonable amount of support she received. Though moderately able to verbalise her emotions, she allowed her preoccupations to impinge on to Hester, especially between 15 and 18 months, when the conflict over feeding was at its height (Graph 6.2). Yvonne made numerous representations about Hester's states of mind and her developing character (Graph 6.3a). These were a mixture of positive and negative observations and comments, and showed a high degree of persistence (Graph 6.3b). Her appreciation of Hester's key events in her development was slightly more positive in Hester's second year than her first (Graph 6.3a).

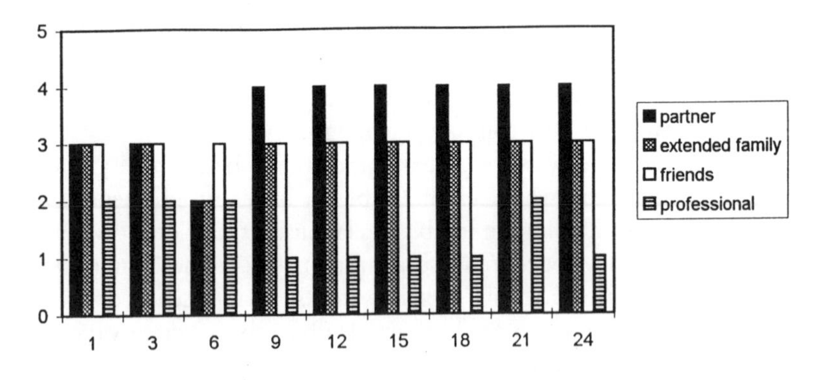

Key: 5=very high levels of support; 4=good; 3=moderate; 2=fairly low; 1=low

Graph 6.1

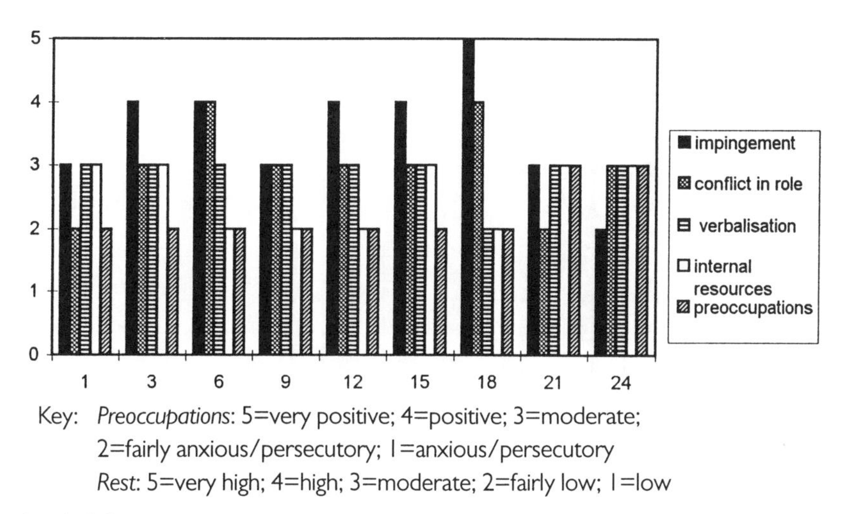

Key: *Preoccupations*: 5=very positive; 4=positive; 3=moderate; 2=fairly anxious/persecutory; 1=anxious/persecutory
Rest: 5=very high; 4=high; 3=moderate; 2=fairly low; 1=low

Graph 6.2

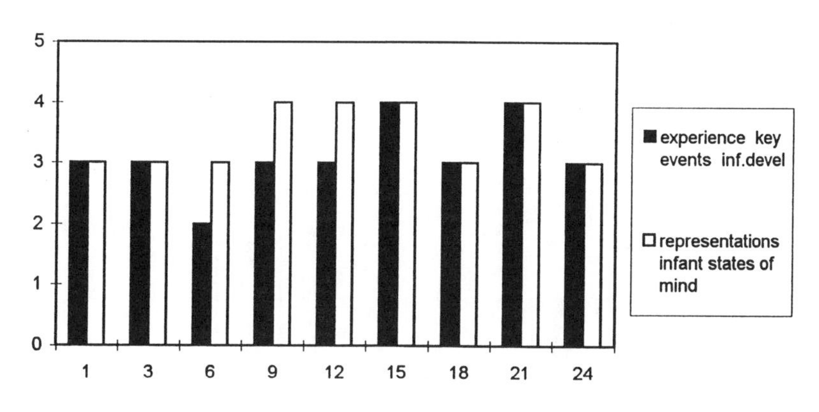

Key: *Experience of events*: 5=very positive; 4=positive; 3=moderate; 2=fairly negative; 1=negative
Representations: 5=very frequent; 4=frequent; 3=moderate; 2=fairly infrequent; 1=infrequent

Graph 6.3a

In her parenting, she was rated as less aware of, and less able to meet Hester's emotional than her physical needs. She was moderately able to show understanding of Hester's communications of her needs; meeting emotional needs was rated as fairly low for periods of the observation (Graph 6.4). Overall the picture provided by this grid was of a somewhat troubled mother (persecutory and anxious preoccupations), with limited resources, who was moderately able to meet Hester's needs and communicate with her.

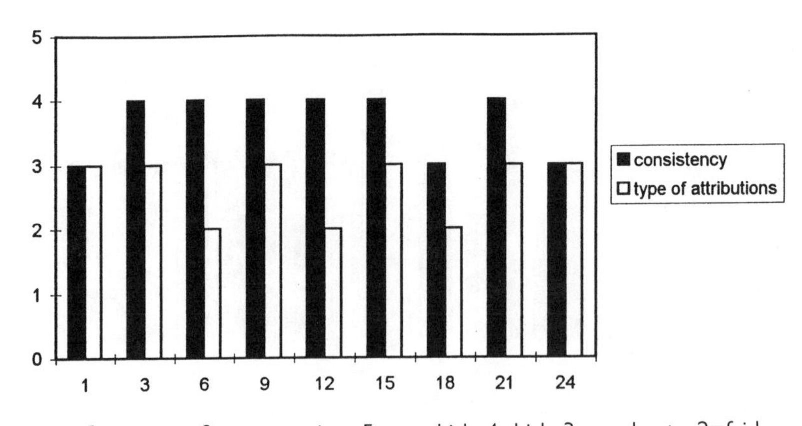

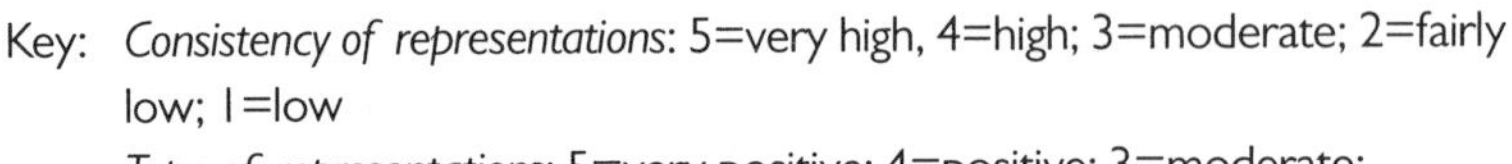
Key: *Consistency of representations*: 5=very high, 4=high; 3=moderate; 2=fairly low; 1=low
Type of representations: 5=very positive; 4=positive; 3=moderate; 2=fairly negative; 1=negative

Graph 6.3b

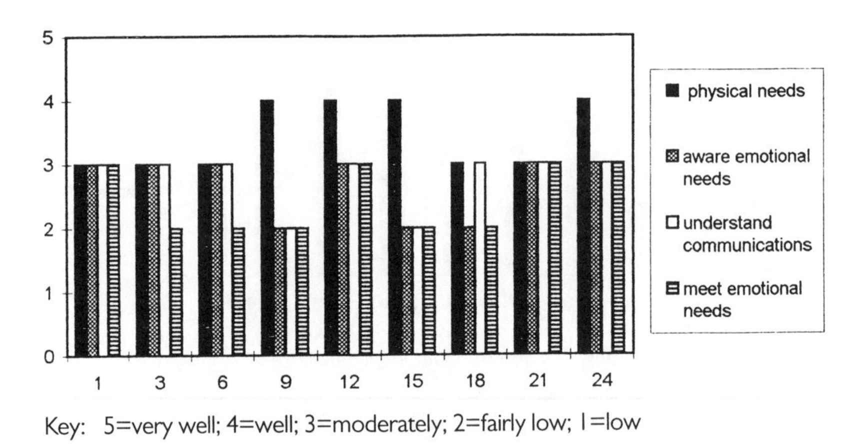

Key: 5=very well; 4=well; 3=moderately; 2=fairly low; 1=low

Graph 6.4

6.8.2 Mother–infant relationship

Levels of intimacy, attentiveness, sensitivity and intimacy were rated fairly low until after Hester reached 18 months. A fairly high degree of conflict was scored in the mother–infant relationship (Graph 6.5). Grip relations between Yvonne and Hester scored at rather low strength at the levels of mouth–nipple/teat, eye–eye, body–body and mind–mind. The voice–ear link was fairly strong (Graph 6.6). Ratings for intensity and capacity to maintain emotionality, were rated as increasing from fairly low to high. Levels of 'in-tuneness' were rated fairly low to moderate (Graph 6.7).

The 'fit' between Hester and Yvonne was rated to include a moderate degree of containment, very little accommodation after six months and a considerable degree of conflict (Graph 6.8). Mother's containing shape showed a moderate to high convex pattern. Concave and flat containing shapes were rated moderate to fairly low (Graph 6.9).

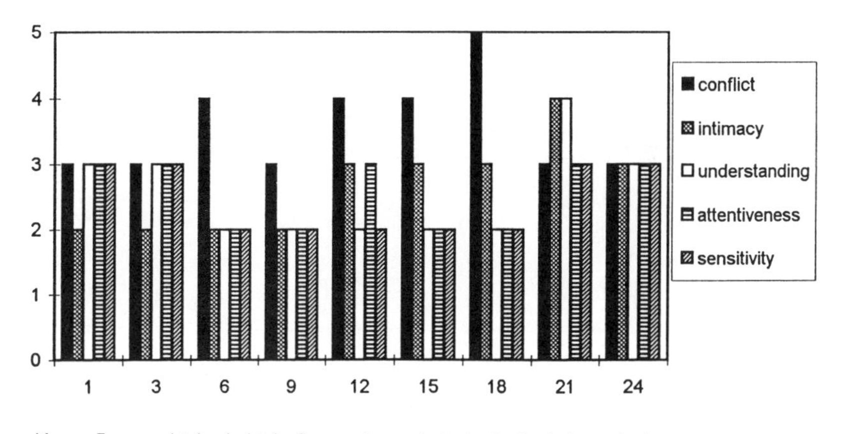

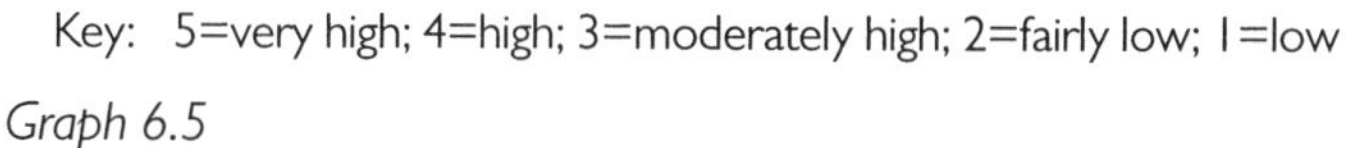
Key: 5=very high; 4=high; 3=moderately high; 2=fairly low; 1=low

Graph 6.5

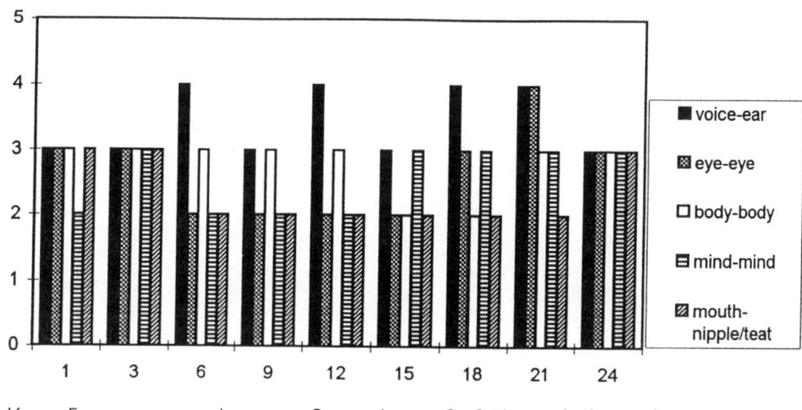

Key: 5=very strong; 4=strong; 3=moderate; 2=fairly weak; 1=weak

Graph 6.6

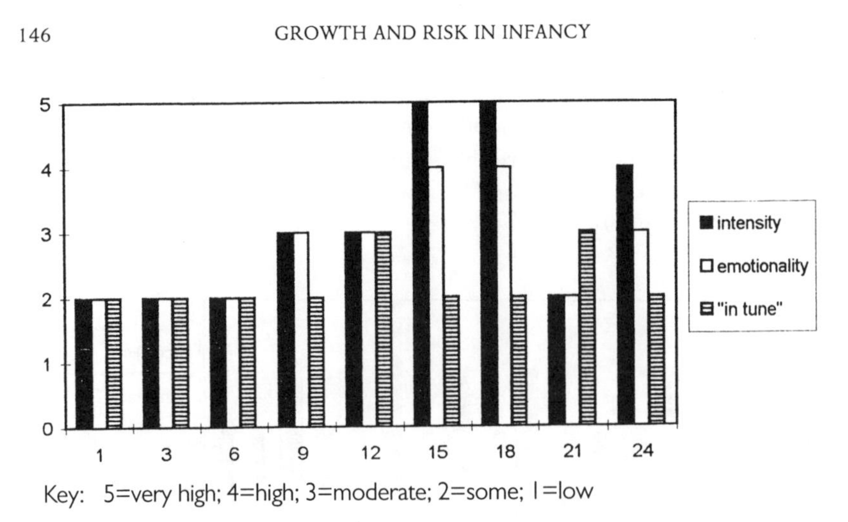

Key: 5=very high; 4=high; 3=moderate; 2=some; 1=low

Graph 6.7

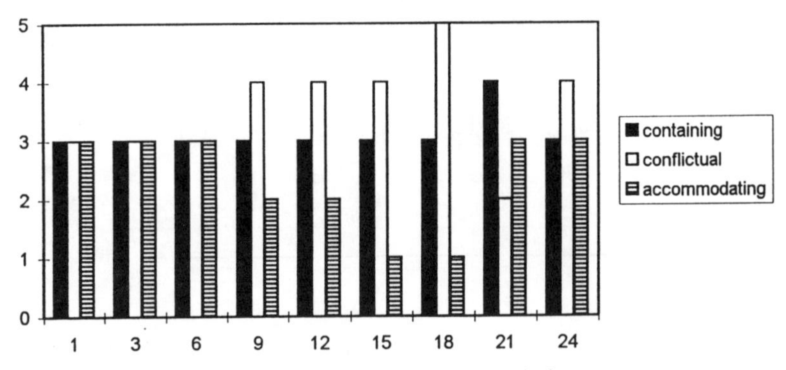

Key: 5=very high; 4=high; 3=moderate; 2=fairly low; 1=low

Graph 6.8

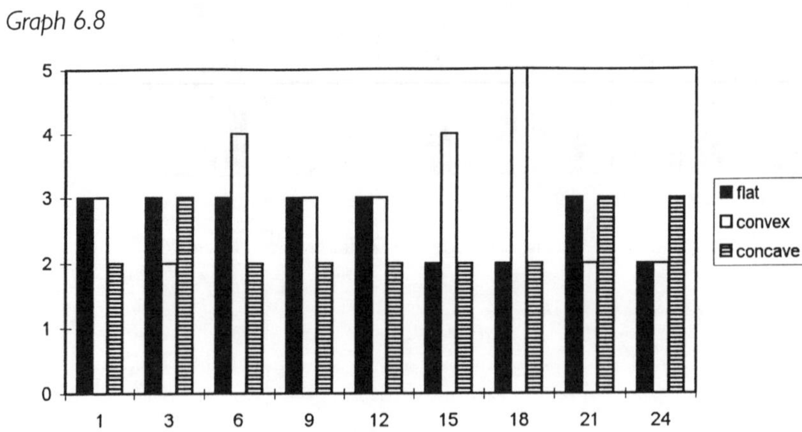

Key: 5=very high; 4=high; 3=moderate; 2=fairly low; 1=low

Graph 6.9

6.8.3 Father–infant relationship

Kevin, Hester's father, showed levels of attentiveness, sensitivity and intimacy that rose from fairly low to moderate and high in his relationship with Hester in the second year (Graph 6.10). The grip relations showed ratings of moderately strong to strong at the levels of voice–ear and eye–eye, and fairly weak at other levels (Graph 6.11).

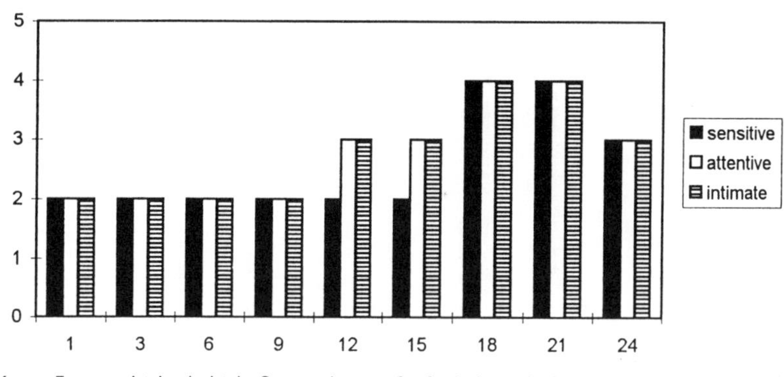

Key: 5=very high; 4=high; 3=moderate; 2=fairly low; 1=low

Graph 6.10

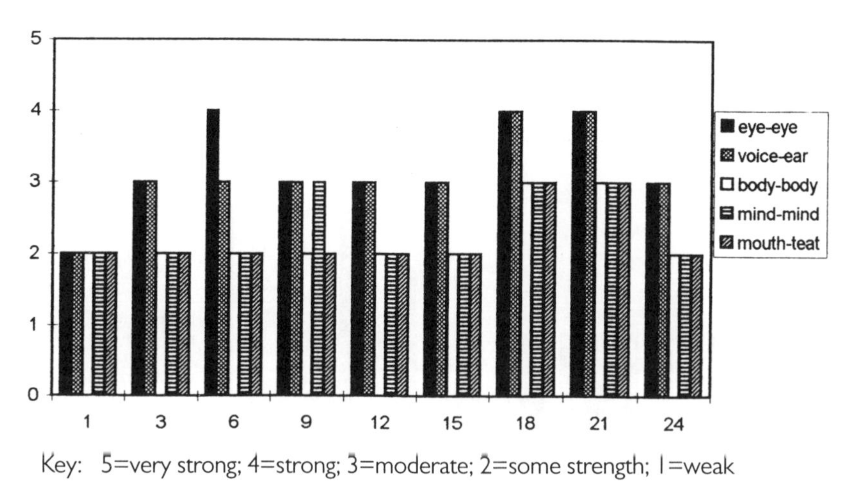

Key: 5=very strong; 4=strong; 3=moderate; 2=some strength; 1=weak

Graph 6.11

6.8.4 Parental Relationship

The grid recorded fairly low levels of conflict and harmony in the relationship between Kevin and Yvonne. Conflict was verbalised to, at best, moderate levels (Graph 6.12). The categories for describing the way parents together met the containment needs of infants all scored at moderate or less frequent. The exception was that there were hints in the rating that there were greater levels of problem solving ('bridge building') in the last six months of the observations (Graphs 6.13, and 6.13 b).

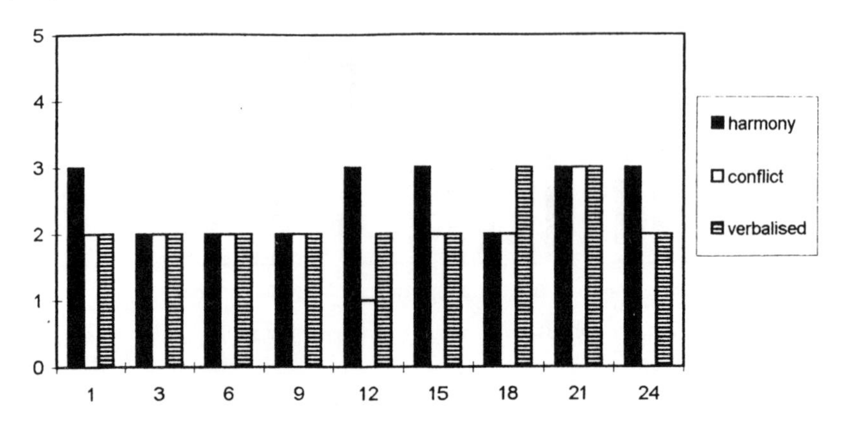

Key: 5=very often; 4=often; 3=moderate; 2=fairly infrequent; 1=infrequent

Graph 6.12

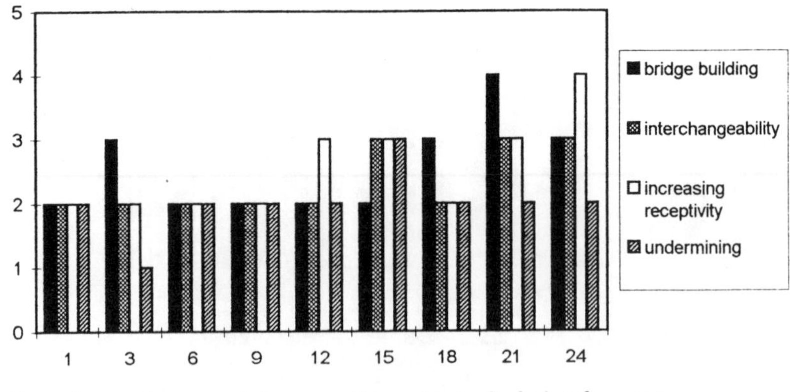

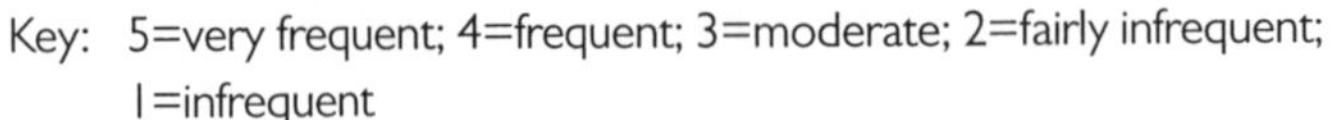

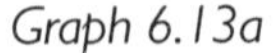
Graph 6.13a

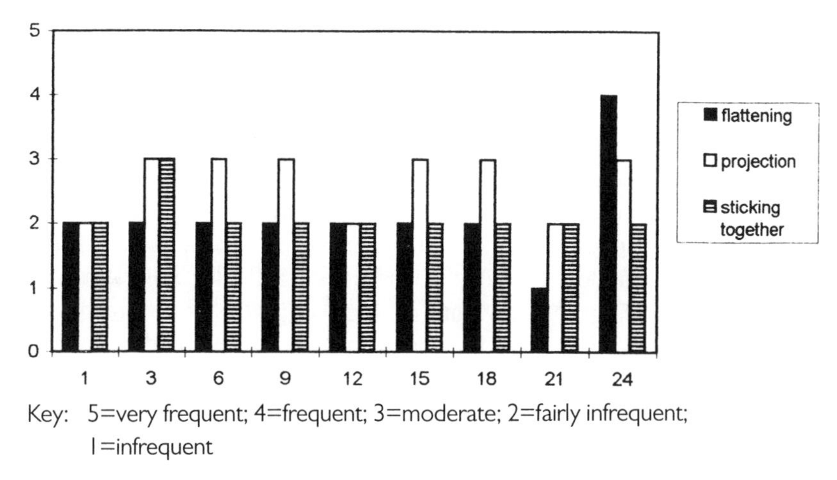

Key: 5=very frequent; 4=frequent; 3=moderate; 2=fairly infrequent; 1=infrequent

Graph 6.13b

6.8.5 Infant development

Hester's physical development, initially somewhat slow, became very advanced. She was sitting at five months, crawling at seven and a half months, standing at nine months and walking at ten and a half months. The context of these developmental features is considered in detail above (section 6.5). She was rated as having continuing and worsening difficulties with feeding, and physical health. Her sleeping patterns were rated satisfactory, though the ratings showed some fluctuations, indicating she was subject to some periods of nocturnal disturbance (Graph 6.14):

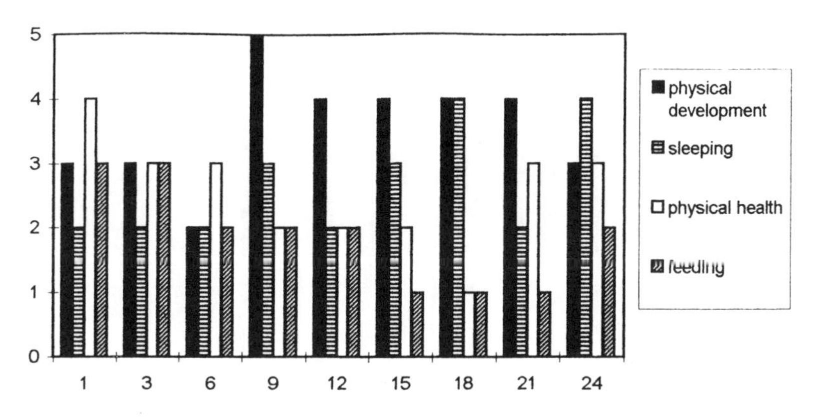

Key: *Development*: 5=very advanced; 4=advanced; 3=in time; 2=slightly backwards; 1=backward
Rest: 5=very well; 4=well; 3=OK; 2=some difficulties; 1=difficulties

Graph 6.14

Hester's grip relations rated as strong to very strong. Her voice, eye and mouth grips in particular came into these categories. (Graph 6.15a). Her grip relations with her hand and body showed, also, a capacity to reach considerable strength at various points in her development, and to be at least moderately strong. Her mind grip was also moderately strong (Graph 15b). Hester's levels of protest and expressiveness reached high ratings after a rating of fairly low in her first six months. She maintained moderate to high frequencies of object relating. Her defensiveness was also moderately frequent, and the quality of her defences were scored within moderately flexible/tending to rigidity levels (Graph 6.16). Hester achieved ratings of moderate to high capacities for memory and recognition, but her ability to recall others with affection was rated at moderate or below this level (Graph 6.17).

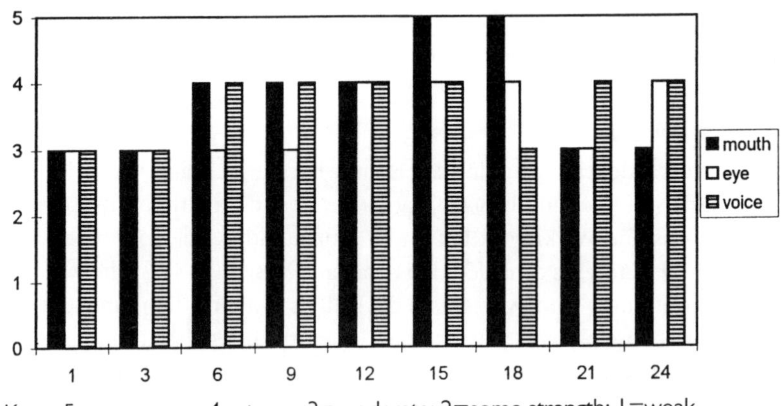

Key: 5=very strong; 4=strong; 3=moderate; 2=some strength; 1=weak

Graph 6.15a

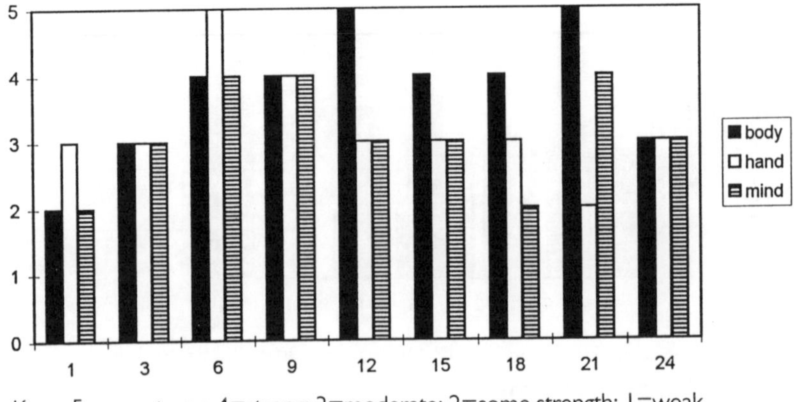

Key: 5=very strong; 4=strong; 3=moderate; 2=some strength; 1=weak

Graph 6.15b

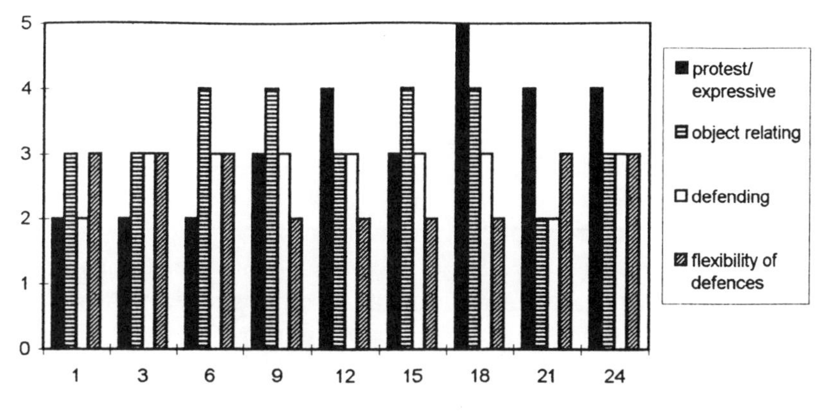

Key: *Flexibility of defences*: 5=very flexible; 4=flexible; 3=some flexibility; 2=tending to rigidity; 1=rigid
Rest: 5=very high; 4=high; 3=moderate; 2=fairly low; 1=low

Graph 6.16

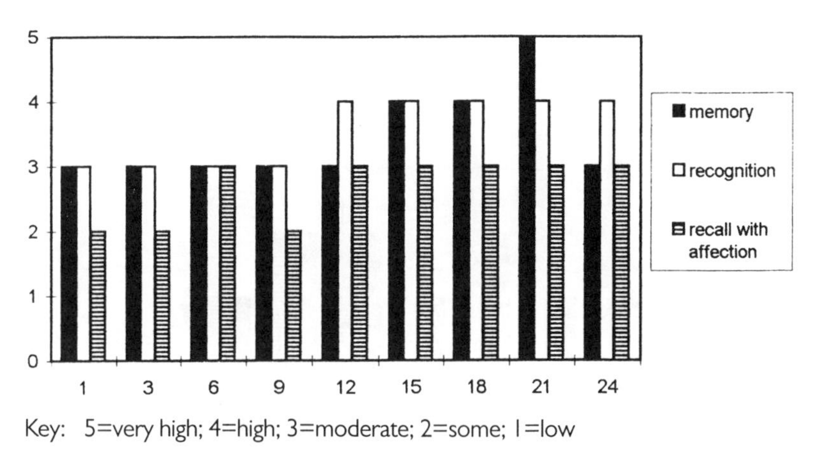

Key: 5=very high; 4=high; 3=moderate; 2=some; 1=low

Graph 6.17

Her demonstrations of proximity seeking were scored as reaching high levels; her capacity to discriminate between people and for thinking were scored as moderate, whilst her reactions to separation were mainly below moderate levels (Graph 6.18). Hester's language development and capacity for symbolic expression in play reached moderate levels, and her play which was recorded as expressions of unconscious phantasy was also rated at the moderate level (Graph 6.19). Hester's overall quality of internalisation was recorded as being a combination of benign and persecutory elements, and there were periods when the rating placed her internalisation towards the persecutory end of the grid (Graph 6.20).

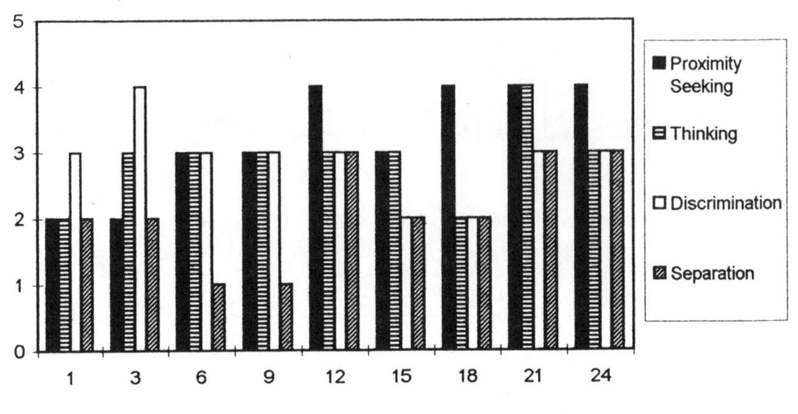

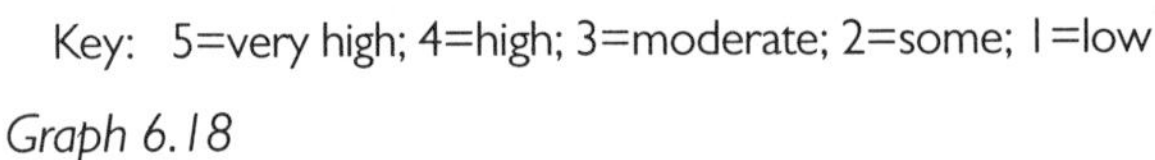

Graph 6.18

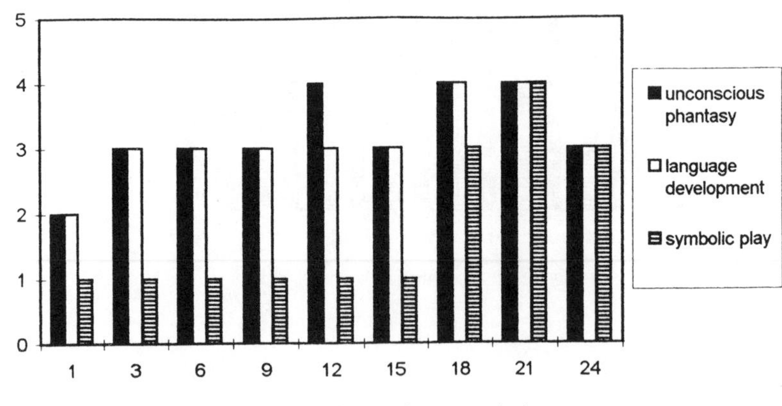

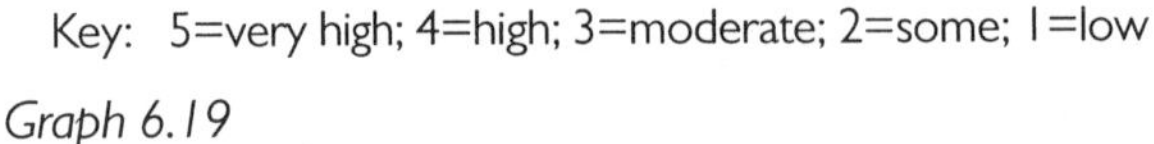

Graph 6.19

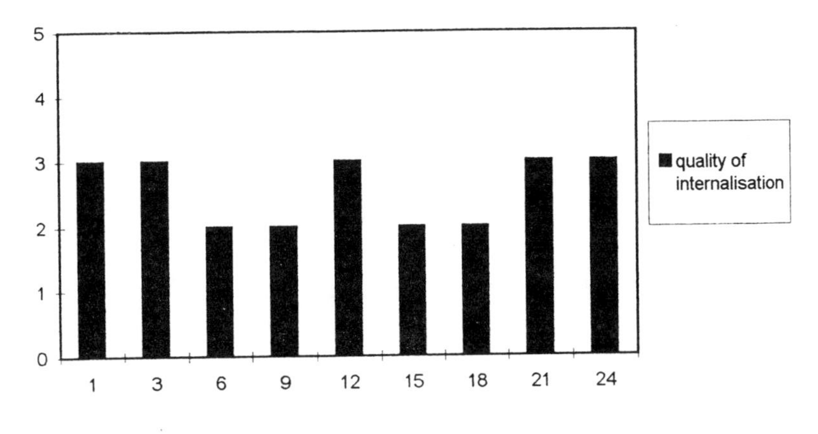

Key: 5=very benign; 4=benign; 3=mixed; 2=tending to the persecutory; 1=persecutory

Graph 6.20

6.8.6 Summary of the grid

The grid for Hester records the particular quality of parenting that is a central focus for this case study, namely convex containing shape (Graph 6.9). The 'peaks' of this convex containing shape at six and 18 months are explored in detail in the descriptive case study. Hester's repertoire of grip relations, her capacity to maintain object relations and her expressiveness, which increased through her second year are also clearly seen in the grid (Graphs 5.15a, 5.15b, 5.16). The impact of Hester's difficult experiences in the face of convex container shape is seen in her limited capacity for recall with affection (Graph 6.17) and her moderate to low capacity to react to separation (Graph 6.18). On the other hand, resilience is seen in her development of symbolic functioning (Graph 6.19) and her capacities for thinking, seeking proximity, remembering and recognising (Graphs 6.17 and 6.18).

The role played by father in Hester's second year is seen in Graph 6.10, and the parents' capacity to link in a problem solving way ('bridge building') is recorded in Graph 6.13. Thus the factors associated with both risk and resilience are shown in these grids.

CHAPTER 7

Samantha

The observation of Samantha provided the opportunity to follow the development of an infant whose family, through their professional lifestyle, as a family in a diplomatic service, were subject to regular moves. Before contacting the family it was thought that such a feature may have bearing on the family's sense of belonging, and therefore possibly on the development of the infant (Williams 1997). In this family there was immediate evidence that the first child, Donald, was experiencing considerable difficulties in his development, particularly with regard to language development and his characteristics of being 'switched off' from relationships.

Samantha's development occurred in the specific context and lifestyle of the family, and in the shadow, as it were of the difficulties already experienced by her parents with Donald. Samantha developed similar 'unadventurous' characteristics to Hashmat and Michael, but a gradual willingness of the mother to make use of the observer led to the observations containing detailed material about the thinking by mother and infant about a key emotional issue, namely belonging and separation, with consequences for the infant's resilience. This then adds to the exploration of the concept developed in the observations of Hashmat and Hester of the relationship between different 'Russian dolls' of experience. The progress Samantha made developmentally during the observation permits a close study of the development of an internalisation of a relationship which endures in the absence of the other person. This study pays careful attention to these developments especially during Samantha's second year. The result is a perhaps more intricately written study than for the other infants.

7.1 The family

Samantha's family were in transit; her father Martin worked at the embassy and when I first met them mother Anne was still in the throes of unpacking. They left Great Britain within a year of the observation finishing, for Martin's next posting in the Middle East.

When I first met Anne she greeted me with the news that her belongings had gone astray; 'it is chaos,' she said, 'the wrong things are arriving and the right things are not.' She seemed understandably very loosely connected to her circumstances, pleased to be in Britain rather than other postings they could have been given, but disappointed not to have been given time in her home town. She was very verbal, expressive, but giving the impression that there was an edge to what she was saying, an emotional content which was barely concealed to herself. In a short time at our first meeting, when she was six months pregnant with Samantha, she had told me about her home, her current circumstances, her previous moves, her family background, the parenting methods she had experienced, and the birth and difficulties she had with her first child, Donald.

Anne told me that Samantha's conception was an accident; one which defied logic, since she had only just stopped breast-feeding and was using contraception. In a defiant, make the best of it tone, she said that 'This baby just needs to be born'. After some time together Anne's torrent of words eased and she became more thoughtful, talking about planning the house for Samantha's arrival. She became disquieted by these thoughts, perhaps suggesting an overwhelming amount to think about so soon after moving, but when she said that she would welcome my presence, because she was isolated and because she 'often did not know what to do or what was best' with babies, she conveyed something more anxious, or unsure of herself as a mother. The accidental conception of Samantha was, despite her brave face, a problematic event for her. She suggested that she would not want to have time to think too often, and she said that she planned to arrange some childcare help so she could go out without the children in the afternoons. Again, the quite reasonable comment hinted at an absence of joyful anticipation of the birth.

Anne was herself 38, and her husband Martin 40. I met him too before Samantha's birth. Both were from an English-speaking country. Whilst Anne was talkative, expressive, and quite largely overweight, Martin was dark, with a sonorous deep voice, speaking slowly and distinctly. Anne attributed to him the reputation of being able to hide behind a newspaper, and he gave the impression he was not easily ruffled, in a quite formidable way. Martin expressed interest in the observation from the point of view that he had some psychotherapy when he was a student. Anne was dismissive, proclaiming a kind of Woody Allen critique of spending many years thinking about the past. 'Why spend so long going over such a short period of childhood,' was her view, 'Ugh, get on with it!' She added that perhaps she should have had counselling, she had 'been through it all', but she had 'just got on with it'. Anne said that Martin's family had not been good at expressing emotions. Hers was, but her parents divorced when she was in her teens and she did not see her father after that. She was one of eight siblings, and had a brother less than two years younger, who interestingly was also called Donald. Anne said she wanted to be different from her parents who had 'hit first and talked afterwards'. Speaking in her rapid way and passing over subjects quickly, she hinted at factors which could have contributed to a disturbed or deprived childhood.

Anne telephoned to tell me that Samantha had been born and to arrange the first observation. She told me in this conversation that Samantha had turned to breach presentation and Anne was then offered a Caesarean. She repeated that since her previous labour had been 24 hours she was not unhappy with this form of childbirth. Again I was struck by the overt acceptance of events, which also held a sense of flattening, or reducing its emotional content, with the implication that birth was too painful, and the pain lasted too long.

7.2 Quality of containment

Three distinct modes of parenting emerged during the course of observations, through the evidence of parent–infant interactions.

First, there were moments of tender interaction. Anne often referred to Samantha as a 'sweet thing', or 'sweet girl' (Graph 7.3a). She held her, and there were interactions in which Anne initiated close contact between them, smiling and gazing at her. Anne showed interest in the idea of the bond she was making with Samantha, and used the observation to talk about this. In this mode her parenting formed a concave containing shape (Graph 7.9).

These 'concave' moments appeared somewhat fleetingly in the face of a depression in which multiple preoccupations seemed to crowd Anne's mind (Graph 7.2a). In this mode, Anne's relating to Samantha was characterised by an approach to emotionality in which the more difficult and powerful emotions which Samantha expressed were treated as unwanted, and Anne did not respond to them, or she responded in a way which left the emotional experience unthought about. Alternatively she seemed to bypass the processes involved in receptive, concave containment. This mode had the effect of flattening, or muffling the emotionality in the relationship between her and Samantha and is categorisable as a flat containing shape (Graph 7.9).

Knowing without experiencing and resorting to practical solutions for emotional problems were other characteristics of this 'flat' mode of parenting. This was a shared approach between Anne and Martin (Graph 7.13). For example: 'Anne said that Samantha has been very unhappy for the last few weeks, crying a lot, and she had found out that the problem was that she did not like – and Martin interjected to complete her sentence, "Thames water"' (O14: Samantha at four months one week five days). This empiricism also contains the idea that, in a travelling life, water can never be one's own; the converse, so to speak, of Brooke's foreign field. The issue of belonging or not belonging was central to the family, and closely linked with the third mode of parenting, producing a convex container shape (Graph 7.9). Observed through Anne's undigested states of mind, such as homesickness (O4) and feeling shattered (O12), these states of mind were projected on to Samantha (and Donald). In this mode there were frequent expressions of hostility towards dependency and emotions connected with it. These feelings, it became clear, emanated from Anne's difficult early experiences, and included her low status as a 'dependent relative' in the embassy (see Miller 1993).

These patterns of relating took place within the context of the culture of the family, that is in the diplomatic community, which connected them with 'great' events. During the Gulf War Anne informed me that the war could not have started, as she had not received a phone call and Martin was inevitably called upon to work long hours during the crisis. The war did touch them personally as well as through this sense of self-importance. British friends went with the army to Kuwait, and there was relief – mingled with regret – that they were not at that time in the Middle East.

Probably more central to the events of the family was the pattern of reunion and separation. Visits from relatives and friends punctuated the two years of the observational period. Maternal and paternal grandmothers made significant visits, as did Anne's sister and some friends (Graph 7.1). The family spent one Christmas with friends in Germany. There were thus two levels of social contact; that with the embassy community and that provided by the wider circle of friends and family, who were seen less often, but whose relationships were longer term. However, all visits of friends, family and embassy contacts were thought about in the same way. That is to say that Anne anticipated the visits as both a welcome event, and one which she felt would include difficulties, both in terms of the qualities of relationship that would ensue and of her capacity to withstand the demands on her. With her sister's visit, for example, she anticipated they would be fighting within a week; her mother-in-law was described to me as a difficult person, and her mother, though more welcomed, was given a vote of no confidence as a help with the children (O2). Similarly, at the end of the visits, the parting was described as a relief, accompanied by a narrative about the mechanics of leaving – the journey to the airport, for example. Feelings about separation were not expressed, or muted. For example, when some friends left for Ghana, there was a matter-of-fact exchange of foods, and little emotional resonance about the parting (O50). Loss was difficult to take into account when moves were so frequent and when a sense of one's own belonging was so tenuous.

In this historical level of the observational period, two other events were particularly significant. First, the family's 'home leave' was a climacteric, occurring between Samantha's 14th and 16th months. This occasioned considerable anxiety in Anne, particularly about how she would be received by relatives, and how she would be viewed as a parent. Second, after this home leave, she began to work herself in the embassy, thus giving herself another dimension to her life, and improving, in her own estimation, her status. She was no longer simply a dependent relative, but rather a colleague of her husband, and an employee. Martin expressed the hope that she could spy for him through her position in the embassy!

7.3 Samantha's early development

Samantha's early development took place therefore within these patterns of relating, and within the context provided by Donald's difficulties in his relationship with his mother. Samantha was an extremely attractive newborn baby, immaculately and tastefully dressed. I first met her asleep in Anne's arms, then:

> Anne moved a little and Samantha, still asleep, moved with her so that her head was lying back, almost out of Anne's arms in a slightly unsupported way. Anne told me she felt a lot of pain after the Caesarean and this was the first day she had not thought about having a painkiller. Samantha stirred, opening her eyes slowly, quietly. She looked towards Anne's face. Anne said she was awake at last and said 'I'm just going to feed her'. She offered the right breast to Samantha and made a grimace as she took the nipple. She readjusted and Samantha lost the nipple, then took it again and sucked steadily. Anne sat cross-legged on the sofa, holding Samantha quite low down so that her face seemed to be hidden in Anne's top. (O1: Samantha at 13 days)

This sequence illustrates three themes that were prevalent in Samantha's early development. First, she was loosely held in mother's arms, and the pose they maintained, with her head not firmly supported holds the quality of a 'sculpt' of the fit between Samantha and her mother. Second, Samantha was seeking her mother with her eyes, demonstrating her wish to make contact with her, and this was taken to mean she wanted feeding. Third, in the feed, Samantha sucked steadily, making a good grip on the nipple. She was not perturbed by needing to start the feed twice. On the other hand, for Anne, the feed was preceded by her reporting pain from the childbirth and the process of making contact with Samantha was also painful, that is to say she grimaced. Finally, as the feed progressed, Anne's conversation followed a wide range of subjects all of which seemed to reflect on her lack of confidence. She then returned to the subject of breast-feeding:

> Anne said she had found she was running out of milk by the evening, and Donald had always been hungry. She said that when Donald had been a baby she had not closed the curtains of the room which led to his waking at 4 a.m. Samantha stopped sucking, holding the nipple in her mouth and Anne looked down at her and then lifted her away from the breast and held her over her shoulder. Anne looked at her again and said 'you're hungry, that's what you are'. She said she thought she would go and make a bottle for Samantha. (O1)

The thoughts of her experience with Donald eventually disturbed the feed, though Samantha continued to hold the nipple in her mouth. She again showed no sigı of the hunger mother reported, and this seemed more nearly to fit her state of mind. The anxiety Anne displayed in her conversation and in her supplementing her feed, appeared based on previous rather than current experience. Whilst mother was preoccupied with feeding, and her previous baby, Samantha was interested in relating to mother; this miscommunication between them became a feature of the first three months of Samantha's life, in which her development became increasingly characterised by sequences of interaction that suggested the emergence of defensive patterns of relating. From these first three–four months I wish to concentrate on three themes:

First, the development of an eye grip, which appeared to move through a number of stages; alertness, precocity and blankness (Graph 7.15a).

Second, feeding difficulties, where the combination of breast and bottle had the sense of a self-fulfilling prophecy of failure, and where Samantha frequently vomited feeds (Graph 7.6b).

Third, Samantha's development of methods of holding herself together, as she retreated from object relations and developed a marked defensive pattern (Graph 7.16).

In the first observation, quoted above, it was noticeable that Samantha's first gesture of relating was with the eye contact she made with mother. This continued through the first four observations, conveying a sense of alertness and willingness to make relationships. By the third observation the eye grip conveyed a sense of searching, of looking for a response from mother which was not there, and her sucking gestures show she and mother have missed each other: 'Anne laid Samantha on the sofa and Samantha lay there, her eyes searching a little, her mouth sucking and she made some slight murmuring noises' (O3: Samantha at three weeks six days).

In the next observation Samantha's eye grip is striking in its clarity of focus. At one point she focused across the room, some 15 feet or so; a quite precocious feat for an infant of under five weeks. As with the feed in the previous observation the direction of her gaze was towards me (O4: Samantha at four weeks six days). Whilst in O3 the eye grip contained a suggestion of Samantha thinking in the circumstances of the temporary absence of mother, the second showed a very active searching out, suggesting a wish to hold on to an object (other than mother). Similarly, in O2 (Samantha at two weeks six days) her eye contact, which was briefly reciprocated by mother before she went out, was accompanied by arms stretching and some small murmurs. She was the youngest infant in the sample to vocalise.

By the time she was two months, her eyes had begun to lose expression, and the blank, unfocused and uninterested appearance this gave her predominated through her third month. In O8, O9, and O10, her eyes either look away from mother or appear blank or both. In O10 (Samantha at three months and one day) she 'lay against Anne's shoulder, looking away, not really focusing', whilst in O8 (Samantha at two months two weeks) she 'looks up at Anne, quite expressionless'. A brief respite was provided by a moment in O10 when mother was less self-preoccupied:

> She sat Samantha up, supported and said to her 'yes you like that, you like looking around' and Samantha pulled a very windy face. She looked towards the other side of the room not at any thing in particular but focusing clearly… Mother said it was not easy to spend this kind of time with Samantha, as she often had '29 other things on her mind'. She continued to talk about Donald, quite anxiously, and Samantha's eyes closed. (O10)

Though mother made a space in her mind to think about what Samantha liked, it did not last long, before the other worries – particularly about Donald – closed in again. Samantha, without continuous attention for herself, switched off and turned to sleep. Mother reported her sleeping for long periods – sometimes 12 hours at night (Graph 7.14). The signs Samantha showed in these observations was of a baby trying to relate in the face of a preoccupied and depressed mother. Not only did she sleep for long periods, but she did not smile. The first smile I saw was when she was three months three weeks. The first infant to vocalise in the sample, she was most certainly the last to smile! The blank, expressionless face indicated that she was internalising the depressed, or inattentive mother, whose contact with her was usually briefly maintained (Graph 7.7).

The development of the eye grip related closely to the pattern of feeding that Anne followed. Early feeds were frequently interrupted either by the presence of Donald, or by his presence in Anne's mind. In O3, Anne was not prepared for the feed. This was the only occasion that Samantha showed a wish to be fed, rather than to relate. In O4, the feed was vomited, and this appeared to relate to the indigestibility of mother's state of mind. The feeding sequence ended with Samantha having hiccups, unheld, 'home alone' in the cradle. Vomiting had become a feature by the time Samantha was two and a half months, as Anne's comments showed: 'Anne took Samantha from Ruby (her helper/nanny) and placed her in the cradle. She said "wait for it (the milk) to come back, it will be projectile time"' (O8: Samantha at two months two weeks).

By this time Ruby was regularly feeding Samantha, and feeding her to excess; she was determined Samantha would finish her bottles:

> Ruby held Samantha behind her head and Samantha sucked. Ruby then took her hand off the bottle holding her under her legs so that the bottle was resting on the back of Samantha's clenched fist. She continued to suck. Her arm, fist clenched, was held out towards the room. Ruby said to Samantha: 'come on, you can manage it, you can finish it all'. Samantha continued to suck, but looked bloated, gazing mainly at Ruby' (O8)

Both Anne and Ruby fed with little holding of the bottle, so that from O4 onwards, she held the bottle herself. The third theme of her first three months was an increasing propensity to find ways of managing the times when she was not held or contained by mother. There were moments in the observations when she put her fingers in her mouth (O10), when she clenched her fists (O8 – see above) and when she appeared to make a grip on herself both with her hand in her mouth, and by rubbing her tummy (O10). Her hand grip on her bottle was also part of this gestalt, and appeared as precocious as her eye grip in O4. When distressed, her hands, up to the knuckle, appeared to go further into her mouth, filling the space, as it were, and making a firmer grip on herself (O11: three months three weeks). In this observation she shivered in the aftermath of vomiting, and this preceded an event where she held herself together through holding her breath. Though this happened after she was three months, the event was the culmination of the trend towards her self-holding and heralded the emergence of the main theme of her development after three months, namely a rigid grip on herself:

> (Samantha has just been sick). Anne laid Samantha in the changing tray and took off her Babygro. Samantha put both her knuckles into her mouth with a slight shiver. Anne wound up the musical horse and let it play, continued to change Samantha, put her nappy on and turned her over. Anne talked to her, calling her a sweet thing. She lifted her up and Samantha looked down at me with the same bland expression. Anne said she would lay her down in her cot. She laid her on her back, and wound up the musical toy. She then said she must go and check on Donald. She went out leaving Samantha lying on her back in the cot. Samantha looked blankly upwards and shook a little. She put her fingers towards her mouth and then held her breath. She made an exhaling noise and then held her breath, going quite rigid. She exhaled noisily again, her fingers held close to her mouth, going limp as she breathed out. She held her breath again, and went rigid and shook a little. She looked at the musical mobile going round above her head, not focusing on it, or taking it in. Anne returned and said the mobile did not seem to be working any more. (O12: Samantha at four months less two days)

These gestures, or series of gestures, had the impact of holding herself together through her breathing and of sending – or expelling – anxiety into me. Mother's departure, following the vomiting and the nappy change which Samantha clearly experienced as a loss of a protective 'skin' (Bick 1968) provoked this rigid, repeated breath-holding sequence, with the suggestion that the underlying issue was one of life and death. As a summary of the trends of Samantha's early development, it raised the prospect of her facing an increasing struggle to maintain object relationships. The fact that mother remained unaware of her breath-holding 'spasm' suggested that Samantha had to some extent already ceased to believe that mother was someone who could embrace her projections of the extremes of her emotional experiences. The implication, in that I was aware of this event, was that I was being invited to act as the recipient for these states of mind.

It was quite clear that Samantha used this withdrawal from her relationship with her mother as a means of defending herself, rather than, say, becoming more vigorous in her protestations to her mother. The pair, mother and daughter, were fitting into a pattern where mother offered little containment of extremes, and Samantha did not put up a fight to put these more on the map. It is true that she was reported to cry on occasions between observations, but the trend appeared to be towards switching off from emotionality rather than maintaining an emotional engagement. The object – mother and breast – was relinquished quite easily, rather than being fought for, and the question raised for her future development was whether a low intensity of relationship in which deep emotionality was being sacrificed, was being chosen as a mutual fit between them (Graph 7.7, 7.8). That this in itself 'fit' with the 'diplomatic culture' of measured response indicated a blueprint for future development had been established. Here was entry into a world without passion, with the membership fee paid in a currency of avoiding anxieties which could not be integrated. Samantha appeared to take this course through her propensity to be open to mother's projections. That is to say that when mother's containment was of a convex shape, the emotional content of these projections from mother found a 'home' in Samantha. She appeared therefore to be a sensitive infant, who was porous, rather than impervious to the emotional events around her.

7.4 Development from 3 to 12 months

When Samantha was between three and 12 months, moments when mother began to enter thinking about emotional issues for Samantha appeared more readily. She reflected on how little 'she liked her self' during Samantha's first three months (Graph 7.2a, 7.2b).

For Samantha, the emergence of her propensity to hold on tightly, or rigidly, became increasingly evident. The way in which she held her body rigid through holding her breath has been described above (O12). In O14 she was tense when Anne picked her out of the high chair: 'Anne stopped feeding her and picked her up, laying her over her shoulder. Samantha seemed to become tense in the face, as if thinking about defecating and Anne said she would go and change her' (O14: Samantha at four months one week five days). Her grip on her bottle as she fed herself became firmer. In O18:

> Samantha picked up her bottle and tried to drink from it. Anne said, 'see, she is trying to feed herself' and Samantha lifted the bottle to her mouth but could not drink from it. Anne laid her back on the sofa, holding the bottle at arm's length, while Samantha sucked and held the bottle with one hand. With her other hand she scratched her head. Her face was turned towards Anne, who said she was being lazy. She

> lifted Samantha and put her on the floor, gave her the bottle to hold and she sucked from it, holding it between both hands. (O18: Samantha at six months two weeks)

Mother's avoidance of the intimate contact of feeding was met by a willingness on Samantha's part to try to feed herself. By eight months she fed herself alone, sadly, firmly holding on to the bottle:

> Anne tried to get Samantha's hands to hold the bottle and she gripped it firmly. Samantha's eyes looked towards Anne, but focused on the ceiling. She rolled her eyes a little as Anne moved. She sucked steadily, and rhythmically with a sound of air and milk together. Anne spoke about Donald. It was very sleepy in the room and Anne yawned. Samantha stopped feeding and pushed the bottle out of her mouth, looking at me sadly, and she let the bottle fall to the floor. (O23: Samantha at eight months less three days)

As well as holding the bottle herself, Samantha had to be a receptacle for mother's feelings about Donald. The depression appeared shared between them both, Anne and Samantha, with Samantha's look towards me being poignantly sad. The bottle seemed to be dropped, or discarded in the face of these feelings. She was still expected to deal with her distress alone, to 'work some of that out for herself', and mother reported to me that she cried a lot, and that she was unhappy (see O32 below). Nevertheless the crying and the firm grip on the bottle appeared to represent an increase in the vigour of Samantha's hold on emotionality (Graph 7.15). In the above extract she seems to be very much in touch with mother's feelings, and at other times she – literally – held on to mother in the moments Anne was available to her. Both these features – an apparent awareness of mother's feelings and conversation, and her holding on to mother – are seen in O25:

> Samantha looked at Anne, her fingers in her mouth. Anne, sweeping up, said that Samantha had started to give up the bottle, and that she liked juice. Samantha said 'mama' and then cried. Anne picked her up and carried her round the room and Samantha held on to her with a firm grip on her shirt (O25: Samantha at eight months two weeks two days)

This grasp of mother expressed possessiveness:

> Anne sat Samantha on her lap and Samantha looked at me – with more warmth – whilst holding the bottle and drinking from it. Anne talked to her and Samantha smiled and put her hand firmly on Anne's breast. She smiled quite broadly as she sat on Anne's lap, her hand on her breast (O27: Samantha at nine months less one day)

Meanwhile, Samantha showed an increasing propensity to smile. In O14: 'Samantha lay on her back looking at the mobile. Anne spoke to her and smiled, and Samantha broke into a big smile' (O14 Samantha at four months one week five days).

At seven months her smile was followed by loss of large motor control: 'Samantha, lying in her cot, lifted her head suddenly, looked at me, and then turned her head further until she could see Anne. She smiled and seemed to lose control of her head, which fell back on to the mattress' (O21: Samantha at seven months six days). She was somewhat slow to reach developmental milestones, rolling over at five months, and sitting at six and a half months. She stood unaided for the first time 11 days after her first birthday (Table 7.1; Graph 7.14). Here (O21, above) the effect was to demonstrate that she smiled at a cost to muscular control, and this gave a meaning to the relationship between her increasingly firm grip on objects, and her equally increasing readiness to smile, namely that smiling, which occasions a 'letting go' of control over (depressed) emotions, required a firm grip on another as a precondition to achieving this degree of letting go. With a degree of grip on her bottle, and on her self, through her muscularity, together with moments when Anne was more available, Samantha went on to differentiate her attitude to mother, from that shown towards others. In the next observation (O22) a smile for mother was given alongside a scowl for me and crying for Ruby: 'Samantha was in Ruby's arms, crying. When she saw Anne she stopped crying and a smile lit her face. Anne took her in her arms and she looked at Anne for some time, then at me, her face expressing displeasure' (O22: Samantha at seven months two weeks).

In this phase of the observation I was frequently the subject of this differential treatment. Samantha greeted me with a slightly persecuted look (O27, O30) indicating that my function was to hold these unpleasant feelings in the service of furthering her pleasurable contact with mother. In the above extract (O22), Samantha's crying appeared to have been brought about by separation from Anne as she came to the door when I arrived, indicating that her aim was to split her feelings for mother and others, at the point of separation from mother. In this way Samantha furthered her relationship with mother, enabling her to enjoy pleasurable contact with her. At this point Anne reflected in a 'depressive' state of mind:

> We went into the living room and Anne sat by the window with Samantha on her lap. She said how the trees were about to lose their leaves and you could look into each other's houses; the trees made a shield; she had seen this before last year. She looked at Samantha and said 'you were not here then.' (O26: Samantha at eight months three weeks)

By eight months, they were both free enough in their relationship to play together: 'Anne sat Samantha at the breakfast bar, lifted her hands above her head and said "so big", smiling at her. Samantha smiled back and clapped her hands a couple of times' (O23: Samantha at eight months less three days). Thus

Samantha appeared to enjoy a much firmer grip on her mother, firmly holding on and more firmly held. She began to develop some sounds and words (Graph 7.19), saying 'mama' at eight months two weeks two days (O25, above), and 'dada' (O28: Samantha at nine months one week). She said 'dada, ga, ga, gaga' (O29: Samatha at nine months two weeks one day) when she was playing with a 'Sesame Street' transparent wheel, an evocative toy, which was seen earlier (O28), and this marked the emergence of play in which Samantha showed an interest in objects where there was an inside space (Graph 7.19). In (O29) she was interested in the washing machine:

> Samantha moved her baby walker to the washing machine. She leaned over the side of the walker and put both hands on the door; she looked intently inside and chattered: 'dada, gaga, gaga, dada' and moved her hands round the door, looking into the glass. Still looking intently, she let go, moved away a little, looked down at her hands and then back to the door of the drier. (O29: Samantha at nine months two weeks one day)

Samantha's attachment to the wheel, the intentness of her play here with the washing machine and the repetition of similar words/sounds suggest the play was informed for her by a similar unconscious phantasy. In the next observation she played with cupboard doors, again showing an interest in the insides, and it seemed apparent that she was thinking about the properties of objects that have an inside and outside, and where the inside can be viewed. That is to say that her thinking was three-dimensional and that she had a curiosity about the inside space, which she experienced as possibly revealed to her. There was a correlation between Samantha's porousness, in touch with mother's state of mind, and Anne's identification with a bare or transparent self (see O26, above). The development of Samantha's phantasy life, through play, continued alongside her increased hold on her mother, and her capacity through splitting and her grip on her self to make the most of the containing experiences that Anne was able to offer.

By 11 months these themes occurred in close proximity to each other. In the following sequence mother's leaving Samantha to cry alone, her rigid grip on the high chair and a firm grip on mother were juxtaposed:

> Samantha started to make some screech-like noises. Anne said that she had been crying a lot lately and not sleeping. She had woken several times during the night, including 5 a.m. when Anne had let her cry for 20 minutes and then she went back to sleep. Last Sunday she had screamed and there had been nothing Anne could do and she left her, and eventually she stopped screaming and started playing. Ruby played with Samantha's feet and talked to her, and she was unresponsive. Anne came to lift Samantha out of the high chair and Samantha screamed and held on. She then let go and let Anne lift her out. She put Samantha

> on the floor and sat down herself, and then lifted Samantha on to her lap. She leaned forwards and put her head down between Anne's breasts, holding on to her with both hands. (O32: Samantha at 11 months less six days)

Samantha's contact with mother was followed by some exploratory play, perhaps provoked by Donald taking her place on mother's lap:

> Samantha looked at them (Donald on Anne's lap) and turned away. She found a small toy, a piece of Lego, and looked at it. She put it down and leaned her hand very tentatively to a small basket with bibs in. She pulled the string of one of the bibs – gently – and then let it go. She looked at Donald and Anne and leaned over looking at the basket, reached out her hand more definitely and pulled the string and the basket fell off. She put her hand over the basket and then let go. She got herself into a crawling position and then could not move forwards or backwards, and swam on the slippery surface of the floor, going backwards until her feet touched the kitchen cabinets. Anne, watching, said they ought to have her on a different floor where she would not slip. (O32)

In Samantha's play an object dropped and then she had a loose grip on the floor. Her rigid grip on the high chair and her firm grip on mother, briefly, were in contrast to this loose grip. In the observations of this period, anxiety about falling regularly appeared:

> Anne laid Samantha on her changing mat. She reached out and grasped a toy with her hand and then rolled on to her side. At the point where she may have rolled off the changing mat and on to her back she tensed and a touch of fear appeared in her face. Anne said 'it's all right, you weren't going to fall, you can roll over' (O25: Samantha at eight months two weeks two days)

Mother sensed Samantha's fear of falling, or going too far, beyond the limits into extremes that, uncontained, held anxiety. This phantasy of falling, as though falling from mother's mind through entering an area for which mother offered flat containment, was followed by Samantha actually falling, when being noisy and uncharacteristically adventurous physically:

> Samantha started to shriek – very controlled and in the back of her throat, looking at Ruby as she did so, and then she ended her shriek with a tuneful 'baa, baa, ga, dada' and Anne said 'He's not here, he's never here, he said we'd have these babies together'. The phone rang and Anne answered it. Samantha, standing on the floor and leaning against a chest reached and touched the key of the chest and suddenly fell backwards. Ruby and I stood to go to her, and Anne moved too,

> saying 'the baby's fallen, got to go!' (O30: Samantha at nine months three weeks)

This was the last but one observation before a break for Christmas, and father's absence, which Samantha invoked and Anne 'flattened' (Graph 7.13), was possibly linked with my impending absence over the break. Anne confirmed this by later inviting me to call in over Christmas (O30). Samantha meanwhile demonstrated sequentially the persecutory part of her inner world, as suggested by the shrieks, and the subsequent fall in the face of mother withdrawing her attention to the telephone conversation (Graph 7.20). Samantha's noisy shrieks accompanied observations through this period. In O32 she strongly resisted leaving the high chair and equally firmly made a grip on mother. In O33 she shrieked and cried when her nappy was changed. Anne said she would put her in her high chair 'if she could do this without Samantha screaming at her'. Then she again held on to the arms of the high chair:

> Samantha cried and Anne said 'did I wipe your face too roughly?' She tried to pick Samantha out of the high chair but Samantha cried and held tightly to the arms of the chair. Anne persisted, and eventually Samantha came away from the chair, and settled in Anne's arms, and stopped crying. (O33: Samantha at 11 months one day)

That Samantha stopped crying when in mother's arms indicates that it was not the movement towards being with mother that led to her resistance to leaving the high chair. There was considerable evidence to support the notion that being with mother was experienced by Samantha as a pleasant and desirable state of affairs. The repeated reluctance to leave the high chair must be seen rather as Samantha's need to maintain a firm grip on herself, a grip which was threatened by change, such as moving from one place to another, and having a nappy changed. The high chair, and the nappy, provided an external structure offering support, in place of the internal structure provided by experiences of concave container shape. Anne's parenting was working towards increased independence of her infant, and Samantha had been weaned from the breast. The bottle was also viewed by Anne as increasingly undesirable.

It was change itself to which Samantha objected, change which meant letting go of the external structure and which meant a momentary journey into the unknown of not being held, at the extreme of the emotional range, initiating anxieties about falling. As with her smile (O21, above), letting go meant losing the structure which provided the antidote to her limited internalisation of mother, and seemingly absent father.

At 12 months, Samantha's development, though complex, revolved around this particularly striking constellation, and the explicitly rigid grip that had emerged during this stage of her development. The outlook suggested by these features was limited development, limited adventurousness and development towards independent mobility which, though not markedly backward, was restricted. On the other hand, the repertoire of grip relations and the internalisations implied by these observations provided Samantha with the capacity to maintain an area of good relationship with mother, and the capacity to think and verbalise through her depressed state of mind (Graph 7.18). It was significant how much Samantha had maintained an interest in, and capacity to persist with object relations (Graph 7.16). She was by 12 months a much more vigorously protesting baby. Her persecuted shriek was a dominant and intensely attention-achieving cry. Her good moments with mother were characterised by tenderness and by mutual 'in touchness' with the emotional state of the other (Graph 7.7). She was by 12 months less switched off from relationships than at three months, and markedly more in contact with others than her, by then, three-year-old brother, Donald.

7.5 Development from 12 to 24 months

There was a caesura in the observation between Samantha's 14th and 16 months, when the family took home leave. Between 12 and 14 months there was a very difficult period when Anne, anxious about the return to her family, appeared very worried about the prospect of criticism of herself as a mother. For Samantha this period saw a heightening of the defensive aspects of her personality that were evident before her first birthday. Anne's worry about her possible reception at home led to her devoting energy to preparing her children for the event. Her main aim was that they should reach key milestones, and in particular, Donald was expected to be weaned from the bottle and toilet trained, a task which Anne approached in a quite forceful way. Donald was painfully depressed, limp and withdrawn. Samantha also became more difficult for Anne to manage, her rigid grip being prominent, and Anne told me she was so resistant to nappy changes that it 'usually took two of them to manage to change her nappy' (O40: Samantha at one year 19 days). In this observation the forcefulness of Anne's approach, and the rigid resistance of Samantha were to the fore: 'Anne wiped her face and hair with a flannel, and Samantha's head jerked back, her eyes closing. Anne tried to lift Samantha from the high chair but Samantha called out protesting. Anne had to lift her definitely, almost forcibly before Samantha would let her arms free of the chair' (O40).

After the home leave, however, mother was more relaxed and the period from 16 months to two years was concerned with Samantha's increasing capacity to be interested in developing object relations and to maintain these at increased levels of intensity. That is to say that she became more passionate, or vibrant, as the year progressed. Second, she became adept verbally, and the quantity and quality of her language appeared to be very much in the service of addressing her emotional preoccupations. Alongside this language development grew a capacity to play, to phantasise and to form symbols. My role as observer became an important one in this respect, both because Samantha developed a closer relationship with me and because the relationship was directed towards addressing a particular emotional issue, namely, absence and separation. Anne too took a greater interest in my relationship with Samantha and encouraged it. She became more able to hold Samantha in her mind and to persist in staying with her emotional needs for longer periods of time. The 'loosely held' quality of their relationship remained in evidence and Samantha's pathway through her second year had as its primary theme the conflict between having a firm grip on relationships and being loosely held, a theme which began to focus clearly both on the physical attributes of her character, and on her mental capacities, particularly her capacity to concentrate and think versus a tendency to become aimless and lose concentration. In following her development through the second year I shall focus on these themes.

When I arrived for the observation when Samantha was one year and 19 days (O40) she greeted me, for the first time, with a smile: 'Samantha was in the high chair. On seeing me, she flapped her hands on the side of the chair, smiled and bounced up and down with excitement' (O40). This was a significant contrast with the previous blank, expressionless or slightly hostile looks she had given me on greeting. When I ended the observation, however, she surveyed me with a blank expression. This pattern, of greeting me with a smile and looking blankly on leaving, was repeated through the observations until the home leave (i.e. O40–45). The repetitiveness suggests that Samantha was using my coming and going to express her thinking about separation and recognition (Graphs 7.17, 7.18). By O42 (Samantha at 13 months 15 days) she greeted me with clear recognition. Her facility for recalling, and recalling with affection seemed very much in place in her internal repertoire. In contrast, separating continued to be a 'no-go' area, unmetabolised, and beyond the range of her contained experiences.

At this point (O40) Samantha's experiences in observations were consistent with the picture described in the previous section, describing her development up to her first birthday. Her rigid grip and her expression of persecution at every change were evident. Additionally, her attitude to food appeared contemptuous, negativistic or rebellious. Where previously she verbalised as she ate (O33), now she squeezed, threw and spat out the food:

> Samantha squeezed the toast in her hand and rubbed it on the high chair. Anne said 'that's it, eat it like that!'... She drank a little juice from the beaker, and then tipped the juice upside down on her tray... She squeezed the toast and ran it threw her fingers, picked up a bit and spat it out, picked up another piece and held it in her mouth for a long time before swallowing it. (O40: Samantha at one year 19 days)

Her distribution of the food and drink, and her very rigid grip on the high chair combined to form a picture of her at this point in time either relinquishing or attacking her dependency on her mother. Instead there was a pseudo-independence (Bick 1968) and perceiving her survival depending, not on mother but on her own capacity to contain herself (Symington 1985). Later in the same observation she fell, and twice banged her head, and then wriggled away from mother's grasp. The smiles were now for others, not mother. She then engaged in a monotonously repetitive piece of play, driving a pedal car backwards and forwards for nearly 20 minutes:

> She went backwards and forwards in the car, trying, it seemed, to get into one of the corners of the patio, failing, and then persisting, but giving the impression that she did not expect to get into the corner, nor did she attempt to change the direction of the car, except by this regular backwards and forwards movement of it. (O40)

This game then conveyed stuckness, and her incapacity to think about the problem of the car's direction. Something similar was conveyed by her blankness at the end of the observation. The act of separating was a crucial variable for Samantha and when mother helped her think about a separation she made verbal progress:

> Samantha held on to the chair which fell over and she fell with it, landing on all fours, softly. She did not complain but crawled back to Anne who lifted her on to her lap. Samantha clapped Anne's hands together and smiled. Anne said 'bye' and Samantha waved to me (O42: Samantha at 13 months 15 days)

It is also noteworthy that Samantha's response to the word 'bye' followed a fall and that it was made in connection with me. Following the home leave and the break in observations caused by this family event, it was possible to chart Samantha's progress from making a pleasurable greeting but a blank parting, to her way of registering a farewell, and then to indications that she was thinking about someone in their absence. The regularity of the observational visits provided the possibility for this to be demonstrated through Samantha's relationship with me.

Samantha was willing to spend time meeting me again in the first observation after the home leave:

> Ruby answered the door to me and Samantha stood in the hallway. She was quite motionless staring straight at me. She held my gaze for a long time and I stopped, looked, smiled and talked to her. Ruby bustled around trying to hurry us into the kitchen but Samantha ignored her and continued to stand and look at me. Eventually Ruby took her hand and led her into the dining room, and Samantha walked with her but turned her head and looked over her shoulder at me, gazing at me steadily. Ruby let her hand go and Samantha took a few steps towards me, still looking at me, then she seemed to relax, floppily sat down and looked away. (O46: Samantha at 16 months five days)

Samantha's concentration on me constituted a definite if low-key reunion, in which she appears to be taking time to place my appearance in her memory. The effort of continually taking me in leaves her floppy. At the end of the observation she said 'bye': 'Anne carried Samantha to the door. Anne said "bye" and Samantha repeated it, looking at me, and then quietly said "bye" again' (O46). In the next observation there was direct recognition with pleasure: 'Anne came to the door with Samantha in her arms. She looked at me and smiled, engaging me with her eyes. Anne put her on the floor and she stood still, looking towards me' (O47: Samantha at 16 months 12 days). She went to sleep before the end of the observation and carefully marked the parting: 'Anne picked her up, still holding her bottle and Samantha opened her eyes and looked at me. She waved and said "bye" quietly, looked at me and again said "bye"' (O47).

The relationship between us continued to gather substance and intensity. At 17 months the smile she gave was a warm one: 'Samantha was coming backwards down the stairs. She stopped, saw me and smiled warmly at me' (O49: Samantha at 17 months seven days). She then sat on my lap: 'Samantha came up to me and put her arms out to sit on my lap. I lifted her up and she sat there quite still and snuggly for a time' (O49), and then she took my hand:

> Anne said to Samantha, 'look who's here' and Samantha sat on the steps and looked at me pleasantly, a bit coyly. Anne said she told Samantha a few minutes ago I would soon be here. Samantha stood up, held out her hand and I took it, and we walked into the kitchen hand in hand. Anne said she was pleased the strides Samantha was making in her friendship with me. (O50: Samantha at 17 months 11 days)

Anne was instrumental in this sequence, both anticipating my arrival and conveying her interest in Samantha making a 'friendship' with me. Thinking in absence was occurring between mother and daughter. The link Samantha made with me, concretely expressed in her hand holding, was followed by her finding ways of using me in her interactions. First, she played give and take with her food:

> Samantha reached for a can. Anne said it was probably empty, and Samantha put it to her mouth. She passed it to me and I put it to my mouth and then passed it back to her. She repeated and we both pretended to drink from the can in turn. Samantha then repeated 'give and take' with a red drinking beaker and then she sucked from a bottle which Anne had passed her. She paused for a moment, considering and passed me the bottle. I pretended to drink from it and passed it back. She took more and passed the bottle to me. Again I pretended to drink from it and passed it back. Anne asked Samantha if she wanted a biscuit. She passed one to Samantha, who took a bite and passed the biscuit to me. I pretended to take a bite and passed it back to her (O50)

Samantha's capacity to share, to let go and take back both feeding objects and food, including her bottle, showed a contrast with the rigid grip she maintained on her high chair, for example. Later in the same observation she gave me clear instructions: 'Samantha watched the washing going round in the washing machine. She turned, saw me, fetched a low stool and said "sit down". Anne said, "she is very imperative, she wants you to sit down"' (O50). Her firmness, and the wish to place me firmly next to her expresses her central emotional issue, namely, of having or taking a firm grip, and she has now prepared to have this contained in her relationship with me. There then followed sequences of imaginative play in my presence which dominated the last six months of the observations. She has also prepared the way, alongside mother, for holding on to and letting go of objects, and for thinking about me in my absence. Most humorously, Anne reported the following event: 'Anne said they had gone to McDonalds and Samantha had seen someone who looked a little like me. She had called out loudly "Hi Steve"' (O66: Samantha at 22 months less three days)

Perhaps saying that Samantha had 'prepared' this pattern in her relationship with me attributes too much motivation to her. Nevertheless there was a clear progression towards the emerging centrality of her relationship with me, which seemed, at the time and on rereading, very definitely achieved. Mother too was quick to grasp the opportunity so that her encouragement of Samantha's relationship with me had a purposeful feel. Particularly this was so in O50 above where Samantha was prepared for my arrival. Mother's preparation was in contrast with the early months where it seemed the observation took her by surprise, suggesting Samantha came into her mind with my arrival. There had thus been a reordering of the dynamics of the observation. Just as Samantha began to play in my presence, so mother found more time to be with and think about Samantha, and to play with her.

The content of Samantha's play fell into three categories; play where the insides of objects was the source of enquiry, and for a time this play concentrated specifically and clearly on representations of birth; play in which there was an element of falling, dropping, losing or where there was an anxiety about separation; play which was about separating and/or joining up. Samantha's play usually took place in connection with her relationship with either mother or myself and was often accompanied by an interaction with one or both of us which provided a context for thinking about the meaning of her play. Additionally, Samantha's development of language followed a course in which the words she used, and later phrases, were connected with emotional themes. These themes were similar to and linked with her play; namely, addressing issues of separation and absence, and, by continuation, lost, dropped or missing things and people; words which expressed possessiveness and words about feelings.

Samantha showed her first preoccupation with the insides of objects when she was nine months (see O28, O29 above). Her second period of play revolving around this theme was between 17 and 19 months. Mother Anne was explicit that at this time she was thinking of having another baby: 'Samantha lifted the seat of the pedal car and put her juice beaker inside. She closed the seat, opened it again and looked inside. Anne said this is the age when you think about having another baby, they are so delightful' (O49: Samantha at 17 months eight days). Samantha's play illustrated mother's wish, the inside of the car and the juice bottle representing, probably, a pregnant mother. Anne's thoughts about pregnancy were contemporary with her being more involved at work. She told me '...about the house she lived in as a child, all eight of them, and how tired she was after work, and that her work was very demanding...' (O51: Samantha at 18 months one day); and then: 'Anne continued to recount what had happened at work and Samantha and Donald had opened a cupboard and taken out some silverware. They looked up furtively when Anne noticed them' (O51). Here mother's conversation, recounting childhood with a sense of an overcrowded house, and her current demanding occupation, was followed by a raid on the insides of the cupboard, by both children engaging in a shared phantasy involving the removal of precious (silver) objects from the container (cupboard/mother). Mother was 'pregnant' with her work and her childhood memories. Thus both the literal and abstract sense of pregnancy appeared to invoke play with insides.

Samantha's play took a more concrete form after this. In O54 (Samantha at 19 months less three days) she simulated giving birth, or having sex, with one of her cuddlies, which mother called 'babies': 'Samantha reached over and took a cuddly. She held it, cuddling it, then she pushed it down her body until it was between her legs. She held it there for a time and then pushed it out and away from her' (O54). She then elaborated a series of games, beginning with a sequence in which the meaning was immediately clear:

> Samantha picked up a see-through ball. She brought it towards me and bent her head, looking into it. She carried it towards Anne, and put it up her pinafore dress. Anne said what have you got up your dress? and Samantha let it fall to the floor, standing back with arms outstretched. (O55: Samantha at 19 months four days)

The ball appeared to represent a baby to which Samantha had given birth. Letting the 'baby' fall suggested a dropped baby, and this theme of dropping appeared throughout this observation: 'Samantha took the apple from Anne, walked round the room and then deliberately dropped it. She picked it up, came over to the table, talking to me softly, saying "apple", then she tried to climb on to a chair and fell, woodenly, on to her bottom, crying out briefly' (O55).

The link between the apple, the ball and Samantha herself falling – or dropping – suggested the dropped baby was herself. Meanwhile, she continued to be preoccupied with birth, and:

> Samantha sat on Donald, who was lying on the floor. He wriggled round so she was lying on his back. Samantha moved forwards, lifting

> her dress, still undone so that Donald's head was between her legs. He wriggled forwards and she moved back so his head emerged and she was sitting on his back again. (O55)

Both birth and sexuality were again suggested by this sequence; Samantha was in all events the 'mother'. She created recognisable, if ambivalent symbols with the ball, apple, and Donald, and demonstrated her projective identification with mother, getting, as it were into her shoes (or bed). Earlier, she had literally tried mother's shoes:

> Samantha pulled out some shoes and put a pair in front of me; a pair that looked like Anne's. She then passed me a pair of Donald's, saying 'Donald'. She selected a pair which was clearly Anne's and put one foot into one of these shoes, looking quite serious, concentrating. She stopped, took her foot out, and ran down the corridor. She ran back with a packet of baby wipes, calling out, 'mummy'. (O50: Samantha at 17 months 13 days)

She seemed to run away from the prospect of being mummy – her projective identification interrupted, as it were – and returned to the role of baby. In her play with insides she maintained the play longer, but by O59 (Samantha at 20 months nine days) she reverted to a wish to be an inside baby: 'Samantha held mother with a hand on each leg and looked at me, speaking incoherently. She put her head between Anne's legs, pushing her backwards. Anne said "you can't go back there. You can't return home"' (O59). Anne certainly took the meaning of this very concrete gesture, which Samantha repeated later in the same observation.

In this theme of play about insides/pregnancy/sexuality Samantha moved between different modes of mental functioning. The last example is of what Segal termed 'symbol equation' (Segal 1957; Klein 1930). The unconscious phantasy behind her play was enacted directly, without representation. On the other hand her play at giving birth was very near to true symbolism, and appeared quite consciously enacted. Samantha continued to move between these modes of mental functioning; from concrete, symbol equation, towards symbol formation whilst her language – significantly – was attached to the latter, but not the former. Samantha, by 21 months, had both a verbal part of herself and a part which was still 'unintelligible' to her, a baby part which was loosely held, and which contained phantasies of being an 'inside baby'. Words were not used in play when she appeared to be enacting herself as a baby, that is to say when her preoccupations were infantile. Alternatively, if she did speak, she was unintelligible. On the other hand, as she extended her interest from insides to every dimension of space, she became increasingly verbal. Anne told me: 'Everything is upstairs, downstairs; inside, outside' (O67: Samantha at 22 months 19 days), and Samantha herself said: '"Donald up," and pointed upwards. Anne said Donald was up now. Samantha said, "Daddy gone" and I said "daddy's gone to work"' (O67).

She continued with the theme: Ruby was out (O69); Donald 'up' (O68); Donald up again, repeated (O69). It was a remarkable feature of Samantha's language development that all her words were formed in connection with emotionally important issues. Even the phrase 'Hi Steve' with which she greeted me was connected with the fact of recognition, and reunion. Similarly, she said 'mummy' when there was a threat of separation, and she communicated her word, to me with anxiety. 'Samantha played with the ball, and some bricks. She was absorbed and then Anne left the room. After a moment Samantha looked at me, said "mummy", anxiously, and followed her out' (O51: Samantha at 18 months one day). Later she added the interrogative 'where?': 'She came over to me and said "mummy where?" in a small voice. I told her mummy was downstairs and would be coming up soon, and she said "mummy?" again in an anxious little voice' (O62: Samantha at 21 months less one day). My function, as the addressee of these anxious questions about mummy, was to hold her worry she was beginning to voice. Words, as we have seen, were used in conjunction with the extension of this theme, locating people in place, and in expressing something about objects which were dropped, lost or broken.

Samantha used words to imply ownership and possessiveness, describing a whole number of objects with the prefix 'my'; for example, 'my Minnie [Mouse]', 'my nappy', 'my Thomas [the Tank Engine]', etc. (O62–O68). In this same period, and belonging to the same category, the word 'no' appeared. Finally, her language development began to include words expressing feelings, and these were addressed to me about Donald: 'Donald, crying, went downstairs. Samantha turned to me and said "Donald's crying". She seemed worried and said it again. She turned to Anne and said "Donald's crying"' (O68: Samantha at 23 months less six days).

The worry, and the description of Donald crying, suggested some worry about her troubled brother. She often told me he was 'up' or 'gone', the latter when he was at play school.

Samantha's emotionally central issue of making a firm grip on another, versus being loosely held, or about to fall, had a continuous presence through the observations. In her interactions between 19 and 23 months she displayed her preoccupation with this issue. In O42, at the same time as she acknowledged the word 'bye' she climbed the stairs, looking down the stairwell. Anne said she always did this and attributed to her not being afraid of heights. She also reported that Samantha dropped toy bricks down the stairwell. In O55 (above) we saw her drop an apple repeatedly and fall over. She also fell repeatedly in a way which suggested an involuntary action, engendering anxiety and suggesting the transposition of the emotional issue 'falling' to a physical, or literal level. The issue held potential risk, suggested by the anxiety which it produced in others, though it was not as severe as in other infants, particularly Hashmat and

Michael. Her movements were generally quite stiff, perhaps ungainly and occasionally 'wooden' (O55). She was not entirely uncoordinated, but rarely graceful. This combination of loose grip, ungainly action and the suggestion of a risk of falling were seen in her play on her rocking horse:

> Samantha said 'horsy' and walked to her rocking horse. She looked at me as she pulled it into the centre of the room. She tried to climb on to it, could not manage and I lifted her up. She rode it vigorously, looking at me and smiling, then she nearly fell off and just caught herself as I reached out to catch her as well. I suggested she went more slowly and held on firmly, and she sat more securely on the horse, then made it go faster and again became more loosely seated on it. She looked around, looked away, and rocked the horse, then she tried to get off and slithered to the ground, lifting her leg awkwardly round the spring of the rocking horse. She wanted to get back up, and managed to climb on herself. She rocked for a time and got down again, awkwardly lowering herself, but holding on to the horse without falling. (O62: Samantha at 21 months less one day)

The loose grip, which she appears here to have internalised as a physical property, evoked falling, but though this was evoked she held on. Loose grip was also expressed in terms of her mental attention. For example, she would at times wander aimlessly, as if unable to think clearly: 'I went upstairs and met Samantha who was alone and wandering around at the top of the stairs, fairly aimlessly. She saw me, and in an absent way said "Hi Steve". Then she focused and came towards me' (O65: Samantha at 22 months less ten days). By O68 she had more control over the issue and could evoke anxiety in others more consciously, and in return take in injunctions to hold tight:

> Samantha rocked on her horse, looking at me with a very alive excited expression until she seemed in danger of falling off. Anne and I both said 'steady' and 'not so fast' to her. She stopped and then started again, rocking with a wide smile and again making the horse go fast, but holding on tightly. (O68)

Conscious control was also the motive behind her play with a pop-up toy: 'Samantha passed me a pop-up toy, and she pressed the button making the head appear, taking both of us by surprise. Samantha then tried to press the button with her hand on the head, so that it appeared slowly rather than quickly. She repeated several times' (O59: Samantha at 21 months nine days). Thus Samantha's development in this phase (O59–O68) showed a trend towards conscious control of her anxiety about falling, beginning with play which symbolised the uncontrolled appearing or dropping object, which was emerging from a container. In sequences she moved between a firm grip on an object, a loose grip and falling. Increasingly during this period I was used as the object on which she had a firm grip. In O54 (Samantha at 19 months less one week), she took a firm grip on my hand whilst Anne expressed anxiety about the way she walked upstairs, and in O56 (Samantha at 19 months 16 days) she held on firmly to my hand, not wishing to relinquish it, to the extent that it became hard to close the door! Then: 'Samantha held on firmly to my hand and we reached the foot of the stairs. I helped her take off her coat, and she bumped into my feet twice before bumping her head against the banisters, as though she was being blown about' (O56). My hand appeared to have the same function as the arms of the high chair had earlier, and her immediate loss of grip followed. Later, Samantha transferred her grip on me to others, notably, on one occasion, with father:

> Anne suggested Martin took Samantha outside. He put her coat on, opened the door and she gripped my finger in her hand, gripping firmly and she walked through the door, holding my hand over her shoulder. Martin joined us and we walked to the end of the street, where Samantha let go of my finger and held Martin's hand. (O63: Samantha at 21 months six days)

Samantha's relationship with me was closely linked with that of a father, and in the above observation she linked us both. I mean that in the observation my role was to have a paternal function (Meltzer and Harris 1984). This contained both the function of holding her firmly, protecting her and being a sexual father. She showed in her play a concept of a phallic father, and a propensity to flirt: 'Samantha passed me a brick and I passed it back to her. She made a tower, after selecting some bricks of the same shape. She looked at me as she finished and said "daddy"' (O62). Then her Oedipal development was vividly seen:

> Anne spoke on the phone to a friend, talking about the friend's new baby. Samantha stood up and started to take off her dress. She took the dress off and started to remove her shirt, standing in front of me and indicating I should help her. She took her shirt off and started to take the vest over her head. (O62)

This 'dance of the seven veils' was distinctly seductive in her tone, posing me also with something of an ultimatum! Though these were the most explicit references to a sexual phantasy about me/daddy, in other observations she showed some excitement, particularly when riding her rocking horse, which indicated also something of a sexual nature. The increase in her vigour and passion was very evident.

As she approached her second birthday, Samantha showed the capacity to manage difficult situations with greater facility, demonstrating a connectedness between the earlier levels of grip, words and her capacity to think. For example, when 22 months 19 days:

> Samantha went into the bathroom where Anne took off her clothes for her to have a bath. She cried as her nappy came off, saying 'my nappy'

> and pointed at it as Anne put it in the bin. Anne put Samantha in the bath and she grimaced and said 'hot, too hot'. Anne told her I was here, and she looked at me briefly. Anne poured water over her head and Samantha looked panic-stricken, gripping the side of the bath and raising herself out of the water. Anne finished and Samantha relaxed immediately, looked at me and said 'Hi Steve'. (O67)

This situation evoked all the problematic features of her development; her grimace replayed the first breast-feed I observed, in reverse, she used words to mediate the impact of her distress at the removal of her nappy, and her grip on the bath when Anne washed her hair evoked her rigid grip on the high chair, and her breath-holding of O12. However, this is borne, and quickly recovered from, as she indicated by greeting me. The episode demonstrates the connective tissue between her early experiences and her current object relations, and the part played in this by the observer. Her internalisation of a firm grip on herself was accompanied by evidence of introjective identification of her relationship with mother. In O56 she worked alongside mother in the kitchen, carefully watching her movements as if taking them in. In O67, she played with her cuddly toys, whilst holding her bottle in her mouth:

> I sat down and Samantha sat in a chair opposite, sucking her bottle. She got up and fetched a toy crib, and took her Minnie Mouse out of the crib. She gave Minnie a bottle to suck, holding Minnie in her arms, while she continued to hold her own bottle in her mouth. (O67)

7.6 Ending

The end of the observation was inevitably difficult, for the issue of separation and loss was the main theme of relationships for Anne and Samantha. Anne found it difficult to accept the date of the last observation, asking me to continue, then saying she would be away after Samantha's second birthday. She then arranged for Samantha to start play school on the date of the last observation, thus ensuring there would be no gap after my visits stopped. I arranged to visit on the regular weekly basis up to the date of Samantha's birthday, and to make a date for a follow-up visit after four weeks.

Samantha herself showed the capacity to understand my impending departure and to work through her feelings about the end of the observations. I told her there were four weeks to go, then three, etc., and she began to be interested in my watch, pointing to it and looking at me (O71, O72). She played making telephone conversations with me, using her toy phone, as if thinking about relating to me in my absence. She then expressed anxiety about whether absent, or missing, meant 'broken': 'Samantha picked up a Duplo truck and said "boken". Anne said it was not broken, it needed joining up with another one. She got another truck and Samantha quietly watched her join them up' (O72: Samantha at two years less 12 days).

Finally Samantha and I said goodbye, in a way which was sad, and where emotionality was maintained:

> Samantha held the teddy (which I had given her) in her hand and looked away from me, looking sad. I spoke to her about her birthday and that we would be saying goodbye now, and I would see her in four weeks' time. Anne said it was very odd they were both at school, and she seemed extremely pained. I said it was heartbreaking, and she agreed, it really was. I said goodbye to Samantha and she put her head down for a kiss. She looked at me and then looked away. She said 'bye Steve'. they walked to the door and I left. Samantha looked at me and then looked down. (O73: Samantha at two years less two days)

7.7 Summary

Samantha's development follows a course from early difficulty, centring on the problems of maintaining intimacy and communication with her mother. This led to a defensive pattern, in which Samantha held herself together in the face of limited containment. Loosely held by mother, that is to say, loosely held in terms of mother's attention upon her, Samantha developed a rigid grip on objects in order to mitigate experiences of the anxiety created by the loss or absence of the containing mother. During her second year, as mother recovered from her depression and was more available to Samantha, her transfer of the firm grip on things to the firm grip on a person, in the shape of the observer, facilitated the development of connective tissue between one level of experience, the earlier, and the later. The 'triangular space' (Britton 1989) in the relationships between mother, observer and Samantha represented a relationship in which the individuals – Samantha and Anne – could be kept in mind, and keep each other in mind. That this process seemed to begin whilst the family were on home leave implied that the distance covered was as wide as an ocean. A sense of belonging could begin to form. Being held in mind, Samantha emerged at two with greater vigour, a capacity to symbolise in the service of thinking, particularly about separation and absence, and a vocabulary which could address these emotional issues. It followed that she demonstrated greater internalisation of containing figures (Graph 7.20).

7.8 Grid

7.8.1 Mothering

Anne, Samantha's mother, was recorded in the grid as receiving moderate to low levels of support from husband, friends and extended family. A feature of Anne's support rating was the professional support which was largely accounted for by the employment of a helper, who combined housework tasks with caring for Samantha some of the time (Graph 7.1). Anne's emotional preoccupations were rated as gradually becoming less anxious and persecutory over the two years, and there were moderate levels of impingement of the emotional preoccupations on to Samantha. Her internal resources were rated between fairly low and moderate (Graph 7.2a).

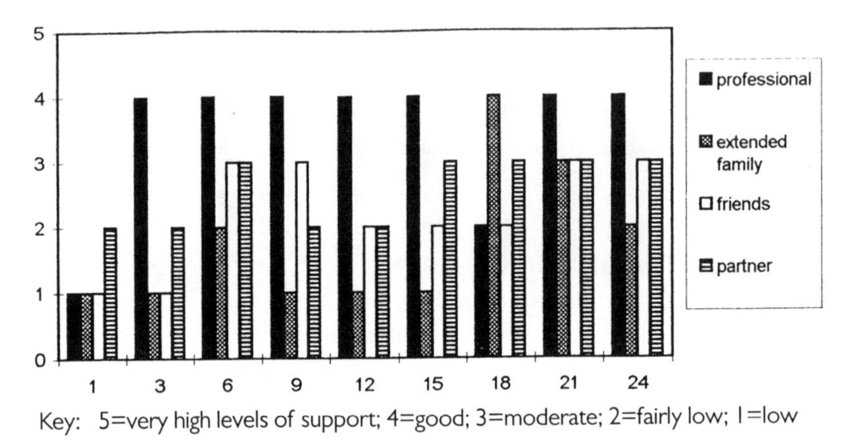

Graph 7.1

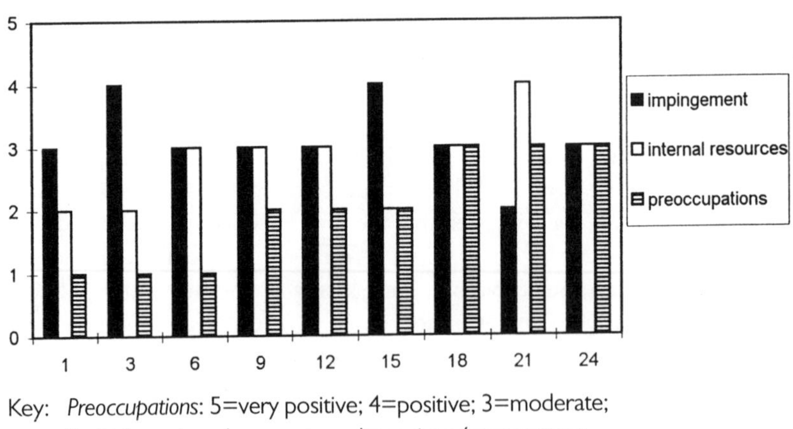

Graph 7.2a

Anne was consistently able to verbalise her concerns to a moderate degree, and the conflict she experienced in her role was moderately high (Graph 7.2b). Anne made numerous representations of Samantha's states of mind and characteristics, and these representations were persistent and consistent, combining positive and negative attributions (Graphs 7.3a and 7.3b). Anne was recorded in the grid as moderately well able to meet Samantha's emotional and physical needs, to understand her communications of need and to show awareness of her emotional needs (Graph 7.4).

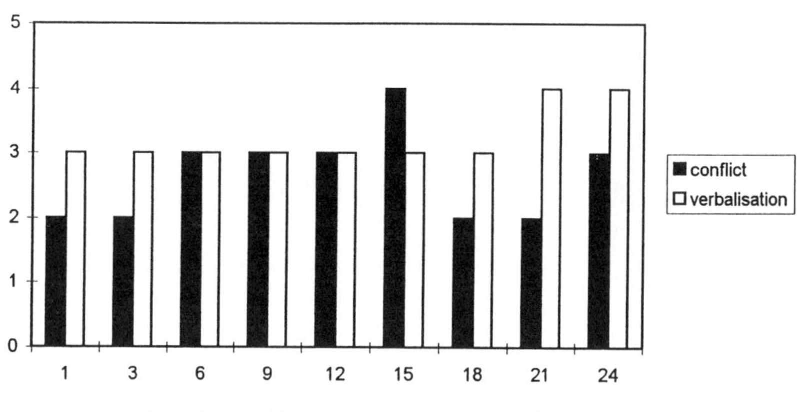

Key: 5=very high; 4=high; 3=moderate; 2=fairly low; 1=low

Graph 7.2b

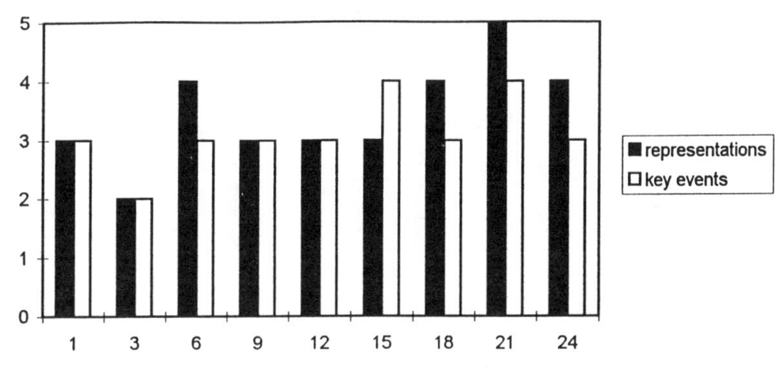

Key: *Experience of events*: 5=very positive; 4=positive; 3=moderate; 2=fairly negative; 1=negative
Representations: 5=very frequent; 4=frequent; 3=moderate; 2=fairly infrequent; 1=infrequent

Graph 7.3a

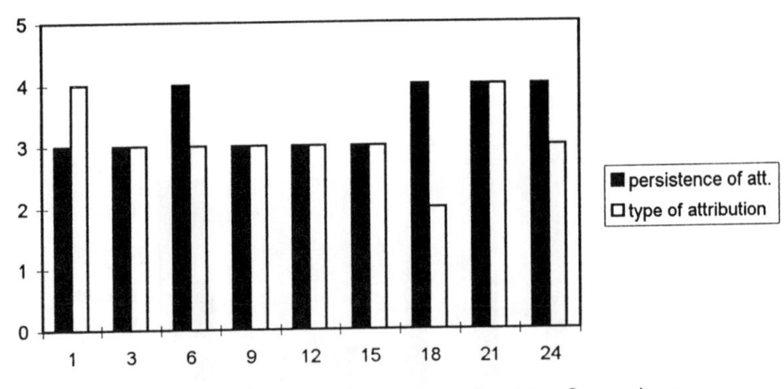

Key: 5=very consistent/positive; 4=consistent/positive; 3=moderate; 2=fairly inconsistent/negative; 1=inconsistent/negative

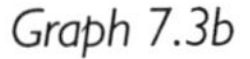

Graph 7.3b

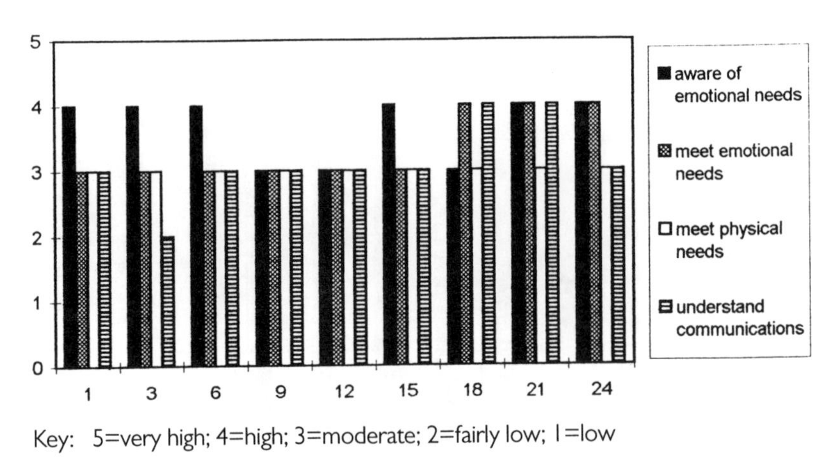

Key: 5=very high; 4=high; 3=moderate; 2=fairly low; 1=low

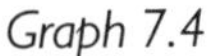

Graph 7.4

7.8.2 Mother–infant relationship

Within the mother–infant relationship grid, qualities of attentiveness, sensitivity, intimacy and understanding and conflict were rated as between moderate and fairly low (Graph 7.5). Grip relations between Anne and Samantha tended to be rated at the moderate and fairly weak categories (Graph 7.6a and 7.6b). The qualities of intensity, being 'in tune' and maintaining emotionality were similarly rated at moderate, or slightly lower strength (Graph 7.7).

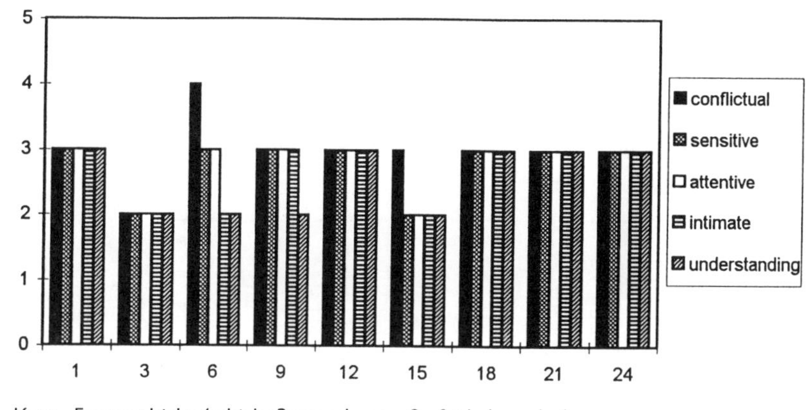

Key: 5=very high; 4=high; 3=moderate; 2=fairly low; 1=low

Graph 7.5

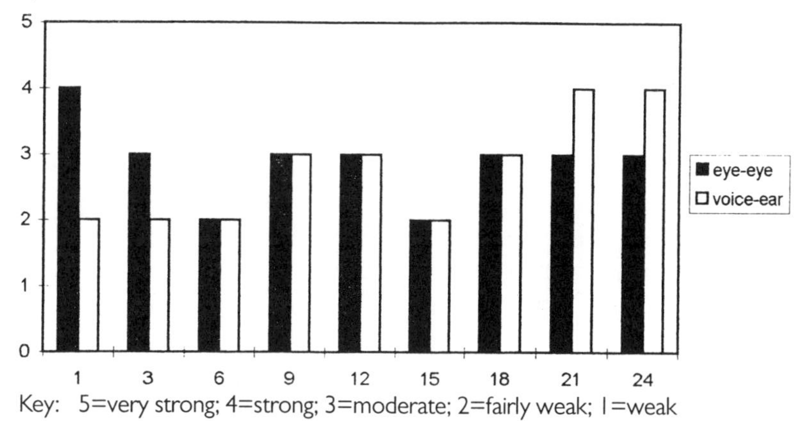

Key: 5=very strong; 4=strong; 3=moderate; 2=fairly weak; 1=weak

Graph 7.6a

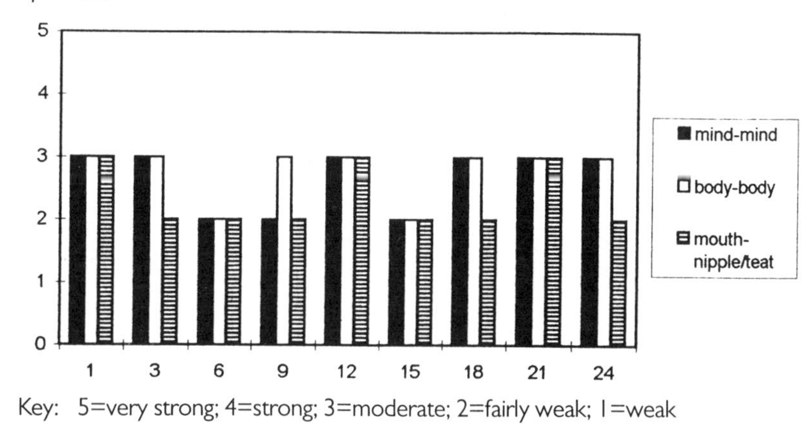

Key: 5=very strong; 4=strong; 3=moderate; 2=fairly weak; 1=weak

Graph 7.6b

The relationship between Samantha and Anne was characterised by a containing fit which did not rise above the moderate category. High ratings for accommodation decreased as Samantha grew. The ratings for a conflictual fit suggested a tendency for moderate to high levels of conflict to be present during nine to 15 months (Graph 7.8). Mother's container shape was scored as moderately flat, whilst convex and concave shapes were overall below the moderate level (Graph 7.9).

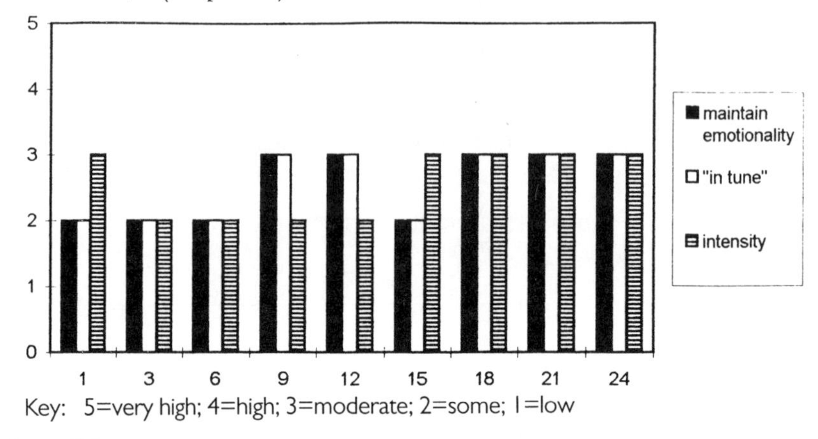

Key: 5=very high; 4=high; 3=moderate; 2=some; 1=low

Graph 7.7

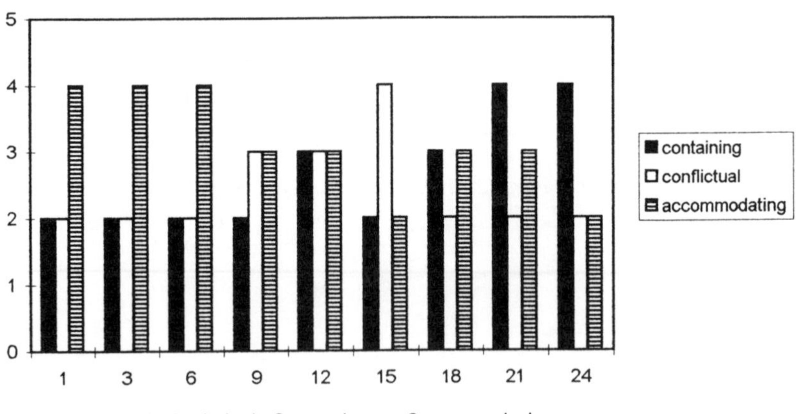

Key: 5=very high; 4=high; 3=moderate; 2=some; 1=low

Graph 7.8

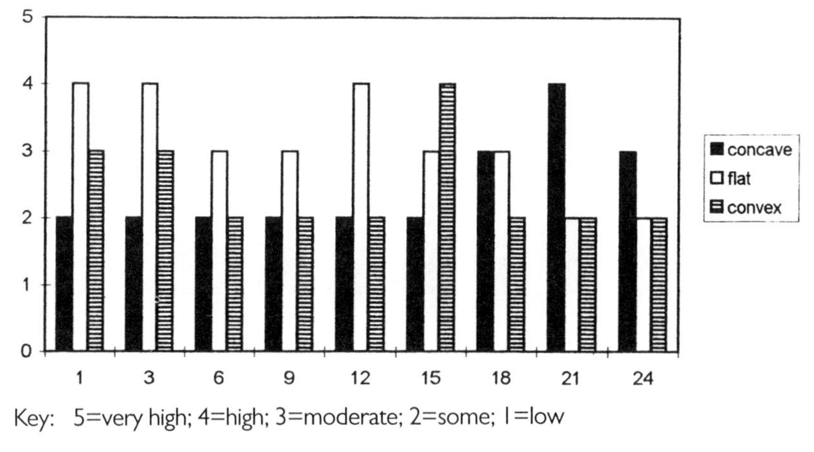

Key: 5=very high; 4=high; 3=moderate; 2=some; 1=low

Graph 7.9

7.8.3 Fathering and father–infant relationship

Martin, Samantha's father, was seen infrequently in observations and there are limited recordings of his containing capacity and relationship qualities with Samantha. His relationship with her was characterised by fairly low ratings for sensitivity, attentiveness and intimacy (Graph 7.10). Similarly, grip relationships were characteristically moderate or below, with the exception of eye–eye grip in the six to nine months period (Graph 7.11).

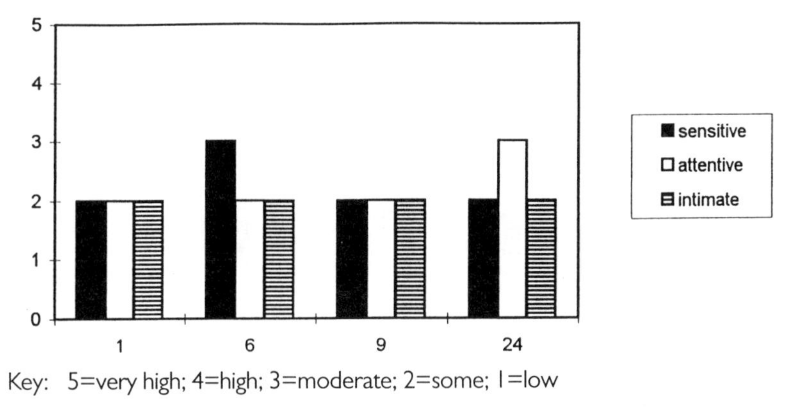

Key: 5=very high; 4=high; 3=moderate; 2=some; 1=low

Graph 7.10

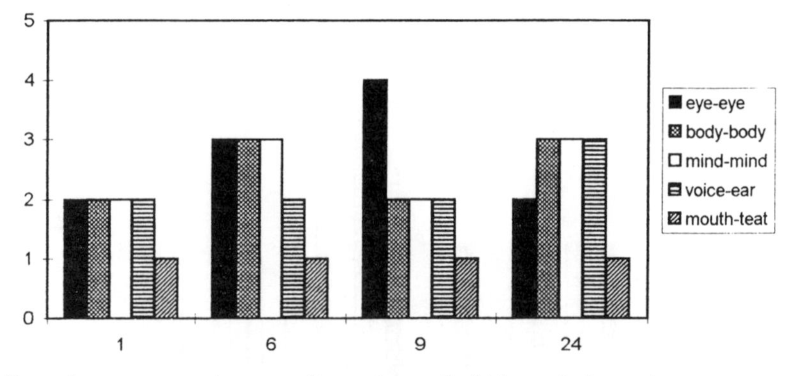

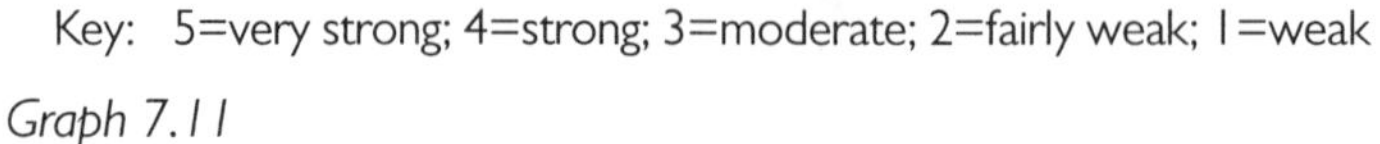

Graph 7.11

7.8.4 Parental relationship

Conflict and harmony were rated as occurring rather infrequently. Where there was conflict, it was verbalised to a moderate degree (Graph 7.12). 'Flattening of affect' and projection of painful experience on to the other were styles of parenting that were rated as occurring frequently. Problem solving ('bridge building') was scored as occurring fairly infrequently for most of the observation.

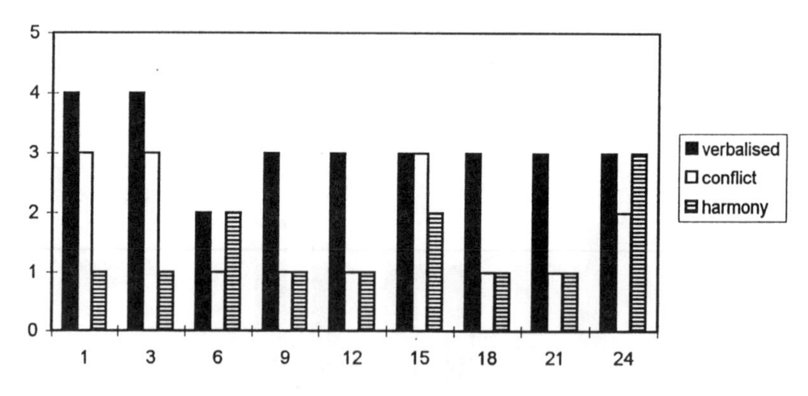

Key: 5=very often; 4=often; 3=moderate; 2=fairly infrequent; 1=infrequent

Graph 7.12

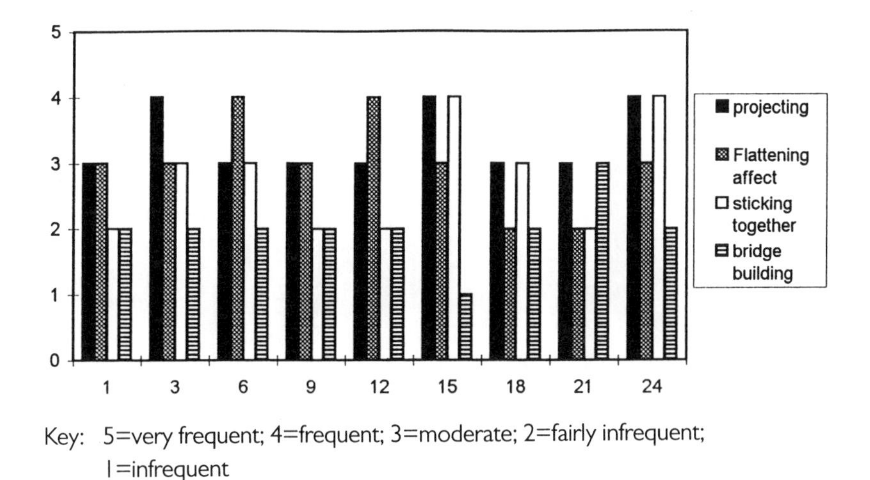

Graph 7.13

7.8.5 Infant development

When Samantha's physical development was recorded, the ratings showed scores which indicated some difficulties in sleeping, feeding and her physical health. Her physical development itself was rated as fluctuating between average levels and above, and some degrees of backwardness. The last correspond with the timing of her reaching mobility milestones (Table 7.1) (Graph 7.14):

Table 7.1

Sitting:	6.5 months
Crawling:	11.75 months
Standing:	12 months
Walking:	14 months

In her grip relations, Samantha demonstrated a very strong hand grip. Her body grip and mind grip were rated to show an increase in strength through her development. Conversely, her mouth grip was shown to decline in strength. Eye, voice/ear and mouth grips showed moderate strength (Graph 7.15a and 7.15b). Samantha was rated as maintaining a high frequency of object relating.

Frequency of defending was scored at moderate to fairly low, and flexibility of defences were in this range too. Frequency of expressiveness/protesting were given high ratings after six months (Graph 7.16).

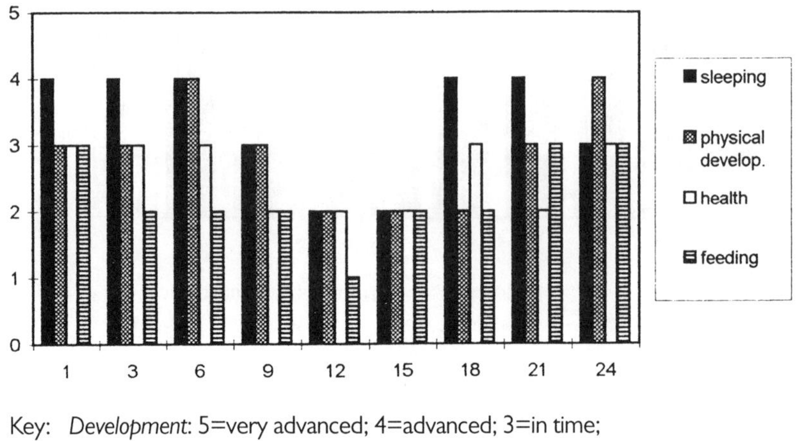

Key: *Development*: 5=very advanced; 4=advanced; 3=in time; 2=slightly backward; 1=backward
Other categories: 5=very well; 4=well; 3=OK; 2=some difficulties; 1=difficulties

Graph 7.14

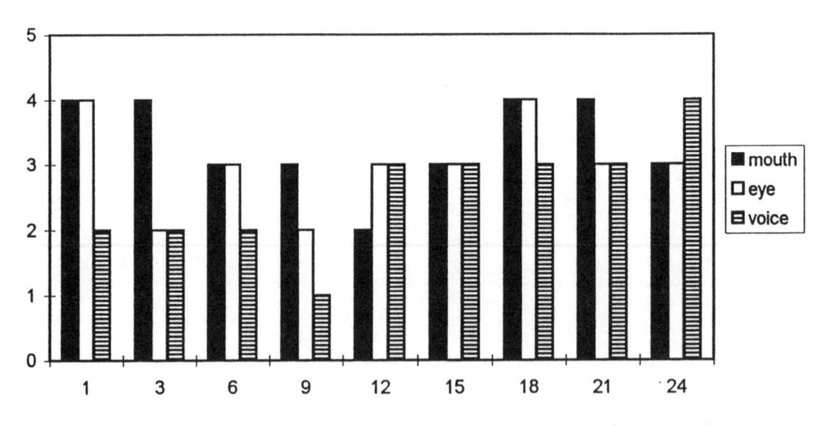

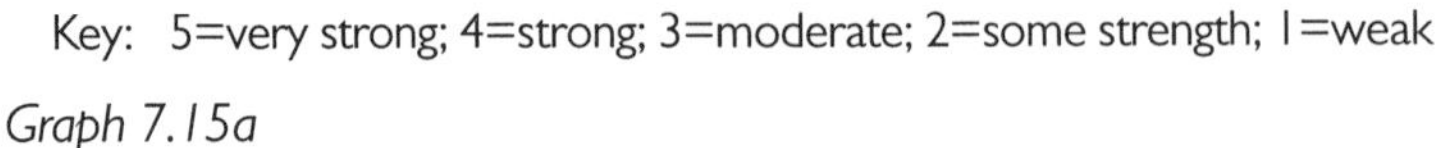
Key: 5=very strong; 4=strong; 3=moderate; 2=some strength; 1=weak

Graph 7.15a

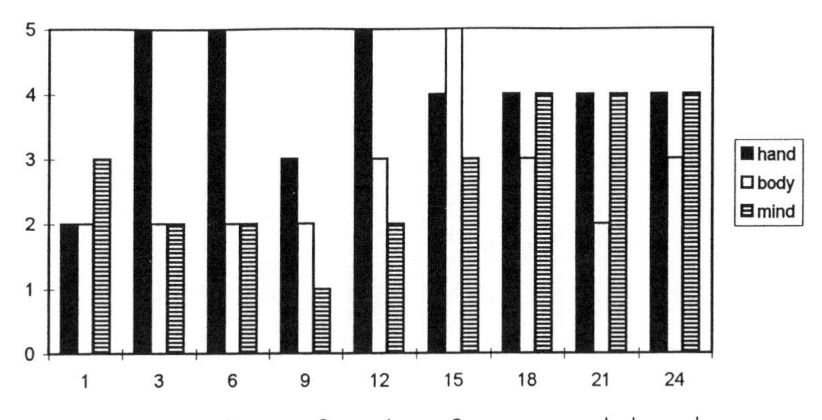

Key: 5=very strong; 4=strong; 3=moderate; 2=some strength; 1=weak

Graph 7.15b

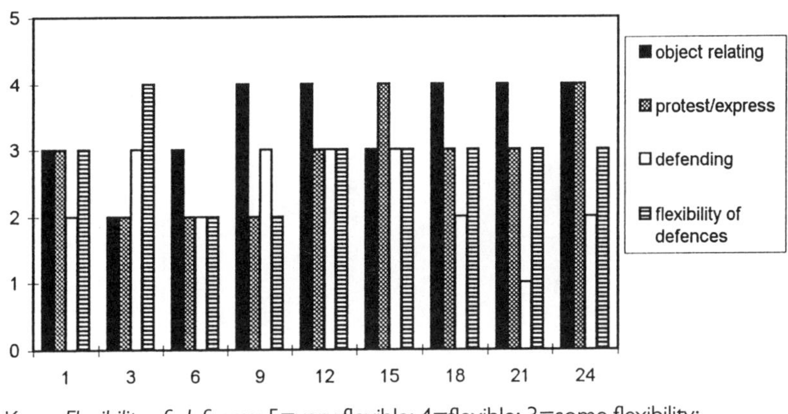

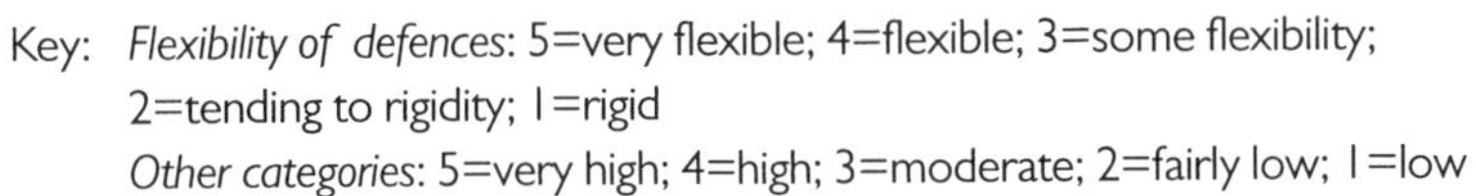
Key: *Flexibility of defences*: 5=very flexible; 4=flexible; 3=some flexibility; 2=tending to rigidity; 1=rigid
Other categories: 5=very high; 4=high; 3=moderate; 2=fairly low; 1=low

Graph 7.16

Samantha's capacity for recognition and recall with affection were rated in terms of a tendency to increase from low and fairly low ratings to moderately high and above during the two years. Her capacity for memory was scored at moderate to high levels (Graph 7.17). Her capacity to think was maintained at moderate levels through her development over the two years, but her demonstrations of seeking proximity, capacity to respond to separation and discrimination between people all registered a low or fairly low rating in the grid after three months. They increased to moderate and above during her second year (Graph 7.18).

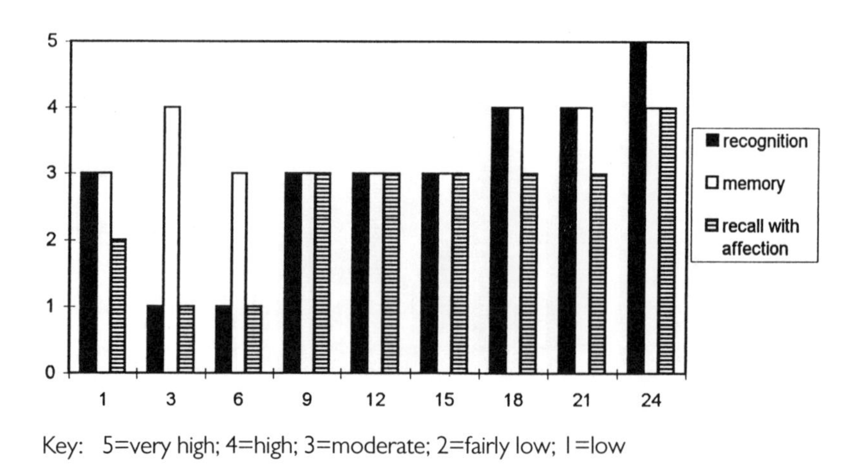

Key: 5=very high; 4=high; 3=moderate; 2=fairly low; 1=low

Graph 7.17

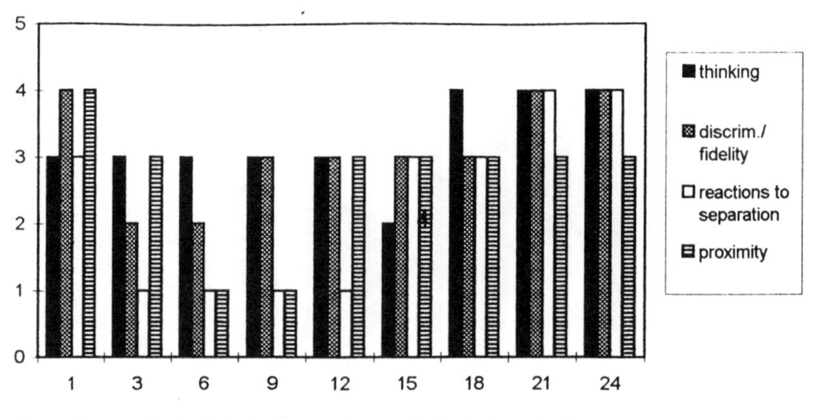

Key: 5=very high; 4=high; 3=moderate; 2=fairly low; 1=low

Graph 7.18

Samantha's capacities for language development and symbolic play were both recorded as moderate or high after 15 months. Expressions of unconscious phantasy in her play were rated at moderate and high levels (Graph 7.19). Her overall internalisation was assessed to include a mixture of persecutory and 'good' aspects in her first year, to be weighted more on the side of a persecutory nature between 12 and 18 months and to recover and be balanced more in favour of a 'good' internalisation by two years (Graph 7.20).

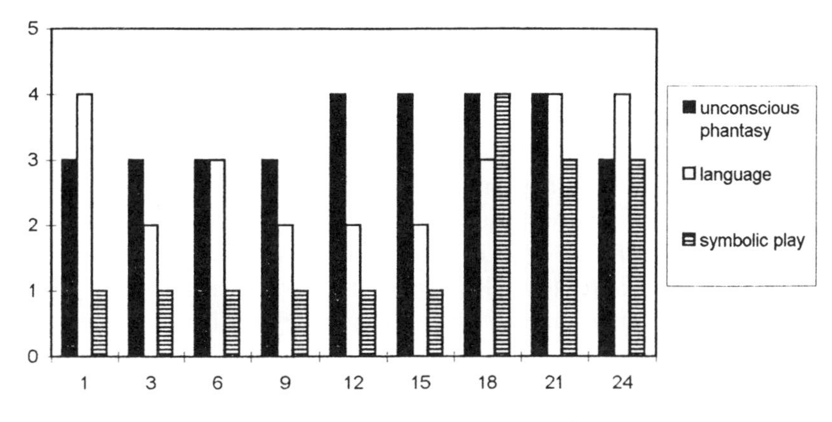

Key: 5=very high; 4=high; 3=moderate; 2=fairly low; 1=low

Graph 7.19

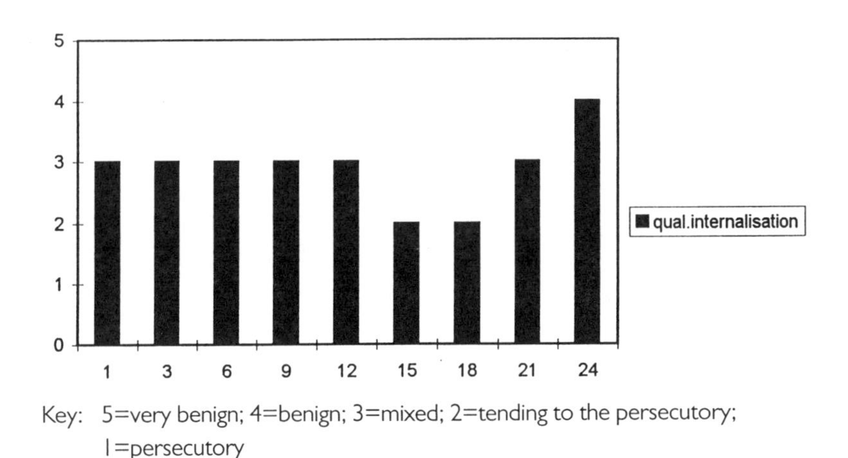

Key: 5=very benign; 4=benign; 3=mixed; 2=tending to the persecutory; 1=persecutory

Graph 7.20

7.8.6 Summary of grid

The grid for Samantha demonstrates the pattern recorded in the descriptive case study of recovery in her second year. Many grid categories record a 'trough' during the middle period (6–15 months) and an increase in rating during 15–24 months. For example, the ratings for Samantha's internalised capacities, such as thinking, seeking proximity, reacting to separation (Graph 7.18) all show an upward trend from a low at 6–12 months. Samantha's grip relations also follow this trend, especially her voice–ear grip (Graph 7.15a) and her body and mind grip (Graph 7.15b). Her capacity to object relate (Graph 7.16) is high from nine months, and her overall quality of internalisation is recorded as moderate/mixed until 21 months. This suggests that a capacity to object relate precedes change and the overall quality of internalisation follows change. This is a pattern for recovery which is intrinsically consistent.

Similarly, there is a picture in the grids of increased parental capacity during Samantha's second year. Mother's trends towards having more positive preoccupations (Graph 7.2a) and the frequency of representation made about Samantha's states of mind and characteristics (Graph 7.3a) both follow upward curves through the observational period. Indicators of increasingly effective containing mothering are seen in the increase of concave containing shape relative to flat and convex (Graph 7.9); mother is recorded as being increasingly able to meet Samantha's emotional needs and understand her communications (Graph 7.4).

CHAPTER 8

Timothy

Timothy's second year provides a contrast with Samantha's. Whilst she was developing language and symbolic thinking he remained speechless and his play had a quite different quality. With Timothy, therefore, there is a return to a case study with a problematic outcome. He was a wanted first baby, whose parents were excited by the prospects of his arrival. Sally, his mother, struggled in his early weeks with her anxiety about her feelings that she doubted her capacity to provide what she felt Timothy needed. The observation, in these circumstances, permitted a study of the relationship between the early experiences of containment and the later developmental achievements of symbol formation and language. In Timothy's relations with his parents there is a variation on the theme of 'triangular space' which formed a central part of Samantha's development.

The context of this observation was that of a middle-class family at the point of transition from marital couple to family, through the birth of the first child. The family was placed, therefore, in a social setting which is often described as 'normal', particularly in psychological and psychoanalytical terms (e.g. Rayner 1978; Box *et al.* 1994; Meltzer 1984, 1988). It was however the only family in this sample within these social parameters.

8.1 The family

I first met the prospective parents just three days before the due date for Timothy's birth, and both parents were in a state of heightened anticipation. Sally, slimly built, with short light-brown hair and a young-looking face, looked straight at Neville, the father to be, and said she was excited about the baby. She touched Neville with her toes, curling them round his calves. Neville, slightly older looking, with receding dark hair and an alert face, said that they were prepared both for the baby to be on time, or late. Sally added that she had thought labour was beginning the previous evening, but it came to nothing. They had been to antenatal classes together, were hoping for a natural childbirth and Neville expected to be present at the birth. Some anxieties were expressed by both of them; Sally was aware she had not been in hospital before, and she conveyed a sense of an anxious journey into the unknown. Both of them asked a number of questions about the observations, Neville being concerned about what would happen in the eventuality that they moved house, which they hoped to do. Sally wanted to know if I had children, or whether I had observed before, suggesting that it would be enough for her to have one person experiencing a new role for the first time. In return I was careful to ask them if they had thought about the prospect of my observing breast-feeds, and Sally said she was not sure how she would feel. Neville suggested I might withdraw at these times, and Sally said that this would not give me the opportunity to observe. We established that it was something we could continue to think about.

The mixture of anxiety and excitement; of curiosity and uncertainty, together with their physical closeness suggested all the elements involved in the emotions of a couple imminently expecting their first child. Neville told me that he worked in the centre of the provincial city in which they lived, commuting from their small, one-bedroom flat in a suburb, whilst Sally had recently given up work to stay at home with the baby. Both their extended families lived in provincial towns and were in regular contact with them. They seemed organised, planned and able to share the warm feelings in anticipation of the birth; intelligent and thoughtful, their curiosity about the observation seemed entirely appropriate. After the initial meeting they soon telephoned to confirm they would like to go ahead and agreed for me to observe for two years.

The events of the birth changed the hopefulness of this picture, and cast a shadow through it, to the extent that their warm anticipation began to seem fragile idealism. Neville telephoned to say that Sally had been admitted to hospital with high blood pressure, and the baby had not yet been born. Nine days later, having not heard from them, I phoned and spoke to Neville's mother, who told me that Timothy had been born five nights before, and that he had been placed in an incubator because of jaundice. Instead of staying in hospital for the planned five nights, Sally was expected to stay for 11. I spoke with Sally when she returned home, and the first observation was arranged for Timothy's 13th day. During this observation Sally and Neville told me that, after two admissions to hospital because of her high blood pressure, she had been induced with pessaries and had her waters broken. There had been a long labour (18 hours), Sally remembered falling asleep during labour, and Timothy was placed in an incubator, next to her bed. Sally then described Timothy as 'dozy' and that there was a tremendous sense of rush to feed him in the hour she was allowed to have him out of the incubator. She would tickle his toes to keep him awake for long enough to take the feed. She had been upset by the suggestion that she supplement his feeds, and had insisted that he was fed through nipple-shaped teats, so that he did not come to prefer the bottle. She was pleased he had not taken to the bottle feeds. Neville mentioned Timothy also needed antibiotics because of a 'sticky eye'.

The contrast could not have been greater between the hopes and expectations both Sally and Neville had for the birth, and the disillusion and annoyance they conveyed about the actual course of events. Not only had there not been a natural childbirth, but the baby, Timothy, had been born with two illnesses, and the stay in hospital, prolonged by five days, had been an ordeal. Having to respond with speed to Timothy when he was in the incubator was painful for her, leaving her with little time to get to know her baby, and she gave me a feeling that she had experienced this as rejecting of her. Whilst Sally wanted to know if my children, too, had been induced, Neville expressed his annoyance through a thinly veiled attack on me. He said that 'babies have lots of infections, and this was because we observed babies and therefore the problems showed. If we were observed in this way we would also be found to have lots of ailments' (O1: Timothy at 13 days).

Neville's sense of persecution at being observed was important to take into account, and it contrasted with the enthusiasm with which they planned the observation with me. It seemed that when there was idealisation, an observer was welcomed; when on the other hand this birth led to disillusion for them both, the observer became seen as the cause of the problem. Neville thus conveyed a sense that difficult feelings, the loss of the ideal, were not easily thought about. Similarly, the strength of his feeling conveyed the degree of their joint disappointment. This hint of difficult feelings which were not easy to contain proved a foretaste of the first months of the observation.

8.2 Quality of containment

Observations of Timothy took place within one of three permutations of the setting; observations when Sally was present, and Neville out; observations when Neville was at home and Sally was not; observations when both parents were at home. Each of these permutations produced a different tenor.

The norm for Timothy's first year was that Sally was at home without Neville. In this permutation there was characteristically considerable anxiety and rivalry on Sally's behalf (Graph 8.2a). Her anxiety took the form of a fear of intrusion from outside: 'A gust of wind made a moan down the chimney and Sally looked towards it saying she feared the cardboard would fall down in the wind bringing with it "dead birds and other mess"' (O7: Timothy at 11 weeks two days). She discussed with me some of her anxieties about the 'outside', particularly her fear of animals:

> Sally said she had made a mistake buying a book about animals because she does not like them and she feared she will have to take Timothy to the zoo. When she sees a cat outside she crosses the road as she cannot stand being near it. She said she knew she would have to change as Timothy grows. (O8: Timothy at 12 weeks two days)

Though this seems a distinct transformation for the cat, from domestic into wild animal, the cat became a leitmotif during the observations, a persecutory animal which seemed to represent a somewhat hidden 'ghost' for Sally.

Second, her anxieties took the form of feeling that she could not give Timothy what he needed to satisfy him. She showed him a mirror: 'Sally picked him up and held him, and he stopped crying. She took him to the mirror and told me he liked to look at himself in the mirror; it made him smile' (O6: Timothy at ten weeks two days). The mirror, a flat reflective instrument, stood as an image for the quality of containment between them, namely that, stirred up in the early weeks by her own anxieties, and seeking to satisfy Timothy through feeding rather than attention to his emotional states, Sally did not have the means to mediate or modulate Timothy's communications. Her flat containing shape was characterised by missing or mistiming communications, and was a recipe for distress, and for Timothy having to hold himself together (Graph 8.9).

Third, Sally was rivalrous of others who had Timothy's attention, including me: 'Sally became aware of this and looked at me and then Timothy. "Yes, that's a funny man is he? What's he got that I haven't got?"' (O8: Timothy at 12 weeks two days). Not only was this rivalry or envy, directed to me but to things to which Timothy became attached: 'Timothy took a corner of the jumper and put it in his mouth to suck. Sally said sharply "what are you doing?" and took the material out of his mouth with a quite sudden movement of her hand' (O7). She had been adamant that she would feed Timothy in hospital, insisting that the bottle he was given was nipple-shaped, so that he would continue to take the breast. This anxiety was, of course, not without foundation, but it also suggested an exclusive possessiveness. Competition was also observed in the relationship between Sally and her mother. This revealed a clear contrast in parenting styles. Whilst her mother had bottle-fed Sally, she was breast-feeding Timothy. Sally believed that her baby should be fed on demand, whilst her mother felt some crying, or time between crying and feeding, was preferable. Whilst her mother held Timothy tightly wrapped in his shawl, Sally left him with his arms free. And whilst Sally used charts and diagrams from the clinic to establish her baby's weight curve, her mother thought this should be a matter of common sense.

Possibly because of these factors Sally did not find it at all easy to develop an 'observational' approach to her parenting during the hour, unlike, for example, Samantha's mother, Anne. Similarly, I found it difficult to find ways of engaging her to join with me in observing Timothy.

Neville was very much the 'family container', providing materially for the family, being in constant contact by telephone during the day and being involved in the evening after his return from work. Observations in Timothy's second year took place near the time Neville returned from work, and his relationship with Timothy was a consistent part of the observations. He combined a ready acceptance of his fatherly responsibilities with a capacity to attend to Sally's preoccupations. He was frequently evoked in his absence by Sally as a source of help and guidance.

When I did see him with Timothy he displayed a confident physical closeness with Timothy, together with an enjoyment of his baby son's capacities and communications (Graph 8.10).

> Timothy then lay on Neville's tummy and after a few moments Neville allowed him to roll first to his right and Neville held him with his arm around him. Then Timothy rolled in the other direction, and Neville again cradled him, before letting him lie on the sofa, moving himself in a quite languorous and calm way to allow Timothy to go there, looking at him and smiling. Timothy made a gurgling sound, to which Neville responded with a similar one. Timothy made a raspberry noise and Neville made a louder one in return. Timothy stuck his tongue out, looking around, and Neville said 'what are you sticking your tongue out for?' With a note of warm curiosity. (O11: Timothy at 15 weeks three days)

This showed a willingness to get on to Timothy's wavelength, to join him in his expressions and behaviours, and the amplification of Timothy's gestures is an exact example of attunement (Stern 1985). It was no surprise to hear from Sally that Timothy became very attached to his father, particularly over Neville's holiday periods. It seemed from these observations and reports that Neville was holding a considerable role in offering a concave containing shape in his relationship with Timothy.

In the second year, Neville continued to show an interest and curiosity in Timothy's behaviour, though he seemed less easily attuned to the kind of communication Timothy was making. For example, in O53 (Timothy at 15 months less four days) he tolerantly allowed Timothy to explore the contents of his briefcase, and conveyed puzzlement and curiosity about Timothy's urgency of communications without quite reaching out to the quality of feelings Timothy engendered.

When both parents were present the predominant feelings were jealousy and the need to avoid being excluded as the isolated or lonely one. As someone was usually 'left out' when the family became, as it were, a unit, one could feel as though in the presence of a sculpture:

> Timothy climbed on to the sofa next to Sally holding his milk, and sitting so his feet just touched the top of Neville's head. Timothy grinned and tickled Neville's head. Neville turned round and grinned; and Timothy moved closer to Sally and when Neville, sitting on the floor, turned towards them, his arm draped over the sofa, I had the sense of looking at a Henry Moore sculpture. (O50: Timothy at 14 months one week)

This was an impressive moment, but one in which the underlying tensions represented a struggle experienced by both parents over this issue of exclusion–inclusion with regard to Oedipal feelings, in a 'bounded triangular space'

(Britton 1989, p.86.) It raised questions of how the couple could provide a 'link' between them for the benefit of Timothy's development, in the face of the disillusion they experienced after his birth (Graph 8.13).

8.3 Timothy's early development

In the first observation the atmosphere surrounding Timothy conveyed the experience of being in the incubator. He was deeply asleep, and I felt a great distance between his world and that of his parents. Then:

> He seemed less deeply asleep, opening and closing his eyes, as he lay on his side. Then he brought his right arm up and over his face. He was still and then his face puckered, he made a slight sighing noise, his head went backwards and his mouth opened, as if to cry, and he settled, seemed less discomforted, settled down and was still. (O1: Timothy at 13 days)

The feeling of distance between Timothy and his parents and the sense in which he awoke, and managed his own discomfort, gave the impression that he was somehow shielded from others, as though still in the incubator, or in other ways 'inside'. He appeared slow to emerge into the world of others, and the early observations showed vividly how his patterns of relating emerged. He was soon (O2, O3) described by Sally as hungry, crying a lot at night, and this distress related very centrally to the problems within their relationship. As Timothy's capacity to relate to others developed over these first weeks of his life, the most important themes were:

1. his wish to retain contact with another as seen through his hand, mouth and eye grips (Graphs 8.15a, 8.15b)
2. his development of a pronounced muscularity which seemed to serve the purpose of holding himself together in the absence of contact with another, and to maintain contact with another (Graph 8.16)
3. the difficulties he experienced in early internalisation as seen through his distress when losing contact with another person (Graphs 8.18, 8.20).

Timothy's interest in and willingness to maintain contact with another person was seen as early as the second observation (O2: Timothy at 20 days). First, after feeding, he used his hand to make a gesture which suggested searching:

> Sally took her hand away from her breast, and eased the breast from Timothy's mouth, and as the breast and his mouth parted he made a loud sucking noise. She sat him up on her lap and he got one hand out of his shawl. His hand reached out in front of him, searching. He struggled to get the other hand out too, but was not able to. (O2)

Both the sucking noise made by Timothy on the point of loss of contact with the breast, and his hand movement suggested a reaction to the ending of the feed. Sally appeared not to notice this sequence, and instead passed him to her father to hold. He was fed again, then put to bed in a somewhat bloated state, his breathing indicating his discomfort: 'His eyes opened when I approached him, and his breathing was heavy, rapid and noisy. He went red and pulled a face as if to cry, reaching the point of crying but made no noise, settled again and continued in a restless sleep, with his irregular breathing' (O2). In that he tried here to manage his distress himself, Timothy's attempts to maintain contact receded in the context of the 'fit' between himself and Sally, and he returned to the mode of being which evoked the experience of the incubator.

The relationship between Timothy's distress, and his attempts to maintain contact with another person through the grip made by his hand, mouth and eye continued to be observed in these early weeks. His hand was prominent both when he was in contact with others, and when he was alone: 'Timothy slept, quite still and settled, then he made a sudden windmilling of both arms, one after the other. This stopped as suddenly as it began, and then was repeated, and then he continued to sleep' (O3: Timothy at 27 days). His freewheeling hand movements were seen again, this time when he was awake: 'Timothy began to cry, his head moving from side to side and his arms and legs moving, windmilling and grasping the air' (O6: Timothy at ten weeks two days).

In O3 Timothy's arms moved through space, without making contact with an object; in the later observation O6, the similarity of the arm movements was accompanied by large motor movements and evident distress. Moreover in this observation, the distress followed immediately on Sally's leaving the room, and this separation from mother was parallel to the reaction seen when his mouth parted from the breast in O2, above. The movement of his hand, and then arms, legs, and head implied a free falling experience, an inability to hold on to an object in its absence, evoking Bick's idea that he is: 'in the position of an astronaut who has been shot out into outer space without a space suit' (1986, p.296).

In O2, Timothy had attempted to free his hand from his shawl, and Sally and her mother had disagreed about whether he should be tightly wrapped or whether his hands should be free. In O3 (Timothy at 27 days), Sally commented to me that she 'had been advised' that she should leave his hands free. Whilst the freedom of his hands permitted him to seek contact with another, especially at the point of separation from the mother and/or her breast, this freedom introduced the possibility of being object-less, distressed or uncontained. On the other hand, being tightly wrapped had the effect of isolating him from others, as he had been in the incubator.

In O4 he was observed using his hand to push away his sheet: 'He slept on his back, his breathing relaxed. From time to time his arm moved, gently, curling up and then his fist and fingers pushed at the sheet – not gripping, but pushing'

(O4: Timothy at five weeks). This pushing movement imitated his earlier movements to free himself from his shawl, and was again seen later, when awake, in context with his relationship with his mother. In O6, he pushed his hands against the floor, in a precocious display of muscularity:

> He cried again and Sally lifted him up, and, talking to him, turned him on his tummy. He laid his head on the mat and then making an effort lifted it well off the mat, pushing down with his arms. He held the position for some time, looked around and then let go, letting his head down on to the mat. After a few seconds he repeated the process lifting his head off the mat, pushing down with his arms looking round and then lowering himself. He again lifted himself up, held his body up on his arms, pushing strongly, and then he laid his head on the mat. He started to cry again, and Sally came towards him, talked to him, but he continued to cry and she picked him up. She took him to the mirror, and showed him, but he continued to cry. She went to the window and Sally talked to him about the cars outside and he quietened as Sally stood still with him in her arms. Sally said it was hard to keep up with Timothy all the time and sometimes she had to let him cry. (O6: Timothy at ten weeks two days)

The pushing motion of his arms was used to generate mobility, or muscularity, which in this sequence aimed to achieve contact with mother, as the searching with his head indicated. This gesture, of raising himself with considerable physical effort, accompanied by looking around, imitated closely, on a larger physical scale, the movement of his hand when his feed ended in O2. Timothy's muscularity, of which a great deal more will be seen in his subsequent development, then seems to have been created through the need to seek contact with mother, and through the need to contend with anxieties about being 'unheld', when out of contact. Eventually he was calmed by physical holding by mother. She expressed the view that it was hard to keep up with Timothy, indicating the demand she felt in achieving a 'fit' with him which was exact. Timothy's dilemma, produced by the conflict between being tightly wrapped or 'free', demonstrated his need for exactness when emotions, particularly distress, were not contained. Both mother and infant were experiencing distress. Mother's despair, shown by her turning to inanimate objects, such as the mirror (O6: page 196 above) indicate her limitations at this point in terms of reverie, and that she, like the mirror, offered a flat containing shape for Timothy's distress.

In O8 (Timothy at 12 weeks two days) Timothy's physical movements, again 'pushing' towards Sally, when it was difficult to see how closer physical proximity could have been achieved, suggested that he was searching or 'pushing' for closer emotional attention. Similarly, when firmly held physically by mother, he used this experience to make contact with others, in a way which indicated both the availability of curiosity and a need to make use of a third person, or thing, in a triangular mode of relating. This feature was observed through Timothy's eye grip, and largely involved me. In O6: 'Timothy sat still, looking around, and then at me as Sally held him firmly' (O6). This was repeated in O8: 'Timothy looked at me directly, sitting facing me on Sally's lap as she held him round the waist. His hands and arms fluttered, as if skipping, and he held his gaze on my face. I looked back at him' (O8: Timothy at 12 weeks two days). In relating to me in this way, he again demonstrated through reaching forwards his willingness to make emotional contact: 'His wandering, restless look changed to one of interest as he caught sight of me, and he looked straight at me. I smiled at him and he smiled back. He cooed and leaned his head forwards as if reaching towards me' (O8).

Although Timothy's attention for another person produced rivalrous reactions from Sally, the growth of his capacity to maintain eye contact indicated the increasing strength of his ability to relate to others, rather than being withdrawn (Graph 8.16). His tendency was to prefer another person. Sally's wish that he prefer 'things', as she herself turned to 'things' to assist her – the mirror, toys and the cars outside the window – continued a miscommunication between them about the merit of the third person in the 'triangle'. When given the opportunity, firmly held, his eyes explored both Sally and others. When he was not distressed, he would focus on Sally with his eyes, watching her from a state of 'alert inactivity':

> Timothy ran his hand over the row of figures on his bouncing chair, and looked up at Sally. He cooed and called towards her, bouncing the chair as he did so. They kept this up; Sally washing up and then turning and smiling, Timothy watchful until she turned then smiling, cooing and bouncing his chair. (O7: Timothy at 11 weeks two days)

At this physical distance, Timothy demonstrated both his willingness to relate to Sally, and his pleasure in doing so. At the same time he 'excludes' me from his eye contact. In contrast, when the intimate situation of feeding occurred, there was greater tension. In O4 he showed a disinclination to take the breast: 'He lay crying lightly, restlessly moving his right arm and his legs, and turning his face towards and from the breast before holding his face up to take the nipple' (O4: Timothy at five weeks two days).

Timothy's indecision indicated some persecutory feelings present, and his head movements – towards and away from – described the nature of his conflict, namely, being somewhat in a shuttle, between being with (the object) and being away from, or out of contact. Timothy generally sucked well once he had a firm grip on the nipple, and he rapidly put on weight, becoming a large baby. Sally tended to control the feeds, deciding when they began and ended, and using her hand to 'guide' the breast. There was more mutuality in the feed which was observed in O7, and where Timothy was more active in the process of ending the feed:

> Sally's hand was on her breast, more covering than guiding, and Timothy's fingers reached towards her hand. Their fingers entwined and curled around each other. Sally looked at Timothy and let her fingers play with his. Timothy occasionally lifted his hand and tapped Sally's, and his leg stretched and made a rocking movement as if to get nearer. Sally played with Timothy's fingers looking at him, while Timothy patted her fingers. He loudly filled his nappy. Gradually it seemed Timothy stopped feeding and imperceptibly almost he and the breast parted. (O7: Timothy at 11 weeks two days)

This was the feed in which Sally complained of the 'dead birds and other mess 'coming down the chimney (see page 195, above). Timothy again rocked towards her, and mother maintains both a hand and eye grip on Timothy, in a way which replicates the contact Neville and Sally had with each other in the initial visit. Timothy appeared to have internalised this particular contact with Sally for he was later seen, asleep, in a similar pose:

> His breathing got deeper and he moved his arms so that his left hand came over and touched the other hand. With his right hand he caught the fingers of the left hand and they caressed a little. He moved his body and his left hand flew away, like throwing a discus, and it lightly hit the bumper of the cot. (O10: Timothy at 14 weeks two days)

The touching of his hands exactly replicated his hand contact with mother, suggesting internalisation of his grip on her (O'Shaughnessy 1986, p.77). The 'throwing away' gesture suggested an anxiety about weaning, and this had also been the content of mother's discussion during the feed in O7: 'His fingers continued to play with her hand and then his toes and leg arched and rocked. Sally again looked up and said she was thinking of having to wean Timothy as he needed more food now. She would begin to introduce solids' (O7: Timothy at 11 weeks two days). Mother's thought about weaning appeared to be initiated by the rocking movements of Timothy's legs, and this left her with a feeling of not being able to give him enough. She may have translated Timothy's need for emotional containment from the emotional to the physical.

Timothy's attempts to maintain contact and his phantasies (Isaacs 1952) of contact when asleep, or alone in his bed, through his pushing, touching and throwing away gestures, suggest some of the qualities of the internalisation taking place. His repertoire of behaviours which initiate contact, or contend with the absence of contact with another person all appear to be dealing with the impact of separation from another person. Timothy's distress shows both a willingness to protest, to communicate, and that he experienced these object relationships as inherently frustrating. He was thus involved in what Bion described as the choice between 'procedures designed to evade frustration and those designed to modify it' (Bion 1962, p.29). His distress on separation, which was seen frequently in these observations (O2, O4, O6, O8), was immediate,[1] that is to say, as soon as Timothy's grip on the other (external object) was lost, he cried. For example in O6: 'Sally put Timothy down on the changing mat, talked to him soothingly, and then left the room. Immediately Timothy began to cry, his head turning from side to side and his arms and legs moved, windmilling and grasping the air' (O6). This 'grasping of thin air' provides evidence that he has no internal grip on his relationship with mother. The quality of internalisation is suggested by his hand gestures. The problem, it appears, is that gaining or losing contact has to take priority for him. This is a conflict which began with Sally's experiences of his incubator days, when she needed to respond quickly before he was taken away from her.

At three months, though Timothy had shown a willingness to object relate, and to use a number of modalities – eye, ear and his whole body in a muscular way – in order to maintain contact with mother; to make vigorous efforts, at times, as in O6, when both Timothy and Sally were preoccupied with a relationship in which making or seeking contact was predominant. When Timothy was firmly held physically by Sally it permitted him the possibility of demonstrating curiosity. On these occasions he made contact with a third person, the observer. When not firmly held, he resorted to distress and a muscular defence. Loss of contact appeared to have both a physical and emotional component. Emotionally, the inexactness of the fit between them was instrumental in the evidence of distress and defensiveness.

8.4 Timothy's development from 3 to 12 months

The question of how Timothy experienced the absence of a grip on an object continued to be raised in observations after he was three months, and to be focused on his gestures with his mouth and his hand. First, in O9, on awakening he made contact with himself and his surroundings:

> Timothy opened his eyes and lay quietly for a time. He seemed to be listening. He closed his eyes again and his fingers moved playing with the sheet. He turned his head and his hand came towards his face, fingers opening and closing individually, his hand moved until it touched his face. His mouth moved in a faint sucking movement. (O9: Timothy at 13 weeks two days)

---

1 There is a contrast in this material and that of Harris (1975, p.420). She describes an infant (Anthea) who was observed, in her first weeks, taking time between physical separation from her mother, and her need to find an object, and longer before distress appeared. On a larger scale, the same process is seen in the Robertsons' film *John* (Robertson and Robertson 1969), where the child, then 17 months, maintained an inner relationship with his absent mother over several days, before distress, and the need to recontact the mother, became overwhelming.

The sucking movement further illustrated his preoccupation with an experience of contact with the breast, along with his hand making contact with the sheet and then his face. These phantasies link with those previously described (O8, O10), where the motions of his mouth, tongue and hand recreate a sense of his relationship with the breast.[2]

Second, when with father (O11), mother's departure, though not overtly recognised by Timothy, led to a change in the way he related:

> Sally came in to say goodbye to Neville and Timothy, offering a kiss to both. She left and Timothy held his toes, not showing any reaction to Sally. He looked over Neville's head at me and then he started to suck his fingers. He held Neville's hand and put his fingers in his mouth and Neville said 'does it taste nice?' He gave Timothy a rattle to hold and he put this in his mouth, sucking it. Neville moved slightly and Timothy began to cry. (O11: Timothy at 15 weeks three days)

Timothy moved from a relaxed, exploratory way of relating with Neville to one in which he held his toes and put fingers in his mouth. His loss of attention on Neville was signified by his glance at me, and this moved him into a triangular mode of relating. He then became susceptible to a slight change in Neville which led to distress. Although this was a displacement from the central issue of mother's departure, which could not be acknowledged directly, this fragility – that a slight change in the other was followed by distress – was another statement of Timothy's difficulty of holding on to himself in the absence of an exact fit with another person. The fact that his fingers went into his mouth again supports the idea that it is an absence, or loss of contact that is his concern.

Timothy's developing muscularity also conveyed the sense that a very fragile emotional state lay behind some very vigorous activity. He was sitting by five months, and crawling by six months. He stood unaided at seven months and could take six to eight steps by ten months. These were considerable achievements, tending towards the precocious (Table 8.1; Graph 8.14). Not only did Timothy appear to use this increased mobility for a particular purpose, namely moving towards people, especially Sally, but also the development of a muscular mode of relating was seen to occur in specific circumstances in the observations, namely, in response to Sally's physical absence, and/or her engrossment in activities other than holding him. In O12, Timothy reacted to Sally's briefly leaving the room through eye contact on me, and then on a mobile:

---

2 This may have a connection with Tustin's thinking (1990, p.48) of the experience of the nipple or teat slipping from the baby's mouth, and then being 'distressingly gone', leading to the baby experiencing bodily separation from the mother. 'Slipping' would indicate a loose grip. Compare, for example, Samantha's 'slipperiness' on the kitchen floor (Chapter 7 above).

> Timothy looked towards me and up to the mobile Sally had swung before she went out. He caught the fingers of his left hand with his right hand and moved them against each other. He rolled his head and looked again at me. Sally's voice came from the kitchen as she talked on the telephone and Timothy appeared to listen, with an air of concentration. (O12: Timothy at 16 weeks two days)

The movement of his hands repeated the observation of him asleep (O10 above) and his attention on Sally's voice also repeated an earlier observation (O9). As Sally continued to come and go in this observation, Timothy's body tone, or muscularity, increased, showing the relationship between having a grip on mother, with whichever modality, and the threat of losing that grip:

> When she stopped talking he moved his fingers, still holding them together and his head and neck seemed to relax. Then her voice came again and he seemed to stiffen, and looked towards me. Sally came in and went towards Timothy. She put her hands on his tummy, her head close to his, and murmured to him. She went out again and he looked towards me, trying to focus. He lifted his legs in the air and his right hand got hold of his right foot; he lay feeling the foot of his leggings. His legs moved and he got hold of the other foot, and he lay looking at his hands and feet. (O12)

Sally has excluded herself here, as she did when Neville was present in O11. Timothy's means of managing her coming and going was clearly organised around holding parts of his body, so that he ended up almost in a circle, with his eyes focusing on the point at which he 'joined' by his hands and feet. Though he made eye contact with me (as in O11) it appeared in the service of managing the issue of whether contact was made with mother, or whether it was broken. The concreteness of the way he made contact with himself, again suggested his primary preoccupation with the breast, and the contact, or breaking of contact with this particular relationship.

Timothy's muscularity was often accompanied by crying, or frustrated calling. For example in O17 (Timothy at five months less five days): 'He cried and flapped his arms against his body, making frustrated noises, calling out'. Each increase in muscular tension accompanied a movement Sally made away from him. In O19, Sally attempted to do some sewing in the observational time, and Timothy reacted by crying and attempting a physical solution to the problem:

> Timothy continued crying and Sally said to him that she had some buttons to sew on. She got up as he continued to cry and gave him a mirror and a rattle, and a felt rabbit to play with. He looked round, cried, and then lifted himself up, leaning forwards towards Sally. He went right forwards on to all fours and started to cry (O19: Timothy at five months 24 days)

Timothy's aim to move towards Sally was clear, only prevented from being achieved by his physical restrictions. Soon he could crawl, and he used his new skill to make a point: 'Timothy leaned forwards and crawled towards Sally. He got to her feet and started to undo her laces, quickly untying one and then tugging at it' (O23: Timothy at six months three weeks, one day). Not only could he crawl early, but he could also untie shoelaces! This was an apposite accomplishment, since he could thereby attempt to control the part of Sally that took her away from him, namely her feet. He repeatedly untied shoelaces, though Sally prevented him from doing this with me: 'He got to my feet, looked at me and then looked at my shoes. Sally said: "you're not going to have those shoe laces, you can have mine or daddy's"' (O23). Untying shoelaces was to be kept in the family! It was also the case that Timothy slept at the foot of their bed and feet were therefore the first point of contact he had with both parents! It did appear that Timothy was consistent in his wish to untie my laces, since I was part of the appearing/disappearing gestalt with which he was emotionally concerned and preoccupied.

Timothy's muscularity then led to increased mobility, and to furthering his attempts to maintain contact with Sally, and others. Over the same period, from three to six months, he had greatly increased his eye contact with me, smiling at me as I arrived for observations (O12, O16, O18, O19, O20, O21, O22) and showing recognition of me after a holiday break when he was five and a half months (Graph 8.17): 'Timothy looked up at me as I came in and his eyes followed me across the room. I sat down and Timothy still looked towards me' (O18: Timothy at five months 17 days). Sally tried to minimise this reunion by getting him involved in some play, and he became distressed, but continued to make contact with me:

> Sally held him and he tried to find me with his eyes, still crying, peering round her shoulder and holding on. Sally moved towards the window and he kept his eyes on me, now stopping crying. Sally talked about something outside the window, and then sat down on a chair near to me, and Timothy looked towards me (O18)

Timothy's prolonged interest in me in this observation was consistent with his attention for the 'third person' and with his greater curiosity when firmly held. In the next observation, there was a distinct look of curiosity in his face when I arrived: 'Timothy, sitting on the floor, looked at me inquisitively. I took my coat off and he followed me with his eyes, again looking at me inquisitively' (O19: Timothy at five months 24 days).

Timothy's dilemma was that in order to develop his curiosity he had to achieve, as a prerequisite, a minimum amount of holding for himself. Without that degree of grip, he lost muscular control:

> Timothy lay on his back sucking a soft toy and blowing bubbles. He made noises as he blew through his lips, salivating. Sally commented

> on his making lots of saliva. Sally returned to her ironing and Timothy looked at her, craning his neck and seeming to reach out to her. He blew some more bubbles and made more noises, and then the noises turned to cries. Sally came to him and sat him up. He put his fingers in his mouth and she went back to the ironing. He suddenly fell backwards, and fell gently on his back rather than his head. (O16: Timothy at 20 weeks one day)

His sudden falling over was one of a number of occasions (O17, O18) when his muscularity visibly collapsed. Here it appeared to be in conjunction with a 'collapse' of his attempts to obtain closer contact with Sally. In other observations it occurred when he attempted another mode of relating. In O17 (Timothy at 21 weeks two days) he smiled at me, and his head 'fell' on to the floor. In O18 (Timothy at 22 weeks two days), again trying to look at me, he lost his hold on his own body, and lay flat. It was usual for Timothy to replace this lost hold on himself with crying, which, with a struggle, brought greater holding from Sally.

His mouth gestures – salivating, blowing bubbles – appeared to be an additional part of his repertoire for maintaining a grip on himself, whilst being linked with the threat of weaning. Sally introduced solids when he was 12 weeks and my intervention to suggest she might feed him alone (O13) may have contributed to her continuing to feed him until he was seven months. Also in the background were frequent reports from Sally that he was still very distressed at night (e.g. O16).

After weaning there was a greater sense of harmony between Timothy and Sally, less tension and less visible frustration in the observations. In this period, from seven months to a year, there emerged some co-operative games between them, with the ideal compromise appearing to be when Timothy could be involved in her activities. One particular game produced interactions which involved giving and relinquishing:

> Sally said she was doing the washing and fetched a baby bath full of clothes. Timothy sat holding the bath tub with both hands while Sally pulled out the clothes and put them on the drying rack. He stood up, took a shirt and sat down holding it. She took it from him and hung it up, and Timothy got another one, and put it in his mouth. Sally asked 'does it smell nice?' and took it from him with a smile, tugging it gently away from him and saying 'thankyou'. Timothy smilingly let it go, immediately finding another one (O31: Timothy at eight months two weeks)

The acceptance and toleration on both sides was in contrast with earlier tensions between them. Instead, here was mutuality and enjoyment. Yet relinquishing the breast was not without some protest and discomfort:

> Timothy started to cry and Sally picked him up. She sat with him and reached for his 'animals' book. He was slightly sick, Sally rubbed his mouth gently and he smiled. He put the book in his mouth and she took it off him, and he put his jumper in his mouth instead, and held it firmly between his teeth. She tried to pull the jumper out of his mouth but he held on. She started to read to him, but he twisted away. (O25: Timothy at seven months four days)

Timothy's firm, biting grip now shows a capacity to hold on and not be easily satisfied with the substitution of book for breast. In this post-weaning period he displayed tender recollection:

> Timothy picked up a book and held it to his nose in a smelling gesture, then he looked at Sally and me. Sally said, 'yes, that's a flower' and added 'we smelled the real ones earlier'. Timothy stood up and walked towards the flowers, then he turned round and pointed to the fern on the mantelpiece, looked at Sally and made a smelling gesture. (O36. Timothy at ten months 12 days)

Timothy's thinking was clearly intact in this example (Graph 8.18), making links between flowers, plants and the images he had seen of them in books. His capacity to make links in his thinking extended to absent or hidden objects:

> Sally gave him the top of a feeding bottle. He returned it to her and she put it under a cushion. He looked under the cushion for it, found it and gave it to her. She hid it again and he again found it but left it under the cushion. (Some minutes later) he returned to Sally, put some books on her lap, looked under the cushion and found the feeding bottle top (O36: Timothy at ten months 12 days)

There was a display here of Timothy demonstrating his capacity to achieve object constancy.[3] The choice of object and the nature of the game again suggested there was play here in the service of working through the loss and absence of the breast. Timothy extended his range of thinking about absence through some games of 'peek a boo' with me (O35, O36, O41). Usually when playing these games he maintained a firm grip on Sally, as if using her very

---

3 The Piagetian notion of object constancy as a cognitive developmental issue has a dimension in which the issue of internalisation is important, through Bion's notion of absent object/present persecutor (Bion 1967), but also a question of intention (Freeman, Lloyd and Sinha 1980, quoted in Alvarez 1992). Here, the sense is that the intention (of hiding the bottle) is less persecutory to Timothy than when mother left the room (O11, O12). Thus this development shows not only an internalisation of constancy (the *ability* to remember), but that absence itself is less persecutory for him, and thus the internalised figures are also less hostile. This appeared to follow his greater confidence that his grip on mother could be maintained, which was triggered by his greater mobility, and his greater sense of control in the relationship. (See below, Chapter 9.5.2)

concretely to play these games, and interactions became triangular: 'He crawled round behind Sally and peered at me. I said "boo" when his face appeared and he smiled. He repeated this a few times and I said to him that I had been away, and now I am here again' (O35: Timothy at ten months four days).

The fact that Timothy played these games within the closest proximity of mother and that he needed a firm grip on mother in order to be able to wave goodbye (O36) and, earlier, to smile (O13) continued to impress that his 'either/or' choice in relationship to mother left him experiencing a need for 'both/and' in his other relationships. His learning to recognise me, and to greet me with a smile (O12–O22) took place when he was firmly held in mother's arms at the door to the flat. The way father was greeted by Sally and Timothy was seen continually in his second year, but not in this period. It is possible to surmise that father played a similar role to myself, and that Sally and Timothy greeted him in the same way.

Developing a capacity to recognise and communicate about absence, separation and reunion (Graphs 8.17, 8.18) was accompanied by an increased reaction to changes which involved his physical state. He was always unaffected by nappy changes, which was not the case with other babies in the sample, and only in O36 did he show some distress at the removal of his nappy:

> Sally laid Timothy on his back on the changing mat and he looked blankly at me, and with a half-smile at Sally. She said 'Is it a bit soon after you have woken to have a change?' and she removed his nappy with quick movements. As she took the nappy off he cried, and his cries stopped when his new one was in place (O36: Timothy at ten months 12 days)

This distress at the loss of the physically holding clothes suggested a move towards the sense of the importance of being held, rather than the container being an oppressive, solid or impenetrable construct. It was becoming more like a container, in other words, than a shield.

At 12 months Timothy and Sally had made considerable moves towards a greater sense of fitting together; they had both moved towards each other, though this had followed weaning. Sally had become more observant, and more able to meet Timothy on his terms; to accommodate to him and put aside some of her preoccupations. Timothy moved towards Sally concretely through the use of his physical mobility, which had developed with precocity. The muscularity of Timothy's development was seen to equate clearly with the need for a concrete, and exact fit with mother, which, if lacking, led to his holding himself together in a multitude of ways. There was some evidence that loss of intimate aspects of relationships, such as occurred in weaning, leads to denial or reducing the importance of these relationships. There continued to be a question mark about how much the emotional currency between them was the subject of understanding, and how much of misunderstanding (Graph 8.5).

Timothy was more curious and adventurous in mental as well as physical activity. He made few sounds – usually only a sound like 'uhh' – but he demonstrated considerable cognitive achievements. This progress had not been lightly achieved, and the considerable distress, frustration and misunderstanding that had characterised the nursing phase of his relationship with Sally had been experienced with some cost in terms of defensive organisation shown by Timothy in his development.

8.5 Development from 12 to 24 months

Timothy's development during his second year was dominated by the problems he encountered in developing language. The gradual emergence of the fact that his language was delayed added tension to the observations, particularly as Sally and Neville became more aware of and concerned about it. By the end of the observational period, when he was two, Timothy was able to say only a handful of single words. Alongside the difficulties in language development, there was a distinct lack of progress towards play with a symbolic content. This is not to say that Timothy did not play – in fact there was an abundance of play (Graph 8.19) – but rather that the symbolic content of the play was very concretely expressed.[4] Nor was there significant development in the quality of his play during the year. Given these features of his development it is important to follow the nature of Timothy's play and his relationships with his parents in order to explore the states of mind which were central to his development. These appeared to be connected with five themes that were evident in his play and interactions:

1. Play with the insides of objects which was concretely expressed.
2. Play with insides where there was a greater degree of representation.
3. Play with insides which was accompanied by banging and/or throwing away.
4. Interactions with mother/father in which inclusion and exclusion was an issue.
5. Play and interactions where a cat was present, concretely and as a symbol of the outside world.

Timothy's interests in the insides of objects was ubiquitous. He was preoccupied with his baby walker, a Thomas the Tank Engine, with a compartment which

---

4 Following the discussion of Samantha's play, this discussion draws on a distinction between play which expresses an unconscious phantasy (Isaacs 1952), and play which is symbolic (Piaget 1951) and Segal's (1957) distinction between symbol formation and symbol equation.

had some bricks inside it. He placed objects inside, and combined this with some banging and throwing:

> Timothy lifted the seat of the walker and put a book in the space under the seat. He closed the seat and then banged both hands on it twice. He opened the seat and put another book in, closed the seat and banged on the seat with both hands. (O43: Timothy at one year five days)

Books had become a currency between Timothy and Sally since weaning, and reading had been a means of being together. Now the books were firmly kept 'inside'. In O50 (Timothy at 14 months one week) he used the walker again:

> He took a brick from her and aimed it at the compartment, which had its lid open. He missed. He took another one, aimed it casually and it went in. He shut the lid and patted it firmly with his hands. He let some bricks fall on the lid and on to the floor. Sally laughed, and in a very quick movement, he aimed a brick at her. She looked scared and cross for a fleeting second and then he put the brick down (O50)

Timothy's quite violent resentment at this moment appears, as though he could become the 'wild animal' of which Sally was so apprehensive. Yet his play, dropping bricks which may go in and which fall on the lid and cannot go in, suggest a kind of 'hit and miss' approach to connecting with another person.

By 14 months he had made a 'den' in a space between the sofa, the wall, and the hearth, a complete inside space into which he could squeeze between the hearth and the sofa. He spent some time in there in every observation between his first birthday and Sally's miscarriage. He put objects in there, balloons and books, and he brought these objects to show me: 'Timothy put one foot in the hearth and pushed his way into the space behind the sofa. He came out with two balloons tied together. He brought them over to me and as I took them he smiled at me' (O50). This physical inside space resembled both an incubator and a representation of an inside-mummy space (Klein 1930). Neville suggested this was an illegitimate activity on Timothy's part when he said that 'mummy does not like you going in there' (O53).

The question of Sally's pregnancy had been in the air from about the time Timothy was 14 months, and she announced this to me in O55 (Timothy at 15 months 11 days). Previously, in O53 (Timothy at 14 months three weeks) Timothy was very busy throughout the observation searching for objects which were hidden in an inside space:

> Timothy walked over to the corner of the sofa and with lots of 'uhhs' and 'oohs' he started to lift the cushion and put his hand into the corner where he had dropped the objects last week. Sally said, 'yes I heard you put lots of toys down there but we can't reach them'... He picked up a blue ball and put it down the sofa, and started to dig his hand down under the cushion to try to find the toys he had hidden. Sally

> helped him. She pulled out a piece of jigsaw which she gave to him, and he brought it over to me. She found another jigsaw piece and again he brought it over to me. Then Sally found a toy car, which she again gave to Timothy and he brought it to me. (O53: Timothy at 14 months 27 days)

He followed this with some equally compelling searching through containers, in an urgent, nearly frantic way:

> Timothy went to Neville's briefcase and pulled at the straps, calling in an urgent and insistent tone, 'uh, eh, eh'. Neville said to me, 'he's getting demanding'. He helped Timothy undo the straps and Timothy pulled out some papers and brought them over to me, passing them to me with a grin. He went back to the briefcase and took out a sandwich box. Neville helped him to open it and Timothy placed a piece of jigsaw inside the box. Neville, following Timothy's lead, helped to close the box. (O53)

Neville was curious about this play, which continued with Timothy having the briefcase opened and closed, and taking out the contents. Each of these explorations appeared to involve a third person, in a triangular mode of relating. He gave a further clue about his state of mind when he combined this search of the insides with banging and throwing, and when he was involved in interactions in which someone was excluded. He dismantled the handle of the baby walker (O43) and then, when mother was talking on the telephone, he banged the cupboard door, as he had banged shut the lid of the walker: 'He crawled off the sofa, this time moving towards the door. He stopped by the dresser and banged his hand against the doors' (O50). When Neville arrived home from work, Timothy could be seen trying to find ways of relating to both mother and father. A resolution was reached in O50 when they all, Sally, Neville and Timothy, became merged together on the sofa (see page 197 above).

The solution to including both mother and father was a physical one, which seemed to be more about 'sticking together' than making a mind-mind link (Graph 8.13). Togetherness was a temporary feature, and Timothy displayed marked infidelity to father, projecting jealousy after he had been left out:

> Sally left to make tea, and Timothy followed, waving goodbye to me at the door. Sally said he could stay and pointed him back into the room. He cried. Sally returned and Timothy pointed to the row of birthday cards on the mantelpiece. Sally said 'you have another birthday card' and she passed it to Neville. Timothy came between them and got hold of it. He stood in the middle of the room, and with some concentration tore a piece of the envelope. He went towards Sally, handed it to her, and then withdrew it. He came over to me and handed the card to me. I shook my head and told him it was not for me, but for daddy. (O51: Timothy at 14 months two weeks)

By O51, Sally reported that Timothy was excited by the thought of my arrival, just as I saw him excited by Neville's return home. During this period, Timothy's language was still restricted to 'ooh' and 'ahh' sounds. The meaning of his verbal communications with Sally were elusive, shedding no light on his search of insides. Obscurity of communications at a physical and vocal level characterised the 'flat' relationship between them. Timothy, however, expressed considerable emotionality when he hit, banged and searched. The notion persisted that it was hard to reach him in a containing way, that is, with the possibility of being able to reach shared understanding. There was an element of a breakdown of communication between Timothy and his parents.

Sally had a miscarriage, and Timothy's play began to centre more on a theme of throwing away, and/or banging. In O60 (Timothy at 16 months three weeks) Timothy threw pieces of orange on the floor, he dropped a piece of jigsaw in the hearth, and a toy soldier in a wastepaper basket. Then he very concretely put himself between Sally's legs. He repeated this in O66 (Timothy at 18 months three weeks). In O62 (Timothy at 17 months three weeks), the problem of understanding at a verbal level was placed in the forefront of interaction between Sally and Timothy. Sally showed her eagerness to talk with him, and to assume understanding of his sounds and gestures, but there remained a gap between them:

> Timothy walked up to Sally and looked at her through pursed lips, saying 'oooh'. He put his hand on her knee tenderly and then put his other hand up to his head saying 'dada'. Sally eagerly said 'daddy went to work yesterday without his umbrella, and he did not need it today'. Timothy made a throwing movement with his hand and said 'maow' and Sally, quickly and without pause said 'yes we threw orange peel on the garden to keep off the cat'. Timothy said 'dada' and Sally said 'dada did it too'. Timothy lifted his arm and pointed to the window, saying 'maow'. Sally said 'the cat was out there this morning but he's not there now'. Timothy pointed to the door and made an 'uuuh' noise, looking still intently, almost earnestly into Sally's face. She smiled back at him. He pointed to the door and Sally said 'daddy did not take his coat'. Timothy said 'mama' and pointed to the mantelpiece, where there was a cup. Sally said 'mummy's tea', and she made a blowing sound, which Timothy imitated. He said 'baba' and Sally said 'blackbird?' and she went on to talk about the ducks and birds they had seen. (O62)

Timothy communicated clearly that he had a preoccupation with daddy, the cat, and outside. He identified something that was mummy's, the tea. He was closely engaged with her, standing close to her and maintaining a serious, earnest intent in his communications. Sally was willing to talk with him, and offer wide-ranging explanations, which tended to be 'historical' in their content, that is, relaying information about their activities together from the recent past. She had my presence in mind as she spoke. From the point of view of how effectively the interaction tuned into Timothy's inner preoccupations, there was a sense that Sally responded too quickly, replying without pause to assimilate his communications. She was beginning a re-idealisation with Timothy as her alive baby. The final interpretation of 'blackbird' for Timothy's word 'baba', was an act of gaucheness on her part, or even misinformation. Sally translated 'baba' as 'blackbird' again in O66 (Timothy at 18 months three weeks) and in O72 (Timothy at 20 months 15 days), when he was playing in the garden:

> Again he dipped his watering can in the bucket, and thus let it fill with water. He went to water the garden. He found an apple core and threw it towards Sally and me. He came back over to the rug and then pointed at an apple core. 'Baba, baba' he said. 'Yes you put it out for the blackbirds' Sally said. (O72)

Not only has Timothy repeated the word 'baba' over a three-month period (O62–O72) but each time he said 'baba' it was in connection with something which had been thrown out (O72), screwed up (O66) and outside (O62). His preoccupation seemed very much to be with a lost, 'apple core' of a baby. This was a thought which could not be known for Sally.[5] This key word in his vocabulary became linked with misinformation.

Sally reported that conversations with Timothy, such as the one described in O62, took place regularly outside the observational hour. Whilst talking with Timothy in O62, the cat was a central piece of their conversation. The connection between the cat, the outsider, and father (together with the observer), suggested a state of mind, or phantasy behind a state of mind, in which Timothy identified with the act of throwing away, or keeping out, the baby-making qualities of the father. This was seen in observations in his possessiveness of mother, the exclusion of father from interactions between them, and the increasing interest in the cat. The miscarriage seemed to have given him permission to act in breaking the link between the parents in his triangular relationships, an intention which was probably the phantasy underlying his play in separating objects (things), for example, the dining table (O41) and the baby walker (43).

In O63 (Timothy at 18 months one week), Timothy linked the cat with throwing away, and Sally understood this to indicate destructiveness:

> Sally pointed to a picture of a cat in a magazine. 'Here's a nice ginger and white one' she said. Timothy stood up and made a throwing away gesture with his right arm, saying 'ohh' which sounded a little like 'go',

5 Or a 'known' which could not be thought (Bollas 1987).

> or 'away'. Sally said it was hard to explain how destructive cats are when they are on a garden. (O63)

Then he linked them with father:

> (Sally made a tower of bricks, and invited Timothy to place some more bricks on top). He placed a brick on top, gently, as though it were very fragile, and repeated this with another brick, again treating it delicately. He found a plastic model cat and put it on top of the tower. (O63)

If this suggested a phallic, father tower, he then placed the cat in the role of 'inside' baby: 'Timothy got the container of bricks and emptied the bricks from it. He took the cat from the top of the tower and put it in the container. He reached for the lid, took out the cat and placed it out of sight behind him' (O63). The cat was then hidden from father, as Neville arrived home from work: 'Neville came in, but Sally had to draw Timothy's attention to him, as Timothy was now playing with the cat. He turned round in a furtive way, so that his body hid the cat' (O63). It was clear that the cat held importance as a representative of a complex number of themes about inside/outside, and the father–mother–baby constellation. In O68 (Timothy at 19 months ten days) his reactions to the cat reached a frenzy of intensity: 'A cat appeared on the windowsill. Timothy, in Sally's arms turned away from the window, and buried his head in her neck, crying out. He turned to look at the cat, with a shriek of delight, and then he seemed to pull back in fear and excitement' (O68). Timothy reaches an identification with the cat, the dangerous outsider, baby-maker and possibly baby-killer.

In his interactions, Timothy was both possessive of mother and excluding of father. In this observation, O63, Timothy appears not to notice Neville's arrival. In O66 Neville commented on this continuing exclusion:

> Neville said that Timothy had not come to him all day, and he suggested that Sally send him over to him. (I had been struggling with feeling excluded for the past few minutes). Sally asked Neville to join them on the sofa, and with some reluctance he moved over heavily and sat with them. After a few seconds, Timothy got off Sally's lap, and went into his 'den', the space between the hearth and the sofa. He pulled out several magazines, and Sally told him not to do this as Neville had just bought them. (O66)

In the aftermath of the miscarriage, both parents were contending with their feelings of loss and rivalry; there seemed not enough baby to go round, and Timothy illustrated that, in the inside space of his den, that which father plants cannot be allowed to remain for long. Here he was the uprooting boy, ensuring the space inside mother remained for him alone. He seemed to be taking prophylactic action. In O66 and O67 Neville was left excluded, and I experienced feelings of exclusion. The following week the observation was cancelled, totally excluding me. In O72, and O73, Timothy shut a door behind him, leaving me shut out of (or shut in) the room he had left, and leaving himself with Sally. In O77 he watched Sally make a Duplo construction, and then:

> Sally tried to get a car through a bridge, and she found it was too narrow. She took the bridge down and made it wider, and as she pushed the car through Timothy leaned over and broke the bridge. Sally petulantly told him she 'wouldn't play if he was going to break bridges' (O77 Timothy at 22 months three weeks)

Sally was here attempting something of a reconstruction but Timothy appeared to have an investment in bridges not being made good. The baby-making couple appeared to be the object of his attentions; the aim was to keep the father out and the couple apart. The result would probably be that he remained the only baby, and the space inside Sally reserved for him. His confusion about the nature of the internal space, stemming originally from the incubator experience, rendered the inside space an area of solitude rather than a place for containment. The area of misunderstanding between himself and Sally (flat containing shape) combined to ensure that Timothy's intentions were regressive rather than developmental. His play was primarily concerned with the expression of unconscious phantasy (Isaacs 1952) rather than the development of symbolic thinking. Separation from the mother meant a journey across a bridge into the dangerous world of the cat-daddy, and for Timothy, buoyed by a mother who returned anew with idealisation of her alive baby after the miscarriage, the costs of this journey were not immediately appealing.

The failure of symbolic thinking in this period was illustrated by two observations of Timothy with food. First he showed dislike for the food the parents had grown themselves:

> Sally passed him his plate and said it was daddy's courgettes and tomatoes. Timothy took one mouthful and then made a face of distaste and spat out the food. Sally used a spoon to give him a mouthful. He took a fork and took a mouthful from this. Sally tried to sort out what he liked and what he did not, and then she said 'you really don't like it', adding, to me, that he usually ate most things. She gave him an apple and he began to eat it. Then he started to choke. Sally told him to stop, and he did.' (O73: Timothy at 20 months 24 days)

'Daddy's courgettes and tomatoes' appear to have been experienced by Timothy as something much closer to parts of daddy himself, as a concrete symbol equation (Segal 1957). The apple too had appeared in the previous observation as representing the miscarried baby (O72). This was clearly indigestible to him. His being able readily to stop choking suggested that he was able to check what appeared to be a virulent phantasy. The second episode involving feeding occurred when he took a drink:

> He made a noise and followed this with an animated gesture with his arms, and an 'uhh' and he got up and went out of the room. I commented on how difficult it was to understand what he meant just then and Sally said she thought it meant he wanted a drink, but she could not be sure; perhaps it was out of reach... (He returned and) she passed him a drink which he held and drank straight away, looking towards me but not focusing on me, but blankly staring ahead as he drank from the beaker (O77: Timothy at 22 months 24 days)

He moved on to an episode of play which was nearly violent and which demonstrated how forcibly he wished to remain the 'inside baby':

> Sally started talking to Neville and Timothy picked up the box/container for the 'pop-up men' toy. He found a wooden soldier and he banged the soldier into one of the holes with a piece of wood. He picked up another soldier and banged this into the hole where it jammed. He continued with a third soldier, jamming it into the third hole of the box. Sally told him to stop because he would damage the paint. He took no notice and continued banging until all four holes were filled with soldiers. (O77)

Parental 'intercourse' annoyed him and he succeeded in wedging apart Sally and Neville: 'Sally repeated he should stop, sounding more desperate than angry. Neville said "he's all right, leave him" and Sally said "we were getting on all right till..." and she went out of the room to make tea, not finishing her sentence' (O77). Here was three-way dissatisfaction, based on the *almost* expressed view, shared it seemed by Timothy and Sally, that the presence of the father was a cause of difficulties. There was an echo in the projective experience of Neville's blaming the observer for the baby's ills (O1, above). Here, however, the observer's presence was preferable – presumably through relative inaction – to father's realistically-based demands.

8.6 Ending

Whilst Sally, mindful for the last five weeks of the observations of the impending ending, made some attempts at reconstruction and bridge building (O77), Neville appeared to be buckling, complaining of feeling unwell, in a slightly hypochondriacal way. In O79 (Timothy at 23 months seven days), Sally attempted to talk to Timothy about the difference between mending and breaking, as he attempted to bang and dismantle things:

> He got the baby walker, turned it over and banged the wooden base with a plastic beaker, banging at first slowly but then rhythmically and quite hard. He turned the walker on its side and put the plastic beaker on the wheel, spun the wheel and studied it. Sally asked him if he was mending the walker and Timothy grunted in response. He turned it

> over again and recommenced banging. Sally, concerned, said she did not think it was a good idea, he might break it. She came over to check and then said he could carry on, but it was a better game to mend the wheels rather than to break them. Timothy banged again, then he turned the walker over and sat inside it, squeezing himself up small so that he could fit. (O78: Timothy at 23 months)

As Timothy explored the properties of the container, particularly its strength, Sally attempted to mediate (concave containing shape). His actions were clearly describing his wishes, and the concreteness of his placing himself, as a small baby, in the container, demonstrated the regressive nature of these intentions. The play, with Sally's attention to the meaning, offered some hope of working through what had become a very stuck issue for him, though the concreteness of the symbol equation. Timothy forced himself to be small enough to sit inside the baby walker, indicating that the developmental problem still remained. In the next observation, however, there was a glimpse of progress:

> Sally, playing with bricks, made a staircase effect with a bridge in the middle. Timothy leaned over and lifted out the bridge. The staircase fell apart, and the other bricks caved in. He held the bridge brick, looked at it, and then at Sally with some concern and anxiety. Sally offered to mend it and Timothy looked reassured. She took the brick and placed it back in the middle, and renewed her construction. (O79: Timothy at 23 months seven days)

Mother's willingness to repair the damage Timothy has done offered him hope of reparation. His approach to a more depressive state of mind was indicated during the last weeks of the observation of a more tender attitude to me and father. First he played in father's slippers: 'Timothy appeared in the doorway wearing Neville's slippers. He smiled warmly at all three of us, and he walked back into the room' (O79). Over the months since the miscarriage, the very idea of Timothy wearing Neville's shoes during an observation was quite beyond probability. Here, though, it was accomplished with warmth and a sense of humour. The state of mind Timothy displayed suggested that there was affection for father, and identification with him, which, given his demeanour, was more likely to be introjective than projective (Meltzer 1984). With me, he made a deliberate and tender exploration:

> He looked up at me curiously, and then ran his hand through my beard. I told him that it was my beard and he left his hand touching my face for a long time, then he ran his hand through my beard again. He smiled at me and then turned back to his bricks. (O79)

The interaction appeared to show Timothy taking in, internalising something with me, in a way that suggested he was making a picture in his mind for himself, an image that might endure. The ending of the observational period gave this opportunity, for accepting an ending or separation, through trying to remember fondly rather than 'forgetting' or dismissing the value of the relationship. When I saw Timothy just before his fourth birthday, Sally told me she had asked him if he remembered me and he had replied that he remembered I had a beard!

8.7 Summary

In Timothy's first year, Sally had spoken about 'not knowing what to do' and of Timothy 'not knowing what he wants'. The predominant type of parenting, which was evidenced in observations by the emphasis on the physical and the concrete, was a 'flat containing shape', both in terms of Sally's approach to thinking about Timothy's communications and in the way she and Neville 'stuck together' rather than making a thinking link ('bridge building'), which would admit more depressive states of mind (Graph 8.13). Timothy's early development was centrally concerned with the problems of internalising an understanding object (Graph 8.20), and the distressing impact of physical separation, whilst it was difficult for Timothy to achieve a 'firm grip' on mother. His muscularity, as a defensive pattern, was developed in the service of contending with the anxieties which these experiences engendered, and substituted a firm grip on himself for one on another. Timothy was the most 'muscular' infant in the sample.

During the second year, when Sally was pregnant and then miscarried, Timothy became preoccupied with the space inside her, over which he claimed hegemony. His play revolved around the phantasy of attaining an inside space and separating the mother–father baby-making couple. Possessiveness in Timothy was matched by Sally's re-idealisation of him, her projections of dangerousness and destructiveness on to the outside, and this led to an accommodating fit between them, which colluded with regressiveness and an avoidance of developmental needs.

The concrete regressive and physical approach to relationships displayed by Timothy in his second year resulted in a restricted range of identifications. Particularly, there were few glimpses of identifications with parents. The concreteness and restrictiveness ran counter to the development of more symbolic ways of functioning. Both the problems in development of symbolic play and the retardation of language appear to have much to do with the earlier intolerance of separation and separateness, and therefore with the problems of early internalisation.

Timothy's future language development confirmed to a great extent the picture that emerged over his first two years. First, until he was three, he gradually gained some words which were not easily understandable. At three he was very anxious about doors being closed and he would try to lock the front door himself. At four, he had gained considerable language, including sentences, but he had only one consonant – L – and all words were reduced to this sound.[6] The problems of early containment, the defences that Timothy developed and the quality of his grip relations, appear to be consistent with this later development.

8.8 Grid

8.8.1 Mothering

Sally, Timothy's mother received good support from her husband, Neville, and the grid showed moderate support from extended family and low support from friends and professionals (Graph 8.1). Sally's emotional preoccupations were scored as moderate/mixed and tending towards the anxious and persecutory. Her internal resources were moderate to fairly low, and there were moderate to fairly low levels of impingement of her preoccupations on to the infant, Timothy (Graph 8.2a). Sally's verbalisation of her concerns and preoccupations was rated as fairly low, and there was a score of moderate to fairly low for the levels of conflict she experienced in her role (Graph 8.2b).

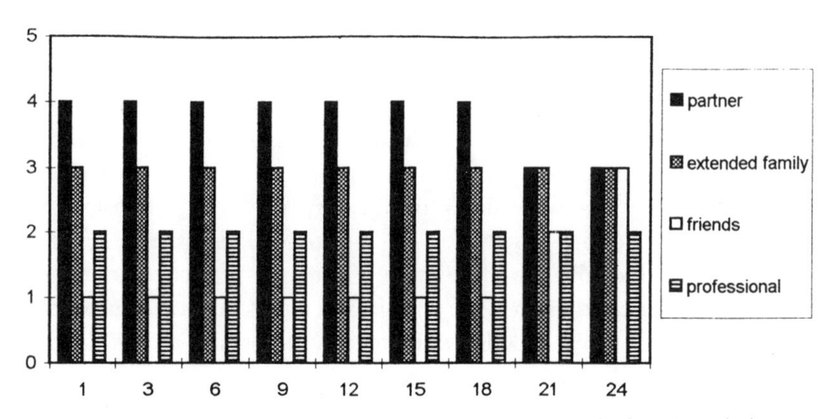

Key: 5=very high levels of support; 4=good; 3=moderate; 2=fairly low; 1=low

Graph 8.1

---

6 The relationship between the kind of sounds the baby makes and the grip relationship with the breast (and the experiences of absence from the breast during breast-feeding and weaning) is one for which there are possible hypotheses, following Meltzer (1984), Meltzer (1975, Chapter VII) and Wittenberg (in Meltzer 1975, Chapter IV). The 'l' sound is consistent with the 'tonguing' seen in O8, O10 (p.204 above) and the looseness of a mouth grip.

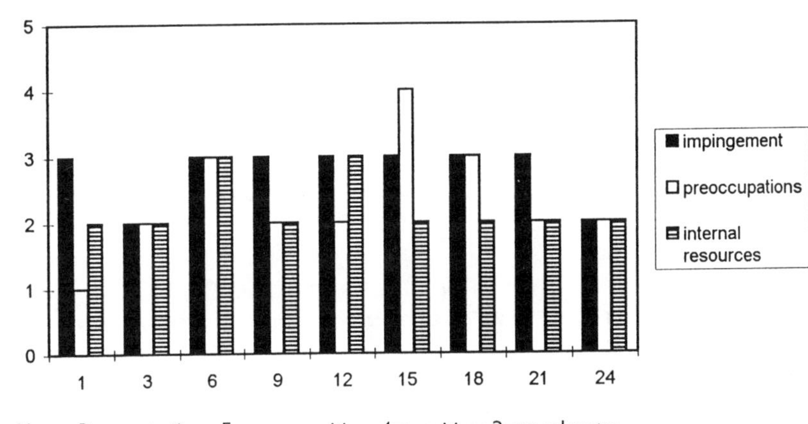

Key: *Preoccupations*: 5=very positive; 4=positive; 3=moderate; 2=fairly anxious/persecutory; 1=anxious/persecutory
Rest: 5=very high; 4=high; 3=moderate; 2=fairly low; 1=low

Graph 8.2a

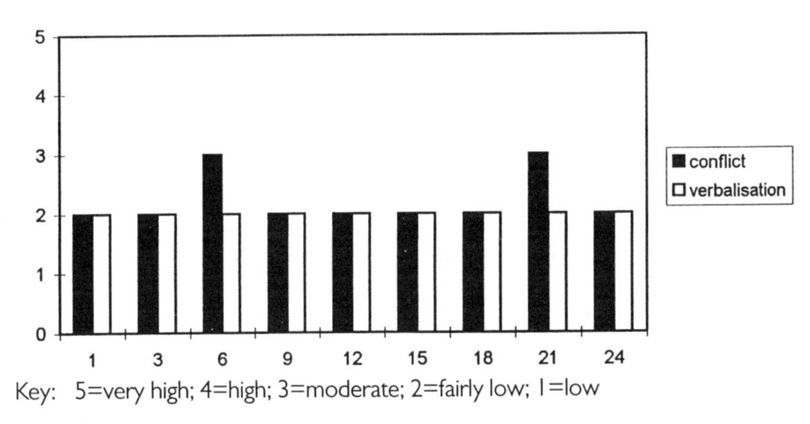

Key: 5=very high; 4=high; 3=moderate; 2=fairly low; 1=low

Graph 8.2b

Sally experienced the key events in Timothy's development in a moderate to fairly negative way, and she made some, but fairly infrequent representations of his states of mind and characteristics (Graph 8.3a). The kind of attribution she made tended to be moderately persistent, or less, and to be neutral, or tending to the negative (Graph 8.3b). Sally met Timothy's physical needs well, and was moderately well/well aware of his emotional needs. She was moderately well able to meet his emotional needs. The grid showed an increase in her capacity to understand his communications from fairly low to moderate (Graph 8.4).

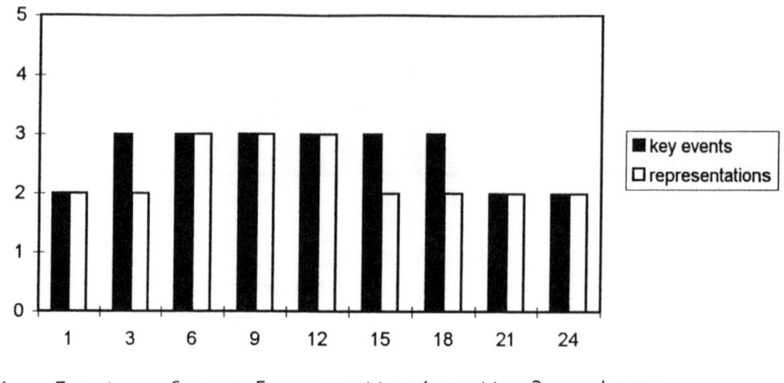

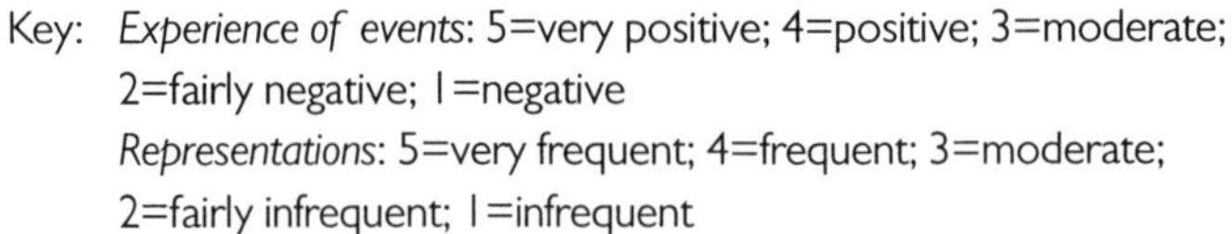

Key: *Experience of events*: 5=very positive; 4=positive; 3=moderate; 2=fairly negative; 1=negative
Representations: 5=very frequent; 4=frequent; 3=moderate; 2=fairly infrequent; 1=infrequent

Graph 8.3a

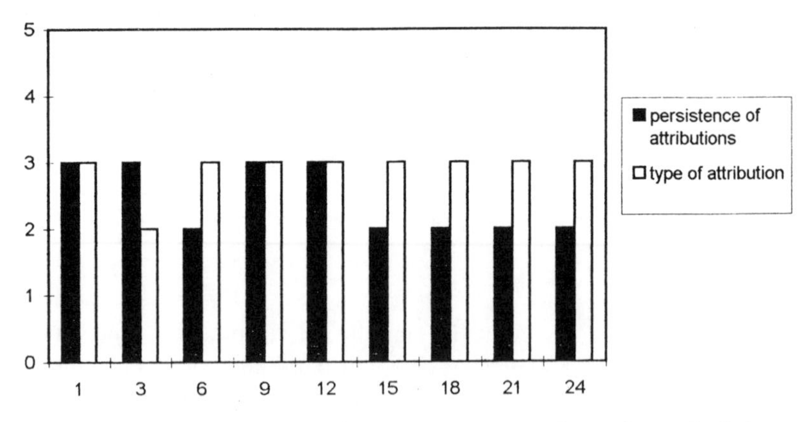

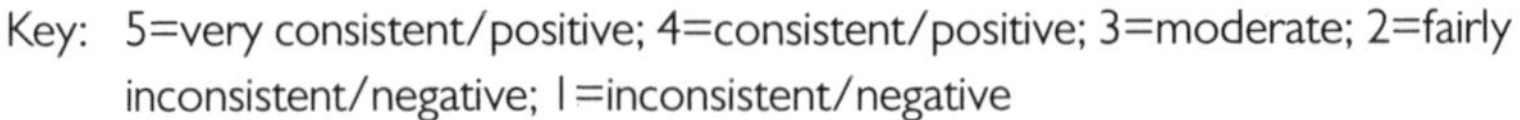

Key: 5=very consistent/positive; 4=consistent/positive; 3=moderate; 2=fairly inconsistent/negative; 1=inconsistent/negative

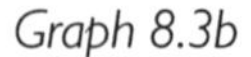

Graph 8.3b

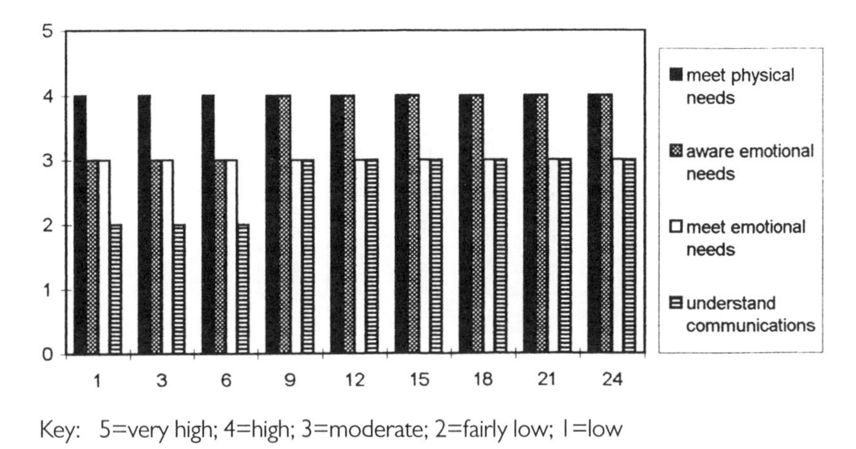

Key: 5=very high; 4=high; 3=moderate; 2=fairly low; 1=low

Graph 8.4

8.8.2 Mother–infant relationship

Sensitivity, attentiveness and intimacy in the mother–infant relationship were all rated at 'moderate'. Conflict and understanding of communications were rated either moderate or slightly low (Graph 8.5). Grip relations between Timothy and Sally were all rated within the moderate and slightly weak categories (Graph 8.6a and 8.6b). Intensity of interactions was rated between moderate and high, and the qualities of 'in tune' and maintaining emotional contact were rated below moderate (Graph 8.7).

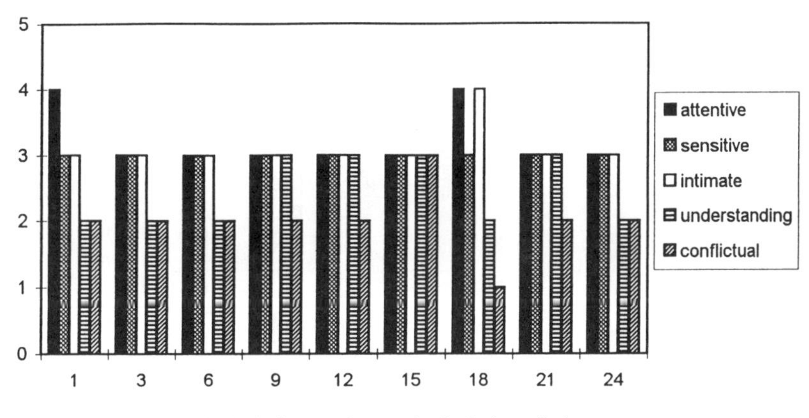

Key: 5=very high; 4=high; 3=moderate; 2=fairly low; 1=low

Graph 8.5

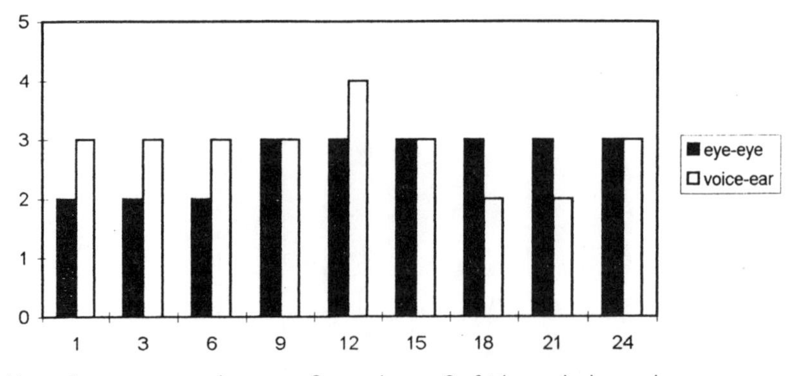

Key: 5=very strong; 4=strong; 3=moderate; 2=fairly weak; 1=weak

Graph 8.6a

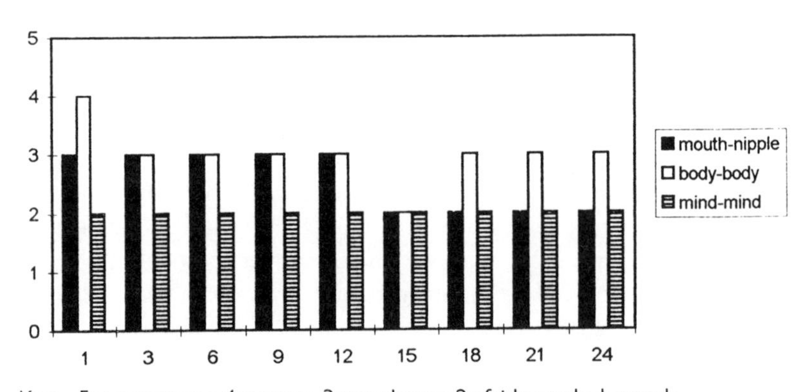

Key: 5=very strong; 4=strong; 3=moderate; 2=fairly weak; 1=weak

Graph 8.6b

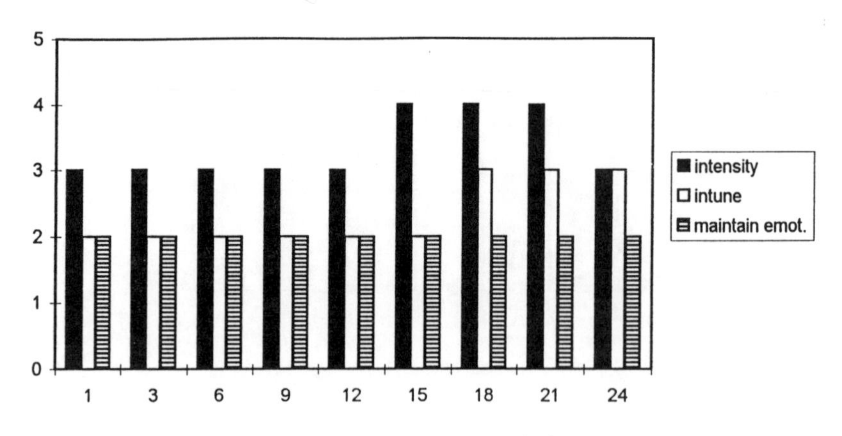

Key: 5=very high; 4=high; 3=moderate; 2=some; 1=low

Graph 8.7

The overall relationship was rated as having moderate degrees of containment, and accommodation, and levels of conflict which were rated between moderate and fairly low (Graph 8.8). Similarly there were moderate degrees of concave containing shape and flat containing shape, whilst convex shape was rated between fairly low and moderate (Graph 8.9).

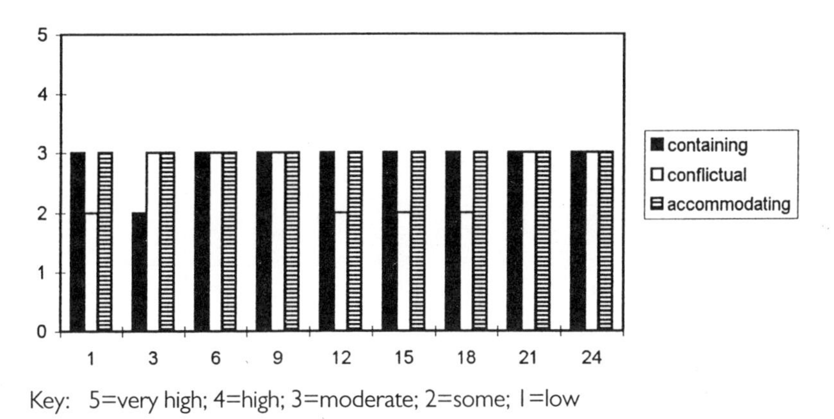

Key: 5=very high; 4=high; 3=moderate; 2=some; 1=low

Graph 8.8

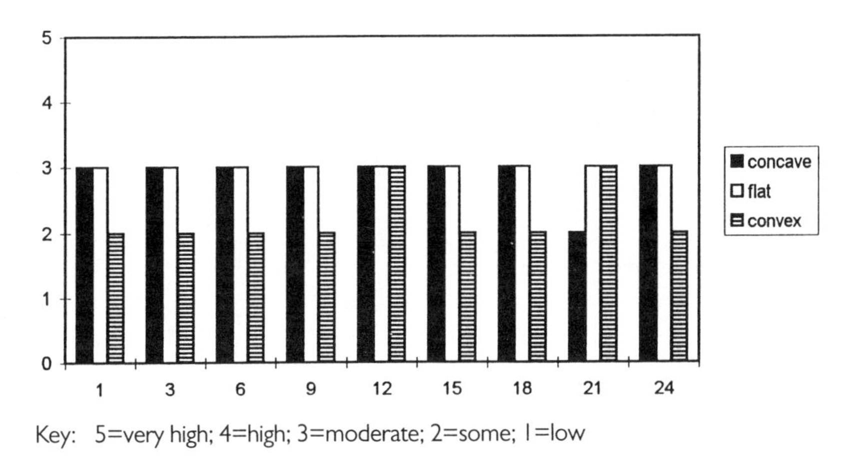

Key: 5=very high; 4=high; 3=moderate; 2=some; 1=low

Graph 8.9

8.8.3 Fathering and father–infant relationship

Neville was seen regularly in observations except when Timothy was between six and 12 months. In the father–infant relationship there were ratings for moderate levels of sensitivity, attentiveness, and intimacy (Graph 8.10). Their grip relations were, overall, moderate, except for mouth–teat, which was low (Graph 8.11).

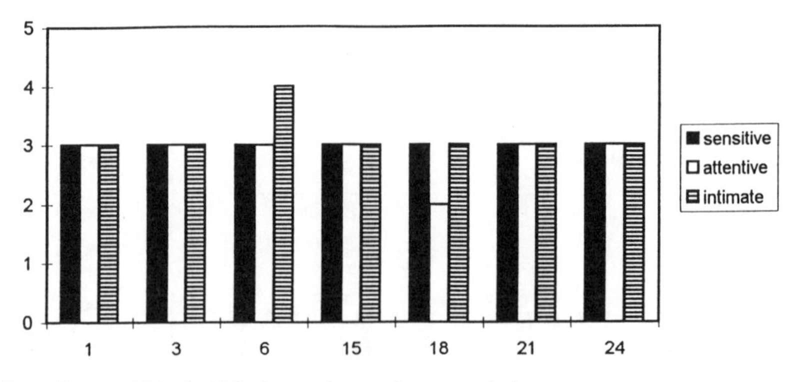

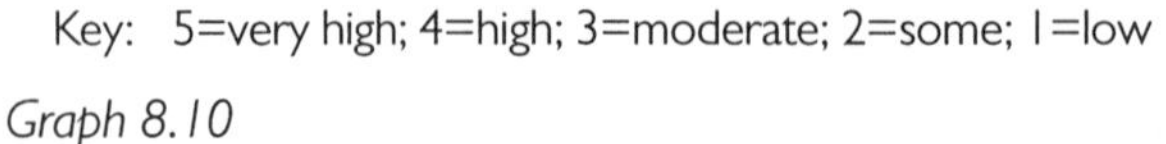

Graph 8.10

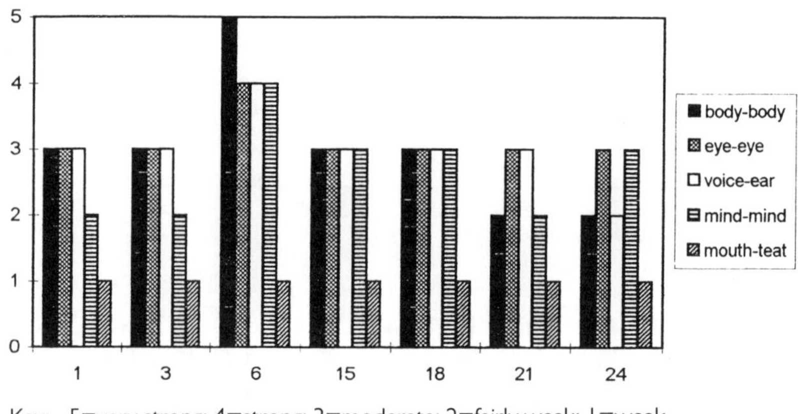

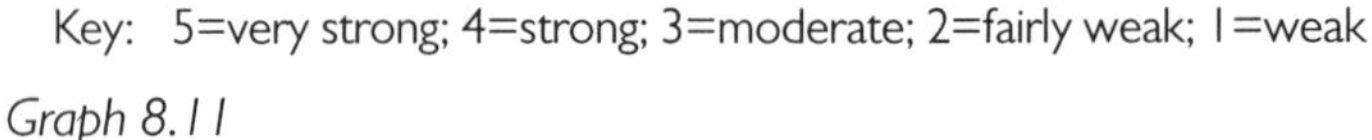

Graph 8.11

8.8.4 Parental relationship

The relationship between Sally and Neville was rated as having low conflict, moderate harmony, and fairly low verbalisation of conflict. From 18 months these levels appeared to fluctuate, suggesting greater conflict, less harmony and greater verbalisation of conflict (Graph 8.12). In their parental styles for meeting Timothy's containment needs, there were high scores for the category 'sticking together', and moderate for 'flattening of affect'. 'Bridge building' scored fairly low. There was a moderate score for the 'nappy changer' category (Graph 8.13).

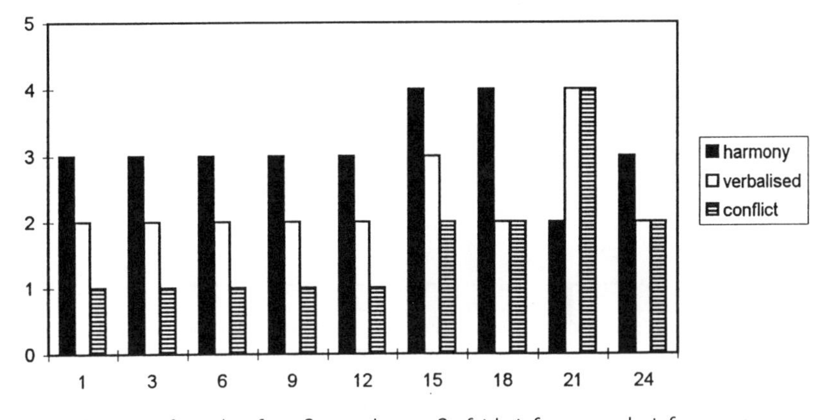

Key: 5=very often; 4=often; 3=moderate; 2=fairly infrequent; 1=infrequent

Graph 8.12

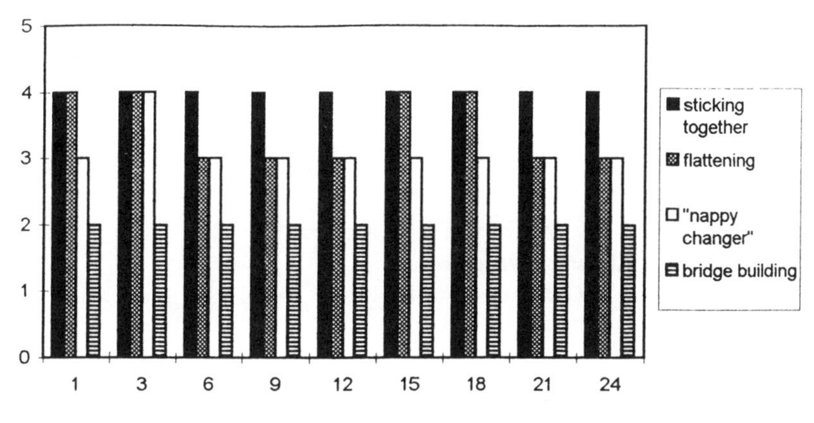

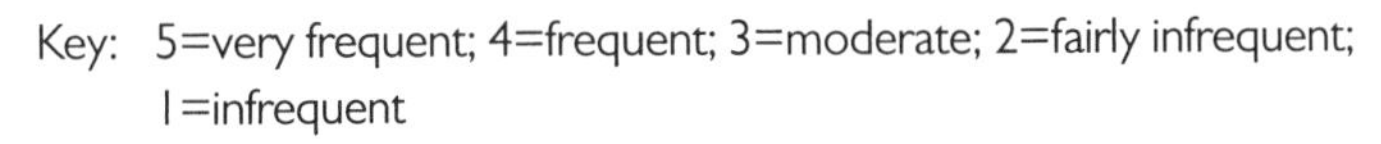
Key: 5=very frequent; 4=frequent; 3=moderate; 2=fairly infrequent; 1=infrequent

Graph 8.13

8.8.5 Infant development

The grid showed Timothy's physical development to be advanced (Table 8.1), particularly in his first year. Feeding was rated moderate, and his sleeping patterns were moderate or below. The grid recorded difficulties in his sleeping patterns particularly in his first year (Graph 8.1).

Table 8.1

Sitting	5 months
Crawling	6 months
Standing	7 months
Walking	9.5 months

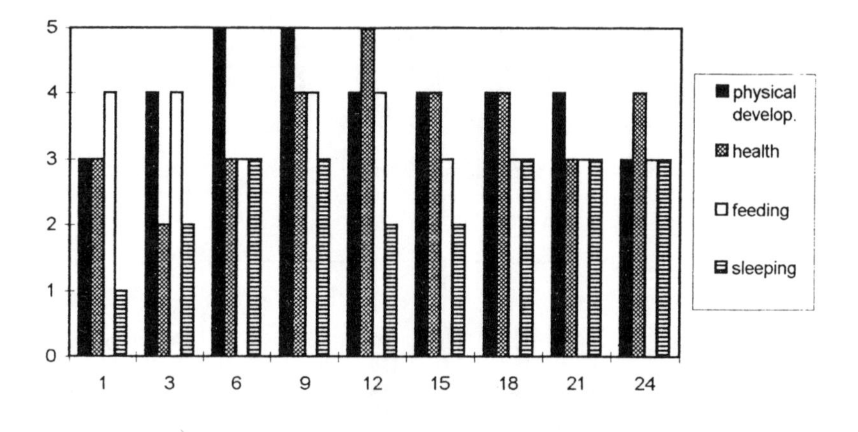

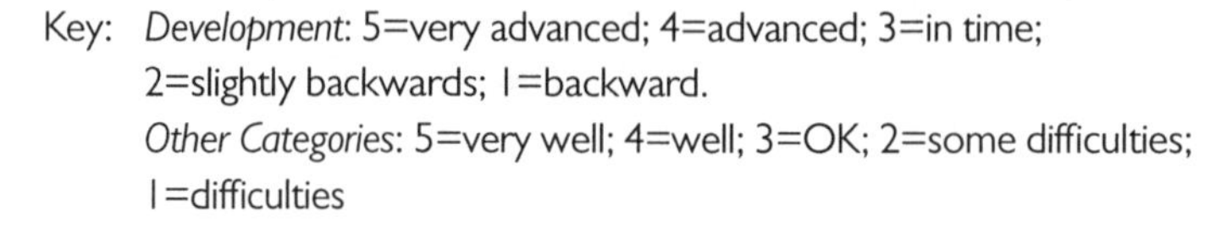

Key: *Development*: 5=very advanced; 4=advanced; 3=in time; 2=slightly backwards; 1=backward.
Other Categories: 5=very well; 4=well; 3=OK; 2=some difficulties; 1=difficulties

Graph 8.14

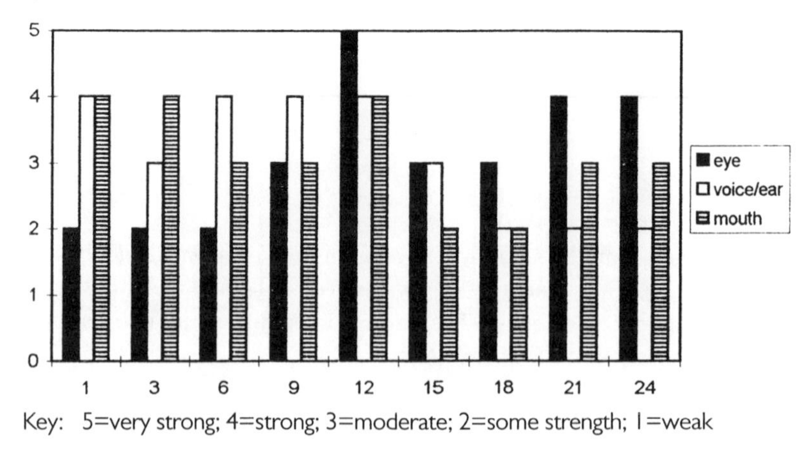

Key: 5=very strong; 4=strong; 3=moderate; 2=some strength; 1=weak

Graph 8.15a

Timothy's strength of grip was rated to show an increasing strength of eye grip, and mouth and voice–ear grips which were scored as falling from strong to fairly weak (Graph 8.15a). His hand and body grips were both rated strong and very strong, whilst his mind grip was moderate or below (Graph 8.15b). Timothy maintained high levels of object relating, and, in his first year, some very high levels of protest/expressiveness. His frequency of defending was scored constantly at a moderate level. His defences tended towards the rigid end of this grid, again especially in his first year (Graph 8.16). Timothy was rated as having high capacities for memory and recognition, and a moderate capacity for recall with affection (Graph 8.17).

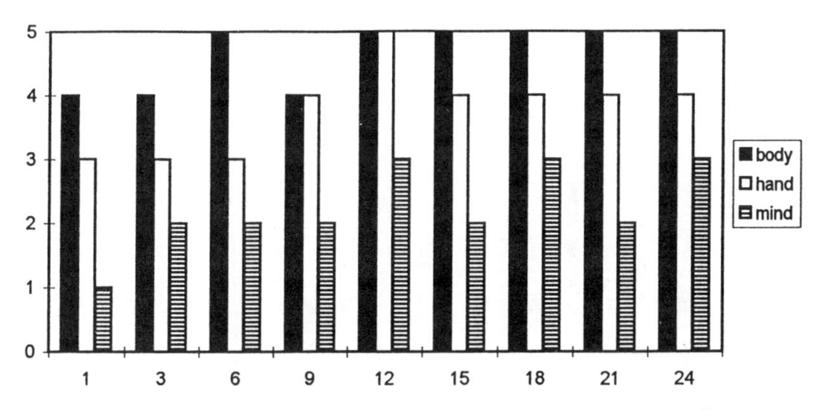

Key: 5=very strong; 4=strong; 3=moderate; 2=some strength; 1=weak

Graph 8.15b

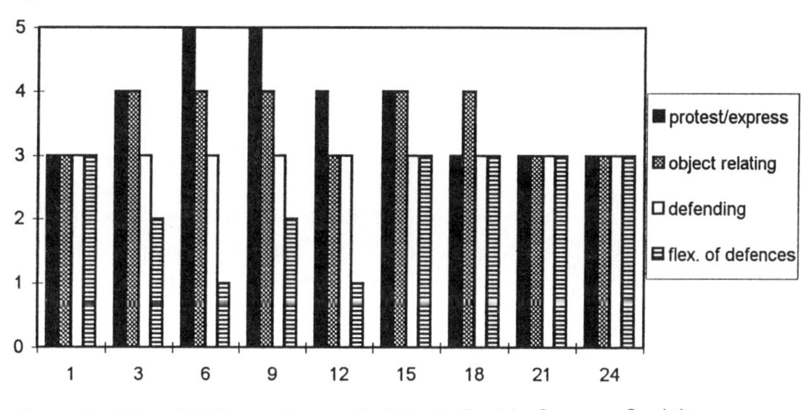

Key: *Flexibility of defences*: 5=very flexible; 4=flexible; 3=some flexibility; 2=tending to rigidity; 1=rigid

Other categories: 5=very high; 4=high; 3=moderate; 2=fairly low; 1=low

Graph 8.16

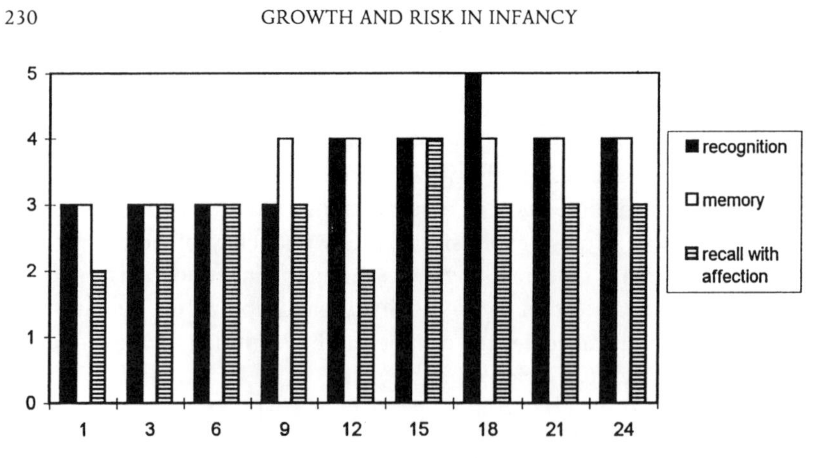

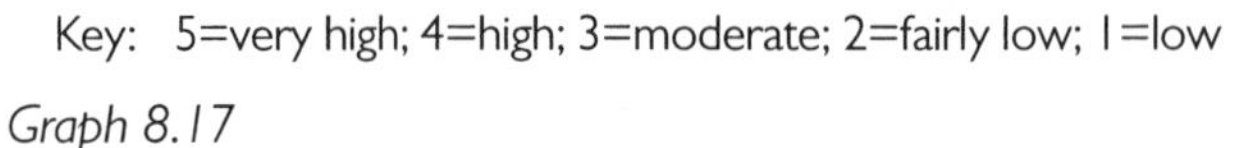

Graph 8.17

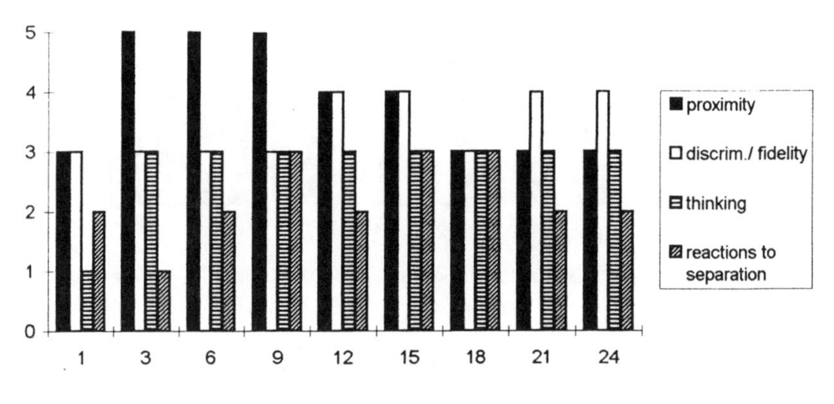

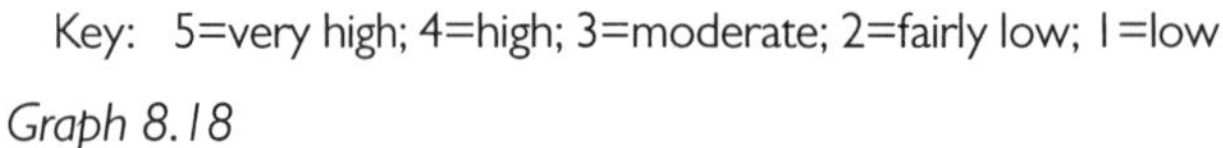

Graph 8.18

He was seen to show high/very high frequencies of seeking proximity and moderate frequencies of thinking and discriminating between people. His reactions to separation were rated as fairly low to moderate (Graph 8.18). Timothy was rated as showing high or very high expressions of unconscious phantasy in play, and his language development declined from moderate to low. Similarly, his expressions of symbolic play were low (Graph 8.19). His overall quality of internalisation tended to the persecutory in his first year, and towards a mixed, or balanced internalisation in his second year (Graph 8.20).

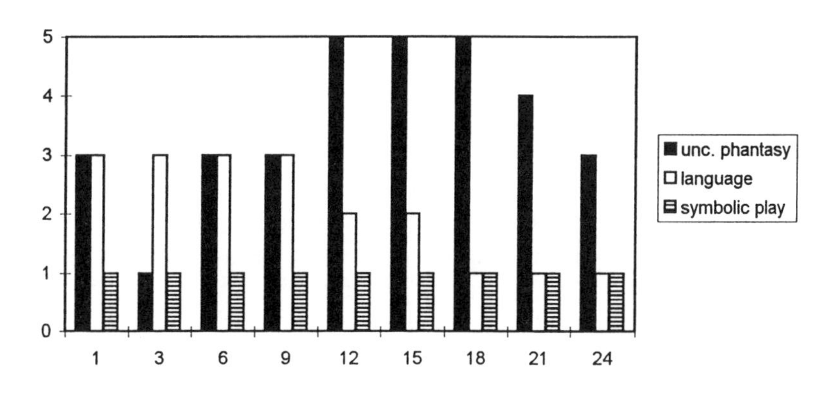

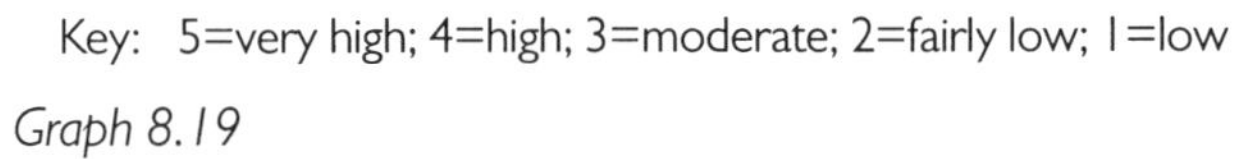
Key: 5=very high; 4=high; 3=moderate; 2=fairly low; 1=low

Graph 8.19

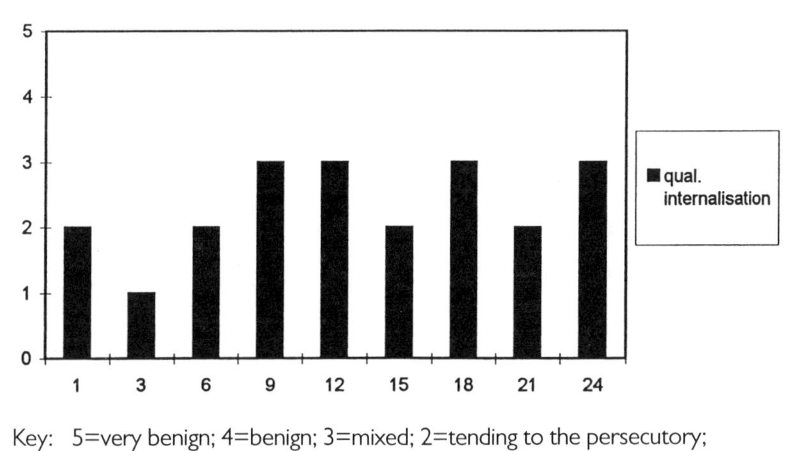

Key: 5=very benign; 4=benign; 3=mixed; 2=tending to the persecutory;

1=persecutory

Graph 8.20

8.8.6 Summary of grid

The grid for Timothy, as with all the other infants, provides categories for structuring the writing of the descriptive case study. Problematic development in the case study concentrated on the lack of language and symbolic play, and these are shown in the grid (Graph 8.19). Although Timothy showed very high levels of proximity seeking, especially between three and nine months, his difficulties in reacting to separation are recorded in Graph 8.18. Declining capacities in his second year in his mouth and voice–ear grip relations are also recorded (Graph 8.15a). These difficulties in development are mirrored by the ratings for parenting, where mother is recorded as having fairly low internal resources (Graph 8.2a), fairly low evidence for verbalisation of her emotional preoccupations (Graph 8.2b) and moderate to fairly low mutual grip with Timothy, especially at a mind to mind level (Graph 8.6b). The parental propensity for 'sticking together' is also recorded in Graph 8.13. The evidence for concave containing shape is also moderate.

Though the grid records problems for Timothy and his mother in maintaining emotionality (Graph 8.7) it also reveals the vigour of his grip relations, with the eye, body and hand especially (Graphs 8.15a, 8.15b), his high levels of protest/expressiveness and his capacity to maintain object relations (Graph 8.16). Timothy's capacities for memory, recognition and the abundance of his play also suggest the potential for positive development alongside the difficulties of language development.

CHAPTER 9

Findings

The five case studies which have been presented here provide a detailed analysis of the five infants' development in their families. It is possible to explore the contribution of these case studies to meeting the series of interrelated aims of the book. The main task is to comment upon the capacity of the model to develop theoretical hypotheses about infancy and in particular to make a contribution to the understanding of risk in infancy. The model, based on the operationalisation of psychoanalytic concepts, used and developed an innovative methodology and it is important to explore how the methodology responded to the purpose to which it was put. Conclusions from the study can therefore be drawn with regard to methodology – the qualities of the descriptive case studies, the functioning of the grid, the role of the observer – and with regard to the model, namely, the capacity of the model to provide descriptive and analytic hypotheses about infancy which relate to the theoretical frameworks described in Chapter 1 and the capacity to generate hypotheses about risk.

9.1 Methodology

The case studies employed the Bick method of infant observation and amended this method to provide comparisons across the sample. They were written in a detailed descriptive format and organised through the descriptive categories in the grid to provide a consistent framework to each case. The grid was developed to provide quantitative data to chosen aspects of each case. Within the restrictions discussed in Chapter 2 and Chapter 3, there is scope here for commenting on the capacity of the grid to develop useful quantitative data.

9.1.1 The descriptive method

The descriptive case studies were written within a framework of categories developed through the operationalisation of theoretical concepts, and as a form of naturalistic ethnographic enquiry they expanded upon the framework along lines suggested by the primary data, the observational reports. Each therefore consists of a number of factors unique to each family, particularly at the level of the social, cultural and situational contexts. These cases were deliberately chosen to represent as wide a cross-section of social situations as was possible.

This has meant that individual cases provide material which relates to that particular case only; for example, being a ninth Bengali baby was of course particular to Hashmat. At another level, the cases also developed material which, though of central interest to the development of that particular baby, affected that baby only. Michael's 'failure to thrive' comes into this category.[1] It is of course inevitable, in a prospective, longitudinal study such as this, that intrinsically interesting data and situations are encountered which are not, however, replicated in the sample as a whole. This was entirely expected and predicted at the outset.

On the other hand, a number of common features did emerge, and these provide the basis for the comparison that follows. Each case study is described within a similar, overlapping framework which shows the development of grounded theory concepts across the sample and how much each case contributed to the development of each concept and its application to the case in question. Some features are highlighted more strongly in one study than another, but the important points of comparison are consistent. Primarily, the case studies demonstrate repeatedly and with a strong degree of conclusiveness that it is possible, using this naturalistic method of observation and employing a 'grounded theory' approach, to provide detailed descriptions of states of mind in infancy. It was anticipated at the outset of the study that the infants, through being observed for an hour each week in their home settings, would be seen in a range of emotional states, and that this was one of the valuable components of this kind of study, namely that it permitted observation of infants in a wider range of emotions than are usually seen in a laboratory-type setting. As there was minimal disruption to the setting through the non-intrusive observational method employed, the fact that the observations of all five infants was accompanied by a context of considerable periods of distress, pain and disturbance provided fewer ethical difficulties than had another setting and method been used.[2]

The observer's attention in observations was directed towards thinking about difficult episodes experienced by the infants and their parents. The role of the observer was modified in particular ways so that some relief of suffering, when this occurred, was provided by the observer's presence and attention. The method therefore permitted sustained study of infants from much younger – a few days after birth – than is usually possible except in the laboratory settings where the observation of infants is constrained to periods of 'alert inactivity'.

Because the observational method gave access to the full range of infant states of mind over significant periods of time, it can be concluded that the psychoanalytic approach to mental and emotional life can be applied to infants

1 Feeding difficulties, through, were common to the sample.

2 In the *Strange Situation,* for example, testing had to be abandoned in the face of excessive distress.

and children younger than those who are usually seen in psychotherapy. Psychoanalytic theories of infancy can therefore be based, not only on reconstructive clinical data but also on direct observation which is prospective and contemporary. The prospects for psychoanalytic theory are that the gap between the 'clinical' and the 'observed' infant will be reduced by this approach, so that observations of infancy may become adept at 'telling us about infants' thinking and feeling and other such matters of especial relevance to psychoanalytic theory' (Spillius 1994, p.18).[3]

Psychoanalytic theorists, it has been seen, have been reluctant to utilise observation as a means of developing theoretical formulations alongside those developed by clinical reconstruction. In the descriptions of infants in this study, it is seen that, if the naturalistic observational method is pursued rigorously, a relationship between observation and interpretation based upon clinical theoretical constructions is possible. In this sense, even the most elusive of psychoanalytical concepts – that is elusive in terms of observation outside the clinical setting – such as phantasy, introjection, projective identification can be discussed in relationship with the observational data. Additionally it is possible that the observational approach is capable of extending and developing psychoanalytical theoretical hypotheses.

It is one matter to urge psychoanalytical theorists to pay more attention to the possibilities provided by observational approaches, and quite another to use psychoanalytical methods in ways which would conform to the specifications of empirical psychology. Operationalising psychoanalytic concepts is – historically – a complex and difficult task. In this thesis the conclusion from the case studies is that, through observing these five infants in a naturalistic methodology, the detailed data about infant behaviour, play and interactions provided the means for describing patterns of infant development, based on repeated observations. The patterns then became the subject for the making of hypotheses in a form consistent with an exploratory methodology, and they are discussed in detail below (9.3 and 9.4). The descriptions of infant development were notable for the way in which they included states of mind, emotional experiences and cognitive development, within a social and situational context. These studies, therefore, suggest that, within a naturalistic observation methodology it is possible to begin to make formulations which link direct observation of infants with a psychoanalytical conceptual framework. An important component of these descriptive formulations is the part played by the concepts developed as substantive theory. These concepts, which, again, are discussed in detail below, perform the function of leading towards a development in

3 The quotation is from Spillius' discussion of the difficulty of achieving this outcome from anything than clinical reconstruction. This study suggests that psychoanalytic theory would be developed considerably through attention to this method of research.

substantive theory which may be capable of empirical testing in the future, and therefore of introducing procedures which can be subject to validity testing.

These case studies suggest that a beginning has been made towards an extension of attempts to link cognition and emotion in studies of infancy. Some of these studies were described in Chapter 1, particularly the work of Murray and Fonagy and his colleagues. The difference between this study and those is that here attempts to extend the methodology are made by attempting to operationalise psychoanalytic concepts. The application of a naturalistic observational approach was an appropriate first step towards this aim, and the outcome has been a rich source of data. Further study is indicated, in which more closed observational methods, quasi-experimental and cohort sequential designs would play a part in further developing the work undertaken here. Reliability and validity would be introduced into the methodology through these more experimental methods.

The process of comparison was facilitated through the study of a sample of cases, the qualitative description of case studies, and the development of the grid.

9.1.2 The grid

The development of a quantitative component of the study was perhaps the most ambitious part of this project. The problems of such an approach which is prior to inter-observer reliability tests has been made clear from the outset. Additionally the procedures used did not follow formally coded standardised formats. They are not measured as basic units of measurement – length, frequency and duration. The naturalistic method was not suited to such measurements. On the contrary, the ratings I have used were judgements made in a scaling procedure. This in itself is an entirely legitimate activity and one which has some parallels – notably in attachment theory – but it does have some considerable implications for issues of measurement and reliability. These have been clearly stated; these are my preliminary moves towards establishing some empirical criteria for future studies.

The quantitative approach was justified, first because the categories which were developed as a framework for writing the descriptive case studies were suggestive of numerical rating, and second, following Fonagy and Moran's view that 'good qualitative analysis invariably precedes good quantitative analysis' (Fonagy and Moran 1993, p.68), in the spirit of the innovative nature of the study, quantification was thought to be a useful exploratory venture. Conclusions from this part of the study are therefore made in full acknowledgement that there have been no interreliability tests. The absence of inter-observer reliability testing and the need to develop working models of causation prior to statistical analysis made statistical analysis of these grids premature. The comments made on the grids are essentially preliminary comments on the viability of the process, and are made in the context of exploration rather than validation. Primarily I would wish to ask the question – if an experimental or quasi-experimental study was designed on the conclusion of this study, where might the starting points be most usefully located? A large number of categories were quantified, partly to provide a wider network of factors which contribute to the operationalisation of difficult concepts, and partly to provide an analysis of which categories appear to have some usefulness for future application.

Statistical analysis of the ratings has not been attempted, and would have been premature. To be effective, statistical analysis requires reliability and an understanding of the problems of measurement and causation (Hartman 1988). As I have explained above, the categories of the grid were formed as a preliminary technique towards the development of closed methods which can be used in future studies. In terms of these preliminary explorations I can comment here on the ratings in accordance with the procedures I have followed. Some of the ratings which I made in the way I have described showed persistence over time of similar ratings, and some recorded changes. Further testing of the reliability and validity of the rating scale would lead to the possibilities of correlating low or high scores through statistical analysis, and the way they change over time with certain outcomes for infant development and risk. In particular, taking comparisons across the cases and over time, were the ratings confirmed in terms of reliability and validity, there would be scope for concluding that there is a relationship between the degree (rating) of container shape, infant capacity to object relate through grip relations and the development of symbol formation in infants. However, as will be discussed below, strength of grip relations is not alone a sufficient category for analysis of the qualities in this concept. Texture and direction are two other aspects which need to be taken into consideration, and which are in principle quantifiable.

The use of the grid in this study partially meets the aims I had. It does provide a framework for comparison across cases which are observed using the naturalistic, Bick method. It does provide categories which are quantifiable and may be useful for testing in future studies some of the hypotheses which are developed here. These are, as I have said, very preliminary explorations of what may form a central arena in future studies.

9.2 The role of the observer

The observer, as discussed in Chapter 2, was a sole researcher, whose recordings were not substantiated by other observers' data, and the descriptions of observations were the sole form of primary data. Video and other forms of triangulation of the primary source were not available. Reliability was provided primarily by the repeated observations, and the consistency of the approach, that is to say, the regularity of the weekly and hourly observation, and the massiveness of the project with observations taking place each week over a two-year period. The aim of the observer was to maintain an unintrusive, receptive stance. The functioning of the observer in each family was made available for scrutiny through the exploration of the observer's activities and emotional experiences. In analysing the findings from the study, the innovative and exploratory nature of the study again need to be stressed. The theoretical findings of this study therefore take into account the role of the observer as participant-observer.

In all the observations the case studies describe the observer becoming active in a particular way, and through this activity developing a combination of roles – and functions – regarding the family, including parents and infants. This modifies the Esther Bick model where 'friendly receptivity' were the constituents of the 'participant' aspect of the participant-observer role. When as observer I was involved in playing with the infants, feeding them, talking to them and, memorably in the case of Hashmat's second birthday, eating meals with them, the role of 'friendly receptivity' seems stretched beyond its reasonable meaning. In Gold's (1958) distinctions of the kinds of participant-observer roles, the observations I conducted became balanced between that of 'participant as observer' and 'observer as participant', rather than 'complete observer'. The role of observing was never abandoned and the additional participative tasks and interactions were – as far as was humanly possible – allied to and responding to the observations that were being made. In the case studies there is discussion of the impact the fact of my observing had on the families, and of the ways observations guided the interventions I made.

9.2.1 Relationships with parents

The expectations of the observation were different in each family. There was an overt acceptance of the observation, and a covert 'agenda', which led to aspects of transference in the relationships with the parents, particularly the mothers. This merits some further discussion. I shall compare the initial expectations, or pre-transference with later developments of the parents' use of the observer.

Hashmat's parents were involved in an ambivalent relationship with a representative of white society. At one level they wished to use me to attain contact with predominantly white institutions (and I did contact the housing department and the GP on their behalf). I was introduced by the health visitor, and Rani described me as being from 'the clinic' well into the observation. There was a wish for acceptance of them, and a scarcely concealed mixture of envy and contempt. Javed Ahmed scoffed at my poor procreative record, while Shakil – who was also influenced by the fact that I was paying attention to his younger brother – explicitly stated the hostile position: 'Me Bengali, you English; fuck off' (O22).

Anne, Samantha's mother, was attracted to the observation through her isolation, and the anxiety she had following her experiences with Donald. She placed me in a role familiar to observers, the expert: 'Anne asked me when the baby's eyes changed colour. I said I was not sure, and Anne said she thought I knew everything. I said I was here to learn from their experience, and Anne said we're really in trouble then' (O3). In the introductory visit she said she was surprised I turned out to be male, and reassured by the thought that she 'got on well' with her father-in-law. I was representative of a missing male – her father – and the 'missing' part of her husband, who was emotionally absent or 'blocking' of emotional experience.

The expectations of Hester's mother, Yvonne, seemed less clear. It did seem that there was a link between the way I was seen as someone who needed help – through needing to have an observation – and her father, who needed her help to find a job. Being needed was important to Yvonne. I also represented a parent or partner who *was* interested in babies, and who could give some space in my mind to her. Here early discussions with me on the telephone after the birth and the speed with which she wanted me to visit indicated the strength of her hope that I would provide this space – and the strength of her fear that something, at a life and death level, may be involved. On one occasion (O3) she was late arriving home for the observation and she reassured me urgently that she would always be there.

Timothy's parents expressed an academic interest in 'research' (without knowing explicitly that this was my purpose!). Before Sally accomplished the social transition from a sentient network of work colleagues, supplementing family relations, to contact with other mothers, I was in effect a bridge between the worlds of family of origin and work and that of being a parent. In their idealisation of the imminent childbirth before Timothy's birth, it seemed that Sally and Neville wished me to record, or bear witness to, the events of their first child. In disillusion, in the early observations, Judy expressed her awareness of the difficulties she faced, the fear of 'wild animals'. Her ascertaining that I had children was also to establish that I was a father, and as a parent I quickly became someone whom she wished to impress and with whom she felt competitive: 'what's he got that I haven't?' (O8).

One of Mary's first reactions was to ask if I would follow Michael after he was two, 'like on *7-up*', a TV series which followed the progress of children at seven-yearly intervals. In this comment she questioned the ending (at two years) of my study, and expressed a sense of importance, rather than rejection and abandonment. The observation provided her with a male figure when she had been abandoned by one (Dave) and a relationship with someone who came and went (and presumably was far more involved with other people than with her). This evoked, as I have shown, the abandoned child Mary, whose mother had died when she was four. Contextually, it also appeared to relate to the unhappiness she expressed about her childhood when her father remarried, namely that he was involved with someone else, rather than her. In the second observation, she likened me to her father: 'Mary asked me to sit down and I said it was easier to stand at the moment. She asked me if I was nervous and she said her dad was nervous of holding Michael, as he feels he might hurt him' (O2).

The beginnings of observations were therefore very much connected with perceptions of me in which gender, cultural context, and specific aspects of parents' past experiences were involved. As the observations progressed, these initial relationships were transformed by experience, and the relationship to the regular, weekly observation became a key variable. This was an event anticapted in a positive way, by for example Yvonne and Anne, especially in her second year, or treated with ambivalence, especially by Mary. In the observations the role that developed was generally that of 'parental container' (most usually here, 'maternal container'). With all the mothers the initial reactions to me as male, and paternal, continued to play a part as the role developed. Not only did mothers use the observational time to comment, report and otherwise air their feelings and concerns over the week, but they also developed a specific 'task' relationship with me. This is best illustrated by reference to Anne and Sally.

Anne began to encourage Samantha to befriend me (page 171), and then in using the observational time to be more involved with Samantha herself. The home leave was central to a process where I was recognised as a person who kept Samantha (and Anne) in mind over this absence, and across an ocean. Her concluding play with Samantha as observations ended (O72) showed that Anne knew that absent did not necessarily mean broken.

Sally's attempt to make a bridge (O77) is clearly a preoccupation of her own, into which Timothy intrudes as bridge-breaker. Bridge building, as an activity for Sally, in the observational time related to her anxiety about linking the outside and the inside, of bringing parts of herself together rather than splitting them off. At the end of observations, unlike Anne, this remained a task not yet accomplished, work in progress as it were. Nevertheless it seemed to represent an awareness, brought on by the observation of the need to make links with absences.

Mother's emotional preoccupations could be expressed consciously or experienced by the observer as unconscious communications. For example, Mary conveyed rage, abandonment and frustration to the observer, both through what she said and her actions. Yvonne communicated an anxiety about hurting – scratching or 'strangling' Hester. She appeared only partially aware of the problem her 'ghost' caused for her, but she communicated about it in her words and actions.

The observer has a rather limited capacity to deal with the manifestations of a negative transference. The existence of a strong negative transference indicates problems these mothers had with the role of the observer. It is also a suggestion of the difficulties they had in their relationships in general. The helpfulness of the observer's role is restricted by the factor of negative transference. On the other hand positive transference is linked with the periods of more positive infant development and mother–infant relationships.

For Sally it was probably the competitiveness with parental figures, the rivalry that she expressed with me and which was evidently related to her internalised relationship with her own parents, which inhibited the potentially helpful impact of the observation. The problems with the relationship with Mary are documented in the case study. The criticism that could be made of this observation was that the transference relationship which was present throughout the observation had a negative impact on Mary and contributed to the eventual collapse of her parenting. Certainly the presence of transference from parents in this setting is difficult to contain, compared with clinical settings, since transference interpretations are beyond the scope and boundaries of the observer's role. The observation of Mary may also have been more manageable for her with a female observer. This is a view which arises from a continuing disquiet with the outcome of this observation, and the importance of gender of the observer for the nature and quality of relationships with mothers. With both Timothy's and Michael's parents, different or additional forms of help were required. It was no coincidence that Mary's collapse came after her social worker had left, and the social worker appeared to represent an active figure, who had authority and who intervened with and on her behalf. On the other hand, it is equally possible that the observation, through containing some of Mary's negative feelings, enabled her to continue parenting as long as she did.

Relationships between fathers and the observer were less intense and less significant. The degree to which the observer was a 'container' for paternal emotional issues was less than that for mothers. Fathers in this sample were relatively uninvolved. Perhaps a greater sense of rivalry could have been expected. By agreeing to the observations at all, fathers could be thought of as having relatively low levels of persecutory feelings. At best, fathers made a constructive link with the observer – such as Javed Ahmed, and Kevin. Martin demonstrated his co-operation with the observer when he 'took over' (O63: page 177above) when Samantha transferred her 'hand grip' from the observer to her father.

Co-operation (and the potential for its corollary, rivalry) demonstrates that the gender of the observer appears to be a significant variable in the quality of the relationship between observer and parents. The observer fulfilled the role of additional or supplementary father/husband figure. The observer's function was similar to Meltzer's description of paternal function (Meltzer 1988, p.61). Concretely, it was seen in the way I intervened to protect infants at moments of risk, and in the very setting itself, the regularity of the observational hour with its clearly defined time boundaries.

The other role that I came to occupy with the parents is best described as 'auxiliary parent'. Here, instead of being a container for mother I was invited by mother (or father) either directly or indirectly to become actively involved in the parenting tasks. In this role I could be said to combine both maternal and paternal functions, in what Klein calls a combined parent figure (Klein 1952a). This role included the active interventions I made. In the case studies numerous examples were given, such as Mary inviting me to undertake the function of reverie on her behalf (page 92 above) and in the relationship I had with Hashmat which Rani and Javed Ahmed enjoyed. Poignantly, the word Hashmat chose for me – 'moma' – and its bilingual associations to an uncle and mother expressed the combined functions.

There was generally a consistently high level of positive feeling towards observer involvement in the role of auxiliary parent. This is not surprising given the circumstances of these parents, namely their vulnerability and the sense of their resources being overstretched. Mary's main complaint was that I offered too little in terms of time and activity. Thus the quality of the relationship between the observer and infant is affected by the parental attitudes to the observer.

9.2.2 Relationships with infants

Close relationships were developed with all the infants in the sample, and the impact of these is recorded in the case studies. In general, the activities in which I engaged were responsive rather than initiating action, though circumstances often led to a particular kind of intervention. My presence in these families where attention and reverie was limited attracted interest from the infants. The dilemma was described in Hashmat's case; attention itself produced interest from the infant, and the opposite of responding would have amounted to a 'blankness' on my part which in 'ordinary' observational circumstances would have been more acceptable because the parent would have fulfilled the infant's needs for attention. Here that was not the case and a total non-response would have been tantamount to a perturbation (Murray and Trevarthen 1986) and a potentially disturbing experience. Rather than consider these relationships in terms of response and non-response, it makes more sense to think about the containing function of the observer. As Sorenson (1997) has shown, this is divisible into three components; observation, resonance and differentiating (naming) things. In the observations I moved along a spectrum formed by these, and this underlies the process of the movement from inactive to active. Activity consists of showing more empathic communications; talking to the infants about what I was seeing, or mirroring and amplifying their communications to me.

Over the two-year observational period infants demonstrated an increasing wish and capacity to us the attentiveness inherent in the observer's role. They were attracted to and made use of the attentive function particularly showing an awareness that the observer was someone with whom they could communicate about inner states. Infants also treated the relationship with the observer in a persecutory way, showing signs of dislike, hostility, avoidance etc., from time to time. Some of the persecutory feelings were described in the case studies as the product of the observer being the recipient of splitting processes (Klein 1946), of bad feelings being split off into the observer. The clearest example of this was Samantha, who between six and 12 months greeted the observer with some quite hostile looks (page 164 above).

In the case studies, infants' communication patterns were described in terms of 'grip relations'. These included patterns of grip relations made between the infants and the observer. For example, the role of Hashmat's and Michael's hand grip with the observer were both seen as a central feature of the development of these infants.

Given the extent to which infants related to the observer with positive affect, that the observer was seen as a source of attention for inner states, and that the infants developed significant patterns of grip relations with the observer, which corresponded to the quality of the relationship overall, it is of interest to think about to what extent the observer made an impact on the developmental worlds of these infants. The case studies recorded the infants responding to the observer's arrival and departure at the beginning and end of each observational hour with varying degrees of recognition. They also showed the infants playing, as it were, in the presence of the observer. The observer, through the process of active attention has a significant role to play in terms of the infants' development.

With these infants the observer's role became therapeutic. That is to say that the observer was used by the infants to make sense of, replay, and to use Freud's (1914b) term, 'work through' experiences. Hester's play with the observer, in which she became an insistently feeding mother and the observer a food-refusing baby (page 138 above) is a particularly striking example. From as early as three to six months, infants were able to express emotionally important issues to the observer with the aim of reworking their experiences. Of course the early examples are simply expressed. Hashmat's dropping his toy as mother left and his subsequent engagement with me when I retrieved the toy (O21: page 70 above) comes into this category. By eight months Hester displayed a complex piece of communication with me (O30: page 131 above) which also had the quality of reliving a previously experienced set of events. In the second year the frequency and complexity of the communications increased. At these times a distinctive atmosphere was introduced into the observations, experienced as a quiet tension, where infants conveyed both that they were alone in their worlds, and that they were aware of my presence. The sense on these occasions appeared to be that I was in the presence of infants' communications of phantasy.

9.2.3 Potential and difficulties in the observational role

The observer made an impact on both the parents and the infants. Here, this has been discussed as fulfilling one of two roles with parents – 'parental container' and 'auxiliary parent'. Second, there was discussion of the way infants developed particular kinds of relationships with the observer and used these to assist in the process of development, specifically, the development of qualities that form the components of internalised functioning. Finally, there was a therapeutic aspect of the observer's role.

The relationships with parents demonstrated that the observer exerted some influence on parenting, particularly in the capacity of the mothers to increase their own observational skills and through this to adapt a more attentive approach to the infant. This is in fact one of the most direct ways that the observer's role can have an effect, the role of attentive observation is taken on by the parents. Parents showed different ways of developing this quality. Rani observed the interaction of Hashmat with me, whilst Anne became more actively attentive towards Samantha herself. Mothers made links with the observer that had positive value for the infant's development. The observer was used to contain a wide range of emotions that were connected with issues which concerned and preoccupied them.

On the other hand, in this sample of vulnerable mothers, there were limitations to the effect the observer had. The observer was not able to contain Mary in her time of crisis and in fact became saddled with a strong negative transference. Clearly the method is not a panacea. The more the mother is able to make a positive relationship with the observer, and have a positive feeling for the role of the observer, the more likely the observer's role will have an impact on parenting. At the other extreme, strong negative transference creates a significant problem for the observation.

The role of the observer with infants makes a case for the potential – and, in this study, actual – capacity of an attentive long-term observer in the family setting influencing and benignly impacting upon infant development. Increased activity in the observer's role was not the main reason for this influence. The impact was as great in relationships, such as that with Hester, where the observer was relatively passive. The observer's role in this respect is best seen as offering different qualities of containment, to the infants. Second, the observer's role is enhanced by a link between parent and observer and diminished by problems in that link. In this study these problems included the presence of parents' rivalry with the observer for the attention of the child, and negative transference from the mothers towards the observer.

The observational relationship is both a flexible and a fragile one. The observer's capacity to maintain attention is its main thread; through this a number of roles, and variations of roles may be taken up, thought about and absorbed. Fragility resides in the relative impotence of the observer to affect issues where in therapeutic practice interpretation would be used, or in preventive practice a more active intervention on behalf of the parent would be instituted. I did from time to time, it is true, intervene in these ways, such as contacting a GP and the housing department on behalf of Hashmat's parents and Mary. I did make comments to the parents that were very close to transference interpretations and which were designed to reduce the tensions felt around my coming and going, particularly with Mary. However I did not make these interventions with the authority that would have ensued from a professional role.

The point for future application of the observational method is that, if it is to be applied in professional practice, preventively and therapeutically, it will be undertaken by professionals taking up professional roles. This will have bearing on the effectiveness and nature of interventions based on observations. What is being said here, in conclusion, is that the potential for influencing development in infancy through an observational approach exists. The potential is centrally connected with the emotional source of attention provided by the observer, and received by both infant and parent. In this study the influence with the infants was a somewhat unexpected outcome.

9.3 The basis for comparison; continuity and change in development

The central aim of the thesis was the establishment of a model through which infant development could be analysed, with particular emphasis on risk. If I turn now to evaluate the functioning of the model developed here, the various components of the model can be discussed in the light of the evidence from the case studies.

The case studies record a complex picture of infant development, clothed in the multiple dimensions of recording naturalistic observations in the home setting, and in the organisational framework of the grid. Descriptions of development and infant relatedness can be said to have been written in multi-layered format. Over the two years of observation, processes of continuity and change formed the fabric of the discussions in the case studies. Therefore the factors of change and continuity and the effect of multi-layering lead to the case studies impacting in different ways, and at different levels of theoretical interest.

There is a level which is idiosyncratic and biographical. Each infant's development is seen in the context of a particular family and there is a specific ending to each 'story'. Alongside the biographical, each observation sets out the detailed processes of infant development in a particular social context, where each family displays its own range of structures, networks, codes, mores, patterns of communication and means of maintaining itself as a unit. Family relationships and the relationships between parents; parental attitudes towards infant care in general and the observed infant in particular; oscillations in parental states of mind; these are all central attributes of the observed canvas.

They relate to, effect and underpin the processes that are the focus of this study, namely the developmental progress of the infants and their relationships with their parents. Development in infancy consists in general terms of the rapid growth and change through milestones and developmental pathways, alongside the more subtle processes of change and development of underlying configurations of emergent personality structure and relatedness which form the internal landscape. Confronted with these different levels of change and continuity a Braudelian approach will be taken here.[4] Using this approach the rates of change and the qualities of change and continuity can be ordered and explored. To do this will lead towards establishing whether, as Emde suggested: 'infant development seems characterised as much by organisational shifts as it does by stability' (1988, p.24). To explore the relationship between continuity and change, and therefore to comment on Emde's conclusions, a differentiation of different levels of the data is required. At other levels, the case studies show the changes in the infants' progress to developmental achievements, the quality of parent–infant relationships in which these took place.

The history of family events and circumstances which affected the families formed a prominent level of change. Miscarriage (Sally), the Bangladesh cyclone, return to the family's home country (Anne and Martin's home leave, Javed Ahmed's return to Bangladesh), death in the family (Kevin's father) and repeated separation from her partner (Mary) all had a major effect on the functioning of family life during the period of observations. In all of these cases the impact of events was greater if the parents were unable to mediate the emotional impact on themselves. This was particularly striking in the way different families 'mediated' the impact of a significant event common to the observations – the Gulf War. Where the war was discussed more, the impact on the infants' and their families was lessened. Martin and Anne talked about it at length in the observations, and little evidence was seen in the children's behaviour of its impact. In contrast, as the war was continually broadcast on TV in Hester's home, the feeding battles at the time were liberally interspersed with images of war – of missiles and bombs (see Kevin's comments, O58, page 137 above). The ways in which parents were able to form a 'skin' between their family and outside events was a part of the process of containment, and leads to thinking about how the parents together worked to meet the containment needs of the infants.

Changes of this kind, in the consequences of family events, had the consequences of altering the fabric of the containing environment. Mothers in this sample, already vulnerable, experienced periodic reduction in levels of support available to them. The qualitative picture of the case studies is supple-

---

4 Fernard Braudel, the French historian, used a distinctive framework for analysing the different levels of change; geological and climate changes were inevitably slower than changes of social institution and individual fortune (Braudel 1975).

mented by the grid in this respect. Graphs 1 shows the periodic levels of support available. Mary and Anne were least well supported at the beginning of the observations, though Anne soon reduced her isolation, which was due to her recent arrival in the country. Mary's low levels of support were a part of her overall difficulties. There was an increase in her support when Dave, Michael's father, was more in evidence, but the social worker's leaving, when Michael was 9–12 months, was a significant loss of support for her. There were fluctuations in the levels of support available to the mothers over the period of the observations. Yvonne experienced a decline in support after Kevin's father's death (Hester at six months). Mothers relied on different kinds of support. Hashmat's family had considerable extended family availability.

That levels of support available to a parent is likely to be a significant factor is well attested (Brown and Harris 1978). The figures here correlate with the qualitative descriptions, but provide a somewhat crude measure alongside the intricacies of the latter. It was important to know not only what levels of support are available, but the use the mother can make of the support which is available. Experiences such as Yvonne's parents needing her as a source of support, Mary's intolerance of absence and Anne's somewhat unfaithful criticisms of her husband Martin were important variables in terms of the mother's capacity to provide containment for her infant. They indicate the capacity of the mother to make use of support available together with being able to manage the needs of her situation and the demands upon her. Mothers' sense of internal resources, including the capacity to make use of relationships were therefore considered (Graph 2), and discussed descriptively. Limitations in the availability of internal resources and anxious and persecutory emotional preoccupations were evidence for mothers' vulnerability.

Mothers gave details of difficult and disrupted childhoods. The case studies provide evidence of 'ghosts' in the nurseries for these mothers, and a considerable degree of unconsciousness about key personal issues. These factors elaborated the struggle mothers had to provide a consistent concave containing shape for their infants.

Maternal attitudes were broadly consistent throughout the observational period. For example, mothers maintained fairly consistent levels of attention for their infants (Graphs 5). They enjoyed brief periods of a capacity – or wish to provide greater attentiveness and suffered similarly with periods of less. Consistency and continuity was also the situation when issues relating to parental relationships, the role of the father with the infant and the quality of parent–infant relationships were discussed.

If the overall picture across the sample is one of continuity, individual parents did develop some consistent trends towards achieving higher levels of functioning in the second year of observations. Mothers experienced less depression and a greater sense of containment themselves in their infants' second years. Positive changes were more focused on Anne, Yvonne and Rani, all of whom enjoyed better relationships with the observer than Sally and Mary. Improvements may be connected to an extent with the impact of observations. Age of the infant is also a factor; these mothers were more comfortable with the emergent toddler than the newborn infant. Sally was anxious about the growing child and the changes she would have to make to contend with these (page 195 above). There were also differences in the qualitative relationship between mothers and their parents/husbands. Categorisation of the way parents operate together led to the idea of parents working together to make a problem-solving link ('bridge building') in contrast with modes of operating which were either maintaining a common front without thinking ('sticking together') or working together to muffle or 'flatten' the affect showed an increase in problem solving in Hester's family, and a reduction of 'flattening' in Samantha's.

This discussion of continuity and change at these various levels of interest provides the background for the comparative analysis of the infants' development in terms of the model and in particular the fine structures of internalisation which are described in the case studies.

9.4 Evaluation of the model: infant development

For each infant in this sample, the case studies successfully described the key features of early development within the model derived from the grounded theory concepts and the operationalisation of the Bion and Bick theories (Chapter 3.3 above). Additionally, the observations of defensiveness, and the categorisation of these defences into 'muscularity' and 'unadventurousness' provide a further dimension to the descriptions of infant development. Comparisons of infant development can therefore be made from the descriptive case studies, supplemented by the data derived from the 'grid'.

9.4.1 Containing shape

The maternal 'shape' in each case included all three types, 'flat', 'convex' and 'concave'. These patterns described in the case studies, that each container shape is encountered in the observations alongside the others suggests that each shape is rarely met in pure culture. In this sample mothers were characteristically struggling with ways of relating and their own states of mind which resulted in different shapes being presented in interaction with the infants. Each mother, it could be said, quickly develops a customary or characteristic response to the infant, combining elements of each 'shape' in individualistic ways.

Mothers were concave to some extent, usually responsive to infant distress, usually holding a crying infant, and in other ways demonstrating some degree of 'concave' containing shape. Limitations of the examples of concave container shape were indicated by the lack of evidence for mothers' 'knowing' intuitively the needs of the infant. Mothers seemed unable to have a deep knowledge of their infants. There were few examples in the observations of mutual joyful interaction. Anne, Samantha's mother, gave an example of awareness of intuitively in-touch mothering when she spoke of 'mother's X-ray hearing' (O3). But she had misheard and the sound was not that of her daughter crying. 'Primary maternal preoccupation' (Winnicott 1965a, p.15) was difficult to achieve when mothers were preoccupied, as Anne, again put it, 'with 29 preoccupations'.

This led to the frequent observations of miscommunicating, misunderstanding and bypassing emotional contact with infants, which are the features of 'flat container shape'. Two particular characteristics were noted throughout the sample. First, infant communications were treated more at a physical than emotional level. Contact made by infants with mothers was treated as a request for food rather than attention (Anne, Sally, Yvonne, Rani). Second, infant communications which aimed at contact were missed or not noticed (Mary, Sally).

Mothers were also seen to bombard their infants with 'convex container shape'. This was seen to take place through hostility (Mary, Yvonne) and to include elements of control and intrusion (Yvonne, Anne). Hashmat was subject to a combination of flat container shape from mother and convex from his father and siblings.

Container shape could be quantified in terms of frequency (Graphs 9) and described in terms of content. For example, Mary's 'flat' containment was characterised as responding mechanically, that is with minimal time, and attention, given to Michael. This point is made in the case study, where the detailed circumstances surrounding Mary's limitations in offering containment for Michael are elaborated. Particular kinds of convex container shape, linked with high levels of impingement of emotional preoccupations on to the infant (Graphs 2) were described. Yvonne's convex container shape was carefully discussed, to include the manifestations in her relating to Hester, the continuities of these emotional factors, and the relationship between her 'shape' and the 'ghost' in her nursery (Freiberg 1980). Hashmat's situation demonstrated that for a complete picture of containment to be established, the 'shapes' of all family including siblings, need to be taken into account.

All family members were involved, therefore, in the containing process. This was seen in all families, and the idea of triangular space was added to the picture developed in the model. 'Flat' container shape included the idea of turning to a third object; in Hashmat's case this was described as a combination of father, siblings and inanimate objects. It was first observed in the early feeding situation (page 66, above). Timothy and Sally were described as turning to father, and inanimate objects such as a mirror (page 196 above).

Convex and flat container shape were associated with risk (see below, 9.6) and there was evidence from both the grid and the descriptive accounts that the greater the frequency of these, and the more intensive the content, the more likely the infant would need to find ways of contending with difficult and stressful experiences. The concept of container shape therefore effectively describes the qualitative difference between parenting which contributes to a 'containing' experience and that which contributes to propensity for risk. These concepts of containing shapes were devised, following Bion's theories, to account for the role of emotionally in parenting. Unavailability for containing emotions and emotions which overspill are therefore seen as central to problems in early development.

9.4.2 Infant ways of relating: grip relations

Container shape was encountered and responded to in different ways by the infants. These were described by using the concept of 'grip relations', which was adapted and operationalised from Bick's theory of 'skin formation'. This facilitated clear descriptions of infant activity, particularly in early relationships and development. Descriptions of grip relations provided the means for identifying key emerging developmental themes. Bick herself used the idea primarily to describe 'clinging' behaviour. In the case studies, the 'grip relations' developed by the infants undertook a wider range of functions than is suggested by the idea of clinging. Primarily, infants were seen activating their perceptual and sensory modalities to accomplish multi-intentional tasks; relating to others, retreating from relationships, relating to inanimate objects and holding parts of the self. The term was used – again particularly in early development – to organise understanding much of the relationship-orientated behaviour of these infants.

Some characteristics and interesting modes of grip relations emerged, often being repeatedly observed so that they could be described as forming patterns of early developmental features. There was such descriptions at all modalities – mouth, eye, voice–ear, hand, body and mind. There were some poignant examples of the infants relating with their hands. Hashmat's hand grip appeared to make a tenuous link with the world of others, Michael's hand grip had a desperate quality, and Hester's conveyed a particular conflict of emotions. Grip relations were described where a change in quality of the grip denoted a change in the quality of relatedness. Hester for example developed a 'blank' eye grip when feeding, and Samantha's eye grip became progressively more blank. Hashmat and Michael shared a weak eye grip. The kind of grip that was observed ranged from very strong to weak, and the grid was used to quantify this aspect of grip relations (Graphs 15). The grid and the descriptive studies together showed infants developing a particular strength of grip in one modality (such as the hand in the examples above) whilst grip in another modality was relatively weak (the eye grip in the examples above). The conclusion that was reached was that some grip relations were employed to compensate for difficult experiences in order to maintain object relations.

This extends the view of grip relations from being used defensively, as in Bick's formulation of clinging. Patterns of grip relations did, however, appear to exist for defensive purposes, and observations of these features enabled the two defensive constellations of muscularity and unadventurousness to be named (see 9.4.3 below). In the former, grip relations were observed as acting with the intention of the infant holding him/herself ('taking a grip on oneself') and making contact with another person or thing. In the latter, unadventurousness, there was a loss of contact with another object or thing, and a withdrawal from object relations.

Grip relations, as I have said, did form observable patterns and they were described in the case studies not only in terms of strength, but also direction and texture. Intentions, which were inferred from sequences and context, followed the way infants moved towards or away from people, things and towards self or away from all objects (people and things). Texture of grip relations described the quality of contact made with an object. In the case studies, a number of terms were used such as 'weak', 'floppy', 'rigid', 'firm', 'loose', 'strong', Michael's very loose mouth grip was a notable example, whilst his hand grip was rigid. Hester developed a very rigid mouth grip and this contrasted with her early loose or floppy eye and body grips. Samantha developed a very rigid hand grip and body grip, which contrasted with the floppiness which was somewhat evident in her mouth, eye, voice-ear and body grips. Levels of looseness/floppiness and rigidity relate primarily to the quality of contact made with other objects (people and things). In the case discussions there were descriptions of infants becoming floppy, losing their grip on themselves, so to speak, in the process of making communications or attempting to accomplish developmental tasks. These included Michael's, Timothy's and Samantha's loss of muscular control. Alternatively, infants developed rigid forms of holding on, through which they demonstrated anxiety about separation. These include Samantha's holding on to her chair and Hester's refusal of food. The texture of grip relations relates very closely to, and illustrates the internalised relationship of container and contained. Grip relations therefore play an important part in processes of internalisation (see 9.5 below). It is therefore an important concept, which is worth further study, and which provides a helpful means for describing infant organisation.

9.4.3 Defensiveness

The case studies documented the appearance in early development of defensive moments. The grid followed the frequency with which infants maintained object relations, and the frequency with which they were defensive. It was interesting how infants maintained a capacity to object relate, and to protest and/or be expressive when there were problems in the relationship with parents (Graphs 16), indicating their willingness to maintain communications about their states of mind, and to be prepared to enter potential conflict in relationships in order to be heard. In this respect, Samantha's increasing capacity for protest/expressiveness were indicative of a rising level of intensity, or passion, in her communications (see page 165 above) and Hester's show the intensity of her conflict with her mother over eating (see Chapter 6). Hashmat reached two peaks of protest/expressiveness, at six and 18–24 months. The former links with his increased vitality when sitting in the chair or walker (see page 69 above) and the latter with his more ebullient development in toddlerhood. Timothy protested strongly in his distress in his first year.

Infants were able to shed defensive patterns when more favourable circumstances occurred. Michael illustrated this; when held he became instantly alert (page 98 above). This also conveyed the meaning that he defended (through switching off) because he was not held.

Defensiveness played a significant role in the development of these infants. The qualities of the defences infants employed, especially with regard to their flexibility or rigidity were followed in the case descriptions and in the grid. Movement from one kind of defence to another, having a range of defences available, and employing them flexibly according to circumstances contributed to a greater capacity to maintain development than if a single form of defence was applied rigidly. Michael's 'blank alertness', Timothy's repeated muscularity and Hester's rigid food refusal all tended towards rigidity for some periods of their development.

Descriptions of the kinds of defensiveness provided categorisation of two different constellations. Michael and Hashmat developed similar characteristics, which were described under the constellation of 'unadventurousness'. This was used to connote lack of contact with others, lack of curiosity and lack of evidence for physical development. It was accompanied by a kind of closing down of the systems for making contact (object relating) and occasioned descriptions of 'frightened animals'. Both Michael and Hashmat had problems with feeding, with considerable vomiting in the early weeks. Both used a grip with the hand to maintain contact with others. Hashmat's appeared to be an 'unobtrusive' link with the world of others, whilst Michael's evoked a more desperate feeding.

As with container shape, these defensive constellations were not met in pure culture. Hashmat was rarely muscular in early months, but his eye grip was directed towards inanimate objects, a feature of 'holding on' rather than 'switching off'. The latter included his eye grip turning away from mother and away from objects altogether. Michael, who was a withdrawing, unadventurous infant, demonstrated his capacity to switch off with his voice-ear, mouth and eye grips. Hester displayed a similar withdrawal from feeding and her eye grip (described as 'blank'), showed a similar pattern to Hashmat's, including the features of turning away from mother, turning to things, and turning away from all objects.

'Muscularity' performed the task of maintaining a vigorous grip on an (external) object – person or thing – in circumstances in which distressing separation was encountered. These features were mainly adopted by Timothy and Hester. In both infants the adaptation of a muscular defence in their first three months was connected with episodes where distress was communicated. With both of them the aim of calming themselves through achieving contact with another object (person or thing; a light, the TV) was clearly observed. A grip on one's own body was a particular feature of this experience. Timothy at one point held himself in a vigorous circle. These observations demonstrate the features described by Bick (1968, 1986) and Symington (1985).

Samantha's early defences lay somewhere between these two 'types'. First, she shared many characteristics of the 'unadventurous' infant; an increasingly 'blank' expression, restricted physical development, limited curiosity. On the other hand she took a considerable role in holding the bottle and herself and her breath-holding experience (O12, page 161 above) performed the task of taking a rigid grip on herself. This was seen through the early rigidity of her eye and the use of her hand to make a grip on inanimate objects and herself.

Grip relations therefore illustrate the development of defensive processes in these infants, within the patterns of object relating, communicating emotional need (protest/expressive) and defending which they established. The variety of grip relations used defensively in early development correlate with the capacity to use defences flexibly or rigidly. The more flexible infants (Samantha, Hashmat, Hester) developed a greater range of defensive grip relations.

9.4.4 Patterns of commensal relationships

The early dynamics of relationships between mother and infant include the concepts of container shape, grip relations, and defensive constellations. The interaction between these elements produced what has been called the 'fit' in the mother–infant relationship, the quality of the commensal relationship. In the descriptive case studies, the processes involved in early mother–infant interactive patterns were described in ways which suggest the formation of distinctive ways of relating, and in which the component parts – container shape, grip relations, and defensiveness – could be described, named and identified. Second, the case studies provided descriptions of the meaning and purpose of these interactive patterns.

Mother–infant relationships (and father–infant relationships) were quantified in the grid through measuring qualities of sensitivity, attentiveness, intimacy, conflict, understanding. These grids showed considerable continuity in mother–infant relationships (Graphs 5 and 10). They did not, however, demonstrate the ways in which relationships were formed and the choices that mother and infant, through their grip relations, exercised in forming and maintaining patterns. Unlike microanalysis, the observations in this study included times when parent and infant interacted, when they moved away from interaction and when they resumed interaction. Timing and rhythm within interactions were seen, and described alongside timing and rhythms of breaking off, ending, and resuming interaction. Mutual bebehaviour and emotions between parents and infants were thus seen in this broader context. Complex patterns of relating and relatedness were formed between parents and infants. These held qualities which were described as containing, conflicting and accommodating (Graphs 8). These overall categories were created from the combination of mother's containing shape and the qualities of grip relations – strength, texture and direction – that developed between mother and infant. In the first observation of Samantha, (page 158 above) the sequence of events as Anne fed Samantha included the following choices:

1. to take in the experience of contact as a 'concave' experience [C <–> g_1]
2. to take in the experience of cessation as a 'convex' experience [<–> g_3]
3. to take in mother's words as the 'familiar talking mother' (as concave) (Bick 1968) [C<–>g_1]
4. to be disturbed by the tenor of mother's voice (as convex) [<–> g_3]
5. to experience non-responsiveness to her holding-on gesture (as a 'flat' experience) [<–> g_2]
6. the mouth grip to be replaced by a protest (voice grip), or a defensive turning away from mother (grip on another object, inanimate object, self, or retreat from contact).

Diagrammatically, this is shown in Figure 9.1.

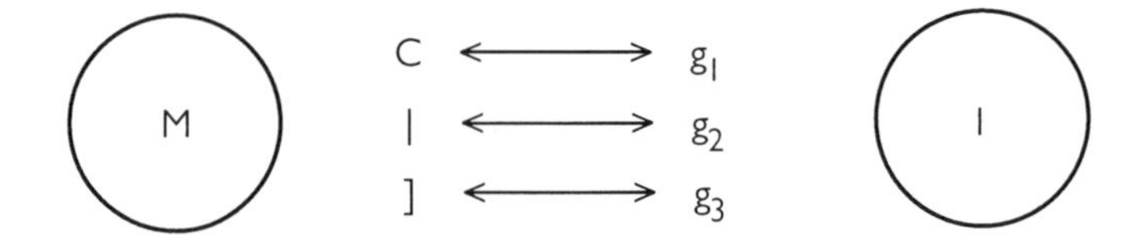

Figure 9.1 Mother–infant interaction

and simplifies to a formula of:

M C_n <–> g_nI.

How and to what degree the infant experiences the various possible permutations of these aspects of mother's responses depends on the relationship between the mother's 'shape' and the infant's use of grip relations. There is a choice – a range even – of options for any mother–infant relationship. The space between the containing shape of mother and the grip relations of the infant hold a potential for different qualities of contact. This is not a linear cause–effect model. When the infant's readjustment is taken into account further stages in the processes of interaction can be added to this schema. They include the infant's defensive reaction and:

1. the infant's adjustment to the mother (an internalisation of experience of contact)
2. the mother's response to the infant's response to the contact ('she's not hungry' or 'she doesn't like this'). The interactive pattern in this way becomes a 'fit' of mutual expectation. The 'fit' between mother and infant is the result, therefore, of a sequence of steps which could be modified, by a move by the mother along the spectrum of concave–flat–convex, and/or by the infant's grip relations changing direction, texture and strength. This could quite clearly be further studies by microanalysis. It adds another axis, so to speak to the kind of observation made by, for example, Trevarthen (page 8 above).

The case studies demonstrated that for all infants, the quality of the fit between mother and infant could be seen in the process of developing, and then characterised as it emerged. The combination of defensiveness and the attempts by infants to maintain contact were powerfully observed. For each infant the 'fit' by three months could be described in terms of the three overall categories – containing, accommodating, and conflictual. The chief characteristics of the interaction – the 'choice' made by mother and infant from the range of actual grip relations at each modality – could be named, and the underlying anxiety identified. Finally, for each infant and mother relationship, a name could be given to the dynamics of containment in each relationship, that is to say the way the concave/flat/convex shape of mother and infant's grip responses worked together. This is tabulated below (Table 9.1).

Table 9.1 Qualities of 'fit': birth to 3 months

Infant	*Type of fit*	*Interaction*	*Anxiety*	*Dynamics in fit*
Hashmat	accommodation	loosely held/ bombarding	'no baby'	affect flattened. projections on to baby
Hester	conflict/ accommodation	bombarding/ loosely held	'has been dropped'; 'hurting and being hurt'	projection/ sado-masochistic
Michael	conflict/ accommodation	not held/ loosely held	'not there baby'	projection (murderousness)
Samantha	accommodation	loosely held	'might be dropped'	flattening of affect
Timothy	conflict/ accommodation	missing each other	'grasping thin air'	sticking together

From three months, mother–infant relationships for these infants were continually involved in negotiating the emotional component of the 'fit', through modification of the quality of the dynamics (moving along a spectrum from thinking and problem solving to flattening the affect/projecting/sticking together); through containing the anxieties; and through a closer match between containing shape and grip relations. All the factors of continuity and change (9.3) and the changing patterns of containing shape (9.4.1) and grip relations (9.4.2 and 9.4.3) were brought to bear on the continuity of 'fit'. The outcome of the 'fit' is, to a considerable extent, commensurate with the qualities of internalisation experienced by each infant and this is discussed below.

9.5 Internalisation

The aim here is to provide a discussion of the nature of internalisation, which, as was noted in Chapter 1, is still not systematically studied. Analysis of the concepts of grip relationship, container shape, and defensiveness which contribute to the fit between mother and infant reveal the processes involved in the qualities of the early internalisation of the infants. These patterns produced configurations in which emotionally important issues were channelled. In the case studies, the detailed descriptions of development and the attention to the components of the 'fit' between mother and infant enabled hypotheses to be made about the qualities of internalisation that were taking place in these infants, and the continuities of these qualities through the two years of observation. Both of these support the central idea that it is through understanding the quality of internalisation that takes place for each infant, that quality of developmental outcome can be inferred. In the discussion of the model (Chapter 3.3) it was suggested that aspects of internalisation could be compared as outcome measures for these infants. These measures, ten in all, were the capacity for memory, recall with affection, recognition, thinking, discriminating between people, reactions to separation and reunion, proximity seeking, language development and the capacity for symbolic play and unconscious phantasy. These formed categories of the grid and were used as a framework for considering the developmental achievements of infants in the descriptive case studies.

From the grid, infants both achieved notable developmental accomplishments in these categories and recorded some difficulties in certain aspects of development. The descriptive accounts provided some detailed elaborations of both difficulties and achievements in development. The discussion of internalisation then needs to take into account the evidence for both accomplishment, or resilience, and difficulties in development, or risk. These two factors suggest the need to consider internalisation chronologically; to explore the factors that developed in the initial stage (birth to three months) and then subsequently.

The comparative analysis of internalisation over time can be organised around the infant's negotiation of developmental tasks, the most significant of which were, first, developing a sense of absence and the permanence of the object (3–12 months) and, second, the development of symbolic functioning in play and language (12–24 months). This correlates with the organisation of the case studies in terms of time and theme.

9.5.1 Early internalisation (to three months)

Many of the features of early internalisation have already been discussed, particularly in the previous section, concerning the development of early interactive patterns. There, the emergence of patterns of grip relations, the tension between object relating and defending, and the 'fit' between mother and infant were elucidated. In the first three months of observations, the infant's qualities of internalisation were seen to be the consequences of specific emotional struggles within the mother–infant relationship. These were, in general terms, between maintaining object relations and taking up defensive strategies in the face of the limited concave container shape available to them. The first three months were problematic for all the infants, and the restricted resources in the environment, particularly the presence of convex and flat container shape, led to the observation of issues which suggested problematic internalisation processes. All infants developed an early defensive pattern, of muscularity or unadventurousness. As part of these constellations the infants' grip relations included high levels of turning to inanimate objects, turning to self and/or away from all objects (people and things). The texture of the grip relations included relatively high degrees of looseness or floppiness. All of these features promoted the central thought that there were problems in the container–contained relationship for all these infants in their first three months.

Infants were therefore held in a conflict which could be summarised as a need to 'take in' from mother (and other family members) and the need to defend against the elements of the mother's containing shape which either missed the infant's rhythms, communications and affective signals (flat container shape) or pushed into the infant the mother's projections (convex containing shape). These dilemmas for the infants were described in the case studies for all the infants.

It has already been shown (9.4.4 above) that complex relationship patterns produced a 'fit' between mother and infant. Moreover, the descriptions of the component parts of these relationships – the type of interaction, the quality and extent of anxiety, the dynamics in the fit and the type of fit – demonstrate the particular problems involved in a fit between container and contained for these infants. These difficulties involved managing anxieties. The infants did experience the kind of unbearable primitive anxieties described by Bion, Bick and Winnicott. Indeed these anxieties were closely connected with the need for the infants to take up defensive alignments. Further, when describing these anxieties, the quality of the emotional issue involved could be categorised, and named. This in turn matched the kind of interaction taking place between mother and infant. Thus Samantha, as a 'loosely held' infant, was developing grip relations which recognised and attempted to contend with the central anxiety which was 'might be dropped'. Michael's absence of fit with mother, the experience of 'not being held' led to, and was based upon, the anxiety of 'not being there', that is of being an invisible baby, and this, in turn was a manifestation of mother's partially conscious wish (that he was not there), resulting in projections of murderousness.

By three months, as I have said, there was a consolidation of issues, that were frequently observed, and the themes were taken up by the infants through their behaviour in general and their grip relations in particular. The qualities of the containing shapes of the mother are therefore internalised through the projection of mother's states of mind into the infants. The channels for the internalisation of these states of mind are one or more grip relation patterns. Thus for example, Hester's hand grip on her mother, which she internalised, became evidently a means for her 'taking a grip on herself', since she used this to achieve further contact with mother (O12, page 127 above) and also a prototypical internalisation of the sado-masochistic relationship with mother (the channel for the internalisation of the 'hurting and being hurt' dynamic). This has been thought about above as the pluralistic nature of the purpose and meaning of grip relations. These descriptions of the emotional content of interactive patterns which are internalised (and then generalised) closely correspond to Stern's elucidation of 'proto narrative envelopes' (see page 11 above).

There was a second 'route' for internalisation, formed by the qualities that were absent in the 'fit'. Like Bower's view of matching (page 7 above) all these infants experienced the missed opportunities of the experiences they did not receive, for which I drew an analogy with Eliot's verse. For some infants the experience which did not take place was more concretely visible; Michael's and Timothy's many 'missed' communications, for example. Hester's experiences of weaning also come into this category, giving her an experience of early loss. Samantha, in contrast experienced a potential loss ('might be dropped'). Fear of loss of the object and actual loss are the subject of Freud's (1917) work on mourning, and Steiner's (1993) recent elaboration of the depressive position. The defensiveness demonstrated by these infants in their first three months indicated that these experiences of loss were not tolerable – or mediated sufficiently by the 'container'. A psychic retreat, to use again Stiener's terminology, was a necessary resort in the face of overwhelming loss. This accounts for the defensive uses of 'grip relations' (9.4.3 above), for the 'sparing' moments and states of mind observed in Hester's play with toys (O4, page 124 above) and Timothy's content in gazing at mother from a distance (O7, page 202 above). The experiences described here relate closely to Braten's distinction between the 'virtual' and 'actual' other (page 9 above). These descriptions of defensive organisation in early infancy – muscularity and unadventurousness – extend Steiner's idea of the pathological organisation, Rosenfield's (1971) narcissistic organisation and Riviere's (1936) 'organised system of defence'.

The 'fit' in which the adaptation of the infant to the actual relationship with mother visited upon the infants experiences of loss, was a crucial component of the early internalisation processes. A third element seen in these observations and demonstrated in the case studies is the quality of contact between mother and infant, container and contained. This has been described above (9.4.2), through the descriptions of texture, 'looseness' or 'floppiness' and 'rigidity'. The quality of contact related to the kind of containing shape the infant experienced, and the kind of grip relations that the infant developed and used. The concept involved here appears to be the rigidity, flexibility or plasticity of the container (Houzel 1990). There could be no clearer example of a 'loose' grip than Michael's mouth grip, which became internalised as a physical, facial attribute, and which correlates to the predominantly convex and flat maternal containing shape. Hester's rigid mouth grip corresponds clearly with Yvonne's increasingly convex shape. Anne's rigidity in her inability to respond to distress, and indeed all emotional extremes, was internalised by Samantha as a component of rigidity, that is, the internalisation of a rigid rather than flexible containing structure, and was seen in the development of her rigid hand and body grips.

Where the mother's containing shape moves flexibly to meet the infant's communications, the grip relations of the infant would be more likely to be wide-ranging, and firm. Flexibility relates to the range of emotionality which the mother can 'contain'; this, together with the infant's capacity to 'hold on' (see 9.4.4 above), determines whether there is a 'firm grip on the nipple', or a grip which was lost, or intrusively experienced. The complexities of the qualities of grip relations – complexities which have been explored in terms of texture, direction, frequency and strength – and the variety of ways in which they can operate ensure that internalisation is never a straightforward introjection of the mother's containing shape, but rather a product of the shared meaning developed between mother and infant in their interaction.

In summary, early internalisation occurred as a product of the components of the 'fit' between mother and infant, together with the quality of contact which is achieved between them. These configurations define not the solution or outcome of the developmental path taken by the infant in respect of internalisation but the issues over which the future relations with others and conflicts over developmental issues will be based. Metaphorically, they define the climate, but not the weather.

The most striking issue of early internalisation was that a configuration emerged – fairly quickly – for each infant, defined through the Mc<–>gI formula, and consisting of patterns of grip relationships and the emotional content of the 'fit' between mother and infant (Table 9.1) which became a continuing and persistent issue for the infant's development and the mother–infant relationship. Thus, for example, Samantha was continually engaged, in the relationship with her mother, in the issue of being tightly or loosely held, and in this way kept in mind. The rigidity of her grip relations (hand, eye, and body), were consequences of, and the means to contend with the 'looseness'. Similarly, Hashmat's early internalisation of 'no baby' developed into a struggle between the dependent 'family child' and allegiance to the gang of brothers, hostile to the presence of babies. His grip relations included a considerable turning away from others, and towards himself and a 'loose' grip, again, as consequences and means to contend with these issues.

Thinking about the persistence of these emotional factors throughout the observational period led, in the case studies to the idea of development being formed through a sequence of Russian dolls where the 'dolls' were permeated by a connective tissue. The connective tissue is an idea of Bion's. Bleandonu described this from *Transformations* (Bion 1965): 'Container and contained should be held in constant emotion which is open to being replaced by another. The recombining of mental systems requires a freedom which depends on the emotions that impregnate the psyche. These emotions materialize a connective tissue enclosing...elements of the container.' (Bleandonu 1994, p.186).

The idea of the Russian dolls was used to describe the process whereby the availability of concave containing shape in the mother in a later stage of development 'contained' the internalisation from an earlier stage, as it was seen in the infant's later (and therefore current) preoccupations, expressions and modes of relating. The development of the idea is followed in the case studies from Hashmat, where the observer fulfils the function of providing the 'connective tissue', through the development of resilience in Hester, to Samantha's capacity to address the issue of being tightly or loosely held (internalised as having a tight or loose hold on another). Michael and Timothy showed a persistence of a regressed or pre-symbolic mode of functioning where the progression from a smaller to a larger Russian doll was not so evident. How these internalised relationships developed can now be discussed.

9.5.2 Internalisation of a sense of absence

Internalisation of a sense of absence was an important process in the infant's development between three and 12 months. The phrase 'a sense of absence' is used here to incorporate the awareness of the permanent existence of an object (thing) – the object concept – and the continued relationship with significant people, or aspects of people, in their absence.[5] In the case studies; a number of different experiences of the infant's sense of absence are recorded. These include the search for hidden objects, reactions to people at the point of separation and reunion, thoughts, actions and emergent vocabulary clearly directed to the task of recognition of people in their presence or absence.

Of the examples in the case studies, Michael failed to find a hidden object – my glasses (O31: page 103 above) and Timothy was interested in hiding his feeding bottle (O36: page 250 above). Timothy's intentionality in the act of hiding the object – and the choice of the object – indicated a link between the act and its emotional and relational content.

Bell (1969) found that object permanence occurs with regard to people before things, and concepts of absence were demonstrated by the infants with regard to relationships with people as much as with 'things'. Michael for example, said 'mama' in the presence of his father (O27: page 101 above) before he could try to find my hidden glasses. The infant's capacity to reach an understanding of absence was observed in the way they displayed recognition towards a returning person, and how they marked a departure. The experiences of separation and reunion were noted particularly in relationship to the observer. Finally, recognition of absence and return was marked by some distinct forms of play – notably 'peek a boo'.

Taking all these measures – searching for a hidden object, recognition of the observer on arrival and departure, playing games such as peek a boo, the following comparative table (Table 9.2) records the infant's development of a sense of absence.

It was also possible to explore the emotional field (Meltzer 1984) in which the infants developed their understanding of absence. The fact and quality of recognition of the observer is recorded in the case studies (e.g. Michael O18, page 100 above; Timothy O19, page 206 above). Hester greeted me at eight months (O30, page 131 above) with a detailed and explicit explanation of her current preoccupations. In contrast Samantha, between seven and nine months, greeted me with signs of displeasure bordering on hostility (Samantha O22, page 164 above). This hostility was felt by the observer to be functional, permitting Samantha to retain a positive sense of her relationship with her mother. The split between mother and others occurred in relation to absence and a third person, particularly father (or father substitute). This led to

5 Piaget's (1955) theory of the development of the object concept, the infant's comprehension of the object's (thing's) permanent existence, despite revisions retains usefulness as a means of assessing the infant's capacity to distinguish between self and other (Murray 1992, p.224). The revision of Piaget's theory by Bower and others (for example Baillargeon 1986, 1991); Baillargeon, Spelke and Wasserman 1985; Baillargeon, *et al.* 1990; Campos and Sternberg 1981) propose the infant's capacity to understand the 'permanence, impermeability and interpenetrability of objects' (Baillargeon 1994, p.10).

discussing the importance of triangular relationships, especially in the case studies of Timothy and Samantha. The emergence of splitting corresponds with a development from part object relations to whole object relations (Klein 1952b), and there was a significant 'split' in four out of the five infants in the fourth quarter of the first year:

> *Hashmat:* tipping away the contents of the feeding bottle whilst retaining a relationship with mother (saying 'mama')
>
> *Hester:* turning away from mother and being seductive with father (singing a 'soliloquy' on the theme of 'daddy')
>
> *Samantha:* splitting 'good mummy' from persecuting, or 'bad' others.
>
> *Timothy:* seeking contact with mother, being in harmony with her, and hiding the bottle.

The fifth infant, Michael hinted at moments of developing a 'split'. That a split was seen to occur and then recede demonstrated, relative to the other infants, his weaker hold on object relations, and the greater slackness of his grip. This also indicated the relationship between the infant's grip relationship configurations and the continuing defensive patterns.

The categories of 'unadventurousness' and 'muscularity' were more accentuated between three and 12 months. The 'muscular' infant achieved rapid, even precocious development (Timothy, Hester) whilst the unadventurous infant was backward in reaching the same milestones (Samantha, Hashmat, Michael).

The patterns of mobility were significant in indicating intentionally. Roger used his large motor activity to seek proximity to mother, whilst Hester, turning away from mother, sought comfort in others (father, myself). When 'muscular' infants lost their grip on the object (person) or on themselves, there was a marked loss of 'tone', experiencing moments of almost complete physical collapse (Timothy O16, page 207 above), or of inconsolable crying (Hester O36, page 131 above). The unadventurous infants developed an increased rigidity of grip to compensate for the intolerable experience of 'letting go'. Samantha held on to the high chair, and Hashmat and Michael used their hand grip. There was a continual conflict between maintaining an emotional response and becoming further withdrawn into defensive 'unadventurousness' or a muscularity which indicated a form of self help, rather than dependence and mutual responsiveness between infant and parent. When the infants experienced degrees of absence or separation which extended them beyond the limits of their flexibility, they sought to renew experiences of containment for the anxieties that were generated. Defences manifested the problems, but resulted in difficulties of communication. Either the infants were responded to with greater receptivity from mothers (as concave container shape increased), and other carers, or there were further experiences of lack of receptivity (flat and convex container shape). The latter produced a new 'Russian doll' of defensive muscularity or unadventurousness; the former a greater propensity to meet developmental tasks, readdressing also earlier experiences (the 'connective tissue'), and preparing the infants for symbolic functioning (see Table 9.2).

9.5.3 Development of symbolic functioning; play and language

The ubiquitous play in which the insides of objects was the major component was seen in these observations as the precursor of symbolic play, but not equated with it. How infants related to the three-dimensionality of objects (people and things) forms the basis of a theory of play between 12 and 24 months (and especially between 12 and 18 months). In the case studies the kind of play seen was carefully elucidated. The infant had a spatial relationship with the content of the play. Primarily, this meant differentiating between play in which the infant put him/herself 'inside' a three-dimensional object, play in which there was an attempt to get 'inside' either a thing or a person, usually mother, and play in which another object was placed 'inside'. Play was then seen to have a bearing upon the infant's current and internalised emotional preoccupations. For these five infants the relationships developed through this kind of play could be summarised as follows:

> Hashmat was involved in play in which there was a concept of a pregnant mother, and in which there was limitation of curiosity about space inside mother (he hits his head against father's chest and mine). Mother is then perceived as having a filled space inside, and she can be categorised as a 'pregnant mother'. Greater curiosity – and less unadventurousness – follows Fashmat's birth, accompanied by identification with a gang of big brothers.
>
> Michael's play showed an interest in insides which demonstrated relating to objects which bump and hurt. He 'takes himself hostage', using himself as a target ('bump him to make him feel better'). He is identified with a bumping big brother. Mother is categorised as a 'dead mother' (Green 1986) and the infant is unprotected. His play was also two-dimensional (p.105 above).
>
> Hester relates to the space inside mother which is filled with sadistic objects which form a convex containing shape, and which are pushed into her. She develops proto-masochistic behaviour, hurting herself, and is identified with a scratching or intrusive mother ('penetrating mother').
>
> Samantha perceives mother as potentially having babies, and from whom she could fall. She tries to get back inside and identifies with mother, in an Oedipal way. The possibility is of thinking leading to symbolic functioning. Mother is a 'pregnant mother'.

Table 9.2 Development of a sense of absence

Infant	*recognition of observer arrival*	*recognition of observer departure*	*searching for hidden object*	*play about absence*	*words relating to absence/recognition*
Hashmat	Looks and smiles at me (4–5 months)	Continues to look as I leave (8–9 months)	Hitting head on my chest and father's (9 months)	Plays with dropped object (6 months)	mama (12 months)
Michael	Looks at me; face brightens (4–6 months)	Watches as I leave (14–16 months); says bye (15 months)	Fails to search (11 months)	Plays with door key (11 months)	mama (10 months)
Hester	Greets with play (8 months)	Waves and says 'bye' (16 months)	Lifts and looks under carpet (11 months)	Plays with mother's purse (10 months)	Daddy (di-ie) 11 months
Samantha	Looks, with persec-ution (7 months)	Waves when prompted (13 months)	Looks inside drawers (11 months)	Toy pushed and pulled (10 months)	mama, dada, (9 months)
Timothy	Looks, (16 weeks to 6 months)	Waves bye (10 months)	Searches for bottle (10 months)	Peek a boo (10 months)	dada (17 months)

> Timothy is preoccupied with getting inside, taking over the space inside mother, which is filled with babies, alive and dead. Mother is pregnant, with a dead baby inside. Timothy totally identifies with being a baby inside, and his behaviour is pre-symbolic, or regressed.

The quality of the infants' internal spaces are demonstrated through this play. The categories of 'fit' which are recorded in this way are; pregnant mother, dead mother and penetrating mother. The fact that three of the five mother's shapes were categorised as 'pregnant' reflects the infant's awareness of the mother's bodily state, supporting Klein's (1930) view that the contents of mother's body are the first objects of infant curiosity. This is very frequently observed. Infant play is often the first indication that mother is actually pregnant or thinking of becoming so.[6] How the infants reacted to the concept of the filling of this maternal space gives evidence to the conceptualisation the infant has formed of the mental space inside mother. Anzieu (1985) comments on the absence in Klein's theory of a means whereby the mental space arises from the physical space. Bion aimed to attend to this problem by the model of container–contained, and the theory of Alpha function. How the infant moves from a 'state of body' to a 'state of mind' is therefore the function of mother's containing shape. Here, the quality of the 'pregnant mother' perception has also a mental context, namely mother's preoccupation with other babies and interests. The actual physical condition of the mother is one which is perceived by the infant through the operation of sensitivity to maternal spaces, physical and mental, and representing a notion of a 'preoccupied' mother (whose shape would be convex or flat). Hashmat was described, for example, as relating to a 'doubly pregnant mother'.

The derivation of three variations of this theme – dead mother, mother filled with alive and dead babies and penetrating mother – also conveys the language of physical and mental properties. These derivatives give a particularly graphic conceptualisation of the 'shape' of mother which is internalised and presented back in the form of play and other interactions, externalisations of the 'fit' between mother and infant.

That these categorisations of the 'fit' – the commensal relationship – suggest problematic, painful and/or damaged areas of development gives some substance to the hypothesis that the function of play includes the expression and externalisation of the most troubled aspects of development. Through play, the infant expresses the pattern of early 'fit' in the relationship given by the formula M(c) <–> (g) I, and thus confirms the continuity of early grip relations.

Change in the infant's development and the pattern of mother–infant relationship is linked closely with the development of symbolic functioning,

---

6 Following my experience with Hashmat's mother's pregnancy I am very disinclined to overlook, when teaching, the potential for this kind of play pointing out a pregnancy!

the development of language and the capacity for play to be received by others with a concave containing shape, facilitating 'working through' (Freud 1914b) in the depressive position (Klein 1940). In emphasising that play which is concerned with the relationship between the infant and an inside space is not of itself symbolic play, the term 'symbolic' is being reserved for play where there is a distinct representation of the self. This is usually understood to mean the replacement of another object for the subject (infant), and a distinctive division between the self and other (see Piaget 1954; Trevarthen 1982; Segal 1957; Fiumara 1992; Hobson 1993). In the case studies use has been made of Segal's distinction between 'symbolism' and 'symbol equation', terms which she developed from Klein's 1930 paper, and between unconscious phantasy (Isaacs 1952) and symbolism (see page 174 above). The play with insides covered a wide spectrum from expressions of unconscious phantasy and concrete 'symbol equation' to play which was bordering on the truly symbolic. Central to these processes was a developmental differentiation by the infant between the mother's mind and her body. With this in mind, it is possible to explore the qualitative differences in the ways in which three infants (Hester, Hashmat and Samantha) took up language and symbolisation, whilst the other two, Timothy and Michael did not. Three factors of importance can be identified.

First, for the three symbolic infants there was evidence of the concept of a problem-solving link between mother and father – or other figures, including mother's mother (Hashmat) and the observer (Samantha). The role of the parental link and specifically the father is widely thought to have connection with symbolic thinking (Lacan 1978; Sarop 1992; Meltzer 1987; Britton 1989). For Bion, the link between two people was the prototype for thinking (Bion 1967, p.102). The link was observed to form distinctive patterns which were categorisable as 'bridge building' – the activity which Sally externalised in *her* play. Kevin fulfilled this function in Hester's second year, and Anne perceived me, the observer, doing this for her. The opposite of bridge building is a non-thinking link – which in Bion's terms is not truly a link. This was seen in Timothy's parents 'sticking together' and Michael's parents avoiding eye contact with each other (staying apart, or withdrawing), and the flattening of affect, or muffling of emotionality achieved by Samantha's parents (see Graph 13).

Second, during the second half of their second years, the symbolic infants had the capacity to arouse tender feelings in mother (Hester), observant and benign responses (Hashmat) and a greater capacity for attention (Samantha), all of which increased the degree of concave containing shape present for them. In contrast, Sally and Timothy remained in a collusion over possession and possessiveness, whilst Michael and Mary were sharing states of mind about 'dying' and the inability to remain together.

Third, and linked with this, as well as there being a shift towards concave containing shape, the infants were able to approach a more co-operative and depressive mode of functioning with their parents. Hester spent time learning language with Yvonne, who became more tolerant, and then weaning from the bottle was accomplished with an accompanying capacity to contain experience of loss. Hashmat's relationship with me was viewed sympathetically and incorporated into the family – I became an 'uncle', and Anne and Samantha shared thoughtful communication, particularly about the difference between broken and separate. This 'depressive' readdressing of relationships was in contrast to the non-symbolic infants' mode of relating (by now Michael was receiving visits from mother in a foster home).

These factors combined to lead infants to the border of symbolic representation in play, and to the development of language, which reached – nearly – appropriate levels for age in the cases of Samantha and Hester. Hashmat, peculiarly, was following the course of a bilingual infant. The development of language meant for the 'symbolic infants' not only forming words, but retaining them for repeated use, and using them as another 'Russian doll' in the service of influencing and relating to emotional issues.

9.5.4 The development of identifications

A range of different kinds of identifications were described in the case studies. The concepts of recognition, memory and recall with affection were operationalised to provide a framework for describing how infants' internalisations were observed. Recall with affection, in particular, was intended to show how a figure was linked with an internal representation, which was regarded with affection. Recall with affection constituted an engagement with an internal representation which was treated with warmth and loving regard (Klein 1957). The grid suggested that in respect of these five infants, Hashmat, Samantha and Timothy had periods in which recall with affection as high; Hester was 'scored' moderate and Michael low/fairly low. The case studies elaborated these features, and repeated observations demonstrated the extent to which the infants internalised and identified with a loving parental figure. There were, therefore, observations of infants demonstrating in their attitudes and play an attachment to a parental figure, based on love and admiration. Samantha was observed carefully watching mother in the kitchen (page 178 above) and Timothy was seen in father's shoes (page 218 above). In this example his attitude was gentle, affectionate and playful, rather than showing serious intent, which signified a more rivalrous or projective identification. This was the case when Samantha put on her mother's shoes (page 174 above). Hester in play with her doll (page 138 above) seemed to be in identification with a mother who cared for her baby, and Hashmat identified with older brother Miral in an admiring way (page 76 above).

There were frequent examples of the rivalrous of competitive projective identification. Samantha identified with a pregnant mother in her play (page 173–174 above), and Hashmat's identification with his father had an illicit quality (taking the betel-nut and the knife from father's pocket) (page 76 above). There were repeated observations across the sample of identifications with harmful or damaging 'objects', such as Michael's identification with a big brother who bumped and hurt (page 102 above) and Hashmat's identification with the 'gang' of brothers who attacked babies. These identifications were closely associated with risk. There were also examples of identifications with parts of the parental container shape which were also associated with risk. Hester was described as becoming identified with a dangerous, biting girl and this was a product of a 'fit' with the convex container shape of mother's fear of hurting or scratching (page 127 above). Timothy, through his relationship with the cat, appeared to be identified with the maternal fear of 'wild animals' and of the outside third person (page 214–215 above). Michael was identified with a baby who would be thrown away and hurt. Hester vividly demonstrated the conflictual identification with a mother who looked after a baby and whose protectiveness was ignored (saying 'get down' to herself) (page 138 above).

Thus, through the fit in the relationship with mother infants developed identifications which were representing of parts of the emerging personality, developing over time through processes of internalisation (introjective and projective) and which related to the infants' capacities to maintain object relations and their propensity to develop defensive constellations. Play, as has been seen, gave the infants opportunities to express these identifications in symbolic or quasi-symbolic (unconscious phantasy) modes, and through repeated or later experiences of concave containing shape develop a capacity to modulate the experiences and make connections between parts of the personality, through the Russian dolls of internalised experience. Identifications were therefore associated with both resilience, positive development and with risk. The nearer the infants approached symbolic functioning the greater the range of identifications they could express, indicating a capacity to move in and out of aspects of their intenalised selves. This accords with Hobson's conclusion that in order to achieve expression of identifications: 'The infant needs to recognise that being a person she can be the source of a variety of attitudes; that is the infant can assume the attitudes of an infinite number of other persons' (Hobson 1993, p.145).

In addition to Hobson's view of the 'affective attitude buried' (1993, p.149) in the development of identifications, the evidence from this study suggests that identifications are expressed symbolically when there is sufficient containment of the earlier emotionality of the fit between mother and infant to permit the infant to be free of the preoccupation with this issue, and/or to be able to express the issues as part, rather than the whole of the self. The development of identifications completes a process of infancy, followed here of movement from grip relations, to states of mind and then to parts of the personality.

9.6 Risk

Through the initial exploration of the theoretical approaches to infancy in Chapter 1, and the development of the model in Chapter 3, it was suggested that risk may be analysed in terms of the parental capacity to manage emotionality. Emotionality which is not taken into account was described as flat container shape, and emotionality which spills over, and is projected into the parent–infant relationship was convex container shape. Second, risk was thought of as consisting in an inability in the infant to find the internal resources to contend with stressful emotional experiences.

These ideas can now be assessed in the light of the evidence from the case studies and the foregoing discussion. First, it can be said that the categories of parental container shape do have a significant role to play in accounting for difficult and potentially risk-involving situations and experiences. Where flat and convex container shape are present, difficulties in developing are likely to be encountered. The greater the degree of flat/convex container shape, both in terms of frequency and intensity, the more likely there is to be developmental difficulty for the infants. Michael in particular was subject to high 'doses' of these container shapes and Hester, who was also significantly bombarded, also received a significant degree of concave container shape.

Maternal container shape is not a clear guide to the extent of the stressfulness to which the infant is subject. As I have said (9.4.1 above) all the family members have the potential for offering a particular containing shape to the infant. The way the family as a whole provides a particular containing environment needs to be taken into account. The discussion of 'triangular shape' is important here. The link the parents have with each other has a significant bearing on the way the infant experiences parental containment. This link was seen either as offering a combined concave pairing, or one which was combined flat ('flattening of affect') or combined convex ('sticking together').

The problems of the parents' internal worlds may then become activated through the particular containing shape to impact on the infant. In the case studies and the discussion of the model in this chapter it has been shown that parental difficulties may be transmitted through the shape of the relationship with the infant, resulting in manifestations of particular kinds of risk. Michael's experiences with Mary, and Yvonne's forcefulness were both associated with near physical damage to the infant as well as creating very difficult emotional experiences. Mothers in these circumstances would appear to become quite identified with parts of themselves, an abandoned girl in Mary's case, and in Yvonne's a damaging or murderous big sister. When these identifications become overwhelming there can be no possibility of concave containing shape.

On the other hand a number of factors appear to be associated with reduction in the power of these parental communications. Greater support, a sense of proportion brought in by a partner, a capacity to engage, through being more contained, with their own internal resources led to recovery. Anne in particular demonstrated the lifting of a burden after her return home (page 168 above).

The element of risk in development was explored here through the operationalisation of the concept of internalisation. Following Bion's theories of the link between early containment and the development of symbol formation there was a particular interest in the capacity of these infants to develop symbolic functioning. Some evidence has been proposed that infants who experienced difficulties in terms of early parental containment did have difficulties in developing language and symbolic thinking. The Bion hypothesis was however modified to include taking into account the effects of a continuous experience of containment, and through the concept of the Russian dolls of internalised experience, a view has been proposed of a configuration of container shape and grip relations (Mc<–>gI) though which early experiences are modulated later. 'Working through' and other expressions of language and play were cited as ways in which resilience occurred and was maintained. What was constantly clear in these observations was that modulation of experience and resilience could not occur without experiences – from at least one source – of concave container shape.

Resilience and propensity to risk were seen also to be dependent upon the infant's capacity to maintain object relations. The alternative was that defensive constellations developed, which eventually became crystallised as 'psychic retreats', in which the infants' development, or part of it, could be entrapped. In the descriptive case studies, considerable attention was paid to the ways in which infants maintained a hold on object relations, and the grip relations they employed to enable them to do this. For these infants, there was at least one category of the grid which was used to follow the infant's developmental progress in which difficulties were recorded. Hester for example was shown to have difficulties around issues of separation. This was carefully followed descriptively throughout her development, from her initial early weaning from the breast to the ending of the observational period.

In the discussion of internalisation and the development of identifications there were drawn together many of the examples of the development of aspects of internalisation in which risk was present. In particular, identifications with murderous older siblings and with aspects of the emotional content of the parental containing shape were discussed. In the descriptive accounts, risk was identified as occurring when the infants put these identifications into practice. Thus Hashmat's attacks on the baby, that is to say the baby in the family (Fashmat) were followed by attacks on his 'internal baby', who tipped away the feeding bottle, joined the 'gang' and then left himself at risk of falling from an open window (page 75 above). Here the formulation is that the attack on the part of the self is as dangerous if not more so than the attack on the other person. Michael was in danger of slipping through the railings of the balcony of the flat – falling as it were through the 'gaps' of his leaky container. Hester bit herself, literally, and in terms of her rigid food-refusing mouth grip as an alternative to 'biting' mother's food. Timothy's preoccupation with an inside space, dead babies and identifications with a mother who feared 'wild animal children' arrested his development. Samantha was at risk of falling but her expressions of this – dropping object down the stairwell – were less risky than the other examples because of the substitution of an object symbolically for the concrete, actual event. Symbolic thought, in other words, is a protection from risk. The greater the capacity for symbolism, the less the risk; the greater the impact of convex and flat containing shape, the greater the difficulties in reaching symbolic functioning. This is the conundrum of risk; this study confirms the importance of the hypothesis of the link between containment and symbolic thinking, modifies it and gives some evidence that there is a link between the quality of container shape, the capacity of grip relations to maintain object relations and the infant's capacity to attain symbolic functioning. At best the infants in this sample were able to maintain development, to mediate difficult experiences and to attain symbolic functioning. At worst, some of the defences and identifications they developed left them more at risk of failing to muster internal resources to contend with development and thus leaving them 'doubly deprived' (Henry 1974).

9.7 Conclusions

I have set out to explore in an innovative way the relationship between certain psychoanalytic concepts, development in infancy and risk. The importance of this kind of study in terms of overall theories of infancy is to link emotionality and cognition. Thus empirical studies which can integrate psychoanalysis with developmental theories of infancy broaden and deepen the understanding of infancy. This study fits into the tradition of recent enquiries, such as those by Stern, Murray and Fonagy in which psychoanalytic theories are applied to an empirical study. It adds to this literature by developing a model based on Bion's theories, operationalising some difficult concepts and following them in detail through the development of the five infants studied here. The study makes a contribution to both developmental and psychoanalytic theory. The model operationalised and developed Bion's theory of container–contained and some substantive theory concepts – container shape, grip relations, 'fit' – in connection with some of the main developmentalist views of infancy, especially those of Bower and Trevarthen. The application of the model creates an axis of emotionality and depth to add to developmental thinking of infant development. In 9.4.4, for example, the components of the development of a 'fit' between mother and infant were described as adding to the models of development proposed by Trevarthen from microanalysis. When mother–infant relationships are studied in naturalistic conditions including observations of infants in all states of mind, the opposing pictures of the infant as either 'rational' or 'anxious' become integrated. The model attempted this integration through the concepts used, such as grip relations, which was derived not only from Bion's theories but also the work of Bower on perception and Trevarthen on mother–infant communication timing rhythms. The model effectively maintained its functioning throughout the five case studies and could therefore be applied in future studies in which more closed observational methods and quasi-experimental methods could introduce the possibility of studying more infants and different samples of infants.

The contribution of psychoanalytic theory is more specific. The theory of container–contained is amplified and broadened. The defensive constellations observed contribute to recent thinking on defensive organisation (9.4.3 above). Discussions of internalisation and identification demonstrate the continuity of development, through the construction of a configuration of concepts which describe that continuity. Early internalisation processes are studied and seen to be complex and in tune with clinical reconstructions. The development of the concept of the 'Russian dolls of internalised experience' modifies the hypothesis of the link between early containment and symbol formation (9.5.1 above). The concepts of grip relations, containing shape and fit have potential application to clinical work and therefore to the body of post-Kleinian theory.

The thesis uses an exploratory methodology through adapting the Bick method of infant observation. Section 9.1 above points to the conclusions that the method is very well suited to detailed, naturalistic descriptions which produce detailed evidence about infant states of mind, and the meaning of their interactions and play. For application to a comparative study the Bick method required adaptation, and the psychoanalytic concepts used here were operationalised, and a grid developed. The grid was partially successful in meeting its objectives. It provided a consistent framework for all five cases and the categories used were quantifiable. The limitations of the methodology have been firmly stated. This was undertaken by a single researcher and there was a dependency on the transcripts of the observations as a data source. There was no statistical analysis and issues of validity were not addressed in this exploratory study. Since the material which has emerged from the study is rich and multi-dimensional, future studies will construct methodologies which lead to testing the qualitative and quantitative data. Future research would, in general, build an eclectic study based on these findings from naturalistic observations.

As well as avenues for future research, there are implications for professional practice. These have been discussed as the writing of the study has progressed, particularly in terms of the role of the observer. The idea that the observational approach could be included in professional practice is not a new one. Here the development of this is to suggest the roles the observational approach can help to develop with parents, the 'parental container' and 'auxiliary parent'. It is also suggested that the role of attention provides the basis for a containing and therapeutic role with infants. There are limits to the method as an intervention and the study has been careful to stress that this is the case (9.2.3 above). Additionally the theoretical findings of this study could lead to the introduction of these concepts into preventive professional practice, clinical work such as mother–infant psychotherapy (e.g. Daws 1989).

The main aim of the thesis was to develop this exploratory, innovative method to see what could be said about potential risk in infancy. The study has therefore established some hypotheses about risk and developed these. The outcome is that some clear statements are made about risk. Bion's theory, as operationalised here does in fact prove a fertile approach to attempting to understand risk. These hypotheses are elaborated above (9.6). There is scope here for future studies to develop these findings, and for testing of them on a larger scale. Risk, it is concluded here, has much to do with the problems parents find in identifying and containing emotions; and the problems infants experience in developing inner resources in difficult and stressful circumstances.

Bibliography

Ainsworth, M., Bell, S. and Stayton, D. (1991) 'Infant–mother attachment and social development: socialisation as a product of reciprocal responsiveness to signals.' In M. Woodhead, R. Carr and P. Light (eds) *Becoming a Person.* London: Routledge. Reprinted from M. Richards *et al.* (ed) (1974) *The Integration of a Child into a Social World.* Cambridge: Cambridge University Press.

Ainsworth, M. *et al.*(1978) *Patterns of Attachment.* Hillsdale NJ: Erlbaum.

Ainsworth, M. and Wittig, B. (1969) 'Attachment and the exploratory behaviour of one year olds in a strange situation.' In B. Foss (ed) *Determinants of Infant Behaviour 4,* 113–136. London: Methuen.

Alvarez, A. (1992) *Live Company.* London: Routledge.

Anzieu, D. (1985) *The Skin Ego: A Psychoanalytic Approach to the Self.* New Haven and London: Yale University Press.

Anzieu, D. (ed) (1990) *Psychic Envelopes.* London: Karnac.

Anzieu, D. (1993) 'Autistic phenomena and the skin ego.' *Psychoanalytic Enquiry 13,* 1, 42–49.

Attneave, F. (1959) *Applications of Information Theory to Psychology.* New York: Holt.

Baillargeon, R. (1986) 'Representing the existence and the location of hidden objects: Object permanence in 6–8 month old infants.' *Cognition 23,* 21–41.

Baillargeon, R. (1987) 'Object Permanence in 3.5 and 4.5 month old infants.' *Developmental Psychology 23,* 655–664.

Baillargeon, R. (1991) 'Reasoning about the height and location of a hidden object in 4.5 and 6.5 month-old infants.' *Cognition 38,* 13–42.

Baillargeon, R. (1994) 'Physical reasoning in young infants: Seeking explanations for impossible events.' *British Journal of Developmental Psychology 12,* 9–33.

Baillargeon, R., Spelke, E. and Wasserman, S. (1985) 'Object permanence in five month old infants.' *Cognition 20,* 191–208.

Baillargeon, R. *et al.* (1990) 'Why do young infants fail to search for hidden objects?' *Cognition 36,* 255–284.

Bell, S. (1969) 'The development of the concept of object as related to infant–mother attachment.' *Child Development 41,* 291–311.

Bell, S. and Ainsworth, M. (1972) 'Infant crying and maternal responsiveness.' *Child Development 43,* 1171–1190.

Bhaskar, R. (1978) *A Realist Theory of Science.* Brighton: Harvester.

Bhaskar, R. (1979) *The Possibility of Naturalism.* Brighton: Harvester.

Bhaskar, R. (1986) *Scientific Realism and Human Emancipation.* London: Verso.

Bick, E. (1964) 'Notes on infant observation in psychoanalytic training.' *International Journal of Psychoanalysis 45,* 184–488.

Bick, E. (1968) 'The experience of the skin in early object relations.' In *International Journal of Psychoanalysis 49.*

Bick, E. (1986) 'Further consideration of the function of the skin in early object relations: Findings from infant observation integrated into child and adult analysis.' *British Journal of Psychotherapy 2,* 4, 292–301.

Bion, W.R. (1962) *Learning from Experience.* London: Heinemann.

Bion, W.R. (1963) *Elements of Psychoanalysis.* London: Heinemann.

Bion, W.R. (1965) *Transformations.* London: Heinemann.

Bion, W.R. (1967) *Second Thoughts.* London: Maresfield.

Bion, W.R. (1970) *Attention and Interpretation.* London: Tavistock.

Bleandonu, G. (1994) *Wilfred Bion; his Life and Works 1897–1979.* London: Free Association Books.

Bollas, C. (1987) *The Shadow of the Object. Psychoanalysis of the Unthought Known.* London: Free Association Books.

Bott, E. (1957) *Family and Social Network. Roles, Norms and External Relationships in Ordinary Urban Families.* London: Tavistock.

Bower, T. (1974) *Development in Infancy.* San Francisco: Freeman.

Bower, T. (1979) *The Perceptual World of the Child.* London: Fontana.

Bower, T. (1989a) *The Rational Infant: Learning in Infancy.* New York: W.H. Freeman and Co.

Bower, T. (1989b) 'The perceptual world of the new born child.' In A. Slater and G. Bremner *Infant Development.* Hove: Lawrence Erlbaum Associates Ltd.

Bowlby, J. (1969) *Attachment.* London: Harmondsworth.

Bowlby, J. (1973) *Separation.* London: Harmondsworth.

Bowlby, J. (1980) *Loss.* London: Harmondsworth.

Bowlby, J. (1988) *A Secure Base: Clinical applications of Attachment Theory.* London: Routledge.

Box, S. *et al.* (eds) (1994) *Crisis in Adolescence: Object Relations Therapy with the Family.* Washington: Aronson.

Bradley, B. (1989) *Visions of Infancy.* Cambridge: Polity Press.

Braten, S. (1987) 'Dialogic mind: The infant and the adult in proto conversation.' In M. Carvallo (ed) *Nature, Cognition and System.* Copenhagen: Kluwer Academic Publishers.

Braudel, F. (1975) *The Mediterranean and the Mediterranean World in the age of Phillip II* (second revised edition). London: Fontana.

Brazelton, T. and Cramer, B. (1991) *The Earliest Relationship.* London: Karnac.

Brazelton, T., Koslowski, B. and Main, M. (1974) 'The origins of reciprocity: The early mother–infant interaction.' In M. Lewis and L. Rosenblum (eds) *The Effect of the Infant on its Caregiver.* New York: Wiley.

Brazelton, T. and Yogman, M. (1986) 'Reciprocity, attachment and effectance: Anlage in early infancy.' In T. Brazelton and M. Yogman (eds) *Affective Development in Infancy.* Norwood New Jersey: Ablex.

Brazelton, T. *et al.* (1975) 'Early mother–infant reciprocity' Parent–infant interaction. CIBA Foundation Symposium 33. New York and Amsterdam: Elsvier.

Brazelton, T. *et al.* (1979) 'The infant as a focus for family reciprocity.' In M. Lewis and L. Rosenblum (eds) *Social Network of the Developing Child.* New York: Wiley.

Brenman Pick, I. (1992) 'The emergence of early object relations in the psychoanalytic setting.' In R. Anderson (ed) *Clinical Lectures on Klein and Bion.* London: Routledge.

Bretherton, I. (1991) 'The roots and growing points of Attachment Theory.' In C. Murray Parkes, J. Stevenson Hinde and P. Marris (eds) *Attachment across the Life Cycle.* London: Routledge.

Briggs, S. (1992) 'Child observation and social work training.' *Journal of Social Work Practice 6,* 1, 49–61.

Briggs, S. (1993) 'Observing when containment fails: reflections on the role of the observer from a study of five infants at potential risk.' Conference paper: Rome 31 May 1993.

Britton, R. (1989) 'The missing link: parental sexuality in the Oedipus complex.' In R. Britton, M. Feldman and E. O'Shaughnessy (eds) *The Oedipus Complex Today.* London: Karnac.

Brown, G. and Desforges, C. (1979) *Piaget's Theory: A Psychological Critique.* London: Routledge.

Brown, G. and Harris, T. (1978) *Social Origins of Depression: A Study of Psychiatric Disorder in Women.* London: Tavistock.

Bruner, J. (1983) *Child's Talk: Learning to Use Language.* Oxford: Oxford University Press.

Cameroff, J. and Cameroff, J. (1992) *Ethnography and the Historical Imagination.* Oxford: Westview Press.

Campos, J. and Sternberg, C. (1981) 'Perception, appraisal and emotion: the onset of social referencing.' In M. Lamb and L. Sherrod (eds) *Infant Social Cognition.* Hillsdale, NJ: Erlbaum.

Chess, S. and Thomas, A. (1984) *Origins and Evolution of Behaviour Disorders: From Infancy to Early Adult Life.* New York: Brunner Mazel.

Cook, T. and Campbell, D. (1977) *Quasi Experimentation: Design and Analysis Issues for Field Settings.* Chicago: Rand McNally.

Crittenden, P. (1987) 'Non organic failure to thrive: deprivation or distortion.' *Infant Mental Health Journal 8,* 1, 51–64.

Daws, D. (1989) *Through the Night; Helping Parents and Sleepless Infants.* London: Free Association Books.

Denzin, N. (1970) *The Research Act.* Chicago: Aldine.

Dingwall, R. (1989) 'Some problems about predicting child abuse and neglect.' In O. Stevenson (ed) *Child Abuse: Public Policy and Professional Practice.* London: Harvester Wheatsheaf.

Donaldson, M. (1978) *Children's Minds.* London: Fontana.

Drotar, D. *et al.* (1990) 'Maternal interactional behaviour with non-organic failure to thrive infants: a case comparison study.' *Child Abuse and Neglect 14,* 41–51.

Eliot, T.S. (1944) *Four Quartets.* London: Faber and Faber.

Ellis, L. (1993) 'The meaning of difference: race, culture and context in infant observation.' Conference paper: Tavistock Clinic Infant Observation Conference; 1–4 September 1993.

Emde, R. (1988) 'Development terminable and interminable.' *International Journal of Psychoanalysis 69,* 23–42.

Escalona, S. (1969) *The Roots of Individuality. Normal Patterns of Development in Infancy.* London: Tavistock.

Evans Pritchard, E. (1940) *The Nuer: A Description of the Modes of Livelihood and Political Institutions of a Nilotic People.* Oxford: Clarendon Press.

Evans Pritchard, E. (1963) *Essays in Social Anthropology.* Manchester: Manchester University Press.

Fiumara, G. (1992) *The Symbolic Function: Psychoanalysis and the Philosophy of Language.* Oxford: Blackwell.

Fonagy, P. (1993) 'Psychoanalytical and empirical approaches: can they be usefully integrated?' *Journal of the Royal Society of Medicine 86,* 577–581.

Fonagy, P. (1994) 'Mental representations from an inter-generational cognitive science perspective.' *Infant Mental Health Journal 15,* 1, 57–68.

Fonagy, P. and Moran, G. (1993) 'Selecting single case research designs for clinicians.' In N. Miller, L. Luborsky, J. Barber and J. Docherty (eds) *Psychodynamic Treatment Research: A Handbook for Clinical Practice.* New York: Basic Books.

Fonagy, P. *et al.* (1993) 'The roles of mental representation and mental processes in therapeutic action.' *Psychoanalytic Study of the Child 48,* 9–47.

Fonagy, P., Steele, H. and Steele, M. (1991) 'Maternal representations of attachment during pregnancy predict the organisation of infant–mother attachment at 1 year of age.' *Child Development 62,* 880–893.

Fonagy, P. *et al.* (1991a) 'Measuring the ghost in the nursery: a summary of the main findings of the Anna Freud Centre – University College London Parent Child Study.' *Bulletin of the Anna Freud Centre 14,* 115–131.

Fonagy, P. *et al.* (1991b) 'The capacity for understanding mental states: the reflective self in parent and child and its significance for security of attachment.' *Infant Mental Health Journal 12,* 3, 201–218.

Freeman, N., Lloyd, S. and Sinha, C. (1980) 'Hide and seek in children's play.' *New Scientist 1225,* 88.

Freiberg, S. (1980) *Clinical Studies in Infant Mental Health.* New York: Basic Books.

Freud, S. (1905) *Three Essays on the Theory of Sexuality.* Standard Edition vol.7, 123–245. London: Hogarth Press.

Freud, S. (1910) *The Future Prospects of Psycho-analytic Therapy.* Standard Edition vol.11, 139–153. London: Hogarth Press.

Freud, S. (1914a) *On Narcissism.* Standard Edition vol.14, 67–102. London: Hogarth Press.

Freud, S. (1914b) *Remembering, Repeating and Working Through.* Standard Edition vol.12, 145–156. London: Hogarth Press.

Freud, S. (1917) *Mourning and Melancholia.* Standard Edition vol.14, 237–259. London: Hogarth Press.

Freud, S. (1920) *Beyond the Pleasure Principle.* Standard Edition vol.18, 1–64. London: Hogarth Press.

George, C., Kaplan, N. and Main, M. (1985) *An Adult Attachment Interview: Interview Protocol.* CA: University of California.

Glaser, B. and Strauss, A. (1967) *The Discovery of Grounded Theory.* Chicago: Aldine.

Glaser, B. and Strauss, A. (1971) *Status Passage.* London: Routledge.

Gold, R. (1958) 'Roles in sociological field observation.' *Social Forces 36,* 217–223.

Green, A. (1986) 'The dead mother.' In *On Private Madness.* London: Hogarth Press.

Hammersley, M. (1990) 'What's wrong with ethnography? The myth of theoretical descriptions.' *Sociology 24,* 597–615.

Harlow, H. and Zimmermann, R. (1958) 'Affectional responses in the infant monkey.' *Science 130,* 421.

Harris, M. (1975) 'Some notes on maternal containment in "Good Enough" mothering.' Reprinted in M. Harris Williams (ed) (1989) *Collected Papers of Martha Harris and Esther Bick.* Perthshire: Clunie Press.

Harris, P. (1994) 'Unexpected, impossible and magical events: Children's reactions to causal violations.' *British Journal of Developmental Psychology 12,* 1–9.

Hartman, D. (1988) 'Measurement and analysis.' In M. Bornstein and M. Lamb (eds) *Developmental Psychology: An Advanced Textbook.* New York: Lawrence Erlbaum Associates.

Heimann, P. (1950) 'On countertransference.' *International Journal of Psychoanalysis 31,* 81–4.

Henry, G. (1974) 'Doubly deprived.' *Journal of Child Psychotherapy 3,* 4, 15–29.

Henry, G. (1984) 'Difficulties about thinking and learning.' In M. Boston and R. Szur (eds) *Psychotherapy with Severely Deprived Children.* London: Routledge and Kegan Paul.

Hobson, P. (1993) *Autism and the Development of Mind.* Hove: Laurence Erlbaum.

Houzel, D. (1990) 'The concept of the psychic envelope.' In D. Anzieu (ed) *Psychic Envelopes.* London: Karnac.

Hoxter, S. (1975) 'The residual autistic condition and its effect upon learning.' In D. Meltzer *et al. Explorations in Autism.* Perthshire: Clunie Press.

Hunt, J. (1985) *Transference and Counter-transference in Fieldwork.* London: Sage.

Isaacs, S. (1952) 'The nature and function of phantasy.' In M. Klein *et al.* (eds) *Developments in Psychoanalysis.* London: Hogarth Press.

Jones, D. *et al.* (1987) *Understanding Child Abuse.* London: Macmillan.

Kant, I. (1964) 'Critique of pure reason.' In A. Zweig (ed) *The Essential Kant.* New York: Signet Classics.

Kempe, H. (1978) *Child Abuse.* London: Fontana.

Klein, M. (1930) 'The importance of symbol formation in the development of the ego.' Reprinted in M. Klein (1987) *Love, Guilt and Reparation.* London: Virago.

Klein, M. (1932) 'The technique of child analysis.' In *The Writings of Melanie Klein, vol.2.* London: Hogarth Press.

Klein, M. (1940) 'Mourning and its relation to manic-depressive states.' Reprinted in M. Klein (1987) *Love, Guilt and Reparation.* London: Virago.

Klein, M. (1945) 'The Oedipus complex in the light of early anxieties.' Reprinted in M. Klein (1987) *Love, Guilt and Reparation.* London: Virago.

Klein, M. (1946) 'Notes on some schizoid mechanisms.' Reprinted in M. Klein (1988) *Envy and Gratitude and Other Works 1946–63.* London: Virago.

Klein, M. (1952a) 'The origins of transference.' Reprinted in M. Klein (1988) *Envy and Gratitude and Other Works 1946–63.* London: Virago.

Klein, M. (1952b) 'Some theoretical conclusions regarding the emotional life of the infant.' Reprinted in M. Klein (1988) *Envy and Gratitude and Other Works 1946–63.* London: Virago.

Klein, M. (1952c) 'On observing the behaviour of young infants.' Reprinted in M. Klein (1988) *Envy and Gratitude and Other Works 1946–63.* London: Virago.

Klein, M. (1957) 'Envy and gratitude.' Reprinted in M. Klein (1988) *Envy and Gratitude and Other Works 1946–63.* London: Virago.

Knorr-Cetina, K. and Mulkay, M. (eds) (1983) *Science Observed.* London: Sage.

Kuhn, T. (1962) *The Structure of Scientific Revolutions.* Chicago: University of Chicago Press.

Lacan, J. (1978) *Ecrits.* Translated by A. Sheridan. London: Tavistock.

Lamb, M. (ed) (1981) *The Role of the Father in Child Development.* New York: Wiley.

Layder, D. (1992) *New Strategies in Social Research.* Cambridge: Polity Press.

Magagna, J. (1993) 'Aspects of the mother–nanny relationship; understanding different ways in which the relationship can influence the development of the baby.' Conference paper: Tavistock Clinic Infant Observation Conference; 1–4 September 1993.

Mahler, M. (1968) *On Human Symbiosis and the Vicissitudes of Individuation.* New York: International Universities Press.

Mahler, M., Pine, F. and Bergman, A. (1975) *The Psychological Birth of the Human Infant.* New York: Basic Books.

Main, M. (1991) 'Metacognitive knowledge, metacognitive monitoring, and singular (coherent) vs. multiple (incoherent) model of attachment: findings and direction for further research.' In C. Murray Parkes, J. Stevenson Hinde and P. Marris (eds) *Attachment Across the Life Cycle.* London: Routledge.

Meltzer, D. (1973) *Sexual States of Mind.* Perthshire: Clunie Press.

Meltzer, D. (1978) *The Kleinian Development.* Perthshire: Clunie Press.

Meltzer, D. (1984) *Studies in Extended Metapsychology: Clinical Applications of Bion's Ideas.* Perthshire: Clunie Press.

Meltzer, D. (1991) *The Claustrum: An Investigation of Claustrophobic Phenomena.* Perthshire: Clunie Press.

Meltzer, D. and Harris Williams, M. (1988) *The Apprehension of Beauty.* Perthshire: Clunie Press.

Meltzer, D. *et al.* (1975) *Explorations in Autism: A Psychoanalytic Study.* Perthshire: Clunie Press.

Meltzoff, A. (1981) 'Imitation, intermodal coordination and representation in early infancy.' In G. Butterworth (ed) *Infancy and Epistomology.* London: Harvester.

Meltzoff, A. and Borton, W. (1979) 'Intermodal matching by human neonates.' *Nature 282,* 403–4.

Meltzoff, A. and Moore, M. (1983) 'The origins of imitation in infancy: Paradigm, phenomena and theories.' In L. Lipsitt (ed) *Advances in Infancy Research.* Norwood NJ: Ablex.

Miller, E. (1993) *From Dependency to Autonomy: Studies in Organisation and Change.* London: Free Association Books.

Miller, L. *et al.* (eds) (1989b) *Closely Observed Infants.* London: Duckworth.

Miller, L. (1987) 'Idealization and contempt: Dual aspects of the process of devaluation of the breast in a feeding relationship.' *Journal of Child Psychotherapy 13,* 1, 41–55.

Model, N. (1987) 'Failure to thrive: A follow up.' *Bulletin of the Anna Freud Centre 10,* 137.

Moore, M. and Meltzoff, A. (1978) 'Object permanence, imitation and language development in infancy.' In F. Minifie and L. Lloyd (eds) *Communicative and Cognitive Abilities; Early Behavioural Assessments.* Baltimore: University Park Press.

Mulkay, M. (1983) 'Why an analysis of scientific discourse is needed.' In K. Knorr-Cetina and M. Mulkay (eds) (1983) *Science Observed.* London: Sage.

Murray, L. (1988) 'Effects of post-natal depression on infant development: Direct studies of early mother–infant interactions.' In R. Kumar and I. Brockington (eds) *Motherhood and Mental Illness 2.* London: Wright.

Murray, L. (1989) 'Winnicott and the developmental psychology of infancy.' *British Journal of Psychotherapy 5,* 3.

Murray, L. (1991) 'Intersubjectivity, object relations theory and empirical evidence from mother–infant interactions.' In *Infant Mental Health Journal 12,* 3, 219–232.

Murray, L. (1992) 'The impact of postnatal depression on infant development.' In *Journal of Child Psychology and Psychiatry 33,* 3, 543–561.

Murray, L. (1993) 'Psychosocial factors associated with the early termination of breast-feeding.' *Journal of Psychosomatic Research 37,* 2, 171–176.

Murray, L. and Trevarthen, C. (1985) 'Emotion regulation of interactions between two month olds and their mothers.' In T. Field and N. Fox (eds) *Social Perception in Infants 137–154.* New Jersey: Ablex.

Murray, L. and Trevarthen, C. (1986) 'The infant's role in mother–infant communication.' *Journal of Child Language 13,* 15–29.

Murray Parkes, C., Stevenson Hinde, J. and Marris, P. (eds) (1991) *Attachment Across the Life Cycle.* London: Routledge.

O'Shaughnessy, E. (1964) 'The absent object.' *Journal of Child Psychotherapy 1,* 2.

O'Shaughnessy, E. (1986) 'Clinical commentary by a Kleinian analyst.' *British Journal of Psychotherapy 13,* 1, 77–79.

Phillips, D. (1977) *Wittgenstein and Scientific Knowledge: A Sociological Perspective.* London: Macmillan.

Piaget, J. (1951) *Play, Dreams and Imitation in Childhood.* London: Routledge and Kegan Paul.

Piaget, J. (1955) *The Child's Construction of Reality.* London: Routledge and Kegan Paul.

Piontelli, S. (1986) *Backwards in Time; A Study in Infant Observation by the Method of Esther Bick.* Perthshire: Clunie Press.

Piontelli, S. (1992) *From Fetus to Child: An Observational and Psychoanalytic Study.* London: Routledge.

Popper, K.R. (1963) *Conjectures and Refutations.* London: Routledge and Kegan Paul.

Raphael Leff, J. (1986) 'Facilitators and regulators: participators and renouncers: mother's and father's orientations towards pregnancy and parenthood.' *Journal of Psychosomatic Obstetrics and Gynaecology 4,* 3, 169–184.

Ravenscroft, K. (1994) 'Changes in projective identification during couples treatment.' Unpublished paper. 23 March 1994.

Rayner, E. (1978) *Human Development.* London: Karnac.

Reid, M. (1992) 'Joshua – life after death. The replacement child.' *Journal of Child Psychotherapy 18,* 2, 109–138.

Reid, S. (1997) *Infant Observation: the Tavistock Model.* London: Routledge.

Rhode, M. (1993) 'Psychosomatic integrations: eye and mouth in infant observation.' Conference paper: Tavistock Clinic Infant Observation Conference; 1–4 September 1993.

Riviere, J. (1936) 'Hate, guilt and aggression.' In M. Klein and J. Riviere *Love, Hate and Reparation.* London, Hogarth Press.

Robertson, J. and Robertson, J. (1969) *Young Children in Brief Separation.* Ipswich: Concord Films.

Rosaldo, R. (1986) 'From the door of his tent: the fieldworker and the inquisitor.' In J. Clifford and G. Marcus (eds) *Writing Culture.* Berkeley and Los Angeles: University of California Press.

Rosenfeld, H. (1971) 'A clinical approach to the psychoanalytic theory of the life and death instincts: an investigation into the aggressive aspects of narcissism.' *International Journal of Psychoanalysis 52,* 169–178.

Rudner, R. (1966) *The Philosophy of Social Science.* London: Prentice Hall.

Rustin, M.E. (1989) 'Encountering primitive anxieties.' In L. Miller *et al.* (eds) *Closely Observed Infants.* London: Duckworth.

Rustin, M.J. (1989) 'Reflections on methods.' In L. Miller *et al.* (eds) *Closely Observed Infants.* London: Duckworth.

Rustin, M.J. (1991) *The Good Society and The Inner World.* London: Verso.

Rustin, M.J. (1993)'A significant step for infant observation: conference report.' *Journal of Association of Child Psychotherapists,* Autumn 1993.

Sarop, M. (1992) *Modern Cultural Theorists.* Brighton: Harvester.

Segal, H. (1957) 'Notes on symbol formation.' *International Journal of Psychoanalysis 38,* 391–397.

Segal, H. (1964) *Introduction to the Work of Melanie Klein.* London: Heinemann.

Segal, H. (1991) *Dream, Phantasy and Art.* London: Routledge.

Shuttleworth, J. (1989) 'Psychoanalytic theory and infant development.' In L. Miller *et al.* (eds) *Closely Observed Infants.* London: Duckworth.

Sorenson, P. (1997) 'The container–contained relationship, with an emphasis on infant–mother interaction.' In S. Reid (ed) *Infant Observation: the Tavistock Model.* London: Routledge.

Spillius, E. (1994) 'Developments in Kleinian thought: overview and personal view.' Scientific Meeting Paper, British Psychoanalytic Society, 20 October 1993.

Spinetta, J. and Rigler, D. (1980) 'The child abusing parent: a psychological review.' In G.J. Williams and J. Money *Traumatic Abuse and Neglect of Children at Home.* Baltimore: John Hopkins University Press.

Steiner, J. (1993) *Psychic Retreats.* London: Routledge.

Stern, D. (1977) *The First Relationship.* London: Fontana.

Stern, D. (1985) *The Interpersonal World of the Infant.* New York: Basic Books.

Stern, D. (1990) 'The role of narrative in understanding development.' Sound recording. Tavistock Clinic Library.

Stern, D. (1994) 'One way to build a clinically relevant baby.' *Infant Mental Health Journal 15*, 1.

Symington, J. (1985) 'The survival function of primitive omnipotence.' In *International Journal of Psychoanalysis 66*, 481–486.

Trevarthen, C. (1979) 'Communication and cooperation in early infancy: a description of primary intersubjectivity.' In M. Bullowa (ed) *Before Speech.* Cambridge: Cambridge University Press.

Trevarthen, C. (1980) 'The foundations of intersubjectivity: Development of interpersonal and cooperative understanding in infants.' In D. Olson (ed) *The Social Foundations of Language and Thought.* New York: Norton.

Trevathen, C. (1982) 'The primary motives for co-operative understanding.' In G. Butterworth and P. Light (eds) *Social Cognition: Studies of the Development of Understanding.* Brighton: Harvester.

Trevarthen, C. (1991) 'Emotions with no 'Theory' of Mind.' Sound recording. Tavistock Clinic Library.

Trevarthen, C. and Hubley, P. (1978) 'Secondary intersubjectivity: confidence, confiding and acts of meaning in the first year.' In A. Lock (ed) *Action, Gesture and Symbol: The Emergence of Language.* Academic Press.

Tronick, E. *et al.* (1978) 'The infant's response to entrapment between contradictory messages in face to face interaction.' *Journal of Child Psychiatry 17*, 1–13.

Trowell, J. (1982) 'Possible effects of emergency caesarean section on the mother–child relationship.' *Early Human Development 7*, 41–51.

Trowell, J. and Miles, G. (1991) 'The application of child observation to professional development in social work.' *Journal of Social Work Practice 5*, 51–60.

Tustin, F. (1990) *The Protective Shell in Children and Adults.* London: Karnac.

Urwin, C. (1986) 'Developmental psychology and psychoanalysis: splitting the difference.' In M. Richards and P. Light (eds) *Children of Social Worlds: Development in a Social Context.* Cambridge: Polity Press.

Urwin, C. (1989) 'Linking emotion with thinking in infant development.' In A. Slater and G. Bremner (eds) *Infant Development.* Hove: Laurence Erlbaum.

Waddell, M. (1988) 'Infantile development: Kleinian and post-Kleinian theory and infant observational practice.' *British Journal of Psychotherapy 4,* 313–328.

Watson, J. (ed) (1977) *Between Two Cultures.* Oxford: Blackwell.

Will, D. (1986) 'Psychoanalysis and the new philosophy of science.' *International Review of Psychoanalysis 13,* 163–173.

Williams, G. (1992) 'Reflections on the process of internalisation.' *Journal of Child Psychotherapy, 17,* 2, 3–14.

Williams, G. (1997) 'Self esteem and object esteem'. In *Internal Lamdscapes and Foreign Bodies.* London: Duckworth.

Wilson, K. (1992) 'The place of child observation in social work training.' *Journal of Social Work Practice 6,* 1, 37–47.

Winnicott, D. (1960) 'The theory of the mother–infant relationship.' In D. Winnicott (1965) *The Maturational Processes and the Facilitating Environment.* London: Hogarth Press.

Winnicott, D. (1965) *The Maturational Processes and the Facilitating Environment.* London: Hogarth Press.

Winnicott, D. (1965a) *The Family and Individual Development.* London: Hogarth Press.

Winnicott, D. (1974) 'Fear of breakdown.' *International Review of Psychoanalysis 1,* 1, 103–107.

Wishart, J. and Bower, T. (1984) 'Spatial relations and the object concept: A normative study.' In L. Lipsitt and C.K. Rovee-Collier (eds) *Advances in Infancy Research (vol.3).* Norwood, NJ: Ablex.

Wittenberg, I. (1970) *Psychoanalytic Insights and Relationships.* London: Routledge.

Wittenberg, I. (1975) 'Primal depression in autism – John.' In D. Meltzer *et al.* (1975) *Explorations in Autism: A Psychoanalytic Study.* Perthshire: Clunie Press.

Subject Index

Adult Attachment Interview (AAI) 12, 15, 23
Affect Attunement 11, 17, 20, 197
Alert Inactivity 14, 17, 18, 46, 201, 234
Alpha function 42, 265
Amodal perception 6, 11
Ancient Mariner, the 141
Anxiety, *see* States of mind, infants and States of mind, parents
  signal 12
Anxieties, infantile 16, 18, 19, 26, 41, 42, 46, 161, 166, 175, 176, 179, 200, 257–258
Attachment, secure 15
Attachment Theory 12, 17
Attunement, *see* affect attunement
Auto erotism 11

Bangladesh 64, 246
Bengali 37, 61, 72, 76, 77, 234
Breast-feeding 61, 123, 135, 155, 158, 178, 194, 196, 198, 201, 202, 220fn
British 37

Child developmental psychology 1–4, 10, 15
Child abuse 2
Childbirth 38, 62, 70, 91, 120, 121, 239
  caesarean 38, 156
  natural 38, 193, 195
  difficult, 121, 194
Child psychotherapist 1, 35
Child psychotherapy 26
Commensal relationships 43–44, 48, 253–256
  patterns of 253–256, 265
see also Fit, in parent–infant relationships.
Concern, stage of 9
Container-contained 12, 19, 20, 21, 22, 40, 41, 42, 43, 47, 48, 56, 67, 257, 258, 265, 271
Container shape 44, 50, 56, 237, 248–250, 254–257, 259,260, 265, 270, 272
  concave 45, 50, 77, 122, 156, 197, 200, 217, 247–250, 254, 255, 262, 266, 267
  content of 249
  convex 45, 50, 56, 63, 66, 77, 92, 120, 133, 141, 162, 248–250, 254, 255, 263, 268, 271
  flat 45, 50, 56, 63, 77, 92, 156, 159, 166–167, 196, 200, 216, 219, 248–250, 254, 255, 271
  frequency of 249
  and risk 249
Counter-transference 29, 30, 31, 75
Curiosity, in infants, *see* States of mind in infants, curious
Deep theoretical structures 24, 32
Defence 15, 17
Defences, autistic 102fn, 108
Defensive constellation 96, 272
  organisation 210, 272
  patterns (of infant) 65, 96, 97, 102fn, 128, 133, 141, 159, 179, *see also* Grip relations, Muscularity, Unadventurousness
Defensiveness, and grip relations 252
  of infant 6, 54, 66, 203, 220, 251–253, 256, 257, 258
Depression, infant
  maternal, *see* Mothers, depression in
  postnatal, *see* Mothers, postnatal depression in
Depressive position 9, 65, 164, 258, 266, 267
Development in infancy, *see* Infant development
Developmental pathway 21, 25, 246,
Dialogic model 9, 16
Dimensionality, two 21, 103, 263
  three 6, 20, 21, 105, 165, 263
Discovery, context of 32
Dyadic organisation 9

Empirical psychology 235
Empiricism, *see* Methodology, empirical
Epistemology, realist 24–25, 31
Ethical difficulties 234
Ethical issues 32, 37, 39

Ethology 13
Ethnography 28, 29, 30–33, 233

Father–infant relationships 12, 64, 83, 113, 122, 129, 137, 147, 185, 225
Failure to thrive 90, 98, 103, 105, 108, 234
Feeding 67, 92, 102, 108, 127, 160, 196
  bottle 65, 71, 97, 98, 124, 131, 162, 163, 167
  breast, *see* Breast-feeding
  difficulties 66, 97, 98, 105, 108, 120, 123, 133, 135–137, 141, 159, 160, 234, 252
  solids 99, 101, 140, 169, 202, 207, 216
Fit, in parent–infant relationship 44, 48, 83, 112, 128, 132, 133, 145, 212, 253–256, 257, 259, 260, 265, 268, 271, 272
  accommodating 44, 66, 128, 132, 162, 219, 255
  conflictual 44, 133, 199, 203, 255
  containing 44, 209, 255
  exact 200, 203
Foster care 90, 108, 267

Gang 63, 65, 260, 270
Generative mechanisms 24, 25, 30
Geneva 4
Ghost in the nursery 14, 15, 127, 247, 249
Grid, assessment 35, 40–41, 48–55, 233, 236, 245, 247, 248, 253, 256, 267, 270, 272
Grip relations 46, 53, 56, 128, 130, 141, 159, 165, 202, 207, 220, 220fn, 237, 243, 250–251, 254–258, 265, 269, 270–272
  clinging 250
  and defensive patterns 67, 257 *see also* Defensive patterns
  direction of 237, 250, 257
  and internalisation 132, 176, 250 *see also* Internalisation
  loss of 97, 100, 203, 205, 206–207
  maintaining object relations 65, 69, 94, 95, 126, 130, 250, 268, 271
  patterns of 67, 97, 125, 126, 131, 167, 198, 199, 251,257
  strength of 87, 124, 177, 237, 250
  texture of (firm, loose rigid) 98, 103, 105, 107, 123, 161, 162, 165, 166, 172, 175–177, 179, 210, 219, 220fn, 237, 250, 257, 259, 260, 262, 271
Grounded theory, *see* Theory, grounded
Gulf War, the 123, 157, 246

Health visitor 35, 61, 62
Hermaneutics 24
'Hypothetical infant' 5fn, 24

Identification, infant 215, 267, 271, 272
  with big brothers 76, 268
  with gang 268
  with harmful or damaging object 268
  introjective 76, 178, 218, 268
  with observer 72, 105
  with parental containing shape 270
  with parental figures 76, 219, 267 271
  projective, *see* Projective identification
  and risk 268, *see also* Risk
  with siblings 75, 76, 77, 103, 108, 270
Infancy, cognition in 4, 271
  emotion in 4, 17, 271
  undifferentiated states in 11
Infant,
  dreams 67, 202
  held in mind 21 179
  inner spaces of, *see* Internal spaces
  proto-masochistic relationships 263 *see also* Proto-masochism
  reactions to separation/reunion 12, 72, 87, 88, 100, 118, 125, 129, 135, 139, 152, 169, 170, 175, 178, 190, 199, 203, 204, 206, 230, 256, 261, 262

states of mind, *see* States of mind
vulnerability of 2–3, 16, 68, 71, 128
Infant capacity, for discriminating between people 88, 118, 129, 152, 190,230, 256
for maintaining object relations 69, 117, 133, 168, 178, 203, 251, 252
for memory 87, 117, 139, 151, 190, 230, 256
for proximity seeking 88, 118, 152, 190, 206, 209, 230, 256
for recall with affection 87, 117, 151, 169, 175, 190, 230, 256
for recognition 47, 87, 100, 101, 117, 131, 139, 151, 170, 175, 190, 209, 230, 256, 261
for thinking 88, 118, 169, 190
Infant development 2, 68, 85, 98, 100, 104, 115, 121, 129, 132, 149, 187, 227
delayed 68, 71, 98, 105, 167, 210
milestones 50, 69, 85, 115, 132, 149, 164, 168, 187, 204, 228, 262
mobility 85, 115, 132, 200, 262
precocious 104, 132, 262
Infant Observation, method of 1–3, 23–34, 233, 272
Information theory, *see* Theory, information
Infantile anxieties, *see* Anxieties, infantile
Intentionality, in infants 6, 16, 208fn
Internal spaces, qualities of in infant 69, 70, 72, 103, 106, 107, 216, 265
Internal working model of mother 13
Internalisation 15, 20, 47, 48, 53, 56, 77, 88, 95, 106, 109, 127, 178, 208fn, 219, 256–270, 272
based on love and admiration 267
benign 141
of damaging/harmful object 106–107, 132
in early infancy 18, 127, 198, 202, 257, 260
and grip relations 251, *see also* Grip relations
of mother's containing function 21
of parent 21, 108, 160, 168, 179
of a sense of absence 139, 154, 260–263
Intersubjectivity 4, 8–10, 15, 17
primary 8
secondary 9,11
Introjection 18, 19, 20, 235

K link 42, 43

Language development 54, 69, 72, 88, 101, 120, 132, 133, 137–138, 142, 154, 165, 168, 170, 172, 174–175, 179, 193, 210, 213–214, 219, 256, 261, 263
bilingual 72, 267
difficulties in 99, 105, 193, 213–214
Life events and difficulties schedule 15
London 4, 61
Longitudinal study 26, 33
Loss 129, 157, 215
in early infancy 124, 139, 162, 258

Matching of stimuli 6
Maternal projections, *see* Projections, maternal
Methodology,
clinical 23, 24, 235
empirical 23, 24, 29, 235, 236, 271
ethnographic, *see* Ethnography
experimental 25, 236, 237
exploratory 23, 235, 272
historical 25, 30, 246fn
laboratory based 23, 25, 34, 234
longitudinal 26, 234
naturalistic 2, 26, 27, 28, 30, 31, 32, 234, 235, 272
observational *see* Infant observation
participant observation 29, 33, 39, 238
reliability of 41, 236, 237, 272
validity of 4, 25, 236, 237, 272
Microanalysis 8, 15, 23, 31, 253

Mindlessness 66, *see also* Infant states of mind, mindless
Model, the 21, 35, 40, 245, 269, 271
Mother–infant psychotherapy 14, 273
Mother–infant relationships 2, 63, 69, 81, 94, 99, 111, 135, 144, 158, 178, 182–185, 223–225, 253, 272 *see also* Fit, Commensal relationships
ambivalent 127
attentive
conflict in 96, 120, 122, 128, 133, 135, 140, 141
containing, 125
cruel 128
emotional struggles in 257
intimacy in 122, 137,163
tenderness in 122, 133,137, 156
Mothers,emotional preoccupations of 78, 92, 110, 128, 143, 155, 156, 160, 168, 180, 195, 196, 221
capacity to observe 121, 179, 196
depression in 15, 16, 38, 63, 67, 92–93, 98, 107, 124, 141, 160, 168, 247
internal resources of 78, 90, 110, 124, 129, 140, 143, 156, 180, 221, 247
levels of support for 38, 78, 109, 142, 157, 180, 220, 247
positive changes in 247
postnatal depression in 38, 91, 121, 160
pregnant 70, 73, 90, 91, 92, 95, 103, 106, 120, 155, 173, 193, 211, 263
Mourning 122, 129, 139, 258
Muscularity 74, 120, 125, 131, 133, 135, 137, 139, 141, 198, 200, 203–207, 219,.248, 251, 252, 257, 259, 262

Nameless dread 44
Narcissism 11
Narcissistic organisation 259
Naturalistic inquiry 26, 233, 245, 272
Nuer, the 30fn

Object concept 5, 15, 16, 103, 208, 260, 261
Object constancy, *see* object concept
Object permanence, *see* object concept
Object relations
theory 13, 14, 16, 17, 18, 20, 22, 41
infants 2, 26, 54, 65, 66, 102, 108, 124, 125, 127, 133, 137, 141, 159, 257, 262, 270
maintained by grip relations, *see* Grip relations
Observation
infant *see* Infant Observation
naturalistic, *see* Methodology, naturalistic
repeated 26, 31, 33, 108, 237
Observer
attentive function of 68, 104, 242, 273
as auxiliary parent 240–242, 244, 273
containing function of 242
empathic communications of with infants 242
impact of, on infant development 243, 244
male 36,
as object of infant's grip relations 98, 130, 177, 243 *see also* Grip relations
as parental container 122, 240–242, 244, 273
persecutory impact of 243
relations of, with infants 68, 72, 98, 130, 131, 132, 134, 139, 161, 169, 170–172, 175, 203, 206, 218, 242–243, 261
relationship of, with parents 61, 92, 104, 134, 135, 169, 195, 196, 238, 244
role of 26, 68, 73, 77, 93, 98, 233, 234, 272
selectivity of recall of 31
therapeutic role with infants of 243, 244

Oedipal development 177, 263
Oedipal relationship 43, 197

Pakistan 61
Paranoid schizoid position 65
Parent–infant relationships, *see* Father–infant relationships and Mother–infant relationships
  conflict in 251 –252
  rhythm in 253
  timing in 108, 253
Parents
  childhood experiences of 38, 91, 92, 121, 155
  identifications 56, 269
  states of mind, *see* States of mind, in parents, *see also* Mothers
Parental 'link' 52, 83, 85, 114, 137, 148, 186, 196, 198, 226–227, 248, 266, 269
  'bridge building' 83, 114, 137, 196248, 266
  flattening of affect in 83, 114, 124, 137, 156, 196, 248, 266, 269
  problem solving 137, 248, 266, 269
  'sticking together' 83, 114, 137, 196, 219, 248, 266, 269
Part object relationship 42, 262
Participant observation, *see* Methodology, participant observation
Pathological organisation 259
Perceptual modalities of infants 6
Perceptual world of the infant 6
Perturbation 15, 16
Play 1, 16, 48, 70, 73, 102, 105, 133, 138, 141, 164, 166, 168, 170, 173, 174, 207, 215, 217, 235, 263, 268, 270, 272
  lack of symbolic content in 210
  peek a boo 74, 208, 209, 261
  pretend 106, 171
  with insides of objects 102, 106, 107, 165, 172, 210–211, 212, 263
  symbolic, *see* Symbolic play
  theory of 263–265
Prespeech 8
Primary intersubjectivity, *see* Intersubjectivity
Primary maternal preoccupation 249
Proto masochism, in infants 128, 130
Projection 18, 19, 20, 62, 212, 217, 219
Projections, infantile 135, 161
  maternal 90, 95, 103, 129, 135, 156, 162, 258
Projective identification 20, 30, 42, 43, 46, 76, 174, 218, 235, 267
Psychic retreat 258, 270
Psychoanalytic theory, *see* Theory, pschoanalytic
  operationalisation of 16, 21, 22, 23, 25, 29, 35, 40, 41, 46, 233, 235, 236, 237, 272

Rational infant, the 6–7
Realism, transcendental, *see* Epistemology, realist
Reciprocity 9, 14
Resilience, in infants 120, 139, 142, 154, 256, 268, 270
Reverie 19, 20, 21, 42, 44, 92, 122, 200
  limited capacity for in parents 242, *see* also Container shape
Risk, and container shape, *see* Container shape
  and emotions 56, 269, 273
  in infancy 2–3, 21, 55–56, 61, 62, 75, 77, 91, 128, 176, 233, 256, 268, 273
  and internal resources 56, 269, 273
  potential 37
  and stressful circumstances 56, 269, 273
Russian dolls of internalised experience 73, 77, 141, 154, 260, 262, 267, 268, 270, 272

Sado-masochistic relationship 258
Secondary intersubjectivity, *see* Intersubjectivity
'Sensitive parent' 13

Siblings
attacks of, on infant 63, 66, 67, 71, 100, 103
cruel 63
jealous relations of, with infant 68, 104
roles of 64,
Skin,
container 47
formation 20, 40
psychic 46, 68, 123, 161
second 46
Social context 235
Social worker 35, 90, 91, 92
Speech therapy 108
Splitting processes 104, 165, 243, 261–262
Strange Situation 12, 15, 234 234fn
States of mind, infant 71, 72–73, 124, 132, 172, 210, 234, 235, 272
aggressive 72, 73, 134
anxious, 121, 171, 175, 193, 195, 196 *see also* Anxieties, infantile
blank 99, 100, 124, 126, 127, 134, 159
claustrophobic 73
curious 72, 100, 101, 102, 108, 138, 165, 201
depressed 133, 168
depressive 218
distressed 15, 70, 94, 131, 136, 156, 163, 198–200, 202, 203, 204, 207, 210, 253
hollow 103
intimate 125
mindless 73, 126, 130
possessive 163, 175
sadistic 72
sparing 124, 128, 132, 258
withdrawn 66, 73, 97
States of mind, parents 158, 245, 248
anxious 121, 127 177, 193, 195, 196
attentiveness 96
claustrophobic 107, 17
depressed. *see* Depression, maternal and Depression, postnatal,
depressive 164, 179 *see also* Depressive position
helpless 63, ,125
hopeful 194
hostile 91, 98, 103, 136
hurrying development 127, 129, 168
overflowing 129
painful 94, 95, 158, 179
preoccupied, *see* Parents, emotional preoccupations
pregnant, *see* Mothers, pregnant
projecting, *see* Projections
receptive 122
Substantive theory, *see* Theory, substantive
Symbolic play, infants 138, 176, 266, 267
infants capacity for 54, 219, 256, 266
Symbol equation 174, 210fn, 218, 266
Symbol formation 20, 48, 168, 174, 179, 193, 210fn, 270, 272
Symbolic functioning 5, 21, 88, 119, 120, 133, 142, 263, 265, 268, 271
Symbolic thinking, father and 216, 266
Symbolism 73, 102, 266

Tavistock Clinic 13, 27, 28
Theory, formal 32
grounded 2, 32, 33, 34, 35, 40, 234, 248
information 6
of play, *see* Play, theory of
psychoanalytic 1–3, 4, 15, 193, 235, 271, 272
substantive 32, 235
Transference 29, 30, 31, 93fn, 238
negative 240, 244
positive 241
Triangular relationships 134, 201, 204, 212, 214, 262
Triangular space 179, 193, 197, 249, 269
Triangulation 25, 31, 33

Unadventurousness 68, 71, 77, 90, 104, 108, 141, 154, 248, 251, 252, 257, 259, 262, 263
Unconscious phantasy 19, 46, 102, 106, 165, 174, 202, 204, 210fn, 214, 216, 219, 235, 243, 256, 266, 268

Validity *see* Methodology, validity of
Validation, context of 32
Violence, threat of, to infant 62, 71

Weaning 123, 124, 128, 139, 141, 202, 207, 208, 209, 267, 279
Whole object relationship 262
'Working through' 76, 243

Author Index

Abraham, K. 5fn
Ainsworth, M. 12, 13
Alvarez, A. 208fn
Anzieu, D. 77, 265

Baillargeon, R. 261fn
Bell, S. 12, 261
Bergman, A. 11
Brenman Pick, I. 19, 21
Bhaskar, R. 24
Bick, E. 1–3, 19–20, 23,26, 28, 29, 31–35, 40, 42, 46, 47, 56, 67, 125, 161, 170, 199, 233, 237, 238, 248, 250, 253, 254, 257, 272
Bion, W. 12, 16, 17, 19–22, 25fn, 40–48, 52, 55, 65, 77, 96, 126, 202, 208fn, 248, 250, 257, 260, 265–266, 270–273
Bleandonu, G. 45fn, 77, 260
Bollas, C. 214fn
Borton, W. 11
Bott, E. *see* Spillius, E. Bott
Bower, T. 4, 6, 7, 10, 12, 15, 16, 17, 18, 20, 47, 258, 261, 271, 272
Bowlby, J. 12, 13, 13fn
Box, S. 193
Bradley, B. 17, 23, 30
Braten, S. 9, 15, 259
Braudel, F. 246, 246fn
Brazelton, T. 9, 10, 14
Bretherton, I. 13
Briggs, S. 27, 93
Britton, R. 43, 52, 179, 198, 266
Brooke, Rupert 156
Brown, G. 15, 38, 247

Campos, J. 261fn
Chess, S. 44, 49
Cramer, B. 14
Crittenden, P. 108.

Daws, D. 273
Denzin, N 25
Dingwall, R. 2fn, 38
Drotar, D 108

Eliot, T.S. 7,258
Ellis, L 28
Emde, R 16, 47, 246
Escalona, S 2, 44
Evans Pritchard, E. 30

Fiumara, G. 261
Fonagy, P. 14, 15, 20, 23, 23, 37, 236, 271
Freiberg, S. 14, 45, 249
Freud, S. 5fn 11fn,12,12fn, 24, ,30, 243, 258, 266

George, C. 12
Glaser, B. 2, 32
Gold, R. 238
Green, A. 263

Hammersley, M. 32
Harlow, H. 47fn
Harris M. 20, 44, 56, 177, 203fn
Harris, T. 15, 38, 247
Hartman, D. 237
Heimann, P. 30
Henry G. *see* Williams G.
Hobson, P. 266, 268
Houzel, D. 259
Hoxter, S. 102
Hubley, P. 9
Hunt, J. 30

Isaacs, S. 106, 202, 210, 216, 266

Jones, D. 38

Kant, I. 22, 24
Kaplan, N. 12
Kempe, H. 2, 38
Klein, M. 9, 11, 11fn, 13fn, 18, 19, 24, 31, 48, 65, 174, 211, 243, 262, 265, 266, 267
Koslowski, B. 9, 14
Kuhn, T. 4

Lacan, J. 266
Lamb, M. 12fn
Layder, D. 23, 32
Leach, P. 104

Magagna, J. 28
Mahler, M. 5fn, 10, 11, 11fn, 18
Main, M. 9, 12, 13, 14, 15,
Marris, P. 12
Meltzer, D. 20, 28, 42, 63, 76, 102, 104, 177, 193, 218, 220fn, 241, 261, 266
Meltzoff, A. 7, 7fn, 11
Miles, G. 27
Miller, E. 157
Miller, Lisa 1, 28
Miller, Lynda 28

Model, N. 108, 109
Moore, M. 7, 7fn
Moran, G. 33
Murray, L. 8, 14, 15, 16, 17, 23, 38, 236, 242, 261fn, 271
Murray Parkes, C. 12

O'Shaughnessy, E. 202

Phillips, D. 24
Piaget, J. 5, 6, 7, 23, 208fn, 210fn, 261fn, 266
Pine, F. 11
Pionelli, A. 28
Popper, K. 24

Raphael Leff, J. 121
Rayner E. 193
Reid, M. 141
Reid, S. 28
Rhode, M. 28
Rigler, D. 38
Riviere, J. 259
Robertson, James 72, 79, 203fn
Robertson, Joyce 72, 93, 203fn
Rosaldo, R. 30fn
Rosenfeld, H. 259
Rudner, R. 32
Rustin, M.E. 27
Rustin M.J. 24, 25, 26, 28, 29,

Sarop, M. 266
Segal, H. 9, 44, 174, 210fn, 266
Shuttleworth, J. 11, 11fn, 18
Sorenson, P. 242
Spillius, E. Bott 5fn, 18, 24, 37, 235
Spinetta, J. 38
Steele, H. 14, 37
Steele, M. 14, 37
Steiner, J. 258, 259
Stern, D. 4, 5, 6, 9, 10, 11, 12, 13, 17, 20, 29, 29fn, 47, 197, 258, 271
Sternberg, C. 261fn
Stevenson Hinde J. 12
Strauss, A. 2, 32
Symington, J. 25, 28, 46, 170, 253

Thomas, A. 44, 49
Trevarthen, C. 8–10, 13, 15, 17, 18, 47, 242, 255, 266, 271, 272
Tronick, E. 15
Trowell, J. 27, 38
Tustin, F. 102, 102fn, 204fn

Urwin,C. 4, 5, 17, 21, 23

Waddell, M. 28
Watson, J. 61fn
Will, D. 24, 25fn
Williams (formerly Henry), G. 27, 45, 47, 75, 141, 271
Wilson, K. 27
Winnicott, D. 5, 5fn, 9, 11, 11fn, 16, 18, 19, 249, 258
Wishart, J. 15
Wittenberg, I. 30, 220fn
Wittgenstein, L. 24
Wittig, B. 12

Yogman, M. 14

Zimmermann, R. 47

NORTHERN MICHIGAN UNIVERSITY
3 1854 005 741 304

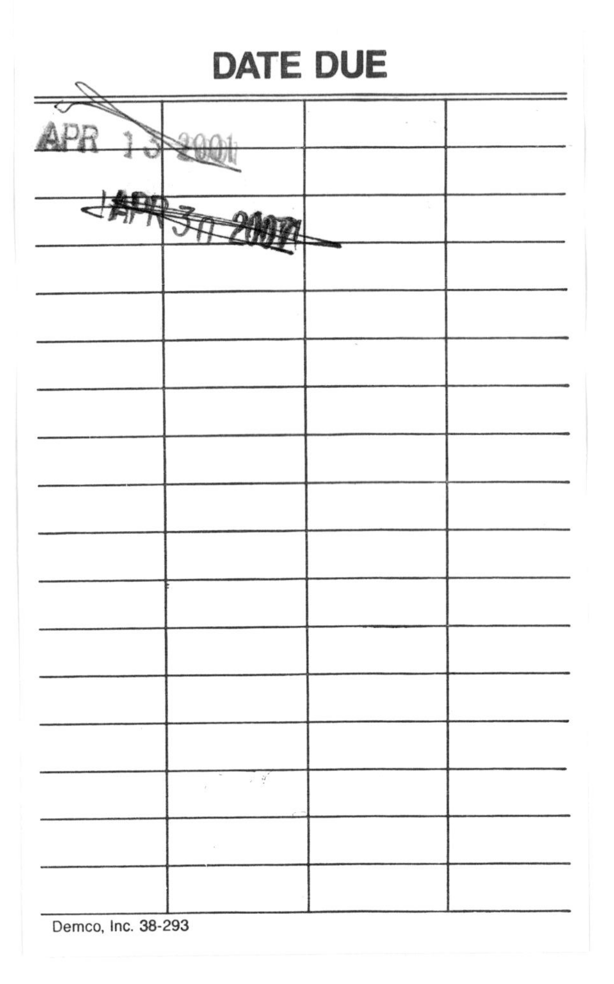
DATE DUE
APR 13 2001
APR 30 2001
Demco, Inc. 38-293